On Decoloniality

**On Decoloniality** interconnects a diverse array of perspectives from the lived experiences of coloniality and decolonial thought/praxis in different local histories from across the globe. The series identifies and examines decolonial engagements in Eastern Europe, the Caribbean, the Americas, South Asia, South Africa, and beyond from standpoints of feminisms, erotic sovereignty, Fanonian thought, post-Soviet analyses, global indigeneity, and ongoing efforts to delink, relink, and rebuild a radically distinct praxis of living. Aimed at a broad audience, from scholars, students, and artists to journalists, activists, and socially engaged intellectuals, On Decoloniality invites a wide range of participants to join one of the fastest-growing debates in the humanities and social sciences that attends to the lived concerns of dignity, life, and the survival of the planet.

A SERIES EDITED BY

*Walter Mignolo & Catherine Walsh*

# On Decoloniality

CONCEPTS

ANALYTICS

PRAXIS

WALTER D. MIGNOLO

*and*

CATHERINE E. WALSH

DUKE UNIVERSITY PRESS  *Durham and London*  2018

Designed by Matt Tauch
Typeset in Minion Pro by Westchester Publishing Services

Library of Congress Cataloging-in-Publication Data
Names: Mignolo, Walter, author. | Walsh, Catherine E., author.
Title: On decoloniality : concepts, analytics, praxis /
Walter D. Mignolo and Catherine E. Walsh.
Description: Durham : Duke University Press, 2018. | Series: On
decoloniality | Includes bibliographical references and index.
Identifiers: LCCN 2017053249 (print) | LCCN 2017056840
(ebook)
ISBN 9780822371779 (ebook)
ISBN 9780822370949 (hardcover : alk. paper)
ISBN 9780822371090 (pbk. : alk. paper)
Subjects: LCSH: Postcolonialism—Philosophy. |
Decolonization—Philosophy. | Imperialism—Philosophy. |
Power (Social sciences)—Philosophy. | Civilization,
Modern—Philosophy.
Classification: LCC JV51 (ebook) | LCC JV51 .M544 2018 (print) |
DDC 325/.301—dc23
LC record available at https://lccn.loc.gov/2017053249

Cover art: Adolfo Albán Achinte, *Marejada,* de la serie
"Andanias"

TO ANÍBAL QUIJANO / *who gave us, and the world,*

*the concept of coloniality.*

*In memory of Fernando Coronil.*

*And in celebration of the 2016 "Standup" resurgence at Standing Rock.*

# Contents

# Acknowledgments

Catherine expresses her gratitude to all those who have formed part of the conversation on modernity/coloniality/decoloniality over more than twenty years. Recalled are the gatherings in various moments and contexts, of those friends and colleagues associated with what has been referred to as the modernity/(de)coloniality group, project, or collective, particularly in its early formations in "Latin" America and the United States.

My thanks to Aníbal Quijano for introducing and pushing reflection on the coloniality of power; to Enrique Dussel for making so clearly visible modernity's distinct moments and global vision, and to Walter Mignolo for illuminating modernity as coloniality's darker side and, of course, for assembling us together. My thanks to Edgardo Lander for concretely bringing to the fore the coloniality of both nature and knowledge; to Nelson Maldonado-Torres, for his meditations on the coloniality of being, his philosophical clarity and force, and his decolonial sensibilities; and to Arturo Escobar for his continuous *sentipensar*. My thanks as well to Fernando Coronil (who lives on in our minds and hearts), Santiago Castro-Gómez, Javier Sanjinés, and Pablo Quintero for their multiple contributions and spaces-places of thought, and Adolfo Albán for his embodied re-existence. A special acknowledgment and recognition to Zulma Palermo, Maria Lugones, Freya Schiwy, and more recently María Eugenia Borsani, Rolando Vázquez, Yuderkys Espinosa, and Rita Segato, whose voices, writings, and thoughts have not only unsettled male centrality, but more importantly, and each in their own way, have pressed for depatriarchalizations in modernity/(de)coloniality's conception, comprehension, praxis, and project. Of course, there are many more from newer generations to recognize and thank, including in other continents of the globe; the list is much too long to include here.

I would be remiss if I did not acknowledge the significance of our doctoral program-project in Latin American (Inter)Cultural Studies at the Universidad Andina Simón Bolívar in Quito. Since its beginnings in 2001, this program-project has deepened collective reflections on the modern-colonial matrix of power, and served as a sort of seedbed of and for decolonial praxis, now reflected in collectives, programs-projects, and knowledge production throughout South and Central America.

Finally, I wish to express my gratitude to the collectives, movements, communities, and activist-intellectuals who, from the different territories, subjectivities, and struggles of Abya Yala, and from the borders, margins, and cracks of the modern/colonial/capitalist/heteropatriarchal order, are planting seeds of life that counter the project of violence, dispossession, war, and death that characterizes the present times. Thank you as well for the possibility, in some cases, of being part of the struggles, conversations, and reflexive praxis, and, in others, of being able to dialogue and/or think "with."

Walter expresses his gratitude to all those who have made possible the structure and arguments of part II. Just after *The Darker Side of Western Modernity: Global Futures, Decolonial Options* was released (December 2011), I faced the task of communicating the works of the collective modernity/coloniality/decoloniality, and my own version of it, to several audiences in Hong Kong and various places in South Africa. Part II has therefore a long story and substantial debts.

Chronologically, my first debt is to Gregory Lee, former director of the Hong Kong Advanced Institute for Cross-Disciplinary Studies (HKAICS) at the City University of Hong Kong. The four public lectures delivered there and titled "Spirit Returns to the East" were a key experience in conveying the meaning of *coloniality* to an audience dwelling in different temporalities. My second debt is to Dilip Menon, director of the Center for Indian Studies in South Africa (CISA), at Wits University, Johannesburg. It was a second opportunity to address, during one month (August 2013) and in four lectures titled "Decolonial Thought," an audience familiar with colonialism no doubt but less familiar with the conceptual specificities of *coloniality* and *coloniality of power* unfolded after Aníbal Quijano introduced the concept in the 1990s.

I owe an even larger debt to Professor H. B. Geyer, director of Stellenbosch Institute for Advanced Study (STIAS). His invitation to enjoy and take advantage of STIAS's wonderful research atmosphere, during two periods of six weeks in July–August of 2014 and 2015, allowed me to write the first and last draft of the second part as it appears here, and that were based on the previous lectures delivered at HKAICS and CISA. During that period I rehearsed the main ideas of my part, presenting them to the STIAS fellows and in a conversation with faculty and graduate studies organized by Nick Shepherd, director of the Centre for African Studies, at the University of Cape Town. Nick announced the workshop as a conversation "On Decoloniality." At Cape Town, I met Daniela Franca Joffe, whose editorial skill and familiarity with understanding of decolonial sentiments in Southern Africa were extremely helpful in streamlining the argument.

Thanks to Rolando Vázquez for his camaraderie and constant conversations to organize and run the Middelburg Decolonial Summer School since summer 2010; and to the crew of the summer school, with whom in the classroom and outside of it, conversations on modernity, coloniality, and decoloniality never stop. They are Jean Casimir, Maria Lugones, Madina Tlostanova, Rosalba Icaza, Ovidiu Tichindeleanu, Jeannette Ehlers, Patricia Kaersenhout, and Fabian Barba.

I did not mention Alanna Lockward, who is part of the team, because my thanks to her are also, and perhaps mainly, for inviting me to be an advisor for her splendid project Black Europe Body Politics (Be.Bop), running since 2012. Decolonial and African diasporic aesthetics, and coloniality in all its forms, have been and continue to be discussed among artists, curators, activists, and journalists. While writing part II, I have both shared and benefited from all those encounters and activities in Europe (the Netherlands, Germany, and Denmark).

Before the work that led to my part of this book began, there were twenty years of experiences with the collective modernity/coloniality/decoloniality that Catherine Walsh mentioned above and that I have already detailed in my latest books. This coauthored book is the consequence of a long working and friendly relationship with Cathy and above all collaborating in the PhD she initiated in 2001 at the Universidad Andina Simón Bolívar (Quito), which was and continues to be a hub for decolonial learning and thinking in conviviality, not in competition.

At home, my debts are to Leo Ching (Department of Asian and Middle Eastern Studies) and to Tracy Carhart (assistant to the director, Center for Global Studies and the Humanities). Two seminars co-taught with Leo in the spring semesters of 2014 and 2015 were invaluable for putting my ideas into conversations with Leo and with students at Duke. The seminars were devoted to exploring the meanings and consequences of *coloniality* experienced in the Eastern and Western Hemispheres.

Together, both of us thank Tracy Carhart for her valuable editorial assistance and to the outside readers for their positive comments and challenging questions. A very special thank you to Gisela Fosado from Duke University Press, who suggested the idea of the book series and then supported it with enthusiasm and flair; she has also been an active part of its conceptualization, development, and coming to fruition, including this first book.

# Introduction

*Catherine E. Walsh and Walter D. Mignolo*

This book opens the Duke University Press series "On Decoloniality." The series' goal is to interconnect perspectives, expressions, thought, struggles, processes, and practices of decoloniality that are emerging in and from different corners of the globe.

Our conception and praxis of decoloniality in this book and series do not pretend to provide global answers or sketch global designs for liberation, even less to propose *new abstract universals*. We are interested instead in relationality. That is, in the ways that different local histories and embodied conceptions and practices of decoloniality, including our own, can enter into conversations and build understandings that both cross geopolitical locations and colonial differences, and contest the totalizing claims and political-epistemic violence of modernity.

Relationality doesn't mean that there is one way to do and conceive decoloniality, and that it happens to be the way we—the authors of this text—do and conceive it. For us to think that we are in possession of a decolonial universal truth would not be decolonial at all but modern/colonial, and for you, the reader, to assume that this is the way we think would create misunderstandings from the very beginning. Relationality also doesn't mean simply to include other practices and concepts into our own. Its meaning references what some Andean Indigenous thinkers, including Nina Pacari, Fernando Huanacuni Mamani, and Félix Patzi Paco, refer to as *vincularidad*. Vincularidad is the awareness of the integral relation and interdependence amongst all living organisms (in which humans are only a part) with territory or land and the cosmos. It is a relation and interdependence in search of balance and harmony of life in the planet. As such, and as we propose in this book and series, vincularidad/relationality unsettles the singular authoritativeness and universal character typically assumed and portrayed in academic thought. Relationality/vincularidad seeks connections and correlations.[1]

Our proposal is for creating and illuminating pluriversal and interversal paths that disturb the totality from which the universal and the global are most often perceived. With this caveat in mind, we open the series with a *local* introduction to decoloniality's praxis, concepts, and analytics. Certainly it cannot be otherwise since all theories and conceptual frames, including those that originate in Western Europe and the Anglo United States, can aim at and describe the global but cannot be other than local.

The proposition here and in the series is to advance the undoing of Eurocentrism's totalizing claim and frame, including the Eurocentric legacies incarnated in U.S.-centrism and perpetuated in the Western geopolitics of knowledge. It is not with eliminating but reducing to size what Michel-Rolph Trouillot describes as North Atlantic abstract universal fictions. Thus while the series does not exclude the United States, the United States is not at the center of its interests, debates, and concerns. The interest more broadly is with *pluriversal decoloniality* and *decolonial pluriversality* as they are being thought and constructed outside and in the borders and fissures of the North Atlantic Western world.

While the Americas of the South (Central and South America) and the Caribbean are part of our location and interests, this is not a "Latin" American studies book series. No one would claim that Martin Heidegger's writings were German studies. He was German, and what he thought had a lot to do with his personal history and language. But he thought what he deemed to be thought at his time and place. So it is for us. Heidegger was not a token of his culture, and neither are we. We are where we think, and our thinking is provoked by the history of the Americas (including the United States) and the Caribbean since the sixteenth century, when the very inception of modern/colonial patterns (i.e., coloniality) began to emerge. Yet our thinking, and the thinking of those who will follow in the series, do not end—nor are they only located—here.

The aim of the series is to make accessible—through short, single- and/or coauthored texts, and edited collections—reflections on decoloniality from different continents, territories, and geographies; from different geobody storytellings, histories, herstories, and transtories; and from different translocal subjectivities, struggles, worldviews, and world senses, most especially of those who have lived—and live—the colonial difference. We hope that these books will broaden and enhance debates, and cultivate conversations among those abandoning modernity's naturalized fictions and imperatives; those in search of the relational and communal over competition, those endeavoring to move beyond the dictates and confines of government politics and uni- or mononational state forms, and those radically opposed to the financial hunting of consumers and corporations chasing for technoqualified workers to increase the armies of unemployed.

Furthermore, the series seeks to interrupt the idea of dislocated, disembodied, and disengaged abstraction, and to disobey the universal signifier that is the rhetoric of modernity, the logic of coloniality, and the West's global model. For us, the pluriversal opens rather than closes the geographies and spheres of decolonial thinking and doing. It opens up coexisting temporalities kept hostage by the Western idea of time and the belief that there is one single temporality: Western-imagined fictional temporality. Moreover, it connects and brings together in relation—as both pluri- and interversals—local histories, subjectivities, knowledges, narratives, and struggles against the modern/colonial order and for an *otherwise*. This is the understanding and project of *pluriversal and interversal decoloniality* that orients the series and this introductory book.

Such perspective does not mean a rejection or negation of Western thought; in fact, Western thought is part of the pluriversal. Western thought and Western civilization are in most/all of us, but this does not mean a blind acceptance, nor does it mean a surrendering to North Atlantic fictions. Within Western thought itself, there have always been internal critiques, Eurocentric critiques of Eurocentrism, so to speak. Bartolomé de las Casas in the sixteenth century and Karl Marx in the nineteenth century are clear examples. But these are not the critiques that we follow here. Our thinking instead is with the decolonial critiques of Eurocentrism that have been present in different moments in time, with the nonacceptances of the West and North Atlantic fictions as the only way. While not accepting could be termed *resistance*, our interest and proposition here (in this book and series) are, more crucially, with *re-existence*, understood as "the redefining and re-signifying of life in conditions of dignity."[2] It is the resurgence and insurgence of re-existence today that open and engage venues and paths of decolonial conviviality, venues and paths that take us beyond, while at the same time undoing, the singularity and linearity of the West. .

This first book introduces the perspective, concept, analytic, practice, and praxis of decoloniality that find their base and ground in the compound concept modernity/coloniality. Modernity, of course, is not a decolonial concept, but coloniality is. Coloniality is constitutive, not derivative, of modernity. That is to say, there is no modernity without coloniality, thus the compound expression: *modernity/coloniality.* Our intent is to help the reader understand how the colonial matrix of power (CMP, of which modernity/coloniality is a shorter expression) was constituted, managed, and transformed from its historical foundation in the sixteenth century to the present. But the intention is also, and more crucially, to push considerations of how decoloniality undoes, disobeys, and delinks from this matrix; constructing paths and praxis toward an otherwise of thinking, sensing, believing, doing, and living. For us, decoloniality and decolonial thought materialized at the very moment in which the CMP was being put in place (from the sixteenth to the eighteenth centuries). Decolonially speaking, modernity/coloniality are intimately, intricately, explicitly, and complicitly entwined. The end of modernity would imply the end of coloniality, and, therefore, decoloniality would no longer be an issue. This is the ultimate decolonial horizon.

We also recognize the legacies of decolonization associated with the Bandung Conference (1955) and the Conference of the Non-Aligned Countries (1961) at the time of the Cold War. However, these legacies are not the central foundation of our project. For us, the horizon is not the political independence of nation-states (as it was for decolonization), nor is it only—or primarily—the confrontation with capitalism and the West (though both are central components of the modern/colonial matrix of power). Our interest and concern, reflected in this book but also in the conversations sustained since the late 1990s within what has been referred to as the modernity/(de)coloniality shared project, are with the habits that modernity/coloniality implanted in all of us; with how modernity/coloniality has worked and continues to work to negate, disavow, distort and deny knowledges, subjectivities, world senses, and life visions.

Here we give attention to the what, why, with whom, and how of decoloniality, to the ways its concept, analytic, and praxis unravel modernity/coloniality's hold; engender liberations with respect to thinking, being, knowing, understanding, and living; encourage venues of re-existence, and build connections among regions, territories, struggles, and peoples. As mentioned above, decoloniality—as we understand it—was born in responses to the promises of modernity and the realities of coloniality, in the sense that Aníbal Quijano introduced it. The conceptualizations and actionings of decoloniality are therefore multiple, contextual, and relational; they are not only the purview of peoples who have lived the colonial difference but, more broadly, of all of us who struggle from and within modernity/coloniality's borders and cracks, to build a radically distinct world. Decoloniality, as we argue in this book, is not a new paradigm or mode of critical thought. It is a way, option, standpoint, analytic, project, practice, and praxis.

The underpinning of this text—and of us, as its authors—is deep-rooted in our sensing of both Americas during the Cold War, one of the Americas (the United States) in the First and the others (Central / South America and the Caribbean) in the Third World. When your life experience is touched and formed in and by the Third World, geopolitics matter; or when you realize that as a citizen of the First World you belong to a history that has engendered coloniality and disguised it by the promises and premises of modernity, you encounter coloniality from the two ends of the spectrum.

Global politics of course is much more complex today than in the Cold War period, or in the sixteenth century when the CMP began to emerge. The election of Donald Trump (and his first 100 days as we write this introduction), and the announced shift from "neoliberal globalism" to "national Americanism," along with the reinstallation of the extreme Right in Argentina and Brazil, the escalating war in Syria, the prominence of North Korea in U.S. foreign policy, and the massive mobilizations in South Africa, among many other emerging geopolitical contexts and "events" (including the election of neoliberal globalist Emmanuel Macron to the French presidency), further complicate the present-day local-global arena. Today the CMP is not simply controlled and managed by the West (the United States and the EU) as has been the case for more than 500 years. The turmoil is now at once domestic, transnational, interstate, and global.

A return of right-wing nationalisms in the West (i.e., in the European Union plus Britain and the United States) is not worse, from a decolonial perspective, than the continuation of neoliberal globalism. However, the New World ordering of global coloniality (including the decline of the United States as worldwide leader), forces us to ask: what do decoloniality and decolonization mean in this junction? The reasons should be obvious: decolonization during the Cold War meant the struggle for liberations of the Third World and, when successful, the formation of nation-states claiming sovereignty. By the 1990s, decolonization's failure in most nations had become clear; with state in the hands of minority elites, the patterns of colonial power continued both internally (i.e., internal colonialism) and with relation to global structures. At that moment coloniality was unveiled; decoloniality was born in the unveiling of coloniality.

Coloniality/decoloniality when introduced by Aníbal Quijano in 1990 was the hinging moment of the closing of the Cold War and the opening of neoliberal global designs (i.e., globalism). Today right-wing nationalisms build on the darker side of neoliberal globalism, and so-called progressive states (e.g., Ecuador, Bolivia, Venezuela) advance a twenty-first-century capitalism grounded in a politics and economy of extractivism that advances the destruction of lands-beings-knowledges, what many understand as Mother Earth. While the rhetoric and politics of right-wing nationalism, neoliberal globalism, and progressivisms may differ, each continues to perpetuate and further coloniality.

Certainly, the current conjuncture calls for urgent and sustained analysis and considerations in terms of the continuing shifts and mutations of the CMP—analyses and considerations not possible in this book but hopefully the subject of future volumes. While decolonial geopolitical and body-political responses—delinking and re-existence, resurgence, and insurgence—continue, decolonial praxis may begin to take on distinct forms in coming years in view of the changing rhetoric of modernity in the confrontations between the United States with the support of the European Union, on the one hand, and China, Russia, and Iran on the other. In the current formation of a multipolar world order the rhetoric of modernity is no longer unidirectional and unipolar.

We—Catherine and Walter—have crossed biographies that both complement each other and define our spheres of interest. Catherine, born and raised in the United States, has lived the majority of her adult life outside the U.S. mainframe, first in U.S. Latino communities and since the mid-1990s, in Ecuador, where she teaches and works closely with activists and social movements. Walter, born and raised in Argentina, after his PhD in France and becoming familiar with Europe, decided to relocate to the United States, where he became a politically engaged scholar who works with intellectuals and activists both inside and outside of the United States. For us both, the common anchor is the concept of *coloniality* introduced by Aníbal Quijano, and explained in detail in part II.

This common anchor connects us, but it does not presume to make uniform—or collapse into "one"—our thinking, doing, and words. This is why we wrote parts I and II of the book separately but connected and in relation. Making visible both of our subjectivities, views, voices, and thought is in fact part of our methodology-pedagogy of conversation that has continued over the last twenty years, reflected as well in our published interviews of and with each other.[3]

In our thinking alone and together, theory and praxis are necessarily interrelated. Theory and praxis are constructions that presuppose the basic praxis of living. Without our daily praxis of living, it would not be possible to make conceptual and second-order distinctions between theory and praxis. Following this line of reasoning, this volume delinks from the modern concept of *theory versus praxis*. For us, theory is doing and doing is thinking. Are you not doing something when you theorize or analyze concepts? Isn't doing something praxis? And from praxis—understood as thought-reflection-action, and thought-reflection on this action—do we not also construct theory and theorize thought? By disobeying the long-held belief that you first theorize and then apply, or that you can engage in blind praxis without theoretical analysis and vision, we locate our thinking/doing in a different terrain.

This terrain is rooted in the praxis of living and in the idea of theory-and-as-praxis and praxis-and-as-theory, and in the interdependence and continuous flow of movement of both. It is in this movement that decoloniality is enacted and, at the same time, rendered possible. Decoloniality, in this sense, is wrapped up with re-existence; both claim a terrain that endeavors to delink from the theoretical tenets and conceptual instruments of Western thought.

If "another world is possible," it cannot be built with the conceptual tools inherited from the Renaissance and the Enlightenment. It cannot be built with the master's tools, as Audre Lorde reminded us a number of years back, "for the master's tools will never dismantle the master's house. They may allow us temporarily to beat him at his own game, but they will never enable us to bring about genuine change."[4] However, Lewis Gordon and Jane Anna Gordon offer a different stance on this same problem. "Not only with the master's tools," they argue. "Slaves have historically done something more provocative with such tools than attempt to dismantle the Big House. There are those who used those tools, developed additional ones, and built houses of their own on more or less generous soil. It is our view that the proper response is to follow their lead, transcending rather than dismantling Western ideas through building our own houses of thought. When enough houses are built, the hegemony of the master's house—in fact, *mastery itself*—will cease to maintain its imperial status. Shelter needn't be the rooms offered by such domination."[5] In both these senses, we seek and posit in this book other conceptual instruments, other ways of theorizing, and other genealogies, all of which—in both the past and present—construct and constitute what we understand as decolonial thinking, praxis, and thought.

Without a doubt, the critique of coloniality and the possibilities of decolonial horizons of praxis, knowledge, and thought (though not always with this same use of terms) have a legacy. W. E. B. Dubois, Anna Julia Cooper, Aimé Césaire, and Frantz Fanon are only several examples of the decolonial thinkers visibly present in the early and mid-twentieth century. However, the list of decolonial thinkers is long: From Guaman Poma de Ayala in the late sixteenth century and early seventeenth in the viceroyalty of Peru to Ottobah Cugoano, in London but reflecting on his experience as a hunted human being enslaved in Jamaica and taken to London by his master, a British man named Campbell. From the abolitionist and activist Sojurner Truth and her famous discourse "Ain't I a woman" in 1851, to Mahatma Gandhi in India in the early twentieth century, to Sun Yat-sen in China and the kichwa leader, activist, and educator Dolores Cacuango in Ecuador a few decades later. From Amilcar Lopes da Costa Cabral in Guinea-Bissau and Cape Verde to Steve Biko in apartheid South Africa; from Audre Lorde in New York, to Gloria Anzaldúa in the borderlands of Aztlán (the U.S. Southwest/Mexican border), Sylvia Wynter in the crossing of the Caribbean and United States, and to the many other racialized, genderized, and borderized decolonial thinkers whose *herstories, transtories,* and *ourstories* of thought have been made invisible by the racism and heteropatriarchy of the modern/colonial order. The genealogies of decolonial thinking and doing (across the spectrums of gender and race) have always marched parallel to the global predatory advance of modernity/coloniality.

Yet it has been the work of what is known today as the modernity/coloniality/decoloniality group or project that has, since the decade of the 1990s and following Aníbal Quijano's introduction of the coloniality of power, more deeply explored the analytic dimensions of coloniality and decolonial thought. This communal project in its initial composition was primarily based in South America and the United States and included Edgardo Lander (Venezuela), Fernando Coronil (Venezuela–United States), Santiago Castro-Gómez and Oscar Guardiola-Rivera (Colombia), Arturo Escobar (Colombia–United States), Javier Sanjinés (Bolivia–United States), Zulma Palermo (Argentina), Maria Lugones (Argentina–United States), Freya Schiwy (Germany–United States), Enrique Dussel (Argentina-Mexico), Nelson Maldonado-Torres, Ramón Grosfoguel, and Agustín Lao-Montes (Puerto Rico–United States), in addition to Quijano and ourselves. Much of its writing was in Spanish. While many of its members have also written extensively in English, the first English-language publications identified with the project or group came out in the volumes of *Nepantla*, including the dossier from 2002, "Knowledges and the Known: Andean Perspectives on Capitalism and Epistemology," organized by Freya Schiwy and Michael Ennis. Another dossier came out in *Cultural Studies* in 2007, and later in a book edited by Walter Mignolo and Arturo Escobar and published by Routledge.[6] Today this decolonial communal project functions as a loosely knit assemblage of socially and politically committed intellectuals with affinities that shift and move, with localizations in most, if not all, of the continents of the world, and with pluriversal perspectives and standpoints on the modern/colonial matrix of power.

Engaging decoloniality as we conceive and enact it in this book, providing a frame for the book series, means to engage in two types of activities at once: the thinking-doing, and doing-thinking of decoloniality. In an earlier draft of this book, we opted to begin with the first, with the analytic of coloniality of power through conceptual elucidation (a familiar task in philosophy). The idea was to establish a conceptual foundation upon which the second activity emerges and is grounded; that is, the processes, practices, and praxis of decoloniality. However, responses from readers made us rethink this order, most especially because our project is to unsettle and disobey—not reproduce—the reign of theory over practice. While we contemplated interspersing the chapters that now constitute part I and part II, our fear was that this would take away from the flow of each part. Our decision then, and reflected here, is to begin with the doing-thinking, with the people, collectives, and communities that enact decoloniality as a way, option, standpoint, analytic, project, practice, and praxis; that is, with the activity of thinking and theorizing from praxis. This does not mean that part I is praxical and part II theoretical. They are both theoretical/praxical in different ways, starting at two ends of the spectrum and working toward the center: theoretical praxis and practical theory. Part I, entitled "Decoloniality in/as Praxis," written by Catherine, is organized around the central questions of the decolonial *how* and the decolonial *for*; that is, on the one hand, the question of how decoloniality is signified and constructed in and through praxis. Of interest here is how those who live the colonial difference think theory, theorize practice, and build, create, and enact concrete processes, struggles, and practices of resurgent and insurgent action and thought, including in the spheres of knowledge, territory-land, state, re-existences, and life itself. And, on the other hand, the question is how this praxis interrupts and cracks the modern/colonial/

capitalist/heteropatriarchal matrices of power, and advances other ways of being, thinking, knowing, theorizing, analyzing, feeling, acting, and living for us all—the *otherwise* that is the decolonial *for*. The geopolitical and body-political context here is Abya Yala, broadly understood as the Americas, and most especially as the Americas of the South (Central and South America) in relation with the Caribbean. Nevertheless, we believe that readers will find interrelation with other regions of the globe.

In this first part of the book, the analytic of the coloniality of power moves in a kind of serpentine fashion, in and out of decoloniality's processes, practice, and praxis, building the connection, conversation, and relation with part II.

In part II, "The Decolonial Option," written by Walter, the order of the above-mentioned activities reverts to thinking/doing. This part is a meditation on *coloniality* (shorthand for *coloniality of power*), a concept as important as those of *unconscious* in Sigmund Freud and of *surplus value* in Karl Marx. Unconscious and surplus value were introduced to deal with and confront issues and problems affecting and afflicting Western European society. *Coloniality* here deals with and confronts issues and problems common to all former colonies of Western Europe in the Third World. The text examines how coloniality of power was formed, transformed, and managed in its history of more than 500 years. Furthermore, it explores how the coloniality of power operates today on a global scale when North Atlantic imperial states can no longer control and manage the monster (CMP) they created, being disputed by *returning civilizations* (commonly referred to as emerging economies).

Once the colonial matrix of power is no longer managed and controlled by the so-called West, it impinges on and transforms all aspects of life, particularly with regard to two interrelated spheres: (a) the coloniality of political, economic, and military power (interstate relations), and (b) the coloniality of the three pillars of being in the world: racism, sexism, and the naturalization of life and the permanent regeneration of the living (e.g., the invention of the concept of *nature*). Part II moves, then, in a kind of spiral (nonlinear) way from the analytic of the coloniality of power to the second, more forward-looking activity. Here the interest is with the variegated processes of delinking from the promises made in the name of modernity: development and growth and the prison houses of coloniality. Part II closes by highlighting decoloniality as interrelated processes of healing colonial wounds that originate in each of us. Each of us, endorsing and embracing decoloniality, is responsible for our own decolonial liberation. The task is not individual but communal. It means that no one should expect that someone else will decolonize him or her or decolonize $X$ or $Z$, and it means that none of us, living-thinking-being-doing decolonially should expect to decolonize someone else. As such, part II complements part I and vice versa. Moreover, each part alone and both parts together evince the interweaving of concepts, analytics, and praxis.

With this book we intend to open up a global conversation that the series will build upon, broaden, and extend. Subsequent volumes will extend the reflection and discussion to other actors, projects, and geopolitical areas and regions, including South and North Africa, the former Western and former Eastern Europe, the Russian Federation and Central Asia, East and South Asia, and Southeast and West Asia (labeled Middle East by U.S. navy admiral Alfred Thayer Mahan in 1902). Global indigeneity, feminisms of color, and decolonial corpo-political-epistemic struggles and standpoints—including those that interrogate gender, sexuality, erotics, and spirituality—will also be the focus of future volumes.

In essence, the series opens to all the people in different parts of the world who are prone, like Gloria Anzaldúa herself, to sense *La facultad* (the power to do). La facultad is sensed by all: "Those who are pushed out of the tribe for being different are likely to become more sensitized (when not brutalized into insensitivity). Those who do not feel psychologically or physically safe in the world are more apt to develop this sense. Those who are pounced on the most have it the strongest—the females, the homosexuals of all races, the dark-skinned, the outcast, the persecuted, the marginalized, the foreign."[7]

Thinking from and with this facultad (undisciplined), from and with decoloniality, and from and with the possibilities of building a radically distinct world, are part and parcel of the project of this series and this first book that introduces it.[8]

## Notes

1    Complementarity and relationality in search of equilibrium and harmony are fundamental concepts in Indigenous philosophy from ancient times to today. For a detailed exposition in decolonial Indigenous thinking, see the argument by Aymara thinker Fernando Huanacuni Mamani, *Vivir Bien/Buen Vivir: Filosofía, políticas,*

estrategias y experiencias de los pueblos ancestrales, 6th ed. (La Paz: Instituto International de Integración, [2010] 2015), 115–68. See also kichwa politician, lawyer, and Indigenous leader Nina Pacari, "La incidencia de la participación política de los pueblos indígenas: Un camino irreversible," in *Las vertientes americanas del pensamiento y proyecto des-colonial*, ed. Heriberto Cairo and Walter Mignolo (Madrid: Trama Editorial, 2008), 45–58; and Aymara scholar and intellectual Felix Patzi Paco, "Sistema comunal: Una propuesta alternativa al sistema liberal," in *Las vertientes americanas*, 61–84. A similar philosophy and pedagogy through the land has been powerfully articulated by the Nishanaabeg scholar, activist, and artist Leanne Simpson, "Land as Pedagogy: Nishnaabeg Intelligence and Rebellious Transformation," in *Decolonization: Indigeneity, Education and Society* 3, no. 3 (2014): 1–25. For a detailed discussion of relationality from a non-Indigenous decolonial perspective, see Rolando Vázquez, "Towards a Decolonial Critique of Modernity: *Buen Vivir*, Relationality and the Task of Listening," in *Capital, Poverty, Development: Denktraditionen im Dialog: Studien zur Befreiung und Interkultalitat* 33, ed. Raul Fornet-Betancourt, 241–52 (Wissenschaftsverlag Mainz, Germany: Achen, 2012).

2   Adolo Albán Achinte, "Interculturalidad sin decolonialidad? Colonialidades circulantes y prácticas de re-existencia," in *Diversidad, interculturalidad y construcción de ciudad*, ed. Wilmer Villa and Arturo Grueso (Bogotá: Universidad Pedagógica Nacional/Alcaldía Mayor, 2008), 85–86.

3   See Walter Mignolo, "Decolonial Thinking and Doing in the Andes: An interview with Catherine Walsh, a propos of *Interculturalidad, Estado, Sociedad: Luchas (de)coloniales de nuestra época*," *Reartikulacija*, Slovenia, January 2011; and Catherine Walsh, "Las geopolíticas del conocimiento y colonialidad del poder: Entrevista a Walter Mignolo," in *Indisciplinar las ciencias sociales: Geopolíticas del conocimiento y colonialidad del poder: Perspectivas desde lo andino*, ed. Catherine Walsh, Freya Schiwy, Santiago Castro-Gómez, 17–44 (Quito: UASB/Abya Yala, 2002).

4   Audre Lorde, *Sister Outsider* (Berkeley: Crossing Press, [1984] 2007), 112.

5   Lewis Gordon and Jane Anna Gordon, "Introduction: Not Only the Master's Tools," *Not Only the Master's Tools: African-American Studies in Theory and Practice*, ed. Lewis Gordon and Jane Anna Gordon (Boulder, CO: Paradigm, 2006), ix.

6   Walter Mignolo and Arturo Escobar, eds., *Globalization and the Decolonial Option* (London: Routledge, 2010).

7   Gloria Anzaldúa, *Borderlands/La Frontera: The New Mestiza* (San Francisco: Aunt Lute, 1987), 63–64.

8   One of the first volumes of the collective modernity/coloniality/decoloniality was titled precisely *Indisciplinar las ciencias sociales: Geopolíticas del conocimiento y colonialidad del poder*, ed. Catherine Walsh, Freya Schiwy, and Santiago Castro-Gómez.

# Decoloniality in/as Praxis / *Part One*

CATHERINE E. WALSH

# 1 The Decolonial *For*

*Resurgences, Shifts, and Movements*

Did you hear?
It is the sound of your world collapsing.
It is the sound of our world resurging.
The day that was day was night.
And night will be the day that will be day.

**—SUBCOMANDANTE MARCOS**

## Openings

Some say we are up against a civilizational crisis, a crisis in which the universalized model or paradigm of the West is crumbling before our very eyes. Others, such as the Zapatistas, speak in a related way of the Storm brewing, the Storm already upon us, the Storm whose force is rapidly growing. This Storm, say the Zapatistas, is the catastrophe that we all feel. It is the war against life in all of its practices, forms, and manifestations.[1]

Many in the Souths of the world, including the Souths in the North, know it well. It is a war of violence, destruction, and elimination, a war that is epistemic and existence based, a war that is feminized, racialized, and territorialized. It is the war of global capital, of coloniality regenerating and reconstituting itself, a war—according to Nelson Maldonado-Torres—indicative of the increasingly violent tendencies of dominant Western ideals (including of the human), and of the constitutive dimensions of dominant conceptions and processes of civilization.[2] It is a war that aims to break the social weave, and to engulf and destroy all—including beings, knowledges, lands, and ways of thought and existence—that obstruct and impede its path.

However, as coloniality-capitalism plot their advance, so too spread re-surgences, shifts, and movements toward a decolonial otherwise, resurgences, shifts, and movements of decoloniality in/as praxis. This chapter opens reflections on decoloniality's otherwise and praxis. And it lays the ground for understanding the potential and prospect of the decolonial *for*.

## (De)coloniality

Decoloniality has a history, *herstory*, and praxis of more than 500 years. From its beginnings in the Americas, decoloniality has been a component part of (trans)local struggles, movements, and actions to resist and refuse the lega-cies and ongoing relations and patterns of power established by external and internal colonialism—what Silvia Rivera Cusicanqui calls colonialism's long duration[3]—and the global designs of the modern/colonial world.

Lest we forget the modes of power that began with the invasion of the Cross and Crown in the Caribbean and in the land and/as myth invented first as America, and later baptized Latin America. This is the land that gave initiation, substance, and form to the coloniality of power, its system of social classification based on the idea of race, of "conquerors" over "conquered," and its structural foundation tied to modernity and Eurocentered capitalism. The control of labor and subjectivity, the practices and policies of genocide and enslavement, the pillage of life and land, and the denials and destruc-tion of knowledge, humanity, spirituality, and cosmo-existence became the modus operandi of this new model and pattern of power that later traveled the globe.

In the America of the North (now Canada and the United States), set-tler colonialism came later, exercising its system of violence and power to accomplish similar expansionist goals. "The form of colonialism that the Indigenous peoples of North America have experienced was modern from the beginning," says Roxanne Dunbar-Ortiz, precisely because it included the "expansion of European corporations, backed by government armies into foreign areas, with subsequent expropriation of lands and resources." In this sense, "settler colonialism is a genocidal policy."[4] While settler colonialism is distinct from the coloniality of power established in the Americas of the South in the sixteenth century, its patterns of extermination, pillage, enslave-ment, racialization, dehumanization, and power are, without a doubt, related.

With colonialism and coloniality came resistance and refusal. Decoloniality necessarily follows, derives from, and responds to coloniality and the ongoing colonial process and condition. It is a form of struggle and survival, an epistemic and existence-based response and practice—most especially by colonized and racialized subjects—*against* the colonial matrix of power in all of its dimensions, and *for* the possibilities of an otherwise.

Decoloniality denotes ways of thinking, knowing, being, and doing that began with, but also precede, the colonial enterprise and invasion. It implies the recognition and undoing of the hierarchical structures of race, gender, heteropatriarchy, and class that continue to control life, knowledge, spirituality, and thought, structures that are clearly intertwined with and constitutive of global capitalism and Western modernity. Moreover, it is indicative of the ongoing nature of struggles, constructions, and creations that continue to work within coloniality's margins and fissures to affirm that which coloniality has attempted to negate.

Decoloniality, in this sense, is not a static condition, an individual attribute, or a lineal point of arrival or enlightenment. Instead, decoloniality seeks to make visible, open up, and advance radically distinct perspectives and positionalities that displace Western rationality as the only framework and possibility of existence, analysis, and thought. Such perspectives and positionalities evoke and convoke what Maldonado-Torres refers to as a *decolonial attitude*. For Maldonado-Torres, this attitude recalls that advanced at the beginning of the twentieth century by W. E. B. Du Bois, that which "demands responsibility and the willingness to take many perspectives, particularly the perspectives and points of view of those whose very existence is questioned and produced as indispensable and insignificant."[5] Such attitude requires attention to what decolonial feminist thinkers such as Sylvia Wynter, Audre Lorde, and Yuderkys Espinosa have referred to as relational ways of seeing the world, including the relation between privilege and oppression.

The interest of this part I is, in a broad sense, with encouraging this relational way of seeing. It challenges the reader to think *with* (and not simply *about*) the peoples, subjects, struggles, knowledges, and thought present here. In so doing, it urges the reader to give attention to her or his own *inner eyes*, what Wynter called the classificatory lens and logic that put limits on how we can see, know, and act on and with respect to the local, national, global order.[6]

More specifically, the interest here is with praxis: the affirmative and prospective thought-actions-reflections-actions that give shape, movement, meaning, and form to decoloniality. The interest is with the praxis that walks decoloniality and, as we will see in the section that follows, with the praxis that gives substance to and elucidates resurgence and the decolonial *for*.

## Resurgence and the Decolonial *For*

Since the Spanish invasion of the "Americas"—what some fallaciously term the *Conquest*—the struggles, movements, and actions of peoples native to these lands and those brought here from Africa by force, have been and still are *against* what the Kichwa intellectual and historical leader Luis Macas calls the colonial yoke or tare. However, they have also importantly been—and continue to be—*for* the creation, and cultivation of modes of life, existence, being, and thought *otherwise*; that is, modes that confront, transgress, and undo modernity/coloniality's hold. It is the for that fosters, signals, and sketches pro-positions of affirmation and reaffirmation that disrupt and unsettle coloniality's negations. It is the for that takes us beyond an *anti* stance. Moreover, it is the for that signifies, sows, and grows the otherwise of decoloniality and/ as praxis.

Central here is that which Adolfo Albán names as *re-existence*, understood as "The mechanisms that human groups implement as a strategy of questioning and making visible the practices of racialization, exclusion and marginalization, procuring the redefining and re-signifying of life in conditions of dignity and self-determination, while at the same time confronting the bio-politic that controls, dominates, and commodifies subjects and nature."[7]

This is the resurgence of "our world" to which the beginning epigraph of the now defunct SupMarcos refers.[8] It is a world radically distinct from that of savage capitalism, imposed Western modernity, domination, and oppression. The reference here is to a collective resurgence—understood as renewal, restoration, revival or a continuing after interruption[9]—of knowledges, life practices, and re-existences that are not only Zapatista but also present and growing in territories throughout Abya Yala and the Souths of the world. For the First Nation activist-thinker Leanne Betasamosake Simpson, the real work of resurgence—and of movement- and nation-building—generates new knowledge on how to resurge from within: "We cannot just think, write or imagine our way to a decolonized future. Answers on how to re-build and how to resurge are therefore derived from a web of consensual relationships that is infused with movement through lived experience and embodiment.

Intellectual knowledge is not enough on its own. . . . All kinds of knowledge are important and necessary in a communal and emergent balance."[10]

My interest in this first part of the book is with the knowledges resurging and insurging *from below* (that is, from the ground up) within and through embodied struggle and practice, struggles and practices that, in turn, continually generate and regenerate knowledge and theory. I find accordance here with Simpson's contention that theory is not just an intellectual pursuit; "it is woven within kinetics, spiritual presence and emotion, it is contextual and relational."[11] I also agree with Sylvia Marcos that to theorize is to live; that is, and following the words of the defunct SupMarcos, "a theory so other that it is practice."[12]

Decoloniality, without a doubt, is also contextual, relational, practice based, and lived. In addition, it is intellectually, spiritually, emotionally, and existentially entangled and interwoven. The concern of this part I then is with the ongoing processes and practices, pedagogies and paths, projects and propositions that build, cultivate, enable, and engender decoloniality, this understood as a praxis—as a walking, asking, reflecting, analyzing, theorizing, and actioning—in continuous movement, contention, relation, and formation.

"Without praxis," Enrique Dussel says, "no pathway is made." It is praxis that makes the path. Yet as Dussel cautions, "the path cannot be made without points of reference that permit one to traverse topographies and labyrinths unknown. One needs a compass and to know in which direction to walk," he says. The compass gives general orientation. However, the "direction is discovered only in concrete application, with the material of day-to-day, militant, and solidarity-based praxis."[13]

It is this praxis, the making of decolonial paths, that is of interest here. While part II will focus on the conceptual frameworks, reflections, and discussions of (de)coloniality's what and why, the focus in this first part is on praxistical questions of the for, the how, and the with whom, and what for. With this beginning, I intend to disturb the notion that theoretical and conceptual frameworks must necessarily precede praxis, as well as the idea that meaning is only conceptually derived. To begin with praxis and the praxistical activity of thinking-doing, is to turn academia and Western modern thought upside down.

Here I ask: How is decoloniality signified and constructed in and through praxis? How—through what actions, processes, practice-based struggles, theory, theorizing, and thought—is praxis enacted, engaged, created, and defined? How, and in what ways, do these actions, processes, practice-based struggles, and thought point to and work toward projects of social, political, epistemic, and (re)existence-based transformation? And, how do they push, provoke, and advance other ways of being, thinking, knowing, feeling, and living? That is, other ways that interrupt, transgress, and fissure or crack modernity/coloniality's matrices of power, and make evident concrete instances and possibilities of the otherwise?

Who are the individual and collective subjects involved? With whom and for what are their propositions, processes, practices, struggles, and projects? What are the aims, intentions, hopes, visions, and horizons? Moreover, how together do the peoples, struggles, propositions, processes, practices, and actions give decoloniality a lived significance and make decoloniality a lived project of/in praxis?

Such questions necessarily make present and bring to the fore voices, bodies, minds, spirits, and thought other than just my own. Here the reader will encounter voices, bodies, minds, spirits, and thought that speak from and to individual and collective standpoints, struggles, projects, propositions, and practices—voices, bodies, minds, spirits, and thought that work to loosen and undo modernity/coloniality's hold; transverse time, place, and space; and put forward an otherwise of being, feeling, thinking, knowing, doing, and living that craft hope and possibility in these increasingly desperate and violent times of global coloniality/global capitalism taken to the extreme.

The intention here, and to paraphrase Gloria Anzaldúa, is to not just tell but also show how decoloniality happens.[14] The intention is not to write *about*, nor is it to develop a narrative by simply citing a plethora of authors, contexts, and texts. Rather, it is to think *from and with* standpoints, struggles, and practices, from and with praxical theorizings, conceptual theorizings, theoretical conceptualizings, and theory-building actionings. It is to think from and with struggles that think and thought that struggles. "Thought that does not struggle is nothing more than noise, and struggles that do not think, repeat the same errors and do not get up after falling," say the Zapatistas.[15] Moreover, it is to think from and with subjects, actors, thinkers, collectives, and movements that are signifying, sowing, and growing decoloniality in/as praxis. This thinking from and with—and especially from and with modernity/coloniality's underside, margins, and cracks—constructs, shapes, and fashions what I understand as, and what I endeavor to assume in my own practice, as a decolonial and decolonizing methodological-pedagogical-praxistical stance.

Such a stance, of course, maintains as constant the dilemma that Anzaldúa so poignantly described: "how to write (produce) without being inscribed (reproduced) in the dominant white structure and how to write without rein-scribing and reproducing what we rebel against."[16] Recognizing this dilemma and continually struggling with it (not expecting that I will ever be able to totally surmount it) are central not only to my pedagogy-method, but also to the ways I conceive, consciously address, and give praxis to my locus or place of enunciation.

As a woman perceived as white, an immigrant (from the America of the North to the America of the South, that is, from the so-called First to the so-called Third World), and an intellectual associated with the university (al-though my militancy and engagement are most often against the institution, in its margins, borders, and cracks), I carry a privilege that I cannot negate. How to write, think, and act in ways that work to dismantle the structures of privilege and the modern/colonial matrices of power (of which privilege is part), how to assume decolonial praxis (including decolonial feminism) in practice, and how to help walk a decolonial *for* (i.e., a decolonial otherwise), are questions that underscore my decolonial and decolonizing intention and methodological-pedagogical-praxistical stance, not only here but in all aspects of my relational being-becoming.

By mentioning this intention and stance, I hope to challenge the reader to shift her or his posture and gaze. The challenge is to not look for theory first. It is also to move beyond a simple reading of and about, toward a thinking from and with, a thinking-doing that requires contemplation of one's own place of enunciation and relation (or not) with the so-called universality of West-ern thought. I am referring to a thinking-doing that delinks, that undoes the unified—and universalizing—centrality of the West as the world and that begins to push other questions, other reflections, other considerations, and other understandings.

The context that orients and grounds this part I is Abya Yala. Abya Yala is the name that the *Kuna-Tule* people (of the lands now known as Panama and Colombia) gave to the "Americas" before the colonial invasion. It sig-nifies "land in full maturity" or "land of vital blood." Its present-day use began to take form in 1992 when Indigenous peoples from throughout the continent came together to counter the "Discovery" celebrations, "to reflect upon 500 years of the European invasion and to formulate alternatives for a better life, in harmony with Nature and Human Dignity." As the then-joint statement of the Confederation of Indigenous Nationalities of Ecuador (CONAIE), the National Indigenous Organization of Colombia (ONIC), and the California-based South and Meso American Indian Information Center

(SAIIC) went on to argue: "With the European invasion and subsequent process of colonization, our peoples became isolated and cut off from each other, breaking a level of development we had attained. Today, our peoples are developing forms of political, religious, cultural, and economic interchange and interrelationships—a continental cultural identity—, a civilization."[17]

It was in this frame of reestablishing a continental identity, relation, and civilization, that Abya Yala became a way to rename, disrupt, and counter "America," a name-idea imposed in, by, and through "conquest." As such, it was a decolonial proposition not only for Indigenous peoples, but more broadly for the continent and to and for the world.

Brought to the fore here are the politics of naming. "To name is to struggle," argues the Kichwa intellectual Armando Muyolema. "First America and later Latin America are the result of those politics of naming and imperial struggles for political and cultural hegemony in conquered territories."[18] Similarly and in reference to European imperial naming, Iris Zavalla sustains that the heuristic code of naming is a form of political cartography or mapmaking that fixes the cultural image, subordinates differences, and radically destroys identities.[19] The European baptizing of the continent drastically modified the heretofore history, plurality, and social, cultural, economic, spiritual, territorial, and existential foundation of these lands, making it—by naming it—a singular unit seen and defined from the European gaze; a naming that as Aimé Césaire argued more than half a century ago, intended to annihilate all that existed before: "I am talking about societies drained of their essence, cultures trampled underfoot, institutions undermined, lands confiscated, religions smashed, magnificent artistic creations destroyed, extraordinary possibilities wiped out, I am talking about millions of men [sic] torn from their gods, their land, their habits, their life—from life, from the dance, from wisdom."[20]

Nevertheless, this baptizing also established, as Vanessa Fonseca maintains, a genitive matrix in its naming. "America, the land of Americo. To name 'her,' he possessed her. To think America as the name of a woman," says Fonseca, "is to insert her—America—as difference in a process of signification that entails a will to power," and a power to name.[21] It is easy to see, in this sense, how "America" has been mutually imbricated with coloniality from the beginning.[22] Moreover, in the same vein, it is easy to understand why the collective renaming as Abya Yala is resurgence, and why it is a clear example of decoloniality in praxis.

Some argue that Abya Yala takes back the original Indigenous concept and name for the continent. Anahuac and "Turtle Island," the latter in increasing use by First Nations peoples, similarly take back North America's pre-invasion conceptual naming. Recalled here as well is Aztlán, the ancestral home of Aztec peoples in the lands of what are now the U.S. Southwest and the Mexican Northwest, a take-back naming present in the works of many Chicanas and Chicanos, most notably Gloria Anzaldúa.

Others see in the renaming of Abya Yala the contemporary exercise of a re-existence-based politics that is decolonial in attitude, posture, proposition, and force. That is, a politics that affirms, constructs, and advances a radically distinct meaning, understanding, and project not just for Indigenous peoples but also for all. Thinking with this politics and naming is part of the decolonial option that Walter will describe in part II. In addition, it is a central part of the conceptualization of decolonial praxis that underscores this part of the book.

Decolonial praxis, of course, is not limited to the context of Abya Yala. Yet it was in the particular sociohistorical and geopolitical context of the "discovery and conquest" of the Americas of the South (i.e., "Latin" America and the Caribbean) and its multiple violences—racialized, gendered, physical, civilizational, cultural, linguistic, ontological-existential, epistemic, spiritual, cosmological, and so forth—that coloniality and decoloniality took form.

As Aníbal Quijano has explained, coloniality developed around two central axes or patterns of power that came to be foundational to modernity and global capitalism. The first was "the codification of the difference between conquerors and conquered in the idea of 'race' . . . the constitutive, founding element of the relations of domination that the conquest imposed." The second was "the constitution of a new structure of control of labor and its resources and products" that articulated "slavery, serfdom, small independent commodity production and reciprocity, together around and upon the basis of capital and the world market."[23] As a matrix of power, coloniality came to operate in Abya Yala, and subsequently elsewhere, in multiple spheres, exercising control over humanity, subjectivity and being, gender and sexuality, spirituality, knowledge production, economy, nature, existence and life itself. Coloniality, in this sense, involves and affects us all. As Maldonado-Torres contends, "as modern subjects we breathe coloniality all the time and every day."[24]

Decoloniality necessarily evokes coloniality. It has its roots and reason in the modern/colonial matrix of power, a matrix that, as Walter will describe, has its base in Quijano's conceptualization. Quijano laid the ground with the concept-term *coloniality*. However, the idea of an ongoing pattern of colonial power can be witnessed in the thought of many, including Frantz

Fanon and the lesser-known Colombian thinker Manuel Zapata Olivella, who both thought from their own colonial difference.[25] The operation of a colonial matrix of power has also been analyzed in differential ways and in distinct contexts by a number of authors, who may or may not identify with the decolonial project.[26]

However, the interest here is not with conceptual genealogies, but with the ways that decoloniality is defined by, from, in and with the struggles—political, epistemic, and existence based—against coloniality and for its otherwise. The interest is with how decoloniality's project and praxis take form in and contribute to the fissures of the dominant order, what I have called its decolonial cracks.[27] While these fissures or cracks are present throughout the world, including in the Global North, the project and praxis of decoloniality are more visibly witnessed, sensed, and felt in what the Pakistani intellectual-activist-feminist Corinne Kumar calls the "wind of the South": "The South as civilizations, . . . as voices and movements, . . . as visions and wisdoms, . . . as the discovering of new paradigms, which challenge the existing theoretical concepts and categories breaking the mind constructs, . . . as the discovery of other cosmologies . . . other knowledges that have been hidden, submerged, silenced. The South as a new political imaginary, . . . new meanings, new moorings."[28]

If it is the South (the South in the South and the South in the North) that, as Kumar suggests, proffers new movements, philosophies, and horizons of and for praxis, then Abya Yala is particularly illustrative. This is because of its 500-plus years of decolonial resurgence, insurrection, rebellion, and agency, and for its present-day shifts, movements, and manifestations that give possibility, sustenance, credence, and concretion to a decolonial otherwise.

## On Decolonial Shifts and Movements

While 1492 marked the beginning in Abya Yala of the model of world power that we now refer to as modernity/coloniality, the decade of the 1990s—of 500 years—began in this same continent a new political moment of decolonial resistance, proposition, shift, and movement. The *newness* of this moment was not in its originality in a lineal sense. Rather it was in its contemporary re-membrance of decolonial struggle and historical continuity in thought, analyses, reflection, and action from the ground up, that is, from the peoples who for centuries have lived the colonial difference, the difference imposed through a hierarchical classification based on the ideas of race, anthropocentrism, heteronormativity, and gender.

The multitudinous public uprisings of Indigenous peoples in Ecuador and Bolivia in 1990, and of the Zapatistas in Mexico in 1994, along with the continental organization against the colonial celebrations of 1992 mentioned above, made visible to the world an agency, initiative, and posture of both protest and proposition. The massive uprising of 1990 organized by the Confederation of Indigenous Nationalities of Ecuador (CONAIE)—sometimes referred to as the awakening of the sleeping lion—disturbed the dominant ethnic imaginary of Ecuador's Right and Left. This imaginary perceived Indians as a passive population tied to the countryside, artisan work, and/or manual labor, and as "disappearing entities anxious to become 'civilized' mestizos."[29] The mobilization of thousands of men, women, and children made present the existence, vitality, and force of Indigenous peoples, but also put on the table the problem—and failure—of the so-called democracy, the homogenizing national project, and the uninational state. Land, self-determination, and ethnic rights were part of their demands; the other part, as I will discuss further in chapter 3, was for a plurinational state and a radically distinct social project for all of Ecuadorian society.

In Bolivia the 500-kilometer March of Indigenous Peoples from the lowland Amazon region to the capital (also in 1990), made visible a peoples that the so-called nation-state had historically denied. It also brought to the forefront debates about the significance of territory, Nature (with a capital *N*), and the capitalist logics of ownership, extractivism, and exploitation.

The public emergence of the Zapatistas in 1994 similarly made visible the historically invisibilized. Moreover, the Zapatistas' call for an end to neoliberal policies and for new visions of social and political participation and democracy in Chiapas and in Mexico as a whole, marked the beginning of a new political moment of decolonial resistance, resurgence, proposition, thought, shift, and movement that continues until today.

Of course these mobilizations, mobilizing acts, and social, political, and economic analyses unsettled traditional leftist class-based perspectives that, throughout the second half of the twentieth century, attempted to fix the identity and social function of native peoples as only rural peasants.[30] Unsettled as well were the anthropologically conceived ideas of, and the anthropological study about, ethnicity and Indios. In Ecuador, Indigenous communities ousted anthropologists; with this loss of "objects" of study, many schools of anthropology closed. Recalled is the poignant analysis of the Maori anthropologist Linda Tuhiwai Smith, on the research-imperialism-colonialism entwine. "The term 'research' is inextricably linked to European imperialism and colonialism," Smith contends. "This collective memory of imperialism has been perpetuated through the ways in which knowledge about indigenous peoples was collected, classified and then represented in various ways back to the West, and then, through the eyes of the West, back to those who have been colonized."[31]

Throughout the decade of the 1990s, Indigenous peoples began to ascertain their own forms of identification and self-representation. They disputed the societal negations of their historicity, perseverance, and self-determination as millennial nations and peoples, and they made visible their presence and intellectual sovereignty as social protagonists and historical and political subjects. In so doing, they challenged the dominant models of society, economy, governance, nation, and state and, in a related sense, their own heretofore anonymity and invisibility in the public sphere. One of the clearest challenges to this anonymity and invisibility has been the collective act of the Zapatistas to cover their faces. "So that they could see us, we covered our faces; so that they could name us, we negated our names . . . reaffirming a collective identity, a movement that is Zapatista."[32]

The decade of the 1990s stands out, not because Indigenous resistance did not exist before, but because of the character and nature of this period of Indigenous-led resurgence and struggle. Throughout Abya Yala, Indigenous people did not just "rise up," but they led public actions, formed alliances with other sectors, and educated the general populace about the lived social, political, and economic problems of neoliberalism and the modern/colonial/capitalist system.[33] They gave substance and form to what Arturo Arias, Luis Cárcamo-Huechante, and Emilio Del Valle Escalante call the "territory of Indigenous agency"; that is, to a linguistic, aesthetic, epistemic, and political project that articulates new spheres of mobilization, subjectivity, and decolonizing production.[34] Additionally, they worked to interrupt the multi-cultural politics of recognition present throughout the continent (discussed in chapter 3), and to work "within," that is from Indigenous communities' own ancestral knowledges and intelligence, what Leanne Simpson calls the necessary knowledge and intelligence for resurgence.[35]

For the Kichwa intellectual and lawyer Nina Pacari, it was in the decade of the 1990s that protest and prospect, theory and practice, and the struggles of land, culture, ideology, and liberation all coalesced in the Ecuadorian Indigenous movements' demands, proposals, and projects for structural transformation and the building of a radically different social order.[36] Yet this is not to suggest that the challenges to coloniality and the propositions of decolonial possibility in Abya Yala have come only from Indigenous movements. Nor is it to simplify or idealize these movements, their propositions, worldviews, and practice or to intimate that indigeneity necessarily implies decoloniality (something I will take up in chapter 4).

Rather, and on the one hand, it is to recognize that in Abya Yala, it has been the social movements of historically excluded, subalternized, and racialized peoples that in the last decades have led and given substance and possibility to what Fernando Coronil referred to as the innovations and ruptures of *el devenir histórico* (the historical becoming).[37] The reference here is to the innovations and ruptures that signal political formations, positions, and practices that extend beyond the concerns of the traditional Left. And it is also to innovations and ruptures that outline new strategies of action and of social, political, economic, epistemic, cultural, and re-existence-based struggle that confront the legacies and contemporary manifestations of the modern/colonial matrix of power and push decolonizing movements. The fact that it has been Indigenous movements, the movements of African descendants, and women—particularly women of color—who have led these innovations, ruptures, and struggles is not fortuitous. Also not fortuitous is the fact that these innovations, ruptures, and struggles have been directed at transformations of and for society as a whole, transformations understood as a historical becoming that undoes the categories that coloniality and its system of hierarchical social classification imposed.

Similarly and on the other hand, it is to recall Arturo Escobar's argument made over a decade ago about "the need to take seriously the epistemic force of local histories and to think theory through from the political praxis of subaltern groups."[38] Escobar's position here was twofold.

First, Escobar made a case for the "flesh and blood" of decolonial struggles; of the need for potential work within what he termed "the modernity/coloniality research program." Here Escobar referred to the work that directly engages "colonial difference and border thinking from the ground up," thus helping to avoid the epistemological traps of disembodied abstract discourse, the risks of logocentrism, and the limitations of academic-intellectual reflection. Second, Escobar argued for a decolonial shift of sorts concerning how we understand theory. Such a shift entails a rethinking of how and with whom we think (and understand) theory, and a recognition of the intertwines of local histories, knowledges, political praxis, and place.

As I have argued, it also entails moving from a posture of "studying about" to "thinking with."[39] This latter move necessarily demands the enunciation of the researcher herself or himself, and the making visible of his or her presence in this thinking. Challenged here are not only the scientific precepts of distance, neutrality, and objectivity, but also importantly the Western modern/colonial frames of theory, knowledge, research, and academic thought. As I will argue in later chapters, such shifts are important steps in individual and group work toward a decolonial perspective, but also, and more broadly, in terms of praxis itself, including in opening decolonial cracks and fracturing and fissuring modernity/coloniality's hold on knowledge, thinking, and learning within the university.

The problem, however, is when theory, theorizing, knowledge, and thought are considered as only—or predominantly—the purview of academics and the academy. This is not to slight the worth of decolonial praxis and movement within academia (see chapters 3 and 4). Instead, it is to prompt considerations that take us beyond the centrality of academia and its subjects, contexts, and confines. It is to confront the idea of historically excluded, subalternized, and racialized peoples as "objects" of study. In addition, it is to open consideration about the ways in which subjects, peoples, and movements who live the colonial difference not only *act* but also produce knowledge and construct theory.

Here, theory, as knowledge, is understood as incarnated and situated, something that the university too often forgets. Theory—as knowledge—derives from and is formed, molded, and shaped in and by actors, histories, territories, and place that, whether recognized or not, are marked by the colonial horizon of modernity, and by the racialized, classed, gendered, heteronormativized, and Western-Euro-U.S.-centric systems of power, knowledge, being, civilization, and life that such horizon has constructed and perpetuated. The production of knowledge and theory through embodied practice and from the ground up—that is by subjects, identified or not as women and men, who live the colonial difference—turns the dominant precept of reason and its geography and geopolitics on its head.

The interest then, and to paraphrase Escobar, is to give attention to the ways those who live the colonial difference think theory through from political praxis, theorize their own practice, and take (very) seriously the epistemic force of local histories and struggles. Such attention takes us beyond postures that simply associate social movements and subalternized groups with social and cultural resistance, and resistance as an end goal. More critically, it urges considerations of the praxistical or praxical. Specifically, it urges considerations of insurgent political, epistemic, existence-, and re-existence-based constructions, productions, creations, practices, and action-reflection that generate alternatives, interpolate the instances of hegemonic power, including neoliberalism and what the Zapatistas have recently termed the *capitalist hydra*,[40] and give route to shifts and movements toward decoloniality's otherwise. The chapter that follows explores what all this means in concrete terms.

## Notes

Epigraph: Subcomandante Insurgente Marcos, "Comunicado del Comité Clandestino Revolucionario Indígena-Comandancia General del Ejército Zapatista De Liberación Nacional del 21 de diciembre del 2012," accessed July 22, 2017, http://enlacezapatista.ezln.org.mx/2012/12/21/comunicado-del-comite -clandestino-revolucionario-indigena-comandancia-general-del-ejercito-zapatista -de-liberacion-nacional-del-21-de-diciembre-del-2012/.

Unless otherwise specified, translations of Spanish-language quotations are those of the authors.

1   See Comisión Sextra del EZLN, *El pensamiento crítico frente a la hidra capitalista I* (Chiapas, Mexico: EZLN, 2015).

2   Nelson Maldonado-Torres, *Against War: Views from the Underside of Modernity* (Durham, NC: Duke University Press, 2008).

3   Silvia Rivera Cusicanqui, "La raíz: Colonizadores y colonizados," in *Violencias encubiertas en Bolivia: Cultura y política*, ed. Xavier Albó and Raúl Barrios, 27–139 (La Paz: CIPCA-ARUWIYIRI, 1993).

4   Roxanne Dunbar-Ortiz, *An Indigenous Peoples' History of the United States* (Boston: Beacon Press, 2014), 6.

5   Maldonado-Torres, *Against War*, 8.

6   Sylvia Wynter, "No Humans Involved: A Letter to my Colleagues," *Forum NHI: Knowledge for the 21st Century* 1, no. 1 (1994): 42–71.

7   Adolfo Albán Achinte, "¿Interculturalidad sin decolonialidad? Colonialidades circulantes y prácticas de re-existencia," in *Diversidad, interculturalidad y construcción de ciudad*, ed. Wilmer Villa and Arturo Grueso (Bogotá: Universidad Pedagógica Nacional/Alcaldía Mayor, 2008), 85–86.

8    At dawn on May 25, 2014, the Insurgent Subcomandante Marcos, Zapatista
     spokesperson and military chief, died a symbolic death. The collective decision by
     the Zapatista National Liberation Army (EZLN) to end SupMarcos's existence, an
     existence created by the EZLN in 1994, was strategic. "We have come to realize that
     we now have a generation of Zapatistas that can look us straight in the face, that can
     hear us and speak to us without waiting for guidance or leadership, without pretend-
     ing submission or following. . . . The figure of Marcos is no longer necessary. . . .
     The figure was created and now its creators, the Zapatista women and men, destroy
     it. If you are able to understand this lesson, then you have understood one of the
     foundations of Zapatismo." See EZLN, "Entre la luz y la sombra," Chiapas, Mexico:
     EZLN, May 25, 2014, http://enlacezapatista.ezln.org.mx/2014/05/25/entre-la-luz-y
     -la-sombra/.

9    Walter Mignolo, "Foreword: Anomie, Resurgences, and De-Noming," in *The Anomie
     of the Earth: Philosophy, Politics, and Autonomy in Europe and the Americas*, ed. F.
     Luisetti, J. Pickles, and W. Kaiser, vii–xvi (Durham, NC: Duke University Press, 2015).

10   Leanne Simpson, "Land as Pedagogy: Nishnaabeg Intelligence and Rebellious
     Transformation," *Decolonization: Indigeneity, Education and Society* 3, no. 3
     (2014): 16.

11   Simpson, "Land as Pedagogy," 7.

12   In Sylvia Marcos, "La realidad no cabe en la teoría," *El pensamiento crítico frente a
     la hidra capitalista III*, ed. EZLN (Chiapas, Mexico: EZLN, 2016), 21, 27.

13   Enrique Dussel, *16 Tesis de Economía Política: Interpretación filosófica* (Mexico City:
     Siglo XXI, 2014), 322.

14   Gloria Anzaldúa, *Light in the Dark, Luz en lo Oscuro: Rewriting Identity, Spirituality,
     Reality*, ed. Analouise Keating, 7 (Durham, NC: Duke University Press, 2015).

15   In Sylvia Marcos, "La realidad no cabe en la teoría," 15.

16   Anzaldúa, *Light in the Dark*, 7–8.

17   CONAIE, ONIC, and SAIIC, "A Call to Indigenous People: 500 Years of Resistance,"
     *Native Web*, South and Meso American Indigenous Information Center, April 1989.

18   Armando Muyolema, "De la 'cuestión indígena' a lo 'indígena' como cuestion-
     amiento: Hacia una crítica del latinoamericanismo, el indigenismo y el mestiz(o)aje,"
     in *Convergencia de tiempo: Estudios subalternos/contextos latinoamericanos,
     estado, cultura subalternidad*, ed. Ileana Rodríguez, 328 (Amsterdam: Rodopi, 2001).

19   Cited in Muyolema, "De la 'cuestión indígena,'" 328.

20   Aimé Césaire, *Discourse on Colonialism*, trans. Joan Pinkham (New York: Monthly
     Review Press, [1955] 2000), 43.

21   Vanessa Fonseca, "América es nombre de mujer," *Reflexiones* 58, no. 1 (1997): 3–4.

22   Mignolo, *The Idea of Latin America* (Malden, MA: Blackwell, 2005), 47.

23   Aníbal Quijano, "Coloniality of Power, Eurocentrism, and Latin America," *Nepantla:
     Views from South*, 1 no. 3 (2000): 533–34.

24   Maldonado-Torres, "On the Coloniality of Being: Contributions to the Development
     of a Concept," in *Globalization and the Decolonial Option*, ed. Walter Mignolo and
     Arturo Escobar (London: Routledge, 2010), 97.

25   See, particularly, Manuel Zapata Olivella, *Las claves mágicas de América* (Bogotá: Plaza and Janes, 1989).

26   See, for instance, Rivera Cusicanqui, *Oprimidos pero no vencidos: Luchas del campesinado aymara y qhechwa 1900–1980*, ed. Silvia Rivera Cusicanqui (La Paz: Hisbol, 1986), 168, and Patricio Noboa, "La matriz colonial de poder, los movimientos sociales y los silencios de la modernidad," in *Pensamiento crítico y matriz (de)colonial de poder: Reflexiones Latinoamericanas*, ed. Catherine Walsh, 71–109 (Quito: Universidad Andina Simón Bolívar and Ediciones Abya-Yala, 2005). In a subsequent text, Rivera elaborated the idea of a colonial matrix of *mestizaje* (see "La raíz: Colonizadores y colonizados").

27   Catherine Walsh, "Pedagogical Notes from the Decolonial Cracks," *e-misférica* 11, no. 1 (2014), accessed May 24, 2016, http://hemisphericinstitute.org/hemi/en /emisferica-111-decolonial-gesture/walsh.

28   Corinne Kumar, "Introduction," in *Asking We Walk: The South as New Political Imaginary. Book One, In the Time of the Earth*, ed. Corinne Kumar, 2nd ed. (Bangalore: Streelekha, 2010), xiii–xiv.

29   Walsh, "The (Re)Articulation of Political Subjectivities and Colonial Difference in Ecuador: Reflections on Capitalism and the Geopolitics of Knowledge," *Nepantla: Views from South* 3, no. 1 (2002): 68.

30   One of the clearest contestations to this imposition can be read in the 1983 "Political Thesis" of Bolivia's CSUTCB, the labor union arm of the katarist movement. "Our oppressors have tried through diverse means to systematically plunder our historical identity. They tried to make us forget our true origins and reduce us to only *campesinos* or peasants, without personality, without history and without identity. . . . In this liberation struggle, we have maintained our personality as Aymaras, Qhechwas, Cambas, Chapacos, Tupiguaranis, etc., and we have learned that we can reach our liberation without losing our cultural identity and our identity as nations." CSUTCB, "Tesis política 1983," in *Oprimidos pero no vencidos: Luchas del campesinado aymara y qhechwa 1900–1980*, ed. Silvia Rivera Cusicanqui (La Paz: Hisbol, 1986), 196.

31   Linda Tuhiwai Smith, *Decolonizing Methodologies: Research and Indigenous Peoples* (London: Zed Books, 1999), 1.

32   Letter from Subcomandante Marcos to "Hermanos," March 1995, http://palabra .ezln.org.mx/comunicados/1995/1995_03_17_b.htm.

33   For a detailed description of these struggles, see Walsh, "The (De)Coloniality of Knowledge, Life, and Nature: The North American-Andean Free Trade Agreement, Indigenous Movements, and Regional Alternatives," in *Globalization and Beyond: New Examinations of Global Power and Its Alternatives*, ed. Jon Shefner and Patricia Fernández-Kelly, 228–48 (University Park: Pennsylvania State University Press, 2011).

34   Arturo Arias, Luis Cárcamo-Huechante, and Emilio Del Valle Escalante, "Literaturas de Abya Yala," *Lasa Forum* 43, no. 1 (winter 2012): 7–10.

35   Simpson, "Land as Pedagogy," 16. On the struggles against the politics of recognition, particularly among Canadian First Nations, see Glen Coulthard, *Red Skin,*

*White Masks: Rejecting the Colonial Politics of Recognition* (Minneapolis: University of Minnesota Press, 2014).

36  Nina Pacari, talk given in the Forum on the "World Crisis and the Exhaustion of Progressive Models," Universidad Andina Simón Bolívar, Quito, October 12, 2015.

37  Fernando Coronil, "¿Globalización liberal o imperialismo global? Cinco piezas para armar el rompecabezas del presente," *Comentario Internacional, Revista del Centro Andino de Estudios Internacionales*, no. 5 (2004): 117.

38  Arturo Escobar, "Beyond the Third World: Imperial Globality, Global Coloniality and Anti-globalization Social Movements," *Third World Quarterly* 25, no.1 (2004): 217. Also see Escobar, "Worlds and Knowledges Otherwise: The Latin American Modernity/Coloniality Research Program." In *Globalization and the Decolonial Option*, ed. Walter Mignolo and Arturo Escobar, 33–64 (New York: Routledge, 2010).

39  See Walsh, "Political-Epistemic Insurgency, Social Movements and the Refounding of the State" in *Rethinking Intellectuals in Latin America*, ed. Mabel Moraña, 199–211 (St. Louis: Washington State University, 2010).

40  See Comisión Sexta del EZLN, *El pensamiento crítico frente a la hidra capitalista I*.

## 2 Insurgency and Decolonial Prospect, Praxis, and Project

### On Decolonial Insurgency

In his inaugural speech in January 2006, Bolivia's president Evo Morales proclaimed: "We are here to say enough with resistance. Of the resistance of 500 years to the taking of power for 500 years, Indians, workers of all the sectors to end with this injustice, to end with this inequality, to end above all with this discrimination and oppression to which we have been subjected. . . . Today begins a new life of justice and equality for the Bolivian people, a new millennium for all the people of the world."[1]

Similarly, but in a very different context and project, the Insurgent Subcomandante Marcos spoke in 2008 of the movement within the Army of Zapatista National Liberation (EZLN) and Zapatista communities from a posture of resistance and a historic and emphatic "no" toward concrete proposals and courses of action. "The 'no' that now rises up does not just resist, but also begins to propose, to determine," said the now defunct SupMarcos.[2] Suggested here is a relation between resistance and re-existence, that is, "to resist re-existing" and/or "to re-exist resisting," both of which imply the propositional *for* discussed in the previous chapter.

*Resistance* has been a defining term used by social movements themselves and by those who purport to study these formations. Here both the posture and theoretical-conceptual lens most often denote oppositional-defensive and reactive-social action. Yet as both Marcos and Morales make clear, the emphatic *no* understood as defensive opposition—a social, cultural, and political reaction *against*—has moved in recent years toward a propositional and insurgent offensive *for* that challenges and constructs. This is the relational protest-prospect-proposition to which Nina Pacari referred in the previous chapter, one that Euro-U.S.-centric thinkers (and their followers in the Latin American academy) generally still fail to see. Certainly this can be observed among those associated with the study of the so-called new social movements defined by the relation of culture, identity, ideology, and politics; Alberto Melucci, Alain Touraine, Ernesto Laclau, Chantal Mouffe, Jürgen Habermas, and Manuel Castells are only some examples.

It is in the *for*, in the postures, processes, and practices that disrupt, transgress, intervene and in-surge in, and that mobilize, propose, provoke, activate, and construct an otherwise, that decoloniality is signified and given substance, meaning, and form. I recognize this pro-positive and creative force as insurgent, and refer to it in this chapter as *decolonial insurgency*. My conceptualization of insurgency here is simultaneously political, epistemic, and existence based; insurgency urges, puts forth, and advances from the ground up and from the margins, other imaginaries, visions, knowledges, modes of thought, other ways of being, becoming, and living in relation.[3] It does not negate the resurgence discussed in the last chapter but instead builds upon and extends it. More than a simple renewal, restoration, or revival (of knowledges, life practices, and re-existences), insurgency here denotes the act-action of creation, construction, and intervention that aims toward an otherwise.

The concept of *insurgency* is certainly not new. It has been used to refer to insurrections and rebellions, to contestatory actions and historical initiatives that confront the structures, politics, and practices of power and domination.[4] Yet seldom are such references conceived with relation to knowledge and (re)existence. That is, as offensive actions and proactive protagonisms of construction, creation, intervention, and affirmation that purport to intervene in and transgress, not just the social, cultural, and political terrains but also, and most importantly, the intellectual arena. Moreover, and seldom yet is insurgency understood from the composite of the political, epistemic, and existential, an amalgam conceived interrelationally (and ancestrally), and revitalized and resignified in the present-day struggles and actions of historically excluded communities, groups, peoples, and movements.

Such struggles and actions have, as we will see, opened paths that lead to new arrangements of thought, knowledge, theorizing, and thinking within and toward the political, and to new constructions of life, living, and societal articulation that give significance, concretion, and substance to decoloniality's otherwise. Recalled here are both the Jamaican philosopher Sylvia Wynter's call for correlation,[5] and the Chicana-feminist Emma Pérez's idea of the *decolonial imaginary*, the latter understood as a political project and an alternative model of (re)conceptualization (for Pérez: of history, historiography, and oppositional conscience).[6]

Nonetheless, it is in the concrete making and doing of insurgency and insurgent praxis—that is, in the multiple contexts, manifestations, and *hows* of political-epistemic-existence-based resistance, rebellion, struggle, action, and prospect in Abya Yala today—that this imaginary, reconceptualization, and correlation begin to take tangible form. It is in this concrete making and doing, in embodied practice, that theory is crafted and that theorizations are continually made. Moreover, it is also in this concrete making and doing—particularly that which creates hope and advances projects of life against and in spite of the projects of violence, death, war, extermination, and attempted extractivism (of lands, nature, life, and knowledges)—that decoloniality is constructed and unfolds. Certainly the examples are many and varied. Here I share a few from different but related contexts and spheres of collective insurgent praxis, and from the voices and perspectives of those actively involved.

## Life, Territory, and (Re)Existence in Relation

The struggles for and on territory and land as the base and place of identity, knowledge, being, spirituality, cosmo-vision-existence, and life, have long organized the collective insurgent praxis of ancestral peoples, identified as Indigenous, Afro-descendant, or Black,[7] and sometimes as peasant or *campesino*. Such struggles are lived today throughout Abya Yala in both the South and North. The Native American resurgence and struggles at Standing Rock against the Dakota pipeline access (in 2016–17 and as I complete this text) is one example in the North. Another is the "Red Line Action," a collaboration among the Indigenous Environmental Network and other groups taking form in 2017 in the United States. "Defend, Protect, Renew, Resist. We are Mother Earth's Red Line . . . a red line of protection against capitalism, militarism and racism," organizers said.[8] However, the references in this chapter are predominantly to collective struggles and contexts much less known to English-language readers, contexts and struggles that defend life against violence taken to the extreme, against the capitalist death project, and for an otherwise of re-existence and life in relation.

One such context is that of the territory-region of Colombia's Pacific coast. The Afro-Colombian decolonial feminist Betty Ruth Lozano makes present the insurgent subjectivities, voices, postures, and thought of *blackwomen* (her way of emphasizing the impossible separation of being a woman and being black) in this territory-region and most especially in Buenaventura. This region, long referred to in national documents as a *wasteland*, has a black matrilineal heritage tied to territory, a history that predates the Colombian state, and a reality marked by the ongoing conflicts and violences of extractivism, development, and capital interests. The presence of guerrilla bands in the region dates back to the 1980s. Yet it was in the '90s when paramilitary groups and drug traffickers began to dispute control that the situation of violence, forced displacement, and death became especially acute. In recent years the situation has become extreme, despite so-called peace agreements.

For Lozano, today the Pacific in general and Buenaventura in particular are laboratories where the new pattern of the global coloniality of power is expressed. It is not fortuitous that Buenaventura is the city with the highest level of unemployment, lowest level of educational opportunities, and the greatest levels of violence (especially against women). It is also not fortuitous that Buenaventura is the city most impacted by evangelical churches (key actors today in the capitalist/heteropatriarchal/modern/colonial project), territorial expropriations, transnational megaprojects, and a destruction of cultural codes, values, and norms. Here, and in the midst of an unstoppable avalanche of violence, the cutthroat moral is that only the most powerful survive.[9]

In this context, Lozano argues, "life becomes unsustainable up against the fear of death, sexual abuse, kidnapping, prostitution (including of young girls), disappearances, impalements that include cutting off the buttocks of women and playing football with them, . . . and killings that include cutting women up in pieces and throwing the parts in the estuaries, rivers or streams."[10] In concrete and lived terms, Lozano constructs the significance—for her and the other Afro-Colombian or blackwomen that make up the collective Red Mariposas de Alas Nuevas Construyendo Futuro (the Network of Butterflies with New Wings Constructing Future)—of insurgency as a political, epistemic, and (re)existence-based strategy of living of and for life itself. Insurgency here refers to those processes and possibilities of collective analysis, collective theorization, and collective practice—all intertwined—that help engender an otherwise of relational being, thinking, feeling, doing, and living in a place marked by the extremes of violence, racism, and patriarchy in today's matrix of global capitalism/modernity/coloniality. In this context, "Blackwomen are not just impotent victims, they also exercise power beyond resistance and survival; they are insurgents," Lozano contends.[11]

Similarly, Vilma Almendra (Nasa-Misak) from the collective Tejido de Comunicación para la Verdad y la Vida (Weave of Communication for Truth and Life), speaks of the life-based practices of *palabrandar* (walking words) that work to confront and overturn the death project strategies that continue in the Indigenous territories of Cauca, Colombia; strategies of terror and war, of dispossession-based legislation, of ideological submission, and of capture–co-optation of leaders. This collective walking of words—without owners—marks a community-based ethic grounded in the defense of dignity, territory, and life; in the revitalization of ancestral thought; and in the resurgence/insurgence of what Almendra refers to as an "other" communication, a communication otherwise.

"Our *palabrandar,* that is to say our other-communication, must lead us to recognize the external aggression, but also the ethical, political, and strategic challenges that emerge from our own contradictions," says Almendra. *Palabrandar* is that communicative action-analysis-reflection-thought-action that organizes the Tejido de Comunicación in the Indigenous territories of Cauca. It both names and constructs processes of consciousness raising, collective analysis, and collective action, readings from within territories—from the land, elders, adults, and youth—of the contexts and realities of struggle against the agents of transnational capitalism, and for strategies and actions to strengthen, re-create, and defend territory and/as Mother Earth, and/as life. As such, it is a concept conceived communally, from the outside and underside—the *below*—of the dominant system. Its meaning derives from the action itself, from giving word to the path of struggle and walking these words, weaving relations of communication, dialogue, critical thought, and shared reflection and action that disturb the spoliations of capital (including its capture of territory), build resistance, autonomy, and community, and construct-and-walk re-existence and its decolonizing otherwise.[12]

This same proposition, prospect, and horizon underscore, orient, and shape Pueblos en Camino (roughly translated as Peoples Walking or Peoples in Route), self-described not as an organization but as a collectively woven *we* of peoples and collective actions of resistance, autonomy, and mobilization from Patagonia to Canada. This *we* posits itself as a proposal, wager, and challenge against "capital, permanent conquest, and the transnational corporative-speculative phase of dispossession that threatens all of life. . . . Activism, militant and critical writing, research, teaching, and diverse forms of direct struggle, communication, responsibilities in Indigenous, popular, and social movements, and political party militancies are only some of the examples that illustrate our being/becoming through that which we do."[13] By generating spaces of encounter, word, and action, including online, Pueblos en Camino impels, links, and spreads embodied thought-analysis, as well as shared reflection and action. It weaves a praxis of political-epistemic-existence-based prospect as a way, this *we* argues, to sow life against the growing project of death of these times.

The defense of water, territories, and life against the ramped imposition and expansion of state and transnational projects of extractivism (mining, energy, gas, and oil) and the commodification of nature organizes and gives reason and form in Abya Yala today to an increasing variety of practices of insurgent action. Yamile Alvira, for example, tells us of the use of orality and song by *campesina* communities, and particularly women, in the Andean Cajamarca region of Peru in their struggle to resist and in-surge against the impositions of extractivism, capitalism, neoliberalism, and patriarchy (all understood as complicit and interwoven), and for an other-condition of living. The "sung word" emerges from and expresses the collective feeling, thinking, and doing of this struggle, says Alvira, but also reveals and transmits Andean knowledges and wisdoms that configure and reaffirm life and existence in relation with all of nature, and in a recurrent and daily pedagogical practice of resistance-insurgence of decolonial character and intent.[14]

From a somewhat different sphere of insurgency and praxis, Arturo Arias, Luis Cárcamo-Huechante, and Emilio del Valle Escalante help us see how an insurgent agency has begun to take shape in and through Indigenous-written literature, most especially in Peru (Quechua), Chile (Mapuche), Guatemala (Maya), and Mexico (Maya, Zapoteca, and Nahuatl). "The struggle for the restitution of territorial sovereignty and autonomy at the political and social levels articulated today in the mobilizations of native peoples is anticipated in the terrain of written literature," they argue.[15] Indigenous literatures increasingly represent and construct a political positioning and a place of enunciation from which Indigenous subjects articulate their languages and politics. The insurgency, in this sense, is manifest in the ways Indigenous writers and texts question the hegemonies of *national literatures*, and theoretically and politically challenge the conceptual bases and still colonial frames of literature, letters, and literary studies. But it is also manifest in the ways these literatures reconfigure Indigenous subjectivities; reconceptualize modes of interpretation and of reading, seeing, and being in and with the world; and negotiate, construct, and advance possibilities and prospects that are intercultural and decolonial in effort, project, and orientation.

## Decolonial Feminisms

Decolonial feminisms mark, constitute, and construct another terrain of insurgent prospect and praxis. These feminisms, increasingly emergent in Abya Yala today, displace the Western rationality and hegemonic discourse of white, Eurocentered feminism and the unitary category of *woman*. They confront, as Betty Ruth Lozano portends, the "modern colonial habitus" that has naturalized the Western-ethnocentric idea and category of both gender and patriarchy within feminism itself, subsuming and subordinating other cosmogonies to the known (Western) universe.[16] And they situate *feminisms* as plural.

Central, of course, are the critical debates opened by Maria Lugones more than a decade ago on the coloniality of gender, the modern/colonial gender system, and the relation between sex and gender. Here and in her more recent work, Lugones elucidates the "subjective-intersubjective springs of colonized women's agency" with respect to the racialized and capitalist oppression of gender. "I want to understand," says Lugones, "the resister as being oppressed by the colonizing construction of the fractured locus" of colonial difference, a process of active engagement and "subjective resistance," rooted in the possibility of overcoming the coloniality of gender.[17]

It is this possibility of overcoming the coloniality of gender that Lugones defines as decolonial feminism. Yuderkys Espinosa, Diana Gómez, and Karina Ochoa further expand and situate decolonial feminism as "The coming together of the productions of feminist thinkers, intellectuals, and activists, of lesbian feminists, Afro-descendants, Indigenous, and poor *mestiza* women, as well as some white committed academics, with the task of the historic recuperation of our own naming of an antiracist feminist theory and practice in Abya Yala."[18]

Decolonial feminisms, in this sense, name, situate, and articulate the pluri- and interversals of feminisms, understood as spheres not of unification (or uni-versalization) but of pluralism, plurality, and possible interrelation. As such, decolonial feminisms disrupt and transgress the white feminist *universal* as they pursue insurgencies, standpoints, and propositions of decoloniality and decolonization. [19] Central here are interrogations of race, ethnicity, gender, and patriarchy, but also of the heteropatriarchal frameworks and norms that organize social structures and institutions, as well as most aspects of everyday life. In this sense, Ochy Curiel's analysis of the "Heterosexual Nation" is particularly illustrative and revealing. For the Afro-Dominican Curiel (who identifies as an antiracist and decolonial lesbo-feminist), heterosexuality is a political regimen that affects practically all social relations, including the conceptions that historically have defined Latin American and Caribbean nations, and these nations' "others."[20]

Indigenous feminists in both the North and South have questioned in recent years the heteropatriarchal norms that operate within Indigenous communities, and within the contexts and practices of Indigenous organizations and decolonizing struggles. The Nishnaabeg decolonial feminist Leanne Simpson, for instance, challenges the perpetuation of heteropatriarchy and heteronormative exclusions in First Nation movements, and calls for a *queering resurgence* as a necessary component of nation-building work. Her astute analysis and critique draw from a number of First Nation feminists and LGBQ2 thinkers challenging the still colonial exclusions within Indigenous communities, nations, and leadership.[21]

Recalled are the multiple ways that native peoples (in both the North and South) have always transgressed the imposed binaries, gender categories, and sexual norms of Christianity and the West, institutions whose logics and projects are undoubtedly entwined. The presence before the conquest-invasion and well beyond, of the androgynous, of the *trans* (transgendered and transdressed), of sacred dualities (sometimes referred to as *third gender*, *two-spirit people*, and/or *berdache*), and of more fluid notions and practices of sexuality, are well known. Irene Silverblatt's now classic text, *Moon, Sun, and Witches: Gender Ideologies and Class in Inca and Colonial Peru*, is one example from the Andes. Black feminists such as Lozano maintain that in African-descended communities, sexuality and gender have also often gone against the imposed norms, obeying instead other cultural, ancestral, cosmo-existential, and spiritual beliefs, philosophies, and practices, as well as other concepts of seduction, pleasure, erotics, and sexuality. However, this is not to contend or suggest that heteropatriarchy is simply a Western colonial invention.

Similar to Simpson, the Indigenous communitarian feminists Julieta Paredes and Lorena Cabnal also question the heteropatriarchal norms within Indigenous communities, this time in Abya Yala's South. Their questioning illuminates the ethnocentricity and homogeneity of the gender and patriarchy categories, the historical origins of these categories, and the complex ways they have been used over time. The Bolivian Aymara Paredes speaks of the historical structures of oppression created by patriarchies, in plural, understood as an *entroque* (link, relationship, or juncture) of patriarchies of ancestral origin and of the West. "Gender oppression did not only begin with the Spanish colonizers," Paredes contends. "It also had its own version in pre-colonial societies and cultures. When the Spanish arrived both visions came together, to the misfortune of we women that inhabit Bolivia. This is the patriarchal *entroque* or junction."[22]

Akin to Paredes, Lorena Cabnal—Maya-Xinka communitarian feminist from Guatemala—describes the construction and presence of a communitarian feminist epistemology in Abya Yala that affirms the existence of an ancestral origin patriarchy "that is a millennial structural system of oppression against native or Indigenous women. This system," says Cabnal, "establishes its base of oppression from its philosophy that norms cosmogonic hetero-reality as a mandate, so much for the life of women and men and for both in relation with the cosmos."[23] With the penetration of Western patriarchy, ancestral origin patriarchy was refunctionalized, Cabnal contends.

Paredes and Cabnal not only complicate and deepen debates about patriarchy and gender (something that the Argentinian decolonial feminist Rita Laura Segato has also done), but they also, and more crucially, push critical debate within Indigenous communities about ancestral cosmologies. By challenging the idealization of gender duality, parity, and complementarity, making visible the present-day simplification and recuperation of these principles by men as mandates to control, order, define, and subordinate women, and recuperating what Cabnal calls the "femeology of our female ancestors,"[24] these and other Indigenous communitarian and decolonial feminists exercise an insurgence of decolonial feminist prospect, understood, in Paredes's words, as "the struggle and political proposal of life."[25] Such struggle crosses the Indigenous territories of Abya Yala North and South.

Of course *feminism* is not always the term that women use to describe, define, or orient their insurgent actions. Lozano argues that the nonnaming of feminism is also part of the "feminisms otherwise" that are "constructed in the struggles for the defense and reproduction of nature, territory, and collective rights, . . . in the transformation of conditions of life."[26] For her as well as for the Afro-Colombian activist-intellectual Libia Grueso, the otherwise of the feminisms of blackwomen in the Colombian Pacific, for instance, and the particular situatedness of their insurgence, can best be understood within the long horizon, historical frame, and contemporary embodied standpoint-theory-practice of *cimarronaje*, or *marronage*.

### Cimarronaje as Embodied Standpoint-Theory-Practice

For Libia Grueso, *cimarronaje* is "a way to rethink oneself against the form of colonialism which is structured on the denial and negation of the other—slave—and which determines a sense of gender as an imposed category."[27] As she goes on to say, "The relations of gender between black men and black women were not constructed from the scheme of patriarchal power relations and submission typical of white, Western families, but instead from the black being subordinated by the historical conditions of enslavement."[28] The challenge to this subordination by both black women and men marked, in different ways, a cimarronaje, or marronage, of strategy, practice, attitude, thought, being, and project. Recalled here is Stephen Nathan Haymes's powerful description and analysis of *slave pedagogy* understood as strategies and practices that helped articulate a vision of the slave's humanity and life affirmation against the physical and ontological violences of dehumanization, what Fanon referred to as the zone of nonbeing.[29]

"From the time of slavery, black women exercised a *cimarronaje* of cultural resistance and an insurgency of knowledges (cultural, ancestral, spiritual) . . . as a project of life," explains Lozano.[30] It is this legacy of cimarronaje that orients the agency of black women in the Colombian Pacific and their stance of feminism *otherwise*," she says. Here we can also observe an organizational cimarronaje, Lozano argues, or a *cimarron habitus* to use the term introduced by Adolfo Albán. Albán builds upon Bourdieu's notion of *habitus* understood not as a repetitive or mechanical custom but as a socialized subjectivity, an active and creative relation with the world. The concept of a *cimarron habitus*, says Albán, is useful in that it helps us comprehend how black maroon communities resisted the violence of the colonial system, how they confronted this system, and the ways in which these communities developed strategies of survival, social unity, and social organization. Moreover, it offers ways to analyze how these strategies and social practices of resistance were passed on and incorporated into each generation.[31] For Lozano, this includes the "practices conditioned by colonial history that have pushed blackwomen to seek autonomy in reactive and creative ways. The *cimarron habitus* is a social practice of resistance-insurgence incorporated within subjectivity."[32]

Black or Afro-descendant activists, social movements, and critical intellectuals in the America of the South increasingly employ *cimarronaje* today as an embodied standpoint and practice that disobeys the reign and rule of coloniality and its axes of dehumanization, racialization, negation, and condemnation. It affirms collective being, memory, and knowledge; generates theory; and denotes, as Edizon León argues, a radical option, decolonial action, and political project of existence, thought, knowledge, and life.[33] As León and I have explained elsewhere, to speak of *cimarronaje* and *cimarron* thought

> Is to underscore an essence, an attitude, and a collective consciousness of thinking aimed at reconstructing existence, freedom, and liberty in the present but in conversation with the ancestors. It denotes a politically and culturally subversive thinking (a thinking that in dialogue with Nelson Maldonado-Torres has a de-colonial attitude)[34] that confronts the dehumanization and nonexistence that coloniality has marked and, in so doing, works toward a "decoloniality" of knowledge, power, and being.[35]

Juan García Salazar, known as the grandfather of the Afro-Ecuadorian movement and the guardian of collective memory and tradition, and self-identified as the "worker of the process," describes *cimarronaje* as "a tool to re-think ourselves, an attitude of resistance and disobedience, and a teaching and pedagogy for the new generations, particularly in urban areas." Cimarronaje, understood in this way, "makes present collective memory, legacies of knowledge and thought, and the ever present struggle for existence and freedom."[36] In this sense, it is part of the posture, attitude, act, action, and thought *casa adentro* (or in-house) of disobedience, rebellion, resistance, and insurgence, and also of the decolonial construction and creation of freedom. That is "of cultural plantings and re-plantings to not only strengthen us as people of African origin, but also to recognize and understand why territory has been and continues to be a vital space, a space where all has been and where all still is planted, including the acts of resistance and ancestral tradition."[37]

The notion of *casa adentro* is not simply a signifier of identity politics or of Afro-centrism as it has been understood in U.S. terms. "To learn *casa adentro* means to learn from the elders," García says. *Casa adentro,* for García, references "collective memory, philosophies and knowledges inherited from the ancestors, histories of acts of resistance, and other elements that mark and permit our difference, our forms of life in community."[38] As such, it is always a collective and community stance. It is the memory built in community, from the insurgence of resistance and re-existence, and from the sowing of territory, dignity, and freedom-liberation. As García and *Abuelo* Zenón contend, "collective memory and sowing started when we began to construct ourselves without the other, without the intervention of the other," in essence, as an act of cimarronaje, self-reparation, and rehumanization.[39] Casa adentro recalls, in this way, what Lewis Gordon and Jane Anna Gordon refer to as "transcending rather than dismantling Western ideas through building our own houses of thought. When enough houses are built," the Gordons say, "the hegemony of the master's house—in fact, *mastery itself*—will cease to maintain its imperial status."[40] Present here is not only Albán's idea of a *cimarron habitus*, but also, and more broadly, a decolonial habitus of sorts in which cimarronaje or marronage (as an in-house standpoint, attitude, act, action, and thought) is included.

In a similar vein, Jerome Branche uses *malungaje* as a sort of foundational trope and counterideology to the psychic annihilation of the travesty and social death of slavery, and as a transhistorical concept that takes into account the agency of Black peoples in antisystemic movements and struggles that affirm survival and life. For the Guyana-born Branche, malungaje (a Bantu word with roots in Central and Eastern Africa) conjures up the liberatory and freedom-based impulse, past and present, of cimarronaje or marronage. Malungaje marks an immanent alterity in terms of memory and sensibility that works today, Branche contends, "to detain the homogenizing and alienating tendencies of state discourses and dominant literature, and promote a premise based in rights and a recuperative trajectory, even against state attempts of co-optation under the precept of so-called multiculturalism."[41] As Branche as well as other Caribbean scholars have argued, the freedom-based impulse and struggle of marronage crosses space and time. "Marronage philosophy runs counter to the idea of fixed, determinate endings," Neil Roberts contends, in that "freedom is perpetual, unfinished and rooted in acts of flight that are at moments evanescent, durable, overlapping."[42] For Roberts, marronage is the epistemology and theory of freedom. And, in the context of the arguments here, it is an embodied standpoint-theory practice of decolonial insurgency, prospect, praxis, and project.

Of course the examples of insurgency and its decolonial prospect are many, and way too numerous to continue to name here. They are embodied in the political, epistemic, territorial, ontological-existence-based struggles against capitalism and the modern/colonial order and for life itself. But they are also constructed and made manifest in a myriad of other spheres, including the erotic, sacred, and spiritual; in ancestral memory, art, performance, music, literature, and the word, to name just some;[43] and by actors in a variety of social contexts struggling against the dominant order and for an otherwise of being and becoming, of thinking, sensing, feeling, creating, doing, and living.

Decolonial praxis has no geographical limits. It is present in the civilizations of the "Souths," in Asia, the Pacific, the Arab world, and Africa as well as Latin America; the South that Kumar poetically describes as insurrection of subjugated knowledges, history, memory, and new political imaginaries.[44] Decolonial praxis traverses the Souths, including the Souths in the North. Recalled are the perspectives that Chicanas and other U.S.-based feminists of color have given to decoloniality and decolonial praxis (e.g., Gloria Anzaldúa, Chela Sandoval, Emma Pérez, and Maria Lugones, among others). Similarly brought to the fore are the decolonizing standpoints of numerous Native, First Nation, and Black diaspora intellectuals in the so-called First World. Recalled as well is the decolonial analytic that orients the Caribbean Association of Philosophy's project to shift the geopolitics of reason (see, e.g., the work of Lewis Gordon, Jane Anna Gordon, Paget Henry, and Nelson Maldonado-Torres, among others).

In Abya Yala and particularly in the territories of Central and South America, as well as in the Caribbean, decoloniality's propositional praxis continues to weave actions and relations of insurgence and resistance against the modern/colonial matrix of power broadly understood, and most especially against global capitalism's new and ongoing patterns of domination. The visible dynamics of the accumulation of global capital—including drug mafias, megatransnational projects (e.g., energy and tourism), extractivism, water and land contamination, deterritorialization, violence, and death—are what most often drive, organize, and orient community- and movement-based struggles, struggles that are for life and for a radically different social order. While these struggles are not always labeled by their participants as *decolonial* (nor necessarily framed by the concept of *decoloniality*), they can be understood as such because of their propositional and prospective praxis toward an otherwise. This is not to impose decoloniality as a conceptual scaffolding or analytic, nor is it to transform insurgent struggles in classificatory objectifications. Rather it is to broaden the spheres from which we can understand decoloniality as action, insurgence, prospect, praxis and project.

Before finishing this chapter, let's explore in a bit more detail, and from the present-day context of the Zapatistas, the ways resistance and insurgence weave a decolonizing praxis of action, reflection, and thought.

Insurgency as described here, and with relation to decolonial praxis, does not negate resistance. The necessity of resistance and rebellion by no means disappears. Yet to rebel and resist in reactive terms are increasingly understood as not enough. Today the practice and attitude of resistance and rebellion are being articulated from below (from the grassroots, from a historically incarnate and intersubjective ground)[45] by insurgents in insurgent terms in ways that call forth, construct, and display strategies, possibilities, and a concept-analytic of an otherwise and of the lived significance of its praxis. Certainly one of the clearest examples is that of the Zapatistas.

In their more than thirty years of organized struggle (more than twenty years in the public eye), the Zapatista Army of National Liberation (EZLN) and Zapatista communities, organized since 2003 in five *caracoles*, or autonomous municipalities each with their own *buen gobierno* or "good (just) government," have shown to Mexico and the world a lived proposition, practice, and praxis of insurgent resistance toward an anticapitalist and decolonizing otherwise.[46] However, as capitalism has changed, so too have the forms, practice, and praxis of Zapatista struggle.

For both the Insurgent Subcomandante Moisés (now Zapatista spokesperson) and the Insurgent Subcomandante Galeano (collectively born with the death of SupMarcos in May 2014),[47] the present-day challenge is to understand both how and in what ways capitalism—described as a multiple-headed hydra—continues to mutate and change, as well as what has not changed. Is it the main head of the hydra that remains the same, or is it the hydra itself and its infinite greed and capacity for regeneration?, these Subcomandantes ask.[48] Such understanding is crucial in thinking and analyzing what to do and how to do it, that is, in orienting resistance and the strategies and practices of an otherwise.

For Zapatismo, capitalism is war.[49] "In its present phase, capitalism is the war against all of humanity, against all of the planet," says SupGaleano. "The genealogy of the hydra can be resumed in one word: war. . . . War is the medicine that capitalism administers to the world to cure it of the ills that capitalism imposes."[50] This war, of course, is not just economic.

> The war also comes in the batons and shields of police in evictions; in the Israeli missiles dropped on Palestinian schools, hospitals, and neighborhoods; in the media campaigns that precede and later justify invasions;

in the patriarchal violence that invades the most intimate corners; in the heterosexual intolerance that stigmatizes difference; in religious fanaticism; in the modern markets of live human flesh and organs; in the chemical invasion of the countryside; in the contents of the press and media; in organized and disorganized crime; in forced disappearances; in government impositions; in the masked dispossession of "progress." In sum: in the destruction of nature and humanity.[51]

In May 2015, the EZLN organized with the participation of the Sixth Commission (part of a national effort begun in 2006 to build an other-way of doing politics), a seminar—or *seedbed*, as they called it—entitled "Critical Thought against the Capitalist Hydra." The organizing concerns of the seminar were the war, the catastrophe and storm that this war is brewing, and the capitalist hydra's changing face.

In the first volume of the book that partially documents this seedbed of reflection, SupMoisés, SupGaleano, the Comandantas Miriam, Rosalinda, and Dalia, and the Zapatista women Base de apoyo Lizbeth and Escucha Selenia, help us understand the crucial role of critical thought in anticapitalist struggle; the ways that rebellion, resistance, and insurgence entwine; and the importance of continuous reflection on and of practice, that is, of praxis. "It is in practice that we get some of the theory," Subcomandante Moisés says,[52] a practice that, as Comandanta Rosalinda adds, is of insurgent women as well as men.[53]

In this practice, rebellion, resistance, resurgence, and insurgence are interwoven. "Our rebellion is our NO to the system, our resistance is our YES to an 'other' possible way," SupGaleano contends.[54] Moreover, with resistance and rebelliousness we have shown, notes SupMoisés, that it is possible to govern and develop initiatives in Zapatista terms. Resistance and rebellion are weapons of struggle, but they are also tools of organization, invention, and creation.[55]

Echoed here is the now defunct SupMarcos's contention that "the 'no' that now rises up does not just resist, but also begins to propose, to determine." The shift in this sense is strategic, pro-positive, propositional, prospective, determinative, and analytically creative. It underscores the *actional* (to which Frantz Fanon also referred), and it urges, fashions, and constructs concrete alternatives.

In the practice of the EZLN and Zapatista communities, and in the context of the larger war of death being waged in Mexico today, resistance and insurgence weave a propositional praxis, and activate political pedagogies of struggle from below. These are struggles *against* the multiple-headed hydra of capitalism, the barbarisms of neoliberalism, and the violences that both exhort, and they are struggles *for* a radically different social order. "The perseverance of resistance and the resistance of below is what terrorizes the dominant order," argues SupGaleano, "because below the calendar is other. Other is the step or walk. Other is the history. Other is the pain and other is the anger. . . . Our struggle and the struggles from below in general depend on resistance," he adds, "to not give in, to not sell out, to not falter."[56] Yet, as SupMoisés maintains, outcry and bravery are not enough, "we have to organize ourselves and struggle, work, create, and invent our form of struggle with resistance and rebellion," he says.[57]

In concert with this perspective, René Olvera Salinas, member of the collective Zapateándole al mal Gobierno and part of the EZLN's Sixth Commission and the previously described Pueblos en Camino, speaks of the "pedagogies of resistance against the war" that, in the current Mexican context, "emerge *from* resistance itself, embodied [resistance], that is to say, in these fleeting moments, or moments of a longer breath, where we are confronted with the relations of production, the hierarchical classification of beings and of hegemonic control, and in which process we construct 'other' relations, very distinct, that do not correspond to 'the other that the system constructs' but rather to an 'other' that negates, that subverts this system, and that can reproduce the life of our peoples."[58]

Resistance and insurgence, in this sense, are not simply gestures, stances, or actions to be described from an objective view or an outside (or outsider's) point of analysis and observation. Their power and potential, as Olvera points out, are in the insurgent prospect and agency of the *how*: the praxistical questions that SupMoisés asks of how to rebel, how to resist so that the evil of capitalism does not destroy, how to once again construct that which is destroyed so that it is not the same but better, how to build democracy, justice, and freedom.[59] Such questions, of course, are not limited to Mexico. More broadly, they voice the concern of peoples, movements, and collectives throughout Abya Yala and the other Souths of the world engaged in decolonial struggle.

For Olvera, the questions of the how exhort and give substance, reason, and direction to what he describes as pedagogies of enactment. These pedagogies are part of what I refer to later in this book as decolonial pedagogies of praxis; pedagogies—understood as methodologies and processes of struggle, practice, and praxis—that are embodied and situated, that confront, that push historical, political, ethical and strategic learnings, and that oblige epistemic, political, ethical, strategic ruptures and displacements.[60] Olvera's call here is to all of us

> To make concretely visible the machinery of war and death, to scrutinize from shame our active participation in this machinery, to highlight the historic, political, ethical, strategic learning of distinct peoples in struggle against the colonial, capitalist, patriarchal system, does NOT put us in a distinct situation from where we began unless there exists, at the same time, a collective rupture and displacement of our own epistemic, political, ethical, and strategic place, a collective rupture and displacement that resounds in each concrete everyday activity; each person in his or her own way, time, and place BUT with the concrete objective of sowing life where there is death. This is just barely a starting point.[61]

As the Zapatista leadership made clear in their 2015 Seminar-Seedbed and book, the questions of the how push deeper analyses, theorizations, and reflections that not only call forth the power and potential of resistance and insurgence but, more crucially, delineate a method of praxis that urges, advances, and enables decolonial shifts and movement.[62]

*Decoloniality* is not the word the Zapatistas use to describe their praxis, proposition, and struggle. The modern/colonial matrix of power is also not the named problem, target, or analytic. However, it is not the use of words that matters here; what matters are the perspectives, processes, prospectives, actions, and thought; that is, the thinking and doing of/in praxis, insurgent resistance, and struggle.

For social movements, communities, and collectives that identify their struggles as from below or from the ground up, *decoloniality* is often not the referent. *Decolonization* is the more usual word for the efforts to confront the ongoing colonial condition; to decolonize, or to undertake and make decolonizing acts and actions (with emphasis in the verb) are the more frequent terms of reference and doing.[63] It is in the praxis of these struggles that decoloniality, as we understand it here, is signified and constructed. Thus while decoloniality can be understood, as Walter describes in part II of this book, as an analytic, its significance (as a verbality and project) is necessarily tied to the lived contexts of struggle, struggles against the structures, matrices, and manifestations of modernity/coloniality/capitalism/heteropatriarchy, among other structural, systemic, and systematic modes of power, and for the possibilities of an otherwise. Praxis, in this sense, is what gives decoloniality a concrete sense of prospect, project, and reason. And it this prospect, project, and reason that gives impetus and ground to a growing body of literature by engaged intellectuals, activists, and feminists in Abya Yala (and elsewhere) that identify with decoloniality and the processes, practices, and praxis of decolonial thinking and sensing, being and becoming, and making and doing.

## Some Final Thoughts on Praxis

Praxis, in a Freirian sense, is "an act of knowing that involves a dialogical movement that goes from action to reflection and from reflection upon action to a new action."[64] It is reflexive and not merely reflective. It is critical and theoretical, and not merely pragmatic. It is intentional in that it acts upon and in reality to transform it, aware of its own processes and aims.[65] And it is grounded in a critical humanism of inquiry and invention that chooses existence and life over the dictates of the colonial, capitalist, patriarchal system. As Paulo Freire once said, "for apart from inquiry, apart from the praxis, individuals cannot be truly human. Knowledge emerges only through invention and reinvention, through the restless, impatient, continuing, hopeful inquiry human beings pursue in the world, with the world, and with each other."[66]

Moreover, as an analytic perspective, sociopolitical standpoint, and pedagogical-methodological stance, praxis enables us to transcend the linear precepts, binary-based suppositions, and outcome-oriented views of Western knowledge, research, and thought. It helps us think from and with the ongoing processes of decolonial shift and movement rather than simply with and from decoloniality as paradigm, consequence, and position. And it helps give presence to relation, the relation—and correlate, to use Sylvia Wynter's term—of action-reflection-action, but also of present-past; the (co)relationality that grounds (ancestral) non-Western knowledges, worldviews, and life practices, and that orients a perspective prospect, and proposition of struggle *for* a different model of life, living, knowing, and being in and with the world. This is the essence of the political, epistemic, and existence-based insurgency referred to here and its decolonial prospect, praxis, and project.

# Notes

1   Evo Morales Ayma, *Discurso inaugural del Presidente Evo Morales Ayma (22 de enero de 2006)*, La Paz: Publicaciones de Cancillería, January 2006, 10. http:// saludpublica.bvsp.org.bo/textocompleto/bvsp/boxp68/discurso-jefes-estado.pdf.

2   Subcomandante Marcos, "Comunicado del CCRI-CG del EZLN: Comisión sexta-comisión intergalática del EZLN," September 2008, http://www.ezln.org.

3   In this understanding of insurgency as an action and proposition "from below," today Morales has no place. From his presidential post "above," Morales and his government have worked to criminalize and eliminate social movements, claim and develop ancestral territories, and advance state capitalism. The Morales government, in this sense, is part of the structural problem of capitalism/moder-nity/coloniality/patriarchy interwined. However, we should not forget that it is the insurgence "from below" that enabled Evo's election, not only as the first Indige-nous president of the majority Indigenous plurination of Bolivia (a historic advance without doubt) but also as a member of a social movement and part of a collective (not individual) project. It is this insurgence that also put in motion the collective project of state decolonizing and refounding. And it is this insurgence of social movements and Indigenous peoples that made possible, not only in Bolivia but also in Ecuador, the radical constellations of thought and life visions that now or-ganize both countries' constitutions and naming of a plurinational and intercultural state, a discussion that I will take up in chapter 3. Suffice it to say that the interest here is not with state, per se, nor with the triumph of coming to state power. Rather, it is with the insurgence of decolonial prospects and praxis, something clearly revealed by the Zapatistas in their practices and praxis of political, economic, and territorial autonomy despite state.

4   In Colombia, insurgency is typically understood as synonymous with the revolution-ary armed forces of the National Liberation Army (ELN) and the Armed Revolutionary Forces of Colombia (FARC); however, these are not references for the discussions here.

5   See Sylvia Wynter, "Unsettling the Coloniality of Being/Power/Truth/Freedom: Towards the Human, after Man, Its Overrepresentation. An Argument," *New Centen-nial Review* 3, no. 3 (2003): 257–337.

6   Emma Pérez, *The Decolonial Imaginary: Writing Chicanas into History* (Blooming-ton: Indiana University Press, 1999).

7   In the context of South and Central America, the reference to Afro-descendants and black peoples is generally interchangeable. After the World Conference against Rac-ism, Racial Discrimination, and Xenophobia held in Durban, South Africa, in 2001, many urban movements, organizations, and individuals chose the former term as a cultural—and not just racial—referent. This is also the preferred term today in state documents, policies, and politics. However, in rural communities the nominal reference often continues to be Black, a naming that some collectives also prefer because it maintains the racialized reference of struggle in racist and racialized societies and a racist and racialized world.

8    See Rise Stronger, "It Takes Roots Red Lines Action," April 2017, accessed July 17, 2017, https://www.risestronger.org/events/it-takes-roots-red-lines-action.

9    Betty Ruth Lozano Lerma, "Tejiendo con retazos de memorias insurgencias epistémicas de mujeres negras/afrocolombianas: Aportes a un feminismo negro decolonial," unpublished PhD dissertation, Universidad Andina Simón Bolívar, Quito, 2016.

10   Lozano Lerma, "Neo conquista y neo colonización de territorios y cuerpos en la región del Pacífico colombiano," talk given at Universidad Andina Simón Bolívar, November 2014.

11   Lozano Lerma, "Pedagogías para la vida, la alegría y la re-existencia: Pedagogías de mujeres negras que curan y vinculan," in *Pedagogías decoloniales: Prácticas insurgentes de resistir, (re)existir y (re)vivir*, vol. 2, ed. Catherine Walsh, 273–90 (Quito: Ediciones Abya-Yala, 2017).

12   Vilma Almendra, "PalabrAndando: Entre el despojo y la dignidad," in *Pedagogías decoloniales: Prácticas insurgentes de resistir, (re)existir y (re)vivir*, vol. 2, ed. Catherine Walsh, 209–44 (Quito: Ediciones Abya-Yala, 2017).

13   See "Somos" at http://www.pueblosencamino.org.

14   Yamile Alvira Briñez, "El lugar del canto y la oralidad como prácticas estético-pedagógicas para la reafirmación de la vida y su existencia en los Andes-Cajamarquinos," in *Pedagogías decoloniales: Prácticas insurgentes de resistir, (re)existir y (re)vivir*, vol. 2, ed. Catherine Walsh, 245–72 (Quito: Ediciones Abya-Yala, 2017).

15   Arturo Arias, Luis Cárcamo-Huechante, and Emilio Del Valle Escalante, "Literaturas de Abya Yala," *Lasa Forum* 43, no. 1 (winter 2012): 7.

16   Lozano Lerma, "El feminismo no puede ser uno porque las mujeres somos diversas: Aportes a un feminismo negro decolonial desde la experiencia de las mujeres negras del Pacífico colombiano," *La manzana de la discordia* 5, no. 2 (2010): 7–24, 13.

17   Maria Lugones, "Toward a Decolonial Feminism," *Hypatia* 25, no. 4 (2010): 747. Also see my discussion of Lugones's classic text "The Coloniality of Gender," *Worlds and Knowledges Otherwise* 2 (2008): 1–17, in Walsh, "On Gender and Its 'Otherwise,'" in *The Palgrave Handbook on Gender and Development Handbook: Critical Engagements in Feminist Theory and Practice*, ed. W. Harcourt, 34–47 (London: Palgrave, 2016).

18   Yuderkys Espinosa Miñoso, Diana Gómez Correal, and Karina Ochoa Muñoz, "Introducción," in *Tejiendo de "otro modo": Feminismo, epistemología y apuestas decoloniales en Abya Yala*, ed. Yuderkys Espinosa Miñoso, Diana Gómez Correal, and Karina Ochoa Muñoz, 13–40 (Popayán, Colombia: Universidad de Cauca, 2014).

19   The postures and perspectives of decolonial feminisms are, of course, not limited to those mentioned here, nor are they only located in Latin America/Abya Yala although the reflections and debates among Indigenous, Black, and mestiza feminists in Mexico (e.g., Sylvia Marcos, Aida Hernandez, Karina Ochoa, Maria Teresa Garzón, Xochitl Leyva, among many others), Central America (e.g., Eveling Carrasco,

Aura Cumes, Breny Mendoza, and more), and South America (with too many to list) are especially vital and centric. Decolonial feminisms are emerging throughout the world. See, for example, in the U.S. and in addition to the work of Lugones, Xhercis Mendez, "Notes toward a Decolonial Feminist Methodology: Revisiting the Race/Gender Matrix," *Trans-Scripts* 5 (2015): 41–59. Also see the discussion of "Planetary decolonial feminisms" (including with respect to the U.S., Bolivia, Korea, Japan, Hindu Nationalism, and Parisian women of color), in the dossier with this name in *Qui Parle: Critical Humanities and Social Sciences*, 18, no.2 (spring/summer 2010). In addition, see Madina Tlostanova, Suruchi Thapar-Björkert, and Redi Koobak, "Border Thinking and Disidentification: Postcolonial and Postsocialist Feminist Dialogues," *Feminist Theory* 17, no.2 (2016): 211–28; and the presentation by Muslim feminist Varsha Basheer, "Decolonial Feminisms: Exploring Religion as Methodology," https://www.youtube.com/watch?v=3Jq8JVRcal4, to name just a few.

20  Ochy Curiel, *La Nación Heterosexual* (Bogotá: Brecha Lésbica and *en la frontera*, 2013).

21  Leanne Simpson, "Queering Resurgence: Taking on Heteropatriarchy in Indigenous Nation-Building," *Mamawipawin: Indigenous Governance and Community Based Research Space*, June 2012, http://leannesimpson.ca/queering-resurgence-taking -on-heteropatriarchy-in-indigenous-nation-building/." Also see Glen Coulthard, *Red Skin, White Masks: Rejecting the Colonial Politics of Recognition* (Minneapolis: University of Minnesota Press, 2014).

22  Julieta Paredes, *Hilando fino: Desde el feminismo comunitario* (Querétaro: Colectivo Grietas, 2012), 66.

23  Lorena Cabnal, "Acercamiento a la construcción de la propuesta de pensamiento epistémico de las mujeres indígenas feministas comunitarias de Abya Yala," *Feminismos diversos: El feminismo comunitario*, ed. Feminista Siempre (Madrid: Acsur–Las Segovias, 2010), 14. "Heteroreality" is understood here as the ethnic-essentialist norm that establishes that all of the relations of humanity, and with the cosmos, are based in principles and values of heterosexual complementarity and duality that harmonize and balance life. See also my discussion of the androgynous erotic force in Walsh, "On Gender and Its 'Otherwise.'"

24  Cabnal, "Acercamiento," 24.

25  Paredes, *Hilando*, 70. See as well my discussion in Walsh, "Life, Nature, and Gender Otherwise: Feminist Reflections and Provocations from the Andes," in *Practising Feminist Political Ecologies: Moving beyond the "Green Economy*," ed. Wendy Harcourt and Ingrid L. Nelson, 101–28 (London: Zed, 2015).

26  Lozano Lerma, "El feminismo no puede ser uno," 348–49.

27  Libia Grueso, "Escenarios de colonialismo y (de)colonialidad en la construcción del Ser Negro: Apuntes sobre las relaciones de género en comunidades negras del Pacífico colombiano," *Comentario Internacional: Revista del Centro Andino de Estudios Internacionales* 7 (2006–7): 151.

28  Grueso, "Escenarios de colonialismo," 148.

29 Stephen Nathan Haymes, "Pedagogy and the Philosophical Anthropology of African-American Slave Culture," in *Not Only the Master's Tools: African-American Studies in Theory and Practice*, ed. Lewis Gordon and Jane Anna Gordon, 173–204 (Boulder, CO: Paradigm, 2006). Also see Frantz Fanon, *The Wretched of the Earth* (New York: Grove Press, 1968).

30 Lozano Lerma, "El feminismo no puede ser uno," 346.

31 See Adolfo Albán Achinte, *Más allá de la razón hay un mundo de colores: Modernidades, colonialidades y reexistencia* (Santiago de Cuba: Casa del Caribe y Editorial Oriente, 2013), 233–36.

32 Lozano, *Tejiendo*, 185.

33 Edizon León, "Acercamiento crítico al cimarronaje a partir de la teoría política, los estudios culturales y la filosofía de existencia," PhD dissertation, Universidad Andina Simón Bolívar, Quito, Ecuador, 2015.

34 For a discussion of decolonial attitude, see Nelson Maldonado-Torres, *Against War: Views from the Underside of Modernity* (Durham, NC: Duke University Press, 2008), 105. Recalled here as well is a Brazilian intellectual-activist collective that took form in the decade of 2000 in Bahia with the name Atitude Quilombola (Marron Attitude). See http://atitudequilombola.blogspot.com/.

35 Catherine Walsh and Edizon León, "Afro-Andean Thought and Diasporic Ancestrality," in *Shifting the Geography of Reason: Gender, Science and Religion*, ed. Marina Paola Banchetti-Robino and Clevis Ronald Healey, 211–24 (Newcastle, UK: Cambridge Scholars Press, 2006).

36 Juan García Salazar, conversation, July 31, 2015.

37 García Salazar in Juan García Salazar and Catherine Walsh, *Pensar sembrando/ Sembrar pensando con el Abuelo Zenón* (Quito: Cátedra de Estudios Afro-Andinos, Universidad Andina Simón Bolívar y Ediciones Abya-Yala, 2017), 36.

38 García Salazar and Walsh, *Pensar sembrando*, 165.

39 García Salazar and Walsh, *Pensar sembrando*. Abuelo or Grandfather Zenón is a symbolic-ancestral figure, considered the grandfather of all the women and men of African origin born in the territory-region of the Gran Comarca, Ecuadorian-Colombian Pacific. While García's maternal grandfather, also named Zenón (Zenón Salazar) had an important influence on García, this Abuelo Zenón traverses the Western logics of the individual as well as of time. Abuelo Zenón is the voice not of one person but of collective memory, of the elders and ancestors present, past, and future. "Zenón is the black community's intellectual property," García says—in Catherine Walsh and Juan García Salazar, "(W)riting Collective Memory, (De)spite State: Decolonial Practices of Existence in Ecuador," in *Black Writing and the State in Latin America*, ed. Jerome Branche (Nashville: Vanderbilt University Press, 2015), 258. Grandfather Zenón is a decolonial manifestation of sorts, a reference, figure, and voice of decoloniality in/as praxis.

40 Lewis Gordon and Jane Anna Gordon, "Introduction: Not Only the Master's Tools," in *Not Only the Master's Tools: African-American Studies in Theory and Practice*, ed. Lewis Gordon and Jane Anna Gordon (Boulder, CO: Paradigm, 2006), ix.

41 Jerome Branche, "Malungaje: Hacia una poética de la diáspora africana," in *Peda-gogías decoloniales: Prácticas insurgentes de resistir, (re)existir y (re)vivir*, vol. I, ed. Catherine Walsh (Quito: Ediciones Abya-Yala, 2013), 185–86. In English see *The Poetics and Politics of Diaspora: Transatlantic Musings* (New York: Routledge, 2015).

42 Neil Roberts, *Freedom as Marronage* (Chicago: University of Chicago Press, 2015), 174, 181.

43 See, for example, M. Jacqui Alexander, *Pedagogies of Crossing: Meditations on Feminism, Sexual Politics, Memory, and the Sacred* (Durham, NC: Duke University Press, 2005); Audre Lorde, *Sister Outsider* (Berkeley: [1984] 2007); and the edited volume of Raúl Moarquech Ferrera-Balanquet, *Erotic Sovereignty at the Decolonial Crossroads* (Durham, NC: Duke University Press) soon to be published in this same book series.

44 Corinne Kumar, "Introduction," in *Asking We Walk: The South as New Political Imaginary. Book One, In the Time of the Earth*, ed. Corinne Kumar, xiii–xxii, 2nd ed. (Bangalore: Streelekha, 2010).

45 Lugones, "Toward a Decolonial Feminism," 746.

46 For a discussion of how the Zapatistas have shifted the geography of reason, see Mignolo, "The Zapatistas' Theoretical Revolution: Its Historical, Ethical, and Po-litical Consequences," in *The Darker Side of Western Modernity: Global Futures, Decolonial Options*, 213–51 (Durham, NC: Duke University Press, 2011).

47 Subcomandante Insurgente Marcos, "Entre la luz y la sombra" (Chiapas, Mexico: EZLN, May 25, 2014), http://enlacezapatista.ezln.org.mx/2014/05/25/entre-la-luz-y -la-sombra/.

48 Comisión Sexta del EZLN, *Pensamiento crítico frente a la hidra capitalista 1* (Chi-apas, Mexico: EZLN, 2015).

49 On the paradigm of war and the possibility of its underside seen from the vantage point of decolonial politics and ethics, see Maldonado-Torres, *Against War*.

50 SupGaleano in Comisión de la Sexta del EZLN, *Pensamiento crítico*, 316.

51 SupGaleano in Comisión de la Sexta del EZLN, *Pensamiento crítico*, 326.

52 SupMoisés in Comisión de la Sexta del EZLN, *Pensamiento crítico*, 98.

53 Comandanta Rosalinda in Comisión de la Sexta del EZLN, *Pensamiento crítico*, 117.

54 SupMoisés in Comisión de la Sexta del EZLN, *Pensamiento crítico*, 221.

55 SupMoisés in Comisión de la Sexta del EZLN, *Pensamiento crítico*, 139.

56 SupGaleano in Comisión de la Sexta del EZLN, *Pensamiento crítico*, 188.

57 SupMoisés in Comisión de la Sexta del EZLN, *Pensamiento crítico*, 369.

58 René Olvera, "Pedagogías de la resistencia: De los *cómo* sembrar vida donde está la muerte," in *Pedagogías decoloniales: Prácticas insurgentes de resistir, (re)existir y (re)vivir)*, vol. 2, ed. Catherine Walsh, 195–208 (Quito: Ediciones Abya-Yala, 2017), 196.

59 SupMoisés in Comisión de la Sexta del EZLN, *Pensamiento crítico*, 137.

60 Olvera, "Pedagogías de la resistencia."

61 Olvera, "Pedagogías de la resistencia."

62  In a similar sense, María Eugenia Borsani poses the idea of "decolonizing exercises" as an attempt to account for "thought in movement": "a sort of action that is unfolding at the same time that we realize it, that is being and being done; an activity in a state of inconclusiveness." For Borsani, a clear example of this "movement" is the struggle of Indigenous peoples, collectives, and movements in Patagonia against the discourse of development and energy sovereignty. "Indigenous peoples, collectives, and movements are the makers of decolonizing exercises, the real protagonists of actions of insurgency, re-emergence, and re-existence." See her introduction in *Ejercicios decolonizantes en este sur (subjetividad, ciudadanía, interculturalidad, temporalidad)*, ed. María Eugenia Borsani (Buenos Aires: Ediciones del signo, 2015), 20.

63  In this sense, it is important to qualify Walter's statement in part II that decoloniality emerged from the shortcomings of decolonization. In the conceptual-analytic context of the modernity/(de)coloniality collective and project, *decoloniality* has been a more useful term because of the ways it brings to the fore coloniality and the modern/colonial matrix of power. It was in a meeting of the collective in 2004 that we decided to move our attention from the problem of modernity/coloniality to the possibilities of decoloniality and its analytic. Yet for Indigenous, campesino, and Afro-descendant communities and movements, decolonization continues to be an important organizing term and tool. Its conceptualization, in these contexts, calls to the fore the structures of domination and the ongoing colonial condition. And its struggle and project, as the multiple examples presented here suggest, point to an otherwise. As such, and as I argued above, it is the political meaning and project that matter and not the word itself. See the section in chapter 4, "On Decolonial Dangers . . ."

64  Paulo Freire, *The Politics of Education: Culture, Power, and Liberation*, trans. Donaldo Macedo (South Hadley, MA: Bergin and Garvey, 1985), 50.

65  Freire, *The Politics of Education*, 44.

66  Freire, *Pedagogy of the Oppressed* (New York: Continuum, 1974), 58.

# 3  Interculturality and Decoloniality

## On Interculturality's Concept

If decoloniality is the process and project of building, shaping, and enabling coloniality's otherwise, interculturality—as defined by social movements in Abya Yala—is both a complimentary political, epistemic, and existence-based project and an instrument and tool of decoloniality's praxis.

In the late 1980s and early 1990s and in direct response to the emergence of neoliberalism in the region, both the Indigenous Regional Council of Cauca, Colombia (CRIC) and the Confederation of Indigenous Nationalities of Ecuador (CONAIE) identified *interculturalidad* (interculturality) as an ideological principle and a central component of their political and epistemic projects of struggle. Interculturality, as these organizations conceived it, signifies more than an interrelation or dialogue among cultures. More critically, it points toward the building of radically different societies, of an "other" social ordering, and of structural economic, social, political, and cultural transformations.[1] As an Ecuadorian social activist once said, "interculturality is simply the possibility of life, of an alternative life-project that profoundly questions the instrumental irrational logic of capitalism in these times."[2]

Interculturality here, of course, is not synonymous with multiculturalism, broadly understood in Latin America as the recognition of cultural diversity by governments, states, multilateral institutions, and international nongovernmental organizations, effectuated through a politics of inclusion that, more often than not, is tied to the interests of the dominant order. This multiculturalism was introduced in the late 1980s and the decade of the '90s—and continues today—as a component part of the logic of neoliberalism and its project to pacify resistance, fragment movements, and bring the excluded into global capitalism's all-consuming framework and structure. As the First Nation intellectual Glen Sean Coulthard aptly shows, for Indigenous peoples this politics of recognition has meant little more than a repetition and reproduction of colonial relations.[3]

It is this same project, framework, and structure that, in the 1990s, began to co opt and use the term *interculturality*, particularly in countries where it had been signified by Indigenous movements as a counterhegemonic project from below. Interculturality became part of the language of the World Bank, especially in its politics and policies (that began soon after the uprising of 1990 in Ecuador) aimed at Indigenous peoples. Moreover, it became part of state policy and neoliberal Constitutions.

Of course, in its dominant and top-down conceptualization and use, interculturality is neither transformative nor critical of the established social, political, and economic order; it is functional to this order, and to capitalism's present-day multicultural logic aimed at the expansion of neoliberalism and the market. This "functional interculturality" draws from what Raimon Panikkar describes as multiculturalism's still colonialist syndrome of cultural superiority and benign and condescending hospitality, and it extends its project.[4] Through individual inclusion, the facade of dialogue, and the discourse of citizenship, functional interculturality constitutes a more complex mode of domination that captures, co-opts, pacifies, demobilizes and divides movements, collectives, and leaders; impels individualism, complacency, and indifference; and shrouds the structural and increasingly compound convolution of capitalism and coloniality. The fact that this utilitarian signification, practice, and use of interculturality followed—and in some cases paralleled—the Indigenous-defined principle, project, and proposition is, of course, by no means fortuitous. It is part and parcel of the prevailing and modernizing politics of capture, catchment, and co-optation that has characterized the region since the decade of the 1990s and the resurgence with force, in contemporary times, of Indigenous insurgent struggle.[5]

What are the political-epistemic-existence-based issues at stake in interculturality as it is theorized, postured, and defined by Indigenous movements? The critical decolonizing view of interculturality (in contrast to the functional view described above) calls for radical change in the dominant order and in its foundational base of capitalism, Western modernity, and ongoing colonial power. Its conceptualization makes visible lived legacies and long horizons of domination, oppression, exclusion, and colonial difference (ontological, political, economic, cultural, epistemic, cosmological, and existence based), and the manifestations of these legacies in social structures and institutions, including in education and the state.

As such, its challenge, proposition, process, and project are to transform, reconceptualize, and refound structures and institutions in ways that put in equitable (but still conflictive) relation diverse cultural logics, practices, and ways of knowing, thinking, acting, being, and living. Interculturality, in this sense, suggests a permanent and active process of negotiation and interrelation in which difference does not disappear. Sociocultural, ancestral, political, epistemic, linguistic, and existence-based difference is affirmed in collective and community-based terms, and understood as contributive to the creation of new comprehensions, coexistences, solidarities, and collaborations. "The values, principles, knowledges, and wisdom of our peoples should not only be respected and archived," Luis Macas says, "but they also should be offered as a contribution from our peoples to society in its entirety as a function of change, as substantial elements of an alternative plan/arrangement."[6]

Interculturality, from this perspective, is not an existing condition or a done deal. It is a process and project in continuous insurgence, movement, and construction, a conscious action, radical activity, and praxis-based tool of affirmation, correlation, and transformation. As such, it can best be understood not as a noun but, more critically (and as I posed with regard to decoloniality in the previous chapter), as what Rolando Vázquez calls a *verbality* that advances from modernity's margins and outside.[7] That is, from the particularity of local histories, and political, ethical, and epistemic places of enunciation, all of which are marked by the colonial difference and by decolonial struggle.[8] From this particularity, interculturality extends its project of an *otherwise*, a transformation conceived and impelled from the margins, from the ground up, and for society at large. However, while its concept and proposition are thought from the Andean region, its project affords relevance and connection with that of other decolonizing struggles from the ground up in other parts of the world.

Here the reader might ask about what all this means in concrete terms. How has interculturality been signified, constructed, thought, struggled, practiced, and proposed, and through what actions, processes, and propositions and with what project of social, political, epistemic, and existence-based transformation? And how, in what ways, do the projects and verbalities of interculturality and decoloniality, in/as praxis, intertwine?

The response to these questions can best be understood from the concrete experience of Ecuador and within the specific context of two interrelated areas or spheres of proposition, action, and struggle. The first has its ground in the social and political, that is, in the structural and institutional transformation of state and society (which of course is also epistemic), while the second links the sociopolitical with what the Kichwa lawyer Nina Pacari refers to as epistemic decolonization, this understood as nothing more than "the reaffirmation of ancestral knowledges and their inclusion in the dynamic of the coexistence of civilizations in the exercise of public administration." Epistemic decolonization is part of a broader project aimed, as we will see here, at the construction of "a new social condition of knowledge."[9]

## Interculturality, Decoloniality, Society, and State

In chapter 1, I briefly mentioned the massive uprising of 1990 in Ecuador, and its significance as a milestone marker of resurgence against the social, economic, and political marginalization of Indigenous peoples in this country and in Abya Yala as a whole. As Marc Becker describes, "the protest altered the political landscape of Ecuador and gave that country a reputation as home to some of the strongest and best-organized social movements in South America."[10] It was in the context of this uprising led by CONAIE and the subsequent diffusion of this organization's political project that the critical, decolonizing proposition and project of interculturality began to take form. In this political project, published in different versions throughout the decade of the 1990s, CONAIE named interculturality as one of nine ideological and organizing principles: "The principle of *interculturalidad* (interculturality) respects the diversity of Indigenous nationalities and peoples as well as Ecuadorians from other social sectors. But at the same time, it demands the unity of these in the economic, social, cultural, and political fields, with eyes towards transforming the present structures and building a new plurinational state, in the frame of equality of rights, mutual respect, peace, and harmony among nationalities and peoples."[11]

Throughout the decade of the 1990s and up until the Constitutional Assembly of 2007–8, the principle of interculturality guided the demands, actions, and proposals of the Ecuadorian Indigenous movement, which was aimed, in large part, at rethinking and refounding the state. These demands, actions, and proposals established the sociopolitical significance and foundation of interculturality in Ecuador and the Andean region. In so doing, they also made clear that the difference between Indigenous and other peoples is not just cultural, but also historic, civilizational, philosophical or cosmogonic, epistemic, political, and economic; that is, at the same time colonial. The struggles and transformations as such had to be structural, the movement said, decolonizing in project and nature and aimed toward the creation and construction of a social project of political authority and of life, a project with justice, equity, dignity, and solidarity. The demands and proposals called for profound changes in the economic, social, judicial, and political spheres and were aimed toward the construction of a plurinational and intercultural society in which Indigenous and other historically excluded cultures, peoples, and knowledges would be considered constitutive. "The proposal of interculturality for us is profound," argued Macas in 2004, "in that it touches the essence of dominant power and the economic system in force."[12]

During the last decade of the twentieth century and the first decade of the twenty-first, interculturality was the central axis of Ecuador's Indigenous movement's historical project, and a constitutive component of their proposal for a plurinational state. For CONAIE, interculturality was key in the construction of a "new democracy—anti-colonialist, anti-capitalist, anti-imperialist, and anti-segregationist" in nature, one that would guarantee "the full and permanent participation of the [Indigenous] peoples and nationalities in decision making" and in "the exercise of political power in the Plurinational State."[13]

Of course, the idea of a plurinational state is not Ecuador's alone, nor is it always and necessarily a decolonizing project. In its most basic definition, a multi- or plurinational state implies the political recognition of the presence and coexistence of two or more ethnically distinct nations or peoples. Canada, New Zealand, Finland, Belgium, and Sweden, in this sense and each in their own way, can be considered multi- or plurinational states. However, in none of these contexts, has the multi- or plurinational meant a radical alteration of historical conflicts, of power relations, or of the dominant, modern, colonial, and Western state model. In all of these countries, the recognition or consideration of the multi- or plurinational has come from the state itself and, as such, has been a multiculturalist, top-down proposition. Coulthard's analysis of Canada's multicultural politics of recognition with regard to the so-called Indian problem is useful here. As he states, "the politics of recognition in its contemporary liberal form promises to reproduce the very configuration of colonialist, racist, patriarchal state power that Indigenous peoples' demands for recognition have historically sought to transcend."[14]

In Abya Yala's South, in contrast, the plurinational has been postured from the ground up, within the frame of Indigenous movements' demands and decolonial struggles. Bolivia was the first to make this posture and demand beginning in the late 1960s in the context of the Aymara-based Katarist movement, a movement of Indigenous resurgence that challenged the cultural-ancestral blindness of the trade-union-based National Revolution of 1952. The interest of the Kataristas was not with the state per se. Rather, it was more specifically focused on the recuperation of memory in relation to the regional organization of *ayllus*, a dynamic communal system and a form of social, political, economic, and territorial organization and governance native to the Andes. The ayllus, the Katarist movement argued, offered a way to (re)think the state project without the state. Such thinking, while divergent in focus from CONAIE's proposal of a plurinational state, was not dissimilar in political intent.[15]

Both countries' movements in the decade of the 1990s and the first half of the decade of 2000 were engaged in political projects thought from the lived experience of colonial difference, not from state ideology.[16] Such projects challenged the foundational ambiguity of the homogeneous and monocultural nation and its "reductionist *mestizaje*" (racial mixing), what Javier Sanjinés calls mestizaje's discourse of power and what Silvia Rivera Cusicanqui names as mestizaje's colonial matrix.[17] They also put on the table the logocentric and reductionist thinking that (in these countries as well as in South America in general), has given form and meaning to *the national*. By disputing and contradicting the monopoly of the (uni)national state that demands an exclusive loyalty, and by bringing into consideration the existence of multiple loyalties within a decentered social, the plurinational marks an "other" agenda, thought from the subjects historically excluded in the unitary vision of state, nation, and society, and for the country at large. In this sense, the plurinational calls into question the colonial and exclusionary character of the uninational; it calls for a rethinking, refounding, and reconstruction of nation and state from the axes of plurality, decoloniality, and ancestrally lived difference. Moreover, it marks, as CONAIE argues:

> a process of transition from the capitalist, bourgeois, and exclusionary state towards an inclusive Plurinational State that integrates all sectors of society in their social, economic, political, judicial, and cultural aspects. It is the transition from the dominant power's elitist and classist State towards a Plurinational State made up of all social sectors of the society, with representation and power. The purpose of the Plurinational State is to gradually resolve such inherited social scars as illiteracy, poverty, unemployment, racism, incipient production, etc., working to satisfy basic material, spiritual, and cultural needs . . . guaranteeing the exercise of individual and collective rights.[18]

Furthermore, and as CONAIE affirmed in a document from 2007 presented to the then Constitutional Assembly, "the Plurinational State is a model of political organization for the decolonization of our nations and peoples ... that gets rid of the colonial and mono-cultural shadows that have accompanied the model of state for more than 200 years."[19] In this sense, the plurinational goes beyond the state itself; its concept, proposition, and reason are in the broader endeavor of decolonization in which interculturality, as principle, process, and project, is considered a component part.[20]

Together, plurinationality and interculturality have been constitutive elements of Ecuador's Indigenous movement's insurgency and decolonial praxis. Over the course of almost two decades, this insurgency and praxis began to filter into the social psyche and consciousness of other social sectors, thus making possible the debates and discussions that led to the formulation of the Constitution of 2008, considered by some as the most radical in the world.[21] Besides naming Ecuador as a Plurinational and Intercultural State, this political charter evidences three fundamental and far-reaching transformations (transformations that can also be broadly observed in Bolivia's Constitution of 2009).

The first transformation can be witnessed in the destabilization of the hegemony and dominion of Western logics and rationalities set from the outset in the Constitution's preamble. This preamble begins with "we women and we men" and goes on to recognize the millennial roots of the country's diverse peoples, to celebrate Pacha Mama of which we are all part, to appeal to cultural wisdoms, and to evoke the social struggles of liberation against all forms of colonialism and domination. The second transformation has to do with the ways the Constitution transgresses and overcomes the multicultural constitutional reforms characteristic of the 1990s (generally present throughout the region) that recognized diversity and collective rights while strengthening neoliberalism and the uninational and monocultural state structure. The third transformation is in the charter's "thinking with" other logics, rationalities, and sociocultural-ontological-cosmo-existence-based modes of life and living. As I have commented elsewhere,

> Together these transformations disturb and disorder the uni-national and mono-cultural foundations of State and society, and the neoliberal capitalist frame and model. In a re-founding and not simply a re-forming of State, the Constitution [Ecuador's as well as Bolivia's] works to reconfigure the political map, institutional structures and the relation of State-society, and

confront injustices and inequalities not just of peoples but also of their log-ics and rationalities, knowledge systems and systems of life/living. They also work to recognize and build the plurality within the Nation and the plurality and distinctiveness of nations within the nation, that is, the pluri-national State.[22]

Three examples from the Ecuadorian Charter suffice to demonstrate the influence of social movements (most especially the Indigenous movement but also, and relatedly, Afro-Ecuadorians) in the charter. More important, they also show the ways the movements' actions, processes, and propositions of interculturality and social, political, epistemic, and existence-based trans-formation have filtered into and radically altered the sphere of the national in decolonial terms.

The first example is the ancestral principle of *sumak kawsay* in Kichwa, *buen vivir* in Spanish, or what we might translate as "living well" or "life and living in plentitude."[23] Afro-Ecuadorians understand this principle as *el estar bien colectivo*, to be collectively well (or collective well-being).[24] As the Constitution's preamble states: "We have decided to construct a new form of citizen coexistence, in diversity and harmony with nature to reach *el buen vivir, el sumak kawsay.*" This principle is the transversal axis of the charter. It is a momentous milestone in that it questions and transgresses the previous foundational models and practices of the state, the heretofore modernist vi-sions of development, and more recent neoliberal policies focused on indi-vidual welfare and consumption. In the Charter, *buen vivir* is understood as the harmonious interrelation or correlation of and among all beings (human and otherwise) and with their surroundings. Included in this relation are water and food, culture and science, education, housing and habitat, health, work, community, nature, territory and land, economy, and individual and collec-tive rights, among other areas of interrelation.

Evident here is an *interculturalization* that affords a conception and ne-gotiation of life thought from and with the complementarity and relationality constitutive of Andean, Amazonian, and Afro-descendant ancestral philoso-phies, principles, and difference. This interculturalization indicates a distanc-ing from the universalizing and totalizing claims of Western modernity. West-ern modernity here is no longer the only framework or possibility. Moreover, it affords a clear challenge to the modern/colonial/capitalist/anthropocentric system of power that has tried to impose and control the notions, values, and orientation of civilization, living, and of life itself.[25]

The second example is in terms of the rights of nature. As the Constitution states: "Nature or *Pacha Mama*, where life is materialized and reproduced, has the right to an integral respect of its existence and the right to the maintenance and regenerations of its life cycles, structure, functions, and evolutionary processes. Nature also has the right to its reparation and restoration."[26]

The understanding of Nature (with a capital *N*) counters the Western logic of Francis Bacon and Comte de Buffon among others, a logic which, as Walter will make clear in chapter 7, separated nature from Man/Human. Nature in the Ecuadorian Constitution is Mother Nature. It is that which Indigenous communities refer to as Pacha Mama (or Pachamama) and which Afro-Pacific communities typically name as "Mother Mountain" (Madre Montaña). Its meaning is rooted in ancestral philosophies, cosmologies, and cosmo-existence. Nature is a living being with intelligence, feelings, and spirituality of which humans are part.[27] It is a composite of intersubjectivity, of beings in relation. Such view, of course, interrupts the human-defined subject of law and with it the Western, colonial, and Cartesian logic that separates humans and nature. Here nature is neither an object nor a use-based exploitable good controlled and dominated by humans; it is an integral part of life and society that cannot be divorced from women and men, from humanity and society. It is this integration conceived from the perspective of interdependence and equilibrium that also calls forth the frame of buen vivir.

Together, Pachamama and buen vivir are concrete examples of an interculturalized, interculturalizing, and interversalizing constitutionalism that, for the first time in Ecuador and the world, endeavors to think with ancestral millennial cultures and their cosmo-existential and life-based philosophies and principles, as philosophies and principles that can govern society. This thinking with is part of the processes and path of decoloniality and decolonization.

The third example references science and knowledge. As I have explained elsewhere:

> By highlighting science and knowledge as integral to the philosophy of "living well," pluralizing their meaning to include ancestral knowledge— defined as also scientific and technological—, and requiring that these knowledges and sciences be part of the educational system from elementary school to higher education, the new Ecuadorian Constitution turns on its head the dominant geopolitics of knowledge. Moreover, by linking ancestral knowledges with *sumak kawsay*, or "living well," and giving the State

the responsibility of potentializing these knowledges (Art. 387), the Constitution takes on and considers a logic radically distinct from that of the modern, Western, individual, instrumental, and rational means–end. Here knowledge is interwoven with life.[28]

As these three examples make clear, Ecuador's Constitution reflects a "thinking with" Indigenous and Afro-descendant conceptualizations, cosmogonies, and philosophies. The examples, however, also help reveal how interculturality—as a political, epistemic, ethical, and existence-based process and project conceived, postured, and transacted/enacted/impelled from the social movements of historically excluded peoples—has interrupted and intervened in the Western modern, capitalist, colonial design, and helped usher in decolonial shifts and movements. In this sense, we can begin to comprehend not only interculturality's significance in Ecuador but also, and more broadly, the implication, possibility, and project of decoloniality in/as praxis.

With the passage in popular vote of the Constitution in September 2008, it seemed as if a new era were about to begin, an era to be characterized and defined by the work of transformation and change necessary to make the charter's otherwise a reality, not just in discourse but in policy, politics, and practice. The understanding was that this work would involve state government, social institutions, and society as a whole; in essence it was a plurinationalizing, interculturalizing, and decolonizing project. The problem, however, was that the project's decolonial shifts and movements never really got off the ground.

Decolonial shifts and movements, of course, are never stable, precisely because, as Quijano reminds us, the coloniality of power is permanent and continuous.[29] Coloniality is in a constant process of rearrangement and production including, and much more complexly, in the so-called progressive governments of the region. Ecuador is a clear example. By 2010 the disconnect between the Constitution's "otherwise" and the Rafael Correa government was clear. Despite the government's publically named mission to "end the long neoliberal night," neither capitalism nor coloniality were to disappear. Instead, they took on new attributes and force.

In 2016, the government began to name its project "modern capitalism" or sometimes "twenty-first-century capitalism," thus replacing the former designation of twenty-first-century socialism that began to wane with the death of Venezuela's president Hugo Chávez. Ecuador has new partners (China,

South Korea, and some Arab States), and an extractive-based economy (e.g., copper and gold mining, oil, hydroelectric power, African palm oil and other agro-industries, as well as agro-combustible fuels). Modern capitalism is postured as the necessary road to socialism, the elimination of poverty, and the transition to a different social, political, and economic order. Yet with decreasing prices of oil and decreasing cash flow, modern capitalism also justifies the reestablishment of relations with the International Monetary Fund (IMF), other multilaterals, and big business. The *modern* is significant here as an organizing axis of the state project focused on the modernization of infrastructure; the modernization of schools; the modernization of health services; and the modernization of higher education, science, and knowledge for production and economic gain. In all of this, the centralized structure and authority of state are fundamental.

Illustrative is the replacement of community-based education with new large, modern, and standardized "millennial schools." More than ten thousand community-based schools were closed in 2013–14, doing away with local, socioculturally and linguistically appropriate schooling, including Indigenous bilingual education (a collective right reestablished in the Constitution, and officially recognized since 1988).[30] In many rural communities, the school is not only the place of government-sponsored schooling but also of community-based intergenerational education and sociopolitical organization. With the closing of schools, the social fabric and survival of the communities themselves are put in danger. Families are increasingly forced to abandon communities and relocate close to the schools (thus recalling the policies in the 1950s of "missionary" groups such as the Summer Institute of Linguistics, whose ties to the CIA and to Rockefeller oil interests have been well documented).[31] For those that choose to stay in the community, the option, in a growing number of cases, is to not send their children to school. Alternatively, it is to reestablish education outside the state structure.

Of similar concern is the construction of "millennial cities" in the Amazon and in zones of oil exploitation and mining. Families and communities are made to leave their habitat and move to these new modern urban spaces, with paved roads and a wall to keep the jungle out. Here the subsistence lifestyle of agriculture and hunting are prohibited (deemed as not modern), and the alternative offered is employment with the "company."

In higher education, a massive program of scholarships sends students to study in Western universities in careers functional to the government's need;

in 2014, the social and human sciences were eliminated from this scholarship program. At home, new state-run "strategic" universities populated with faculty from the Global North work to replace and eliminate public higher education.

A centralized state and a centralization of authority in the president himself consolidated, during the years of the Rafael Correa government (2007–17), an authoritative, top-down, patriarchal structure that has endeavored to control not only politics, but also people and their everyday lives. Protest and resistance have been criminalized (described as state terrorism), and the heretofore insurgency of social movements has been increasingly fragmented and debilitated. New state-formed, -funded, and -sponsored Indigenous and Afro-Ecuadorian organizations have aimed to replace the historic organizations formed from community ranks and that made possible the decolonizing and interculturalizing shifts in the Constitution, in the idea and structure of state, and in the new orientating and transversal principles of living, society, and co-relation. In all of this, the otherwise of the Constitution of 2008, loses meaning, application, and force. As Boaventura de Sousa Santos has said, today "the primacy of law pleasantly coexists with the primacy of illegality. It is the norm to de-constitutionalize Constitutions in the Constitution's name."[32]

The actual condition and circumstance are much too vast and complex to detail here, nor is this the intent. Moreover, with a new president in power as this book goes to press, and efforts begun to reestablish dialogue with the social movements and sectors that made possible the Constitution's otherwise, the future still remains to be seen. Suffice it to say that the case of Ecuador offers important learnings about the (still) problematic of state. It also prompts critical questions about the directionality, the proposition, and the how, where, and with whom of interculturality and decoloniality and their political projects, particularly concerning the spheres of state and society. Is and should the state be the target and goal of insurgent struggle and decolonial praxis? Alternatively, and asked differently, how should the state be interrogated and thought about from decoloniality's perspective and praxis? How are we to read, understand, and analyze today the ideas originally proposed by social movements in Ecuador and in Bolivia, of state refounding, state transformation, and state decolonization? Similarly, how should we read, understand, and analyze the otherwise of both countries' constitutions? Moreover, if the state is not the proposition of struggle (as the Zapatistas have clearly argued), should and can the state simply be ignored?

Such questions are also relevant for the second interrelated area of Ecuador's Indigenous movement's proposition and struggle aimed at the decolonization of knowledge.

## "A New Social Condition of Knowledge"

The examples of Ecuador's Constitution described above evidence the infiltration of ancestral knowledge, cosmology, and thought into the broader social imaginary of "other" possible futures. This infiltration is the result of the movement's prolonged agency, influence, and praxis that has helped other sectors also see the need to interrupt what the Bolivian Rafael Bautista has called the "monologue of modern-Western reason,"[33] and to seek other logics of thought, knowledge, and living in co-relation. This infiltration is intercultural and interepistemic. It is also decolonial in shift, movement, and orientation; moreover, it recalls the interversality and pluriversality to which we referred in this book's introduction.

At the beginning of the twenty-first century, the historical Indigenous leader Luis Macas began to refer to the movement's agency and struggle as both political and epistemic. Such enunciation reflected the need, identified by the movement at this time, to both intercede in and transform the existent social structures and institutions, and to construct "a new social condition of knowledge."[34]

Amawtay Wasi (House of Wisdom), the Intercultural University of Indigenous Nationalities and Peoples of Ecuador, was founded in 2000 in response to this need and as an educational and epistemological component of CONAIE's political project. This higher-educational project has come to be a reference not only for Ecuador and the Andean region but, more broadly, for the Global South.

For Macas, the university's founding rector, Amawtay Wasi was conceived as a way to shake off the colonial yoke, confront intellectual neocolonialism, and revalue the knowledges that during millenniums have given coherence and personality to Andean peoples. Its project has been to consolidate a space of higher education that helps dismantle the supposed universality of Western knowledge, confronting this knowledge production with that of indigenous peoples.[35] "Amawtay Wasi's fundamental task is to respond from epistemology, ethics, and politics, to the decolonization of knowledge . . . as an indispensable prerequisite to work not from the answers to the colonial epistemological, philosophical, ethical, political, and economic order, but rather from [our] proposal constructed in a base of [Andean] philosophical principles."[36]

In this sense, Amawtay Wasi's project confronts and endeavors to move beyond the traditional model of higher education based "in the reason of Western Eurocentric thought." Such model "is part of the project and will of the colonization of knowledge," in which knowledge is thought to be outside *being*—living beings and the state of being itself—a position that does not understand and, worse yet, denies and negates the "being-becoming" (*estar siendo*) that sums up the dynamic of ancestral thought.[37] Such thought, as Amawtay Wasi contends, offers a distinct way to approach reality. "In its consideration of human beings as the 'thread of a living weave or fabric' [*hebra del tejido vivo*], it [Amawtay Wasi] intends to construct a new way of approaching knowledge from bio-ethical parameters, from the respect for nature, and for all the beings that reside in the cosmos."[38]

In its conceptualization, organization, and logic, Amawtay Wasi finds its ground in a renewed comprehension and use of ancestral science, that is, of an Abya Yalean cosmology and philosophical theory of existence centered on relationality or connectedness, symbolized in the concept of the Andean *chakana*. The chakana orients an educational perspective that has its base in the complementarity, reciprocity, correspondence, and proportionality of knowledges, practices, reflections, lived experiences, and cosmologies or philosophies, all of which, in turn, organize the *pluriversity*'s five knowledge centers, an organization that marks a radical departure from the continental model of disciplinary and "disciplined" faculties, departments, and programs.

From this framework, ancestral and community-based knowledges afford the foundation of learning from a praxis-oriented perspective. "Western" knowledge also has a key role in constructing what Amawtay Wasi has referred to as *intercultural knowledge*; that is, an intercultural co-construction of theory, reflection, and practice—of praxis—that seeks to facilitate a different understanding of global, national, and local realities and, at the same time, articulate diverse rationalities and cosmologies in a "rationality of *Abya Yala* that is fundamentally lived and inter-relational in character."[39]

The problem is when this "other" rationality falls prey to the logic, structure, and requirements of the state. Shortly after its founding in 2000, Amawtay Wasi began the process of state approval. This process, questioned by some sectors of the movement, took practically three years, and many revisions of the university's program, project, and curriculum, before being finally accepted. For Amawtay Wasi's leaders, the importance of state approval, at the time, was twofold. First, it represented the continuation, at the higher-education level, of the system of intercultural bilingual education recognized by the Ecuadorian state but under the semiautonomous control of national Indigenous organizations (one of the movement's victories won in 1988, and the only such case in all of Abya Yala). Second, it demonstrated to the larger society, the political, cultural, and epistemic capacity and right of Indigenous peoples to run their own degree-producing project of higher education, a project open to all.

This logic, of course, operated as a sort of double-edged sword in the sense that it made the otherwise of Amawtay Wasi (including its decoloniz-ing project, Abya Yalean paradigm, and community-based practice) subject to the same structures and institutions that the movement was struggling to transform. Some say that this was the beginning of a distancing between the university and the movement's political project. In this distancing, Amawtay Wasi came to represent an alternative within the established system rather than a community-conceived and -based project of political-epistemic insurgence and decolonial prospect.

Leanne Simpson's critique of attempts in Canada and the United States to "Indigenize the academy" are relevant here. "While Indigenous scholars, students, and leaders have made substantial inroads in some disciplines of the academy in terms of curriculum and programming, we have been much less successful in gaining the academy's recognition of Indigenous knowledge systems and intelligence on their own merits," Simpson says, "and far less suc-cessful in dismantling systems of domination and oppression, dispossession and erasure advanced by the academy. While there are sites of decolonization within academic institutions, they still remain a colonizing force upholding the values of heteropatriarchy, settler colonialism and capitalism."[40] Indige-nous universities throughout the Americas are necessary spaces in this regard (as have been U.S. historically black colleges), not as simple alternatives within academia, but as places that embody, enable, engage, and support a distinct project of existence-and-as-life, and-as-knowledge.

In November 2013, the Ecuadorian government officially closed Amawtay Wasi. The argument was that the university did not meet the minimum qual-ity standards established by the National Council of Evaluation, Accredita-tion, and Insurance of Quality in Higher Education (CEAACES). This state office of higher education evaluated Amawtay Wasi on two occasions. The first evaluation employed the same instrument used to evaluate all public and private universities in 2011–12; the results found the Intercultural University to be below minimum standards. Some of the reasons included the lack of academic departments (Amawtay Wasi's organization was around knowledge centers) and the lack of a centralized campus and faculty (Amawtay Wasi operated within a decentralized and community-based model, in which professors—university trained and community formed, including those considered as wise women and men—offered classes in selected community-based centers). The second evaluation came as a response to Amawtay Wasi's argument about the inappropriateness of the Western standards and framework of the evaluative instrument and process. This evaluation, defined by the government as "intercultural," followed the same criteria and standards with the simple add-on of cultural diversity. Again, Amawtay Wasi "failed."[41]

Made evident here is the difficulty for government and state in understanding and accepting the precepts and praxis of interculturality as a decolonial project, including epistemic interculturality, that is, the intercultural co-construction of diverse epistemologies and cosmologies in which knowledge, as philosophy, is never complete but always "in construction." Made evident as well, and more crucially, are the contradictions involved when such a project becomes subject to state evaluation and validation.

Moreover, and as the intellectual-activist Atawallpa Oviedo notes, "the only anti-colonial, anti-patriarchal, anti-imperialist, anti-civilizatory, anti-capitalist and anti-anthropocentric university was *Amawtay Wasi*"; its epistemologies, structures, pedagogies, methodologies, and symbolisms were all "other." "It will go down in history that it was a government self-named as 'Left' that eliminated it," he adds, while at the same time instituting the multimillion-dollar state-conceived "Yachay University" focused on technology, productivism, and an economistic capital model.[42]

Today Amawtay Wasi continues to function insurgently as part of an Abya Yalean network of Indigenous universities.[43] More appropriately, it has renamed itself as a *pluriversity* and reconceived its status as a "community-based organization for research and ancestral knowledge."[44]

Recalled in this experience of Amawtay Wasi is another intercultural political-educational project: Mexico's Universidad de la Tierra (University of the Earth), with central sites in Oaxaca and San Cristóbal de Las Casas in Chiapas. In contrast to Amawtay Wasi, Unitierra—as it is called—was conceived from the outset (in the last decade of the twentieth century and the first of the twenty-first), as independent, autonomous, and outside the dictates of government, state, and the Western-established university model. Its project-praxis in both sites (and with a somewhat different history and focus in each) is rooted in Indigenous communities; based on autonomy, freedom, and the construction of a more socially just society; and reflective of Ivan Illich's call for deschooling, radical social change, and convivencial learning. *Unitierra* is distinct from Amawtay Wasi in this sense, in that its conceptualization and foundation are thought not *from*, but *with* Indigenous struggles and postulates of knowledge, in conversation with other forms of critical thought and liberation-based theory and praxis. Such is Unitierra's intercultural political-educational proposition and project.

For Unitierra, education and study are not "the means to climb the meritocratic pyramid of formative cycles, academic courses, certificates of attendance, and degrees. In its installations, in principle one learns without the necessity of professors, curriculum, students, textbooks, and degrees."[45]

Gustavo Esteva, the founding rector of Unitierra in Oaxaca, refers to this as "reclaiming our freedom to learn." By "deschooling our lives . . . in this real world, where the school still dominates minds, hearts and institutions" and by building conditions of apprenticeship, of decent living, social fabric, and of the regeneration of community, we are shaping and enabling an "internal and social structure that is a fundamental condition for real freedom . . . and for learning. What we are doing is highly subversive," Esteva says. "In a sense, we are subverting all the institutions of the modern, economic society. In packaging our activities as one of the most respected sacred cows of modernity—education—we protect our freedom from the attacks of the system."[46]

Similarly, and as I discuss in more detail in chapter 4, the Escuelita Zapatista (the Zapatista "little school"), organized in 2013 by the EZLN and in collaboration with Unitierra Chiapas, has opened an "other" ethical, epistemic, political, and educational space, an other decolonizing praxis, and an other social condition of knowledge that turns capitalism/modernity/coloniality on its head. The *escuelita* invites people of all ages to learn to unlearn in order to relearn, from the collective lived practice, experience, thought, and knowledge of Zapatista communities and from these communities' ongoing struggle for autonomy and liberation.

These examples, along with many others that space does not permit me to elaborate on here, give presence to "educations" that are radically distinct from those that most of us know, and study or teach in. They confront the increasingly corporate, dehumanized (at once anthropocentric), and disconnected realities of education, theory, knowledge, and thought in today's institutions of so-called learning. These institutions, as is generally true in both the North and South, have little or no idea of, or interest in, peoples, the world as such, or the otherwise of thinking, sensing, feeling, and being present and emergent in modernity/coloniality's cracks, fissures, and borders.

The examples of Amawtay Wasi and Unitierra, in contrast, bring to the fore the pluriversality and interversality of decoloniality and of interculturality postured from below, including the intertwining of both in building, assembling, and re-membering (putting and pulling together anew and again) other conditions of knowledge(s). As such, they give concrete substance to the possibilities and praxis of an otherwise.

### On the Dilemma of "Outside, Inside, and Against": Some Final Questions and Thoughts

Taken together, the experiences detailed here raise important questions about the *how*, *where*, and *with whom* of decolonial praxis. How are we to consider decoloniality, its stance, project, practice, and praxis with regard to, and in the concrete context of, the dominant system, the state, and its social institutions, structures, and spheres of power, control, and operation? As a posture of struggle that takes form and is grounded in modernity's outside, fissures, and borders, should decoloniality's aim and practice be the strengthening of this *outside* against and despite state and the dominant systemic structures? Alternatively, should its aim and practice also be to intervene and intercede within the system, its structures, institutions, and conditions, including those of knowledge and state?

Such questions, of course, have no simple answer. On the one hand, they recall the tension and dialectic of inside/outside,[47] given a critical consideration in Quijano's construction of outside/inside/against. For Quijano, this construction denotes a continuous flow, filtration, and articulation of subject positions that exceed or go beyond the binary of either/or.[48] It points to strategic shifts, tactical moves, and an intertwined complex of relations that transgress and traverse power domains, all postured and understood as forms of struggle *against* the dominant order. Thinking with Quijano I asked in 2002: "Can a social movement continue to be considered as such once it enters the state structure and institution and begins to assume more than just an outside position? Can it be inside and at the same time against?

How can an outside and against position and perspective operate simultaneously with an inside reality?"[49] In a similar sense, and following Anzaldúa, we can ask whether it is possible to be simultaneously insiders, outsiders and other-siders.[50]

These questions remain pertinent today, most especially in Ecuador. The Ecuadorian Constitution of 2008 and its radical rethinking of society, law, and state, including the recognition of racism, reparation, affirmative action, collective rights, and aspects of Indigenous and Afro life visions (i.e., ancestral knowledges, collective well-being, and nature's rights), ushered in a new era of visibility and inclusionary politics. The interrogatives that seem to naturally follow are: What happens when the historic concerns of Indigenous and African-origin peoples become part of—are assumed by and within—the state? How is inclusion functional to the state, including in its more progressive positioning and construction? Does the *inside* denote and mark a succumbing to state capture, (i.e., the state's capture of social movements and their resistance-insurgence)? Moreover, could and should the naming of a "plurinational and intercultural state" be understood as a pyrrhic victory in this sense, since it is not necessarily transformative of the state's historical relation (or nonrelation) with Indigenous and African-descended peoples?

Recalled are the collective memory–based words of both Juan García and the real and symbolic figure of Grandfather Zenón regarding the problematic inherent in the very idea and practice of state, preceding and current. For both thinkers, such problematic is grounded in, among other concerns, the dis-memory that inclusion and the inside engender especially for African-origin peoples, peoples who predate *state* understood as the imposed referent through which domination, subjugation, regulation, and exclusion have been proffered.

> We cannot forget that our right to live in these territories is born in the historic reparation of the damage/harm that meant the dispersion of our African blood through America, dispersion that through the will of others we had to live these hundreds of years before the configuring of the states, which now order/regulate us.
>
> What we are today as people is what we never wanted to be, because what we are today does not depend solely on our will or desires to be. Today we are what the laws of the state direct and dictate that we will be.[51]

Made evident here is not only the problematic of state but also, and more crucially, the processes, practices, and perspectives that spite state; that is, that which goes on despite state, and in the borders, margins, and cracks of societal structures and institutions.

As the experiences and reflections detailed in this chapter suggest, decoloniality and interculturality are neither given facts or conditions, nor are they idealist states of arrival. They are also not policies to be legislated, managed, or administered from *above*. In such cases, and as we have learned in the recent experiences of Ecuador described (with similar parallels in Bolivia), their meaning and use become functional to the systems of domination and the matrices of modern/colonial/capitalist power. These are the systems and matrices that regenerate and persist in all governments of the region, regardless of their definition as conservative, neoliberal, progressive, or "Left."

Of course, the situation becomes more complex with the capture of subjects and the co-optation and functionalization of terms signified and conceived in struggle, including interculturality and decoloniality. In response to this functionalization and increasing co-optation, Macas argues that the task at hand is not to drop the terms but to take back their processes and projects of struggle, and learn with and from this action. "Experience and history have made us realize that we live a colonized interculturality, seen and created from a Western and colonial logic. As such, we have the huge task of decolonizing interculturality, undoing Eurocentrism, and de-monopolizing life, a task that follows from our resistances and our projects, and that follows the paths of our *taytas, mamas, amawtakunas* [wise people]. It is a task that necessarily begins with un-learning. It then passes through a re-learning, until getting to the re-constitution of peoples, of society, and of life."[52]

Decoloniality and interculturality are, in this way, interwoven projects and entwined verbalities. Understood from and within the context of past and present struggles, they are wagers, proactive propositions, and political, economic, social, epistemic, and existence-based processes and projects in perennial action and continuous movement, actions and movement that purport to fissure and crack, and to construct, create, and "walk" an otherwise.

Of course, the danger here, and as we will see in the next chapter, is to idealize and simplify the actions and terms. Similarly, it is to perceive decoloniality as a point of arrival or an end in and of itself, a perception that works to negate and/or minimize the power of coloniality and its continual regeneration, and shroud the ever-constant struggles, actions, and constructions—the decolonial pedagogies—that fissure or crack the modern/colonial matrix of power.

# Notes

1 CRIC, ¿Qué pasaría si la escuela . . . ? *30 años de construcción de una educación propia* (Popayán, Colombia: CRIC, 2004), 118.

2 Quoted in Walsh, "(De)Construir la interculturalidad: Consideraciones críticas desde la política, la colonialidad y los movimientos indígenas y negros en el Ecuador," in *Interculturalidad y Política*, ed. Norma Fuller (Lima: Red de Apoyo de las Ciencias Sociales, 2002), 139.

3 Coulthard, *Red Skin, White Masks: Rejecting the Colonial Politics of Recognition* (Minneapolis: University of Minnesota Press, 2014).

4 See Raimon Panikkar, "Religion, Philosophy, and Culture," *Polylog*, 2000, accessed September 5, 2017, https://them.polylog.org/1/fpr-en.htm.

5 See Vilma Almendra, "PalabrAndando: Entre el despojo y la dignidad," in *Pedagogías decoloniales: Prácticas insurgentes de resistir, (re)existir y (re)vivir*, vol. 2, ed. Catherine Walsh, 209–44 (Quito: Ediciones Abya-Yala, 2017).

6 Luis Macas, "Diversidad y plurinacionalidad," *Boletín ICCI-ARY Rimay* 6, no. 64 (2004): 2, accessed December 6, 2016, http://icci.nativeweb.org/boletin/64/macas.html.

7 Vázquez, "Towards a Decolonial Critique of Modernity: *Buen Vivir*, Relationality and the Task of Listening," in *Capital, Poverty, Development: Denktraditionen im Dialog: Studien zur Befreiung und Interkultalitat 33*, ed. Raúl Fornet Betancourt, 241–52 (Wissenschaftsverlag Mainz, Germany: Achen, 2012).

8 Such understanding, of course, marks a radical difference with the functional or utilitarian conception of interculturality thought and postured from modernity's inside; that is, from what Mignolo has referred to as the monotopism of modern thought, and the universalism and total validity claims that underscore modernity's double negation. (Quoted in Walsh, "Las geopolíticas de conocimiento y la colonialidad del poder: Entrevista con Walter Mignolo," in *Indisciplinar las ciencias sociales: Geopolíticas del conocimiento y colonialidad del poder: Perspectivas desde lo andino*, ed. Catherine Walsh, Freya Schiwy, and Santiago Castro-Gómez [Quito: UASB/Abya Yala, 2002], 25, accessed May 26, 2016, http://www.oei.es/salactsi/walsh.htm.) For Vázquez, this is "the exclusion of the 'other' and the negation of that exclusion" that is indelibly linked with coloniality's denial of existence and ontological and epistemic nullification of "other" people (see "Towards a Decolonial Critique of Modernity").

9 See Nina Pacari, "La incidencia de la participación política de los pueblos indígenas: Un camino irreversible," in *Las vertientes americanas del pensamiento y el proyecto des-colonial*, ed. Heriberto Cairo and Walter Mignolo (Madrid: Tramas editorial, 2008), 47. For a discussion of the "new social condition of knowledge," see Universidad Intercultural Amawtay Wasi, *Aprender en la sabiduría y el buen vivir/ Learning Wisdom and the Good Way to Live* (Quito: UNESCO/Universidad Intercultural Amawtay Wasi, 2004).

10 Marc Becker, "The Children of 1990," *Alternatives* 35 (2010): 291.

11 CONAIE, *Proyecto Político* (Quito: CONAIE, 1997), 12.

12 Macas, "Diversidad y plurinacionalidad," *Boletín ICCI-ARY Rimay* 6, no. 64 (2004), accessed December 6, 2016, http://icci.nativeweb.org/boletin/64/macas.html.

13 CONAIE, *Proyecto político*, 11.

14 Coulthard, *Red Skin, White Masks*, 3.

15 For a more detailed discussion of the idea of the plurinational in Bolivia and Ecuador, see Walsh, *Existence Otherwise: Decolonial Movement in Abya Yala* (Durham, NC: Duke University Press, forthcoming).

16 Of course with the election of Evo Morales in 2006 and the subsequent Constitutions that named both Bolivia (in 2009) and Ecuador (in 2008) plurinational states, the relationship with the state shifted, but it also became, as I will argue below, much more problematic.

17 See Javier Sanjinés, *Mestizaje Upside Down* (Pittsburgh: University of Pittsburgh Press, 2004), and Silvia Rivera Cusicanqui, "La raíz: Colonizadores y colonizados," in *Violencias encubiertas en Bolivia: Cultura y política*, ed. Xavier Albó and Raúl Barrios, 27–139 (La Paz: CIPCA-ARUWIYIRI, 1993).

18 CONAIE, "Políticas para el Plan de Gobierno Nacional: El mandato de la CONAIE," manuscript (Quito: CONAIE, 2003), 2.

19 CONAIE, "Propuesta de la CONAIE frente a la Asamblea Constituyente: Principios y lineamientos para la nueva Constitución del Ecuador," manuscript (Quito: CONAIE, 2007), 5–6.

20 For a detailed discussion of CONAIE's various proposals with regard to the Plurinational State, and the distinct political moments of their development, arguments, and presentation, culminating with the document of guidelines and principles presented to the Constitutional Assembly in 2007, see Walsh, *Interculturalidad, Estado, Sociedad: Luchas (de)coloniales de nuestra época* (Quito: Universidad Andina Simón Bolívar/Ediciones Abya-Yala, 2009).

21 Particularly important here was the pedagogical process of the Constitutional Assembly led by Alberto Acosta and made up not of political parties but of representatives from social sectors and civil society, a process that I had the opportunity to participate in as a "nonofficial" advisor.

22 Walsh, "Political-Epistemic Insurgency, Social Movements and the Refounding of the State," in *Rethinking Intellectuals in Latin America*, ed. Mabel Moraña (St. Louis: Washington State University, 2010), 206.

23 This principle is also present in the Bolivian Constitution, named as *vivir bien* in Spanish or *suma qamaña* in Aymara.

24 See García and Walsh, *Pensar sembrando/Sembrar pensando, con el Abuelo Zenón* (Quito: Cátedra de Estudios Afro-Andinos, Universidad Andina Simón Bolívar y Ediciones Abya-Yala, 2017), and Walsh, *Interculturalidad, Estado, Sociedad*.

25 As I have argued elsewhere, the Western tradition of the "good life" has base, in part, in the biblical myth of the Garden of Eden and in the Aristotelian vision of the polis. It is also indelibly linked with the economic, political, social, and cultural philosophy and practice of capitalism and its proposition "to have." Together all construct modern

civilization and orient its central project of culture over nature, a project clearly opposed to buen vivir. See Walsh, *Interculturalidad, Estado, Sociedad*.

26  Constitución de la República del Ecuador, 2008, Art. 71 and 72. For the English translation, see http://pdba.georgetown.edu/Constitutions/Ecuador/english08 .html, accessed July 19, 2017.

27  See Walsh, "Life and Nature 'Otherwise': Challenges from the Abya-Yalean Andes," in *The Anomie of the Earth: Philosophy, Politics, and Autonomy in Europe and the Americas*, ed. F. Luisetti, J. Pickles, and W. Kaiser, 93–118 (Durham, NC: Duke University Press, 2015).

28  Walsh, "Political-Epistemic Insurgency: Social Movements and the Refounding of the State," in *Rethinking Intellectuals en Latin America*, ed. Mabel Moraña, 199–211, (St. Louis: Washington State University, 2010).

29  Aníbal Quijano, "Coloniality of Power, Eurocentrism, and Latin America," *Nepantla: Views from South* 1, no. 3 (2000): 533–80.

30  See Catherine Walsh, "¿Interculturalidad? Fantasmas, fantasias y funcionalismos," in *Ecuador. Desafíos para el presente y futuro*, ed. César Montúfar and Fernando Balseca, 269–82 (Quito: Universidad Andina Simón Bolívar and Ediciones de la tierra, 2015) and Rosa María Torres, "Adiós a la educación comunitaria y alternativa," in *Línea de fuego*, November 2013, https://lalineadefuego.info/2013 /11/14/adios-a-la-educacion-comunitaria-y-alternativa-por-rosa-maria-torres/.

31  See Gerard Colby and Charlotte Dennett, *Thy Will Be Done: The Conquest of the Amazon: Nelson Rockefeller and Evangelism in the Age of Oil* (New York: HarperCollins, 1995).

32  Boaventura de Sousa Santos, "Para leer en 2050: Una reflexión sobre la utopía," September 2015."

33  As Bautista argues, "the racist myth that inaugurated modernity, a myth that cancelled modernity's pretention of critical reason, never permitted a real dialogue with the rest of the world, but instead [propagated] a monologue with itself of Western-modern reason." Rafael Bautista, "Bolivia: Del estado colonial al estado plurinacional," January 21, 2009, https://www.servindi.org/actualidad/opinion/6774.

34  Universidad Intercultural Amawtay Wasi, *Aprender en la sabiduría y el buen vivir/ Learning Wisdom and the Good Way to Live* (Quito: UNESCO/Universidad Intercultural Amawtay Wasi, 2004).

35  Luis Macas and Alfredo Lozano cited in Walsh, *Interculturalidad, Estado, Sociedad*.

36  Universidad Intercultural Amawtay Wasi, *Aprender en la sabiduría y el buen vivir*, 280–81.

37  See Pluriversidad Amawtay Wasi, "Quienes somos," accessed September 7, 2015, http://www.amawtaywasi.org.

38  Pluriversidad Amawtay Wasi, "Quienes somos."

39  CONAIE-ICCI, *Amawtay Wasi: Casa de la sabiduría: Universidad Intercultural de las Nacionalidades y Pueblos del Ecuador: Propuesta de camino en camino* (Quito: CONAIE-ICCI, 2003), 18.

40  Simpson, "Land as Pedagogy," 13n29.

41  At the same time as the government closed Amawtay Wasi, it approved (in the National Assembly or Congress) the creation of four new government-controlled universities with huge budgets and a base of administrators and faculty principally from the Global North: Ikiam (Regional Amazonian University), Yachay, the University of the Arts, and the National University of Education.

42  Atawallpa Oviedo Freire, "El neocolonialismo de fe," *Plan V. Ideas*, May 27, 2015, http://www.planv.com.ec/ideas/ideas/el-neocolonialism-fe.

43  This network includes URACCAN on Nicaragua's Atlantic Coast, the three Indigenous universities formed by the Bolivian government, the Autonomous Indigenous Intercultural University (UAIIN) in Cauca Colombia of CRIC, and UNISUR in Guerrero, Mexico. All of these institutions except UNISUR are state approved. While UAIIN is considered part of the state System of Indigenous Education, its recognition within Colombian higher education law is unclear.

44  Acuerdo del Consejo de Desarrollo de Nacionalidades y Pueblos del Ecuador (CODENPE), No. 2884, December 4, 2013.

45  Jon Igelmo Zaldivar, "La Universidad de la Tierra en México: Una propuesta de aprendizaje convivencial," in *Temas y perspectivas sobre educación: La infancia ayer y hoy*, ed. José Luis Hernández Huerta, Laura Sánchez Blanco, and Iván Pérez Miranda, 285–98 (Salamanca: Globalia, Ediciones Anthema, 2009), 286.

46  Gustavo Esteva, "Reclaiming our Freedom to Learn," *Yes Magazine*, November 7, 2007, accessed October 23, 2015, http://www.yesmagazine.org/issues/liberate -your-space/reclaiming-our-freedom-to-learn.

47  David Slater, "Spatial Politics/Social Movements: Questions of (B)orders and Resistance in Global Times," in *Geographies of Resistance*, ed. Steve Pile and Michael Keith, 258–76 (London: Routledge, 1997).

48  Comments by Quijano presented at the workshop "Knowledges and the Known," Duke University, November 2000, and discussed in greater detail in Walsh, "The (Re)Articulation of Political Subjectivities and Colonial Difference in Ecuador: Reflections on Capitalism and the Geopolitics of Knowledge," *Nepantla: Views from South* 3, no. 1 (2002): 61–97.

49  Walsh, "The (Re)articulation," 75.

50  Anzaldúa, *Light in the Dark, Luz en lo Oscuro: Rewriting Identity, Spirituality, Reality*, ed. Analouise Keating (Durham, NC: Duke University Press, 2015).

51  Abuelo Zenón in Walsh and García Salazar, "(W)riting Collective Memory (De) spite State: Decolonial Practices of Existence in Ecuador," in *Black Writing and the State in Latin America*, ed. Jerome Branche. (Nashville: Vanderbilt University Press, 2015), 259.

52  Luis Macas, "Presentación," in *Interculturalidad crítica y (de)colonialidad: Ensayos desde Abya Yala*, ed. Catherine Walsh (Quito: Ediciones Abya-Yala, 2012), 5.

# 4    On Decolonial Dangers, Decolonial Cracks, and Decolonial Pedagogies Rising

## Decolonial Dangers

Decoloniality, as I am posing it here, does not imply the absence of coloniality but rather the ongoing serpentine movement toward possibilities of other modes of being, thinking, knowing, sensing, and living; that is, an otherwise in plural.[1] In this sense, decoloniality is not a condition to be achieved in a linear sense, since coloniality as we know it will probably never disappear.

Decoloniality is also not a condition of illumination or enlightenment that some possess and others do not. Such assumption sets the stage for intellectual disputes over who is more decolonial.

It also leads to simplifications, generalizations, essentializations, and over-subjectifications (particularly by well-intending and conscientious whites) that make decoloniality the natural purview of Indigenous people (most especially Indigenous people in Abya Yala). These simplifications, generalizations, and essentializations reduce the Indigenous to an ethnic category, thus obscuring the political, sociocultural, epistemic, ontological, and existence-based violence and struggle that began with the imposed category of *Indio*, or "Indian." Indio, or Indian, is not an essentialist and ethnic category, says Silvia Rivera Cusicanqui, it is a category of struggle whose very term will end with freedom and emancipation.[2]

These simplifications, generalizations, and essentializations also leave out and obscure the relations of power within Indigenous communities as Lorena Cabnal in Guatemala, Julieta Paredes in Bolivia, and Leanne Simpson in Canada, among others, have argued. They shroud the everyday struggles of Indigenous, *campesina*, and Afro-descendant women against heteropatriarchal structures and growing levels of violence against women and girls (including in community settings). They also overlook and negate the increasingly ramped corruption and co-optation in these communities and organizations, the result, in large part, of capitalism's tentacles and state policies of inclusion. Moreover, they lead us to believe that decolonial struggle is always "ethnic," predominantly rural, and devoid of the institutional and personal *isims* of the dominant system (i.e., sexism, racism, heterosexualism, etc.). Certainly, such posturing is part of what I call emergent and developing *decolonial dangers*. The simplification and oversubjectification of indigeneity and Indigenous communities is one such danger, along with the notion of a decolonial geography of ruralization. Decoloniality in/as praxis knows no territorial, racial-ethnic, or sex-generic bounds.

Another danger is the commodification of decoloniality as the property of a group of individuals (i.e., the modernity/[de]coloniality project) and as a new *canon* of sorts, both of which erase and shroud decoloniality's terrain of political project, praxis, and struggle. Other dangers include the increasing rhetorical use of decoloniality within spheres of power, including its cooptation and use within the contexts of the state (as we saw in the last chapter), and its increasing adjectival lightness as a replacement for the *alternative* and *critical*, all too often devoid of significance, praxis, and struggle. The proposition of this first part of the book is to make evident and think from this praxis and struggle that signify decoloniality, its prospect and project.

Finally, and without denying other present and imminent perils, there is the danger of thinking, imagining, and seeing decoloniality only from the *outside* of the matrix of modern/colonial power. Such thought and visioning not only limit the spheres of action, but they also blind eyesight of the decolonial cracks that exist within this matrix and system and that, in essence, complement and push toward the edges and borders. For many of us, these cracks are the place of our location, agency, and everyday struggle.


## On Decolonial Cracks and the Praxis of Fissure

As the Insurgent Subcomandante Galeano reminds us, while we may want to bring down the wall (of history and of the system), "basta con hacerle una grieta" ([it is] enough to make a crack in it).[3] In a similar vein and more than half a century earlier, Aimé Césaire and later Frantz Fanon referred to the cracks in Western Christian civilization as spaces, places, and possibilities of and for decolonization.[4] Gloria Anzaldúa also found resonance in the cracks: "*Las rajaduras* [the cracks] give us a nepantla perspective, a view from the cracks . . . [that] enables us to reconfigure ourselves as subjects outside the us/them binary . . . to construct alternative roads, create new topographies and geographies . . . look at the world with new eyes, use competing systems of knowledge, and rewrite identities. Navigating the cracks is the process of reconstructing life anew."[5]

It thus seems relevant to bring up once again the question of the *how*. How do we, and can we, move within the cracks, open cracks, and extend the fissures? How can we shift our gaze to see from and through the cracks? How can we remain vigilant that the cracks do not close or that the dominant order does not simply patch them over?

Such questions take us beyond discussions *about* decoloniality per se. They also require considerations of our own explicit locations, of the questions of from where, with whom, and how we—the authors of this text, you the readers, and those (living and in spirit) with whom we walk (the relational *I* of which Édouard Glissant speaks)[6]—act and move within, from, and with respect to the cracks. Similarly, they push reflections of our own cognizance of the cracks and our own participation in the crack making. The cracks, in this sense, enunciate, reflect, and construct another place and postulate of decoloniality in/as praxis.

The best way to introduce the idea of this place and postulate is in terms of my own practice. As I have argued elsewhere, the fissures and cracks are part of my localization and place.[7] They are a component part of how and where I position myself. Moreover, they are constitutive of how I conceive, construct, and assume my praxis.

Although I work in the university, I seldom identify as an academic per se. My identification is as a militant intellectual, and always as a pedagogue, the latter understood not in the formal educational sense of a teacher who transmits or imparts knowledge, but as a facilitator; as someone who endeavors to provoke, encourage, construct, generate, and advance, with others, critical questionings, understandings, knowledges, and actionings; other ways of thinking and of doing *with*.

For me, this notion of pedagogy and of the pedagogical intertwines with intellectual militancy, activism, and action, forming an inseparable whole constitutive of and constituted in praxis, a praxis that I construct and assume both outside the university and within. Such posture began in the United States in my engagement with activist organizations and groups, and with Boricua, Latino, Black, Asian, and Haitian collectives and communities. It was consolidated in the years spent working with Paulo Freire while he was in exile in the United States, and it deepened and matured with my permanent move in the mid-1990s to Ecuador.

It is here in Abya Yala's South, and most particularly through collaborative work with Afro-descendant and Indigenous social movements and communities at their request, that I began to more profoundly comprehend the colonial and the decolonial, but also my own responsibility with respect to political-epistemic insurgence and decolonial praxis. That is a responsibility to think *with and from* the insurgent constructions, creations, practices, and subject-actors that, from the outside, the borders, edges, and cracks challenge and defy modernity/coloniality. This means disobeying the dominant domain that locates academic theory above and over praxis, and it means taking seriously what was argued in the introduction to this book: theorizing from and with praxis. It is a responsibility to open, widen, intercede in, and act from the decolonial fissures and cracks, and to make cracks within the spaces, places, institutions, and structures of the *inside*.

This is the localization and place of my thinking and praxis, and of the way I conceive my work, including within the university. The regional and international Latin American doctoral program that I began in Quito in 2001 is one such example.[8] Here the project has been to disobey, interrupt, and counter— as much as possible and pushing the limits of laws and regulations—the hegemonic Western frame of doctoral study. This means, on the one hand, to engender a thinking from and with the knowledge production—the production of knowledges in the plural—of South America, Central America, and the Caribbean, and with and from its actors/thinkers. It is to push a thinking from and with the social, political, cultural, epistemic, and life-based processes of struggle, movement, and change, making evident one's own place of engagement and enunciation. From this "place," the program-project works to build dialogues and conversations with knowledges produced elsewhere, in other "Souths" and in the so-called Global North. In this sense, the program-project's proposition is pluriversal. Moreover, it endeavors to build an interversality of interepistemic relation.

On the other hand, and relatedly, the doctoral program-project disobeys, interrupts, and counters the individuality and competition characteristic of academia and of graduate study. It builds the possibility of relationality and correlation; a space and place of dialoguing, thinking, analyzing, theorizing, and doing in community and in concert *with*, that encourage alliances, commitments, collaborations, and interculturalizations that cross disciplinary (de)formations, investigative interests, national borders, and racial, ethnic, sexual, and gendered identifications and that extend beyond the classroom and the period of doctoral study. In this sense, decolonial praxis is part of the program/project of the doctorate itself (in which Walter is also part). It is a praxis shared by those involved—students, professors, and interlocutors from social movements and from other places outside the university—all colleagues and *compañeras* and *compañeros* of a process that aims to deepen the fissures in the modern/colonial order. In this sense, and on repeated occasions, the doctorate has served as a base from which to build contacts and conversations with the growing number of collectives from Mexico to Patagonia that define themselves with regard to decolonial thought, praxis, and struggle. It also has worked to build dialogues with collective processes of the Souths in the North.

In my writing, I also endeavor to maintain this praxis and stance. My proposition has never been to study or report about social movements, actors, and thinkers but rather to think with, and, at the same time, to theorize *from* the "political moments" in which I am also engaged. This has meant, in some instances, constructing texts in conversation, writing with, and writing for and from the charges of collaboration and colabor that I have received and assumed from movement leaders,[9] writings targeted for use *casa adentro* (in house), *casa afuera* (out of house), and between houses.

This praxis of fissure, of course, is not limited to the university or to the writing of texts. For me, the political-epistemic responsibility has meant an involvement and engagement with the ongoing and emergent processes of struggle and change in ways that help fracture and fissure the modern/colonial order, and help walk an otherwise. Such processes have at times meant moving within the inside/outside/against articulations discussed in the last chapter, in order to open other conceptualizations, other practices, and other possibilities of reflection, action, and thought. This is how I postured and conceived, for example, my collaborations with Afro and Indigenous leaders and Constitutional Assembly members in the collective making of Ecuador's Constitution of 2008. This collaboration—as a praxis of fissure—focused on the conceptualization of interculturality, plurinationalism, and collective rights and on the praxical significance of these concepts, including as postulates, propositions, and actions that intervene in and crack the dominant monocultural and uninational frames of constitutionalism, law, and state.

Similarly, the work with Juan García Salazar, together with other Black community members, youth, and elders, to document, position, and give lived presence to collective memory and ancestral knowledges (as contemporary, evolving, and in continuous use and construction), has entailed a praxis of fissure inside and outside the institutional frames of both nation and education. This in a country that did not recognize the presence of Afro-Ecuadorians until 1998 (a presence calculated today as at least 8 percent of the population) and where music, dance, and food continue to be used as the principal signifiers and representational markers of cultural (read: colonial) difference. The Afro-Andean Document and Archival Project that Juan García and I established in 2002, as a coagreement between the collective Procesos de Comunidades Negras (Black Community Processes) and the Universidad Andina Simón Bolívar in Quito, is one instance of this shared, collaborative, and collective praxis that both fissures and (re)constructs. The project here has been to preserve, classify, catalogue, and digitize the more than three thousand hours of oral testimonies compiled by Juan and other community-based intellectuals-activists in rural Afro-Ecuadorian communities over a period of more than thirty years, and more than ten thousand photographs. This material is now open to use by the public. However, the project is not just this. It has also been to continue to add to this archive of collective memory and to return this memory to communities in useable form, including in print, visual, and multimedia formats and in educational materials.

Together these examples are part of a pedagogical praxis of accompaniment and engagement that endeavors to move within and connect the cracks while looking toward and pushing to foster, build, and enable decolonial horizons. Yet what these examples do not clearly show are my own processes of unlearning. Illustrative is the following excerpt, taken from a small book of mine organized and published by the Mexican collective Zapateándole el Mal Gobierno and translated here into English.

> In November 2013, I received in an e-mail a personal letter of invitation from the Subcomandantes Marcos and Moisés; it was a letter inviting me to be a first-grade student in the Escuelita Zapatista. This experience, lived intensely during the last week of December 2013 in the *caracol* of Morelia, left an imprint that I still cannot totally capture, describe, or process. Its significance and profoundness are still becoming.
>
> And in this *becoming* I feel the presence of Viejo Antonio (for Marcos and the Zapatistas, a real and symbolic elder), along with my own ancestors-guides, appearing from time to time, as occurred that cold, rainy, foggy, and muddy night, the first in the caracol. With a need to go to the latrine, I got up from my bed, several pieces of wood pushed together on the dirt and

cement floor shared with many other students, including children, adolescents, and adults. It was in the solitude and darkness of the night that I felt a soft, warm, and affectionate wind coming close; it was almost as if a hand was taking mine. At first, I thought, how great—someone has come to help me get quickly to the latrine, to alleviate the growing urge! However, when I turned to look, I saw only, and for a splitting second, a star that seemed to open a small hole, a crack of light in the thick brume. Was this not a signal, I asked? Now I interpret it as an accompaniment and as an admonition of the path unknown on which the escuelita was about to take me.

The path and experience, of course, were not easy. They were made more complicated by the particularity of the community that I was assigned to, a community with only a small number of Zapatista families who face on a daily basis the conflicts caused by the anti-Zapatista majority (i.e., progovernment, paramilitary, and evangelicals, among others). The relative isolation of my living conditions, the difficulties of translation, and my own health problems made the learning ever more difficult. The brume, metaphoric and real, seemed to swallow me.

However, the experience served to evidence—in real life—the strength and grandeur of Zapatista communities, the depth of the fissure that they have opened in the Western civilizatory and capitalist logic and project. It evidenced this *muy otra* (very other) way that has its base in autonomy, freedom, and community as vital praxis, lived praxis. And it evidenced a praxis that effectively undoes the supposedly single order of market, greed, and capital.

But the experience also gave me a lesson in humility, displacing and de-centering what I thought I knew, how I thought I knew it, and how I thought I came to know. It made me confront the assumptions that, despite my own declared criticalness and decolonial positioning, I had not questioned or challenged, neither in my pedagogical practice nor in my identification and authority as professor and teacher.

It gave me a lesson in humility in taking away the clarity of day, in clouding my sight in the mist and brume. And it gave me a lesson in humility by making me assume, at a personal level, what I had been arguing and teaching for many years: unlearning in order to relearn. In this sense, it made me live—not for the first time but certainly in a way particularly "other"—the difficulty, conflict, the discomfort, and pain.

Much happened, and much was lived. I feel in me the political-pedagogical imperative to not only share this experience and learning but, and more significantly, to make it walk asking. This was one of the first lessons that I learned in the Escuelita Zapatista.

Asking and walking questions and, at the same time, unlearning to relearn are, undoubtedly, central components of the pedagogical and decolonial weave, a decolonial pedagogy making itself and becoming, opening and extending cracks and fissures in the dominant world and, at the same time, contributing to the building of a world—of worlds—*muy otro(s)*.[10]

## Decolonial Pedagogies Rising

Pedagogy has been a recurring theme and reference throughout this text. Its reference has not been to schooling or education per se. Instead, pedagogy has been employed as related to and synonymous with the work of resurgence and insurgence, the work of knowledge (in which we all labor), and the work of decolonial praxis.

Pedagogy is understood here in the sense established by Paulo Freire, which is as an essential and indispensable methodology grounded in peoples' realities, subjectivities, histories, and struggles. It is in the social, political, epistemic, and existential contexts of struggle that "leaders and peoples, mutually identified, together create the directive lines of their action [educational, political, and of liberation]," Freire said.[11] As I have argued elsewhere, social struggles for Freire are pedagogical settings of learning, unlearning, relearning, reflection, and action. The educational nature of struggle is what interested Freire most, along with the pedagogical practice of working toward individual and collective liberation.[12] This is an engaged pedagogy. As bell hooks argued a number of years ago, it emphasizes an integral notion of well-being and of healing.[13]

If Freire was still alive, I think he would agree that pedagogy in this sense (and as I suggested above with respect to interculturality and decoloniality), is more of a verb than a noun; *pedagogization* makes pedagogy a *verbality*, to use Rolando Vázquez's term. Furthermore, the pluralizing of both interrupts a singularity and unity in concept, use, practice, proposition, and form. The significance of pedagogies and pedagogizations for me is in what Fanon— another pedagogue—described in *Black Skin, White Masks* as the actional: "the prime task of him [sic] who, having taken thought, prepares to act."[14] I am thinking here of the practices, strategies, methodologies, and ways of making and doing that interweave with, and that are constructed in, resistance and opposition, as well as in insurgence, affirmation, and re-existence (as rehumanization), in imagining and building a different world.

While Freire has offered much for understanding pedagogy as method and political praxis, his limitations from a decolonial perspective cannot be overlooked. Certainly, he was a product of the post–World War II Latin American Left, and of Marxist and humanist emancipatory paradigms, postures, and worldviews. The problem here, as the Maori anthropologist Linda Tuhiwai Smith argues, is that all too frequently paradigms, postures, and views—"often regarded as deriving from Freirian approaches"—have worked to negate and obscure the methodological standpoints, practices, processes, and approaches of feminist theorists of color, ethnic minorities, and Indigenous peoples. This negation applies to the methodologies and/as pedagogies that derive from the lived experience of colonialism, racism, and the struggles for self-determination and decolonization.[15] The Native American intellectual Sandy Grande makes a similar argument against Freirian-based critical pedagogy, including what Peter McLaren names as "revolutionary critical pedagogy." For Grande, the theoretical formulations and assumptions of this pedagogy remain Western, anthropocentric, and largely Marxist informed and thus in tension with Indigenous knowledge and praxis.[16]

Still, and despite Freire's limitations with regard to the modern/colonial matrix of power (something he himself began to recognize in his last years), much of his praxistical liberation-based thought remains relevant. This relevance is, in fact, the subject of attack by Latin America's recently emergent extreme Right, led largely by evangelical movements and transnational interests. Brazil is a case in point.

On June 28, 2016, Paulo Freire's biographical page on Wikipedia was altered, allegedly by SERPRO, the communicative and technology-based network of Brazil's ultra-right-wing federal government. Among the alterations made were those, for example, that associated his pedagogy of liberation with Marxist indoctrination, with the "formation of soldiers willing to defend Marxism, tooth and nail, in the academic sphere."[17] Similarly, the alterations lay blame on Freire for the educational reforms of 1996, the period in which he was minister of education; the claim is that his indoctrination is the reason for and the base of what these attackers conceive as Brazil's still backward and still politicized and ideologized education system. References here, and in a parallel text published by Brazil's Liberal Institute, are to "Paulo Freire Assassin of Knowledge." State legislation that prohibits the discussion and teaching of politics and of gender in schools and in higher education is a reflection and product of the attack on Freire. The authors of this legislation are the evangelical majority now in municipal, state, and federal government as well as the movement "Schooling without [Political] Party" (i.e., the Workers' Party, of which Freire was also part). This legislation and movement intend to de-ideologize education, control curricula, and keep out of universities and schools studies on and discussions about politics, gender, sexuality, feminism, Black, Indigenous, and popular struggle and thought, and even African-based religions; that is to keep out, and even criminalize, elements and postures of decoloniality in/as praxis.

Thinking from and with the lived experience of coloniality and its matrix of power that traverses practically all aspects of life, including the realms of subjectivity, knowledge, being, sexuality, spirituality (including soul-body, spirit-mind, and ancestor-relation), and nature (understood interrelationally as Pachamama), affords a perspective and analytic that challenges many of the presuppositions of Western knowledge and thought. This thinking, for many, is considered both dangerous and heretic. In great part this is because it brings to the fore the decolonial otherwise, its social, political, epistemic, and cosmic-existence-based insurgencies, its pedagogies, pedagogizations, and praxis, an otherwise that stands up to "the racist myth that inaugurated modernity and the monologue of modern-Western reason."[18] Moreover, it is considered dangerous and heretic because it affirms, aligns, and connects that which modernity/coloniality/heteropatriarchy/capitalism has worked to dismember.

In her powerful book *Pedagogies of Crossing,* the Caribbean feminist Jacqui Alexander allies herself with Freire's understanding of pedagogy as method. Yet at the same time, she defines her project as navigating other realms that take her beyond the confines of modernity and the imprisonment of what she refers to as its *secularized episteme.* Alexander's project is to "disturb and reassemble the inherited divides of the Sacred and the secular, the embodied and disembodied" through pedagogies that are derived from "the Crossing," this conceived as signifier, existential message, and passage toward the configuration of new ways of being and knowing.[19] While Alexander does not explicitly position herself from the decolonial, she engages this perspective in her analysis of the material and psychic fragmentation and dismemberment produced by colonization, and in her emphasis on the work of decolonization with respect to the yearning of wholeness.[20] Here she sustains that "anticolonial and Left liberation movements have not understood this sufficiently in their psychology of liberation." "What we have devised as an oppositional politic has been necessary," she says, "but it will never sustain us, for while it may give us some temporary gains (which become more ephemeral the greater the threat, which is not a reason not to fight), it can never ultimately feed that deep place within us: that space of the erotic, . . . the Soul, . . . the Divine."[21] For this author, pedagogies must be conceived in this sense; called forth is the decolonial otherwise of which I have been speaking.

Here Alexander's multiple understanding of pedagogies is particularly relevant:

> As something given, as in handed, revealed; as in breaking through, transgressing, disrupting, displacing, inverting inherited concepts and practices, those psychic, analytic and organizational methodologies we deploy to know what we believe we know so as to make different conversations and solidarities possible; as both epistemic and ontological project bound to our beingness and, therefore, akin to Freire's formulation of pedagogy as indispensable methodology. Pedagogies [that] summon subordinated knowledges that are produced in the context of the practices of marginalization in order that we might destabilize existing practices of knowing and thus cross the fictive boundaries of exclusion and marginalization.[22]

Alexander, it seems, is both thinking with and beyond Freire. She locates her perspective of pedagogies as akin to his; that is, of pedagogies as indispensable methodologies of and for transformation. Yet at the same time, she reveals the limits of the psychology of liberation that, of course, was constitutive of Freire's work. However, in so doing, she does not reject Freire; he is part of the crossroads she evokes and invokes, of the crosscurrents of genealogies, theorizings, politics, and practice that she fashions. In so doing, Alexander makes evident her practice of pedagogization. She stimulates reflection on Freire not as the authoritative source, but as what we might consider an elder and pedagogical guide.

The "guides" in the pedagogical course—or pedagogization—of decoloniality and/as praxis do not end, of course, with Alexander and Freire. Nelson Maldonado-Torres, Lewis Gordon, Sylvia Wynter, Walter Mignolo, and I, as well as others, have highlighted the decolonial and pedagogical contribution of Frantz Fanon, particularly in *Black Skin, White Masks*, but also in *Wretched of the Earth*.[23] In the former text, Fanon speaks from the lived experience of the Black man, analyzing the structures that contribute to his dehumanization, and posing *sociogeny* as a kind of decolonizing pedagogy for humanity. As Maldonado-Torres indicates, Fanon becomes then a kind of pedagogue or Socratic teacher of sorts—a midwife of decolonial agency—who aims to facilitate the formation of subjectivity, self-reflection, and the praxis of liberation. And it is precisely in enabling the sub-other to take a position in which he or she can recognize and do things for himself or herself—that is, to act—that the teaching consists.[24]

Another less-known guide is the Colombian writer, novelist, medical doctor, anthropologist, researcher, folklorist, and educator Manuel Zapata Olivella, called by some as the *abridor de caminos* (opener of pathways) and *ekobio mayor* (wise elder). In his work, which traverses more than fifty years; crosses the fields of literature, art, journalism, history, philosophy, anthropology, culture, and medicine; and connects the lived realities, spirituality, and thought of the African diaspora in the Caribbean and Americas, Zapata Olivella struggled to make visible and confront both the racism and epidermization of his native Colombia, and the broader human and colonial condition. Dehumanization and alienation were constant problem themes that gave impulse and orientation to his insurgent, actional, and pedagogical project. As was the case with Freire, Zapata Olivella was greatly influenced by Fanon.

Until his passing to the other side in 2004, Zapata Olivella struggled with the tenacity of a pedagogue for the vindication of humanity, the epistemic capacity of Afro-descendants, and the horizons of decolonial relation. While his contributions were many, one that particularly stands out is the positioning of the insurgent, ancestral, and living force of "Muntu," understood as "the sum of the deceased (ancestors) and the living, united by the word to the animals, trees, minerals in an indissoluble knot . . . , the conception of humanity that the most exploited peoples of the world, the Africans, give back to the European colonizers without bitterness or resentment."[25]

Together Fanon and Zapata Olivella recall another present-day African descendant pedagogue long engaged in decolonial praxis: Juan García Salazar, who on July 18, 2017, also passed to the other side, beginning the journey to reunite with his ancestors. Popularly known as the grandfather of the Afro-Ecuadorian movement, the worker of the process, and the guardian of the word and the tradition, García has kept alive, over the last more than fifty years, the generational charge to register, document, and circulate *casa adentro* and *casa afuera*, the ancestral knowledges and oral tradition of Afro-Ecuadorian peoples. His conceptualization of this charge was—and is (since in collective memory his words, thought, and practice continue to live)—

both decolonial and pedagogical; his practice constructs a pedagogy of decolonial attitude and intent.

For example, in his conception of *cimarronaje*, or marronage, as a pedagogy for the new urban generations (see chapter 2), García underscores the ways that marronage can be used as a sort of theoretical and memory-based anchor, conceptual analytic, and decolonial code and tool to reread official history and to contribute to it with a new and "other" reading. "This is a *cimarrón* attitude: to always distrust the word written by the dominant other, . . . to closely go over this word and history and compare it with our own, . . . to recuperate elements of the memory of resistance that is born in the *cimarrón* being . . . and to reconstruct a new memory," that is, a history otherwise.[26] Entailed here as well is a learning to unlearn in order to relearn, a central component of decoloniality in/as praxis.

Similarly, in his community-based work with and through oral tradition, García gives life to collective memory and the word. He crafts a pedagogy and pedagogization grounded in the realities and struggles of the present, including the deterritorialization, plundering, and dispossession of ancestral lands, the extraction of natural resources and knowledges, the capture and co-optation of leaders, and the policies and politics of state-sponsored inclusion, among others.[27] As García describes it, it is a pedagogy of sowing seeds. All those who assume the role of guardian and cultivator of collective memory, says García, become sowers. Their task—our task—is to update the words of the ancestors for the new generations, to make them accessible to children (in stories, tales, riddles, and other forms), and to continue the work of the elders by planting seeds of ancestral knowledge and collective memory. That is, to put into practice methods and pedagogies of sowing that plant and nurture a shared and collective decolonial otherwise of cultural affirmation, and of life, living, knowing, and being in relation.

Re-membered here is what Haymes calls the symbolic work—through songs, stories, and rituals—of slave culture, a pedagogical labor and imagination that permitted enslaved Africans and African descendants to forge a community of belonging that, in the process "remade blackness, a Western European white supremacist invention, into a standpoint of historical consciousness and leverage for change."[28] Similarly recalled is what Paget Henry describes as the cosmogonic and communitarian nature of African philosophy and ethics.[29] In a social world still—and increasingly—marked by racialized violence and hostility, and ongoing struggles of legitimacy, affirmation, ethical expectation, re-existence, human freedom, and life-visions, the pedagogical force of collective memory and ancestral knowledge—as knowledge and memory of the present in continuous relation with future and past—becomes ever more relevant.

Re-membered here as well is a learning from and with the land, understood—figuratively and symbolically—as life practice. Such perspective and practice, of course, interweave with those of many ancestral peoples. Leanne Betasamosake Simpson's reclamation of "land as pedagogy" both as process and context for Nishnaabeg—that is, her ancestral community's own—intelligence, is one of the many resurgences and insurgences in this regard long evident among First Nation peoples. The pedagogies of struggle of Brazil's Landless Workers Movement (MST) similarly signify the centrality of land, and the ways that deterritorialization and dispossession have functioned as arms of capitalism and the modern/colonial matrix of power. In a different context but with a project in some ways related, the Take Back the Land movement in the United States, formed in 2006, centered in Miami, and modeled after Brazil's MST, works to disrupt gentrification, block evictions, and rehouse homeless people in foreclosed houses. Recalled here as well are the struggles in many urban centers in both the North and South (the favelas in Rio de Janeiro being particularly emblematic)—struggles to reclaim and retain community (as land space-place) against the tentacles of capital and its present-day entwine (an entwine in continuous mutation and re-formation) with the racialized/gendered/modern/colonial order, an order that prospers by disposing of all that gets in its way and by laying claim to the "riches."

The processes and practices of pedagogization that Wilmer and Ernell Villa detail in the context of the Caribe Seco Colombiano (Colombia's "Dry" Caribbean), offer another perspective, more closely tied to that of García's. For these community- and university-based intellectuals, the *pedagogization* of the word and of listening is a political strategy, an intentional action of mobilization of cultural content that affirms life, existence, and the right of territorial belonging.[30] The word—spoken, cultivated, heard, and situated in-place—transmits cultural knowledges, circulates cosmogonic references, and animates memory as a sowing and rerooting of belonging in a region and society where Black people are increasingly "disembarked," dislodged, and evicted from their own sense of being, memory, and place, and from their network of origins, of extended family, and of relation. "The 'pedagogization of listening,' particularly in intergenerational encounters, animates, heartens, and enlivens life, belonging, and the defense of territory, where the reflection about origins becomes necessary in the moment of asking ourselves about place and about the meaning of experience of the black communities of *Caribe Seco*."[31]

Pedagogies, as I am proposing them here, are the struggles, practices, processes, and wagers for life. They are the praxis of decolonial paths that, as Betty Ruth Lozano describes with respect to blackwomen in the Colombian Pacific, work to regenerate the broken weave of community, territory, ancestral knowledge and memory, spirituality, and existence as life itself.[32] They are manifestations of what Carmen Cariño, Aura Cumes, Ochy Curiel, Bienvenida Mendoza, Karina Ochoa, and Alejandra Londoño call the exercise of spinning threads, to braid knitting from situated places, including from the "epistemic diversity that inscribes this open field that we call 'decolonial feminisms.'" Decolonial pedagogies, in this sense, "imply the possibility of re-knowing the multiple knowledges, thoughts, experiences, existences, cosmovisions, dissidences, and emotions that cross the subjects and populations that produce knowledges from positionalities that locate them as subalternized, exploited, oppressed, etc."[33]

All of the perspectives and practices of pedagogization presented above underscore the *for* that introduced this first part of the book and that has oriented the reflection and discussion of the otherwise of decoloniality in/ as praxis. Recalled once again is Adolfo Albán's concept of and clamor *for* *re-existence*. "Re-existence as the mechanisms that communities create and develop to invent daily life and power, in this way confronting the hegemonic project that, since colonization until our present day, has inferiorized, silenced, and negatively made visible existence.... Re-existence puts off center the established logics in order to look for, in the depth of cultures—especially Indigenous and Afro-descendant—the keys to forms of ... organization and production that permit the dignifying and reinventing of life and its continued transformation."[34]

For Albán, it is in the specific context of the construction of Black subjectivities that re-existence takes meaning and form. Re-existence references the configuration of ways to exist and not just resist—to re-exist resisting and to resist re-existing—as subjects, to build projects of society and life despite adverse conditions (of enslavement, dehumanization, racialization, and discrimination), and to surpass and overcome these conditions in order to occupy a social and cultural place of dignity: a re-existence as subjects and with others in radically distinct terms.[35]

To speak of pedagogies of re-existence, then, is to once again call forth the agency, action, and praxis of the otherwise. It is to raise the existential, philosophic, and lived concerns and pedagogical imperatives of freedom, anguish, responsibility, embodied agency, sociality, and liberation to which Lewis Gordon refers.[36] It is to signal affirmation and hope in spite of—and in the midst of—conditions of negation, violence, and despair, part of the war of capitalism and the reorganization of modernity/coloniality/heteropatriachy. It is to recognize that decolonial re-existence in the circumstances of the present times requires creative pedagogies-methodologies of struggle.

Herein lies the significance, urgency, and insurgency of decolonial pedagogies rising.

## Notes

1   I use *serpentine* here in the sense defined by the Mayan Yucatecan artist and intellectual Isaac Can Carrillo. Carrillo, conversation, February 2013, Duke University.

2   Silvia Rivera Cusicanqui, "Violencia e Interculturalidad: Paradojas de la etnicidad en la Bolivia de hoy," *Revista Telar* 15 (July 2016): 49–70; http://revistatelar.ct.unt .edu.ar/index.php/revistatelar/article/view/18.

3   SupGaleano, Comisión de la Sexta del EZLN, *Pensamiento crítico frente a la hidra capitalista I* (Chiapas, Mexico: EZLN, 2015), 200.

4   See Aimé Césaire, *Discourse on Colonialism*, trans. Joan Pinkham (New York: Monthly Review Press, [1955] 2000), and Frantz Fanon, *Black Skin, White Masks* (New York: Grove Press, 1967).

5   Gloria Anzaldúa, *Light in the Dark, Luz en lo Oscuro: Rewriting Identity, Spirituality, Reality*, ed. Analouise Keating (Durham, NC: Duke University Press, 2015), 82.

6   Édouard Glissant, *Poetics of Relation* (Ann Arbor: University of Michigan Press, 1997).

7   See Walsh, "Pedagogical Notes from the Decolonial Cracks," *e-misférica* 11, no. 1 (2014), http://hemisphericinstitute.org/hemi/en/emisferica-111-decolonial-gesture /walsh.

8   For a description of this effort, see Walsh, "The Politics of Naming: (Inter)cultural Studies in De-Colonial Code," *Cultural Studies* 25, nos. 4–5 (2011): 108–25.

9   See, for example, Juan García Salazar and Catherine Walsh, *Pensar sembrando/ Sembrar pensando con el Abuelo Zenón* (Quito: Cátedra de Estudios Afro-Andinos, Universidad Andina Simón Bolívar and Ediciones Abya-Yala, 2017); and Walsh and García, "(W)riting Collective Memory (De)spite State: Decolonial Practices of Existence in Ecuador," in *Black Writing and the State in Latin America*, ed. Jerome Branche, 253–66 (Nashville: Vanderbilt University Press, 2015).

10  Walsh, *Lo pedagógico y lo decolonial: Entretejiendo caminos* (Querétaro: En cortito que's pa' largo, 2014), 88–90.

11  Paulo Freire, *Pedagogy of the Oppressed* (New York: Continuum, 1974), 183.

12  See Walsh, "Decolonial Pedagogies Walking and Asking: Notes to Paulo Freire from AbyaYala," *International Journal of Lifelong Education* 34, no. 1 (2015): 9–21, and Walsh, "Introducción: Lo pedagógico y lo decolonial Entretejiendo caminos," in *Pedagogías decoloniales: Prácticas de resistir, (re)existir y (re)vivir*, vol. 1, ed. Catherine Walsh, 23–68 (Quito: Ediciones Abya-Yala, 2013).

13  bell hooks, *Teaching to Transgress: Education as the Practice of Freedom* (New York: Routledge, 1994).

14  Fanon, *Black Skin, White Masks* (New York: Grove Press, 1967), 222.

15  Linda Tuhiwai Smith, *Decolonizing Methodologies: Research and Indigenous Peoples* (London: Zed Books, 1999), 167.

16  Sandy Grande, "Red Pedagogy: The Un-Methodology," in *Handbook of Critical and Indigenous Methodologies*, ed. N. Denzin, Y. Lincoln, and L. T. Smith, 233–54 (London: SAGE, 2008).

17  Leando Melito, "Doutrinação: Página de Paulo Freire na Wiki é alterada em rede do governo," *UOL educação*, June 29, 2016, accessed July 19, 2017, http://educacao .uol.com.br/noticias/2016/06/29/doutrinacao-paulo-freire-na-wikipedia-e -alterado-por-usuario-do-governo.htm.

18  Rafael Bautista, "Bolivia: Del estado colonial al estado plurinacional," January 21, 2009, https://www.servindi.org/actualidad/opinion/6774.

19  M. Jacqui Alexander, *Pedagogies of Crossing: Meditations on Feminism, Sexual Poli tics, Memory, and the Sacred* (Durham, NC: Duke University Press, 2005), 7.

20  For Alexander, this wholeness and yearning to belong "is not to be confined to membership or citizenship in community, political movement, Nation, group, or belonging to a family. . . . The source of that yearning is the deep knowing that we are in fact interdependent . . ." (*Pedagogies of Crossing*, 282).

21  Alexander, *Pedagogies of Crossing*, 281, 282.

22  Alexander, *Pedagogies of Crossing*, 7.

23  See, for example, Lewis Gordon, *Fanon and the Crisis of the European Man* (New York: Routledge, 1995); Nelson Maldonado-Torres, "Frantz Fanon and CLR James on Intellectualism and Enlightened Rationality," *Caribbean Studies* 33, no. 2 (July– December 2005): 149–94; Mignolo, *The Darker Side of Western Modernity: Global Futures, Decolonial Options* (Durham, NC: Duke University Press, 2011); Walsh, *Lo ped agógico y lo decolonial*; and Sylvia Wynter, "Towards the Sociogenic Principle: Fanon, The Puzzle of Conscious Experience, of 'Identity' and What It's Like to Be 'Black,'" in *National Identities and Sociopolitical Changes in Latin America*, ed. Mercedes Durán-Cogan and Antonio Gómez-Moriano, 30–66 (New York: Routledge, 2001).

24  Maldonado-Torres, "Frantz Fanon," 159.

25  Manuel Zapata Olivella, *Rebelión de los genes: El mestizaje americano en la sociedad futura* (Bogotá: Altamira Ediciones, 1997), 362. Muntu is linked to what Africa-origin peoples throughout the world name as Ubuntu, and it recalls the Afro and Indigenous life-visions of relationality, expressed also as collective well-being, life in plentitude, and *sumak kawsay* or *buen vivir*.

26  García in *Pensar sembrando*, 128.

27  See Walsh, "Afro In/Exclusion, Resistance, and the 'Progressive' State: (De)Colonial Struggles, Questions, and Reflections," in *Black Social Movements in Latin America: From Monocultural Mestizaje to Multiculturalism*, ed. Jean Muteba Rahier, 15–34 (New York: Palgrave Macmillan, 2012), and Walsh and García, "(W)riting Collective Memory."

28  Stephen Nathan Haymes, "Pedagogy and the Philosophical Anthropology of African-American Slave Culture," in *Not Only the Master's Tools: African-American Studies in Theory and Practice*, ed. Lewis Gordon and Jane Anna Gordon (Boulder, CO: Paradigm Publishers, 2006), 202.

29  Paget Henry, *Caliban's Reason: Introducing Afro-Caribbean Philosophy* (New York: Routledge, 2000).

30  Wilmer Villa and Ernell Villa, "Donde llega uno, llegan dos, llegan tres y llegan todos: El sentido de la pedagogización de la escucha en las comunidades negras del Caribe Seco colombiano," in *Pedagogías decoloniales: Prácticas insurgentes de resistir, (re)existir y (re)vivir*, vol. 1, ed. Catherine Walsh, 357–99 (Quito: Ediciones Abya-Yala, 2013).

31  Villa and Villa, "Donde llega uno, llegan dos," 399.

32  Betty Ruth Lozano Lerma, "Pedagogías para la vida, la alegría y la re-existencia: Pedagogías de mujeres negras que curan y vinculan," in *Pedagogías decoloniales: Prácticas insurgentes de resistir, (re)existir y (re)vivir*, vol. 2, ed. Catherine Walsh, 273–90 (Quito: Ediciones Abya-Yala, 2017).

33  Cariño et al., "Pensar, sentir, y hacer pedagogías feministas descoloniales: Diálogos y puntadas," in *Pedagogías decoloniales: Prácticas insurgentes de resistir, (re)existir y (re)vivir*, vol. 2, ed. Catherine Walsh (Quito: Ediciones Abya-Yala, 2017), 524.

34  Adolfo Albán Achinte, "Pedagogías de la re-existencia: Artistas indígenas y afrocolombianos," in *Pedagogías decoloniales: Prácticas insurgentes de resistir, (re)existir y (re)vivir*, vol. 1, ed. Catherine Walsh (Quito: Ediciones Abya-Yala, 2013), 455.

35  Albán Achinte, "Epistemes 'otras': ¿Epistemes disruptivas?" *Revista Kula* 6 (2012): 30.

36  See Lewis Gordon, *Existentia Africana: Understanding Africana Existential Thought* (New York: Routledge, 2000), and Lewis Gordon, "A Pedagogical Imperative of Pedagogical Imperatives," *Thresholds* (2010): 27–35.

# Sowing and Growing Decoloniality In/As Praxis

*Some Final Thoughts*

As I have argued here, decoloniality is not a done deal, a condition to be reached, or a stage of critical enlightenment. It is also not an abstract academic paradigm, that is, a paradigm and postulate devoid of struggle and praxis. Silvia Rivera Cusicanqui's argument that decoloniality is part of a multiculturalist discourse and a new academic canon with its own "gurus" (in which, according to Rivera, both Walter and I are included), negates the broad range of decolonizing practice that, as this part I has shown, gives substance, significance, and form to decoloniality in/as praxis.[1]

Thus while the term *decoloniality* follows Quijano's naming of *coloniality* in the late 1980s (see Walter's discussion in part II), the matrix of power and the struggles that both mark have a history and "herstory" of more than five hundred years in which diverse forms of decolonial contestation, construction, and struggle (from "the bottom up") are necessarily present and related. Decoloniality is one way—but by no means the only way—to name this contestation, construction and struggle against what Macas called the colonial yoke or tare, and for an otherwise. This "against" and "for" obviously call forth what social movements in Abya Yala often continue to refer to as decolonization, that is, decolonizing struggles, postures, and actions that seek to undo the ongoing and complexly intertwined structures of local-national-global power, and foster, assemble, and support radically other modes of collective re-existence.

María Galindo's claim that decolonization necessarily requires depatriarcalization is fundamental here. "You can't decolonize without depatriarchalizing," says the Bolivian Galindo. This phrase, central to the work, struggle, and public declarations of the autonomous feminist collective *Mujeres Creando*, founded by Galindo, Julieta Paredes, and others, gives credence to the ongoing relation of patriarchy and colonialism. And it also signals the complexity of the transformative work to be done.[2] Recalled here as well is María Lugones's analysis of patriarchy as a component part of the coloniality of gender, as well as Rita Segato's study of the relation of patriarchy, coloniality, and violence against women in Latin America today.[3]

The crucial point here, and as I have argued throughout this part I, is in the action, labor, struggle and toil of decolonizing; that is, in decolonial praxis, in the plural, that continues within the cracks, margins, and borders of the dominant order. Walter's argument in the chapter that follows for the difference between decolonization and decoloniality does not deny this bridging from below. Instead, it points to the dominance of the top-down conceptualization of decolonization constructed with the Cold War, a meaning primarily indicative of and associated with states' political independence. It is in this context that Walter highlights the differential concept, analytic, and significance of decoloniality.

The issue here is not about an ownership of terms or words, nor is it, as the recent arguments of Ramón Grosfoguel would also lead one to think, about who named and/or referred to first the ongoing colonial regime, matrix, or system of economic, racial, gender, and patriarchal power, or who best represents (and re-presents) decolonial theory and practice.[4] I, for one, am not interested in perpetuating these debates, critique, and competition.

For me, and as I have detailed in this Part I, decoloniality is a perspective, stance, and proposition of thought, analysis, sensing, making, doing, feeling, and being that is actional (in the Fanonian sense), praxistical, and continuing. Moreover, it is prospectively relational in that it looks, thinks, and acts with the present-future-past, including with the peoples, subjects, and situated and embodied knowledges, territories, and struggles that push toward, advance, and open possibilities of an otherwise. It is in this sense that decoloniality can be understood as a process, practice, and project of sowing seeds; of cultivating, nurturing, and growing, always vigilant of what the Zapatistas refer to as the Storm brewing, the catastrophe and collapse that is now upon us thanks to the incredible capacity of regeneration of the capitalist hydra, and relatedly, the continual reconstitution of the coloniality of power.

In the EZLN's seminar in May 2015, or "seedbed" of critical thought, the Insurgent Subcomandante Galeano asked participants for "the seed that questions, provokes, encourages, pushes us to continue to think and analyze; a seed so that other seeds listen that they have to grow, in their own way, according to their own calendar and geography."[5] Likewise, SupMoisés called for attention to the seeds themselves, to the ones that will germinate, grow, and give fruit, and for the need for attention, practice, and vigilance in this regard.

From the context of the Afro-Pacific, Juan García and Abuelo Zenón remind us of the seeds sowed by peoples of African origin in the lands of the Americas, seeds of ancestral knowledge, philosophy, memory, and tradition, of resistance, and of and for life. These are seeds, they say, that need to not just be remembered but also resown in contemporary times and with attention to the present-day reality of deterritorializations, dispossessions, expropriations, co-optations, and false inclusions, and the recoloniality of power, being, knowledge, and nature.[6]

Similarly, and from the context of Cauca, Colombia, Vilma Almendra speaks of the *caminar de sembrar*, "of the walk to permanently sow, fertilize, feed, nurture, and harvest pedagogical actions to *palabrandar* life, a sowing and pedagogical actioning that goes beyond the category that defines us as Indigenous" in that it convokes all involved in and committed to transforming the dominant system.[7]

The praxis of decoloniality, subject of this first part of the book, is just this: the continuous work to plant and grow an otherwise despite and in the borders, margins, and cracks of the modern/colonial/capitalist/heteropatriarchal order. The pedagogies of this praxis are multiple. They are sown and grown in the contexts of decolonial struggle, wherever and however this struggle is conceived, situated, and takes form. And they are sown and grown in the methodologies and/as pedagogies of struggle itself. I am thinking of the struggles in Indigenous, Black, and peasant communities, the struggles of racialized subjects, struggles in urban spaces, struggles within feminisms, and struggles in the educational sphere. I am thinking of the struggles of youth, of those who identify as women, men, or as both or neither of the two. And I am thinking of the struggles that challenge and move beyond anthropocentric frames, of struggles that challenge the dominant spheres of reason and thought, of being, becoming, and of existence itself. I am thinking of struggles that walk asking and that ask as they walk,[8] and of struggles that bring to the fore the forces of the sacred, ancestral, erotic, spiritual, and creative. I am thinking of all those struggles against the modern/colonial matrices of power in their myriad manifestations and faces. And I am thinking of all those struggles—and all those efforts, strategies, processes, and practices—to push, enable, create, and construct a decolonizing otherwise.

It is praxis, as Dussel reminds us,[9] which makes the path. And it is the sowing and growing that give root to praxis; a sowing and growing that herald life in an era of death, and that give cause to decoloniality as a process, practice, project, and praxis of radically "other" thinking, feeling, sensing, being, knowing, doing, and living.

In closing this part I, it seems appropriate to ask what all this means for the readers here. If we can understand decoloniality not as a new paradigm but as a way, an option, a standpoint, and a practice (and praxis) of analyzing but also of being, becoming, sensing, feeling, thinking, and doing, how does decoloniality challenge, interrogate, and/or interpolate you? Such a question I believe, and I am sure Walter would agree, gets at the proposition of this book and our series "On Decoloniality."

## Notes

1   Silvia Rivera Cusicanqui, *Ch'ixinakax utxiwa: Una reflexión sobre prácticas y discursos descolonizadores* (Buenos Aires: Tinta limón, 2010).

2   María Galindo, *Feminismo urgente: ¡A despatriarcar! Mujeres creando* (La Paz: Lavaca, 2014), 23. Also see http://www.mujerescreando.org/.

3   Lugones, "The Coloniality of Gender"; Rita Segato, "Patriarchy from Margin to Center: Discipline, Territoriality, and Cruelty in the Apocalyptic Phase of Capital," *South Atlantic Quarterly* 115, no.3 (2016): 615–24.

4   See, for example, Luis Martínez Andrade, "Entrevista a Ramón Grosfoguel," *Analéctica*, December 2013, accessed July 24 2017, http://www.analectica.org/articulos/mtzandrade-grosfoguel/.

5   SupGaleano, in Comisión Sexta del EZLN, *Pensamiento crítico frente a la hidra capitalista I* (Mexico City: EZLN, 2015), 33.

6   Juan Garcia Salazar and Catherine Walsh, *Pensar sembrando/Sembrar pensando con el Abuelo Zenón* (Quito: Cátedra de Estudios Afro-Andinos, Universidad Andina Simón Bolívar y Ediciones Abya-Yala, 2017).

7   Vilma Almendra, "PalabrAndando: Entre el despojo y la dignidad," in *Pedagogías decoloniales: Prácticas insurgentes de resistir, (re)existir y (re)vivir*, vol. 2, ed. Catherine Walsh, 209–44 (Quito: Ediciones Abya-Yala, 2017).

8   Such is the praxis-based method, epistemology, and pedagogy of the Zapatistas, "el caminar preguntando." See Rafael Sandoval, "La epistemología zapatista y el método del Caminar Preguntando," in *La escuelita Zapatista*, 7–16 (Guadalajara: Grietas Editores, 2014).

9   Enrique Dussel, *16 Tesis de economía política: Interpretación filosófica* (Mexico City: Siglo XXI, 2014), 322.

# The Decolonial Option / *Part Two*

WALTER D. MIGNOLO

# 5 What Does It Mean to Decolonize?

Emancipate yourselves from mental slavery
None but ourselves can free our minds.

**—BOB MARLEY**

In the western culture in which modern science and technology has
arisen, we speak in daily life of reality and of the real as a domain of
entities that exist independently from what we do as observers. Furthermore, we act and speak, both colloquially and technically, as if we
knew we were able to make reference to such independent entities. The
flow of normal daily life and experience, in which things appear to us
as if they were there independently of what we do, seems to confirm
this. Furthermore, the use that we make of the operational coherences
of daily life for successful cognitive predictions of the consequences of
our operations in it with objects also contributes to support this implicit
view. This I want to change by reflecting further on the consequences of
accepting the operational separation of the experience and the explanation of the experience in the explanation of the biology of observing.

**—HUMBERTO MATURANA,** *Reality: The Search for Objectivity
or the Quest for Compelling Arguments*

I start here from where Catherine left off in the previous chapter. I would
argue throughout part II that each of us is responsible for our decolonial
liberation, which Bob Marley clearly expressed in *Redemption Song*. Part II
moves between popular music philosophy, of which Bob Marley is a master, and the irreverent scientific thinking of Humberto Maturana. Parallel
to Maturana's in the hard sciences (nomothetic in the traditional division
between human and natural sciences), I take an undisciplinary stance in the

ideographic field of knowing and understanding (humanities, socials sciences, philosophy, and the arts, the epistemology creates ontology).[1] Hence, decolonial thinking and doing aim to delink from the epistemic assumptions common to all the areas of knowledge established in the Western world since the European Renaissance and through the European Enlightenment. Re-existence follows up on delinking: re-existence means the sustained effort to reorient our human communal praxis of living.

Decoloniality is not an academic discipline, which doesn't mean that it cannot be enacted in the academy. It comes from decolonization, and decolonization was not a known disciplinary trend or a new method. By enacting it in the academy (Cathy and I work in the academy; the book is published by Duke University Press), we attempt to reverse the trend and take decoloniality as a disrupter in the academy. For example, if you apply to get grants or fellowships to engage in decolonial praxis, be sure that you will not get them. And to disguise it with the name of *decolonial studies* will be to keep decoloniality hostage of modern epistemology. Decolonial studies could not be decolonial—it's as simple as that—for what would decolonial studies be and above all in what political, ethical, and epistemic frame would it be enacted? As Catherine highlights in the first chapters (as I understand it), decolonial studies what for?

This chapter is built on the distinction between decolonization during the Cold War and decoloniality after the end of the Cold War. Aníbal Quijano introduced the key and groundbreaking concept of *coloniality* right at the edge: both the end of the Cold War and the beginning of neoliberal global dreams of final victory. The first actualized; the second may not. The question then is to find out the task of decoloniality once it became evident that the state can be neither decolonized nor democratized. The end of the Cold War and the invasion of Iraq, justified by the collapse of the Twin Towers (whoever was the planner and whatever the motivations), closed a five-hundred-year cycle of Western mental and physical hegemony. We are living on the planet in the concerted Western effort (the United States and the European Union) to manage and control the colonial matrix of power (CMP) now that hegemony has disintegrated.

To proceed in this direction, the second part of the volume introduces and updates decolonial thinking as it has unfolded from Aníbal Quijano's concept of *coloniality* and the transformation that it produced to the idea of *modernity*. Coloniality—the darker side of Western modernity—is a decolonial concept and therefore the anchor of decolonial thinking and doing in the praxis of living. It is not intended to be an ethnographic report of who is doing and who has done decolonial work, nor is it meant to be a *modern* theoretical proposal pretending to be universal and to dictate to everyone what decoloniality is or should be. It is an introduction for readers not yet familiar with it, and an update for readers already familiar, to the specific vision and practice within the frame modernity/coloniality/decoloniality.

It is not a postmodern conceptual introduction, in the sense of rejecting macronarratives. On the contrary, it claims the necessity of five hundred years' macronarratives of the colonial matrix of power that modern macronarratives disguised and postmodern philosophy ignored. If you just look into macronarratives in the Americas and the Caribbean, you will notice that Indigenous narratives have two beginnings: the memories of the creation of the world and the creation of the ethnic group that tells the story of the creation of the world (i.e., Popol Vuh, Leyenda de los Soles, narratives of Turtle Islands). The other macronarratives would be the moment of the Spanish invasion, between the end of the fifteenth century and the first half of the sixteenth. The disseminated African diaspora, through the Americas, begins instead with the Middle Passage.

The population of European descent in South America and the Caribbean start also from 1500, but while for some that was a moment of salvation and civilization, for others it was the beginning of the historical crimes justified by the narratives of modernity—salvation, progress, development. This is precisely the trajectory that frames the project modernity/coloniality/decoloniality as pursued here. On the other hand, for the population of British and French descent in the United States and Canada, the story will begin by the seventeenth century, with the arrival of the first pilgrims and the establishment of the first settlements.

It is beyond the scope of this book for me to continue around the planet and point out how different regions of the world tell the story from their own millenarian memories and from the moment of the disruption of their respective local histories by Spanish, Dutch, Portuguese, French, or British invasion, and how each of us has related and experienced the continuation of modernity/coloniality under the leadership of the United States since 1945.

## The Many Faces of Decolonization

The usages of *decolonization* (and its verb, *to decolonize*) have been growing exponentially over the past five years; this is, of course, a very good thing. The volume is an introduction to a particular school of thought on decoloniality, and it exposes the different venues that the project has taken; it is not a comprehensive review of various decolonial trajectories based on particular local histories, memories, body politics, and conceptual frames.[2] The answer to the question "What does it mean to decolonize?" cannot be an abstract universal. It has to be answered by looking at other W questions: Who is doing it, where, why, and how?

The book is also one answer to the question from the shared works of a collective (who); which emerged in South America and expanded to other regions of the world (where); to understand the formation and mutation of the rhetoric of modernity and the logic of coloniality to orient decolonial work (why); by working academically on conceptual analysis and shifting away (delinking) from Western epistemology and engaging in nonacademic work where Western epistemology has trickled down framing subjectivities, education, ways of eating, health, and destroyed conviviality (how). More specifically, I explain how I understand and enact the analytic of coloniality and envision decolonial venues.

Therefore what I intend to do is to explain one particular meaning of (de)coloniality, the meaning it has acquired in the works of the members of a collective identified by three key words: *modernity/coloniality/decoloniality*. When necessary I will refer to other decolonial projects grounded on different assumptions, needs, and experiences. In my own decolonial conception, there is no proprietor or privileged master plan for decoloniality. Ours (Catherine and myself) is certainly not; and we will not take seriously any decolonial project that postulates itself (implicitly or explicitly) to be the guiding light of decoloniality. We, and by *we* I mean here the human species, are all today in the colonial matrix of power. There is no outside of it, and there is no privileged location (ethnic or sexual) from which to confront coloniality. For this reason, border dwelling, thinking, doing is the decolonial direction this introduction is taking.

As I have mentioned already, we are not providing here an ethnographic global report on decoloniality. The book series is open to other decolonial projects to be presented by their own leaders, in their own specific local histories, and specific decolonial projects. It is not the aim of this book to *represent* anything or anybody. *Representing* is a toxic word in the vocabulary of modernity and modern epistemology. Why? Because representation presupposes a constituted world or reality that is somehow represented and then different schools or people in daily life provide different interpretations of something that is objective and real. If the decolonial is argued as an option, it is because life is lived among options, and options are built by people and institutions according to their own assumptions and interests. Interests are not bad in and of themselves: being interested and acting in favor of conviviality, harmony, creativity, and plenitude are some of the ideals and interests that decoloniality promotes; being aware, nonetheless, that this is not the direction that states, corporations, finances are taking and mass media promoting.

Having said that, the three key words (modernity/coloniality/decoloniality), and the "/" that unite and separate them at the same time, are in fact one complex concept, articulated by the movements that embed the concept in people praxis of living. Each key word or concept is divided while at the same time connected to the previous one. Decoloniality is at once one of the three concepts, but it is the concept that made visible coloniality as the darker side of modernity.

The triad is, using Aníbal Quijano's felicitous expression, a heterogeneous historical-structural node.[3] It departs (delinks) from the dyad signifier/signified profusely discussed during the 1960s and 1970s as well as from the dyad sign/reference (in analytic philosophy) and from the dyad word/think critiqued by Michel Foucault. The triad places signification on different grounds: decolonial grounds.

Therefore, decoloniality argued here cannot be understood without understanding modernity/coloniality that engendered it. Without modernity/coloniality, there would be no need for decoloniality, because there would be nothing to decolonize. Theories, like cosmologies, aim the totality, but they are not necessarily totalitarian. That is, there is room for other trajectories of engaging decoloniality. "Nothing to decolonize" means here beyond the conceptual frame modernity/coloniality. Hence, if coloniality is engendered by modernity, there cannot be modernity without coloniality; and there would be no coloniality without modernity. To end coloniality it is necessary to end the fictions of modernity.[4] You cannot dispense with coloniality and maintain the principles, assumptions, and belief laid out in the macronarratives of modernity. Thinking *without* modernity, delinking from its fictions, is one major decolonial challenge.

The idea of modernity (cfr. modernity is neither an entity nor an onto-logical historical period, but a set of self-serving narratives)[5] gained currency in the second half of the twentieth century. It was the abstract companion of two more concrete signifiers: modernization and development. Modernity was built as the imaginary of itself and of a world of which modernization and development were the engines. Modernity came to signify a horizon, the horizon toward which modernization and development were driving us—all of us, that is, on the planet.

The concept of "modernity" in the second half of the twentieth century (and postmodernity at the end of the century) recast a horizon of life and history that was devised long before. In its previous guises, it had other names: renaissance, progress, and the civilizing mission. The catch-22 was to make believe that *modernity* is something beyond the narratives that invented the word and the imaginary the word invokes. Decolonially speaking, it is a fiction, a construction made by actors, institutions, and languages that benefit those who built the imaginary and sustain it, through knowledge and war, military and financial means.

*Development* was another key and new concept in the second half of the twentieth century that replaced the ideas of progress and civilizing mission. Development replaced progress and modernization replaced civilizing mission. Hence the discursive rhetoric of modernity was refreshed with a re-description of an older horizon. This older horizon was the renaissance, its very historical foundation. Although *modernity* was not a common word earlier on, what modernity came to mean in the second half of the twentieth century was already embedded in the preceding centuries. It was embedded in the well-known debate in sixteenth-century France between "les anciens et les modernes."[6] *Modern* in the sixteenth century meant "present time." *The ancients* was a classification invented by those who considered themselves modern.

It was, then, a pejorative term: the ancients were behind, backward, the conservative people who did not see the light of the present. But, importantly, "present time" was understood to be the only present, the present of Europe (it could not have been the present of Japan or Africa or South America, for people there had other exigencies), which was also increasingly assumed to be the center of space. This feeling was consolidated in Hegel's *Lectures on the Philosophy of History*, where he argued for a chronological and ascending un-folding of universal history, one that—at the time of his writing—had arrived in Germany. Germany, for Hegel, was the center of geography/space, and the present of history/time.[7]

The idea of modernity in the twenty-first century prolonged and expanded the initial philosophical impulse and attitude of those who self-identified with *renaissants and moderns* back then. A further dimension of development came into being when *modernity* was absorbed by and subsumed under neoliberal *globalization*. Neoliberalism and the Washington Consensus displaced the compromise of development and modernization and replaced it with development and globalization, which displaced and subsumed the liberal connotation of progress, modernity, civilization, and development.

## On Coloniality, Coloniality of Power, and the Colonial Matrix of Power (CMP)

But let's go slowly and elucidate the conceptual frame before getting to the historical unfolding. *Coloniality* is a decolonial concept. Its main thrust is to illuminate the darker side of modernity. By so doing, coloniality emerges as a constitutive, rather than as a derivative dimension of modernity. Hence, the opening theoretical concept of *modernity/coloniality* became the foundation concept of the collective decolonial work as introduced here in this book.[8] Moreover, coloniality and modernity/coloniality were concepts that came into being in the Third World. Better yet, these concepts arose at the chronological moment of the Soviet Union's collapse and, with it, the ideology that divided the world into First, Second, and Third. Coloniality and modernity/coloniality are therefore signposts in the imaginary mutation of the Third World into the Global South.[9]

Thus, our perspective here is based on the memories and experiences of the Cold War and the Third World, in which the decolonial concepts of modernity and modernity/coloniality are embedded. Ours (Catherine's and mine) are not based on the memories and experiences of minorities in the First World, although our lived experiences in the First World are not only undeniable but also relevant. In the crossed experiences (see Introduction) of Catherine and myself, Gloria Anzaldúa's statement is a marker for our argument: "The U.S-Mexican border *es una herida abierta* where the Third World grates against the first and bleeds. And before a scab forms it hemorrhages again, the lifeblood of two worlds merging to form a third country—a border culture."[10] *Borders* are everywhere and they are not only geographic; they are racial and sexual, epistemic and ontological, religious and aesthetic, linguistic and national. Borders are the interior routes of modernity/coloniality and the consequences of international law and global linear thinking.

If coloniality is a decolonial concept, it must be the outcome of decolonial thinking. The tautology here is meant to emphasize that coloniality (in the specific sense Quijano introduced it) is a transdisciplinary concept: it did not come out of any specific disciplinary or interdisciplinary debates, but from the lived experiences in South America, from the 1960s to the late 1980s. Although leading decolonial thinker Aníbal Quijano was a trained sociologist and committed participant in the debates on dependency theory, Eurocentrism, and modernity that were circulating in South America in the second half of the twentieth century, they were beyond disciplinary concerns: they were not a matter of updating or improving a discipline, but embedded in the praxis of living and of liberation concerns. The social sciences frame is certainly undeniable in Quijano's thinking, but what brought about the concept of *coloniality* was not an intent to improve the social sciences but an intent to reveal a hidden side of history in which the social sciences themselves were and still are implicated.[11]

Coloniality, then, is not a concept that emerged in Europe to account for issues of European concern—its economy, sensibility, and history—but a concept created in the Third World, responding to needs prompted by local histories of coloniality at the very historical moment when the Three World division was collapsing. In Europe the concerns were on modernity, postmodernity, and globalization, not on coloniality, the darker side of modernity, postmodernity, and globalization.

The concept of coloniality opened up two trajectories at once: on the one hand, it brought to light the darker side of modernity and, on the other, it mutated decolonization into decoloniality and decolonial thinking. It means that, paradoxically, decolonization during the Cold War was still articulated in terms and sensibility of modern thinking: it aimed at changing the contents rather than the principles in which modernity/coloniality was established. Decolonization focused on specific colonization; the overall logic of coloniality was not yet available. Coloniality is a consequence of decolonial thinking, and decolonial thinking came into being through the concept of coloniality. For all these reasons coloniality is already a decolonial concept: thinking decolonially made it possible to *see* coloniality and seeing coloniality materialized decolonial thinking. The implications of *seeing* two sides of the story, modernity/coloniality, instead of only one side (modernity) are immense. To reiterate: one of the two sides (coloniality) once uncovered reveals the hidden dimensions of life, engendering people's dissatisfaction and anger, while the other (modernity) is the storytelling of good things to come; of the richest families investing part of their fortune for the good of others, for example.[12]

Out of this second side of the equation, the expression "thinking and doing otherwise" emerges. Why? Because of the need to think from the experiences of what modernity disavowed and by so doing to show that modernity is half of the story constantly hiding and repressing what doesn't fit the imaginary and desires of storytellers that legitimize themselves in the name of science, politics, and economy that provides a warranty for the well-being and interests of storytellers. The radical implication is that coloniality is not reducible to a concept that could be applied or an entity that could be studied in the existing social sciences or humanities to investigate certain historical facts or issues. Coloniality it is not "applicable," but rather, always *already calls for* decolonial thinking and forgoes the disciplinary regulations of social sciences or humanities thinking. The stakes are high. It means to change the terms (assumptions, principles, rules) of the conversation and to dispense with the disciplines, rather than updating the disciplines by "including" coloniality.

The vocabulary of any of the existing disciplines, words that denote the field of investigation or are concepts you use to approach the field, have two semantic dimensions. You will find, first, that most of the words/concepts you are using belong to European modern/imperial and vernacular languages and they have been derived from Greek and Latin. You will find, secondly, that most, if not all, of the words/concepts you use in your discipline and even in everyday conversation were translated and redefined around the sixteenth and seventeenth centuries in Europe.

The fact that none of the existing civilizational languages at the time (Mandarin, Hindi, Urdu, Persian, Arabic, Russian, etc.) are relevant in any of the disciplinary formations confirms that Eurocentered knowledge asserts itself at the same time that it disqualifies the vocabulary (and logic) of other knowing praxis and knowledge and belief systems. The *trivium* and the *quadrivium*, framing Renaissance science and scholarship and, later on, Enlightenment science, philosophy, and social sciences, all founded their conceptual vocabulary on the Greek and Latin languages, worked together to disqualify any and all coexisting frames of knowledge and understanding in non-European and -Western civilizational languages.[13]

I would like to add at this point some further comments requested by one of the outside evaluators: what does Quijano mean by *power* in the expression *coloniality of power*?

Coloniality and coloniality of power are shorthand for "patrón colonial de poder," which I have translated as "colonial matrix of power." *Matrix*, derived from Old French *matrice*, means "uterus." Other derivations followed through the century all related to regeneration of life and to a substance from which something else originates. By the second half of the twentieth century, its meaning had expanded. The one I highlight here in the translation of *patrón* is a set of structural relations and flows constitutive of an entity (conceptual and mechanic, like in the film *The Matrix*.) In the film, machines have created a cyberworld making believe that the fabricated illusion is what human beings believe is their reality. Neo, the main character, realizes what is happening and rebels, attempting to end the computer program producing the illusion of reality and using human bodies' energy and heat to feed the machines that create the fantasies in which human bodies live. The analogy with the colonial matrix of power is almost one to one. The exception is that the creators of the illusion are, in the film, not human beings but machines that humans have created. In the colonial matrix of power, the creators of the illusions (modernity), using human bodies (labor) energies as well as energy from the biosphere (water, land, and oxygen) and the cosmos (sunlight and moonlight) are human beings inside the colonial matrix of power but believing, or making believe, that there is an instance outside the colonial matrix from which it can be observed. That instance was the Christian God and the Secular Human Scientific/Philosophical Observer. Decolonially speaking there is no outside and, therefore, decolonial thinking doesn't pretend to be a modern (or postmodern) version of God or of Scientific/Philosophical Observer.

The *matrix* (colonial) created by a minority of the human species rules the life of the majority of the human species. Power is that instance of the colonial matrix in which all of us, human beings, are being ruled, and the ruling includes of course the creators and gatekeepers of the rule: the ruler is ruled by its own desire and compulsion to rule. Decoloniality is the exercise of power within the colonial matrix to undermine the mechanism that keeps it in place requiring obeisance. Such a mechanism is epistemic and so decolonial liberation implies epistemic disobedience. The awareness of the illusion of modernity/matrix is no longer in the consciousness of one modern hero (Neo) but in the growing planetary political society taking their/our destiny in their/our own hands. Decoloniality can no longer be thought out as enacted by a hero, the privileged figure in the individualistic imaginary of Western modernity. The equivalent of Neo in *The Matrix* (the movie) are the globally dispersed decolonial planetary energies becoming interconnected in our diverse local histories, in the present. Decolonial analytics aims at understanding the formation and transformation of the colonial matrix of power, of "understanding the past to speak the present" as explained in the introduction of *The Darker Side of the Renaissance*.[14] To delink requires to know from what and how to delink. That is the power struggle within the colonial matrix of power.

The future doesn't exist, and neither does the past. We all, on the planet, live in a constant and always fluctuating present carrying the burden of the past and the hopes for the future. The future would be what we human beings are doing in the present all over the planet, not only in the North Atlantic, where universal fictions dwell. Decoloniality is one among other options in the present. Some of the options intent to dominate and regulate, and there are conflicts and differences among different ideas of what rewesternization should and could do and what dewesternization should and have to do to prevent rewesternization from ruling unilaterally. Both options are state led: they both actualize the current dispute for the control and management of the colonial matrix of power. Decoloniality is not, cannot be, state-led projects. They are projects by the people organizing themselves in their local histories and needs to delink from the colonial matrix. Furthermore, there are also different options among liberating forces, and these forces multiply today around the globe, but not all of them are decolonial in the sense I described here. And of course they do not have to be. Decoloniality, as introduced here, let me repeat, is not claiming truth without parentheses. On the contrary, it is revealing that without truth in parentheses there are no solutions to the problems created by modern/colonial truth without parentheses. Decoloniality, as introduced here, is one option among many. Each option (regulatory or liberating) has its own imperatives. Imperatives are not universal. They are relevant to the option in and for which imperatives emerge and are enacted. I will return to these issues in chapters 6 and 7. Let's explore further the distinction between colonialism and coloniality and subsequently decolonization and decoloniality.

### Coloniality Doesn't Equal Colonialism

Coloniality shall not be confused with colonialism. The distinction between the two is fundamental to understanding what we mean, in this volume, by decoloniality within the triad of modernity/coloniality/decoloniality.

Let's start by elucidating the meaning of *colonialism*. Not much information is available on the word *colonialism*. The online etymological dictionary tells us that the word was introduced in 1886 and means "the system of colonial rule."[15] The *Stanford Encyclopedia of Philosophy* is more generous. It frame *colonialism* as follows:

> Colonialism is a practice of domination, which involves the subjugation of one people [by] another. One of the difficulties in defining colonialism is that it is hard to distinguish it from imperialism. Frequently the two concepts are treated as synonyms. Like colonialism, imperialism also involves political and economic control over a dependent territory. The etymology of the two terms, however, provides some clues about how they differ.
>
> The term *colony* comes from the Latin word *colonus*, meaning farmer. This root reminds us that the practice of colonialism usually involved the transfer of population to a new territory, where the arrivals lived as permanent settlers while maintaining political allegiance to their country of origin. Imperialism, on the other hand, comes from the Latin term *imperium*, meaning to command. Thus, the term imperialism draws attention to the way that one country exercises power over another, whether through settlement, sovereignty, or indirect mechanisms of control.[16]

The quoted definition is relevant to my argument for two reasons. First, it is very informative. Second and most important, it shows the difficulty the writer of this note runs into. The writer defines *imperialism* in almost exactly the same terms that the etymological dictionary defines *colonialism*. The problem here is that the entry was written from a historical, disciplinary perspective, with the assumption that each word corresponds to a different phenomenon— even though, as the author concedes, it is sometimes difficult to distinguish one from the other. What if we think otherwise—decolonially—and conceive of colonialism as the complement of imperialism, writing imperialism/ colonialism and asserting that there is no imperialism without colonialism and that colonialism is constitutive of imperialism? Doing so is a small exercise in decolonial thinking, delinking from the assumptions of modern/ Western epistemology; or Eurocentrism if you wish.

## On Modernity and Globalism

Let's then elucidate the term *modernity*. *Modernity* is not a decolonial concept, But *modernity/coloniality* is. Coloniality shows that all the narratives and celebrations of modernity are only half of the story. Modernity is an unfinished project, in Jürgen Habermas's expression. And we see it today in the efforts to conquer the Middle East, to control the enormous natural resources of Russia, and to "contain" China from committing the heresy of "developing" on its own; are all instance of the unfinished project of modernity in its rewesternizing stage.

Since modernity has been conceived in one line of time, universal time and universal history, the concept needed the historical moment before: the premodern and it generated also the critical moment after: the postmodern. Decolonially speaking the nonmodern is a necessary concept to illuminate the coexistence of temporalities and modes of living and thinking that are neither premodern nor postmodern. The nonmodern is a flexible concept—not always mentioned—but presupposed and necessary for the invention, in the present, of underdeveloped, uncivilized people: all that has to catch up to become modern or postmodern. Bringing the nonmodern to the foreground helps to understand the salvific narratives and the rhetoric (persuasion) of modernity, which in turn justifies ruling over the nonmodern and casting it as an encumbrance to the modern (and imperial) projects of paving the way for the unfolding of universal "history" and the unfinished project of modernity. Decolonially, however, the casting of modernity as the unfolding of universal history is staged as if it were an entity or a historical period detached outside and independent of the narrative that legitimizes actions and decision making to maintain the march of history, when decolonially speaking it is an illusion created by the very modern concept of modernity (redundant necessary: modernity is a modern concept). The Aztecs, it is often alluded and condemned, sacrificed human bodies to keep the Sun ongoing. Western modernity sacrifices (and it is accepted) whatever is needed to keep Civilization ongoing. The consequences of the word (and the narratives weaved around it) results in the invention of an ontology of history that extends from the origin of humanity to its modern (and postmodern) times and forms. The *new* recently defined era, the *anthropocene*, is nothing other than a scientific narrative fiction of the unilineal universal "history" of humankind. Hence, derived from the imaginary created around the concept of modernity.

When exactly the word *modernity* was introduced as a descriptor of the spirit of Western civilization is not clear, though the idea and the feeling of it can be traced back to the Renaissance and the sense of *newness*. Its first use is attributed to Charles Baudelaire—specifically, to his 1864 essay "The Painter of Modern Life." Baudelaire obviously writes around his own European experience only. In section IV of the essay, titled "Modernity," Baudelaire tries to capture with his prose the nature of a figure that can no longer be called an *artist*, or a *dandy*, or even a *flâneur*, because his sensibility surpasses these categories. Baudelaire suggests that this more modern man be called a "lover of life" and writes this of him:

> And so, walking or quickening his pace, he goes his way, forever in search; in search of what? We may rest assured that this man, such as I have described him, this solitary mortal endowed with an active imagination, always roaming the great desert of men, has a nobler aim than that of the pure idler, a more general aim, other than the fleeting pleasure of circumstance. *He is looking for that indefinable something we may be allowed to call "modernity", for want of a better term to express the idea in question.* The aim for him is to extract from fashion the poetry that resides in its historical envelope, to distil the eternal from the transitory.[17]

At some point, modernity was imagined in contradistinction with tradition. *Modernity and tradition are two modern concepts,* not two ontologies, one modern and the other premodern. As modernity was construed by means of fictional narratives in which modernity itself is the main character, the word names a historical period and a set of norms that defines socioeconomic organization as well as particular subjects and subjectivities. Fiction becomes reality. In these narratives, tradition is construed as a *period* preceding the advent of modernity. In these narratives, coloniality is always absent and therefore "tradition" materializes the hidden logic of coloniality, which is how the rhetoric of modernity operates.

When these constructions are decolonially analyzed (which is one way of decolonizing knowledge and subjectivities)—that is, seeing modernity through the logic of coloniality—*tradition* appears in all its clarity as a term invented in the process of building the very idea and the imaginary of modernity. On the other hand, when it comes to make-believe that it consists of historical periods and good (modern) ways of life, modernity has always been figured as if it were universal and therefore shall be extended globally: it was assumed that the rest of the planet was going through a similar unfolding of history in the inexorable march toward modernity, and that at some point it would go through the same periodization as Europe. Western Europe and more recently the U.S. were the point of arrival for the rest of the planet. Society would be organized the same way, and subjects and subjectivities would all be European clones. Absurd narratives indeed, but they are still with us. Coloniality is not over; it is all over.[18]

For some, the historical point of origination of modernity is located in the European Enlightenment. For others, its point of origination is located in the European Renaissance. Renaissance is in itself a concept and an idea that underlines a change in time—either that or rebirth and moving forward. Both are subsumed in our argument in the modern/colonial world order and its two key concepts: modernity/coloniality. The trope of moving forward, from the creation to the end of the world, to final judgment and ultimate salvation, was already a Christian teleology. Rebirth, though, was not weaved into Christian cosmology. It was an idea that emerged out of an incipient secular orientation that would mature three centuries later in the European Enlightenment. It was in the secular tendencies of the Renaissance that the idea of *progress* struck. That is, the idea of progress as we understand it today first entered into the Western vocabulary: "[L]ate 14c., 'a going on, action of walking forward,' from Old French *progres* (Modern French *progrès*), from Latin *progressus* 'a going forward,' from past participle of *progredi*. Its early use in English was especially 'a state journey by royalty.' Its figurative sense of 'growth, development and advancement to higher stages' is from circa 1600."[19]

Postmodernity came into the picture as a critique of many assumptions of the modern imaginary, chief among them the need of macronarratives. Postmodern critiques of modernity, however, did not originate in China or Namibia, Uzbekistan or Bolivia. They originated, as should be expected, in the same place the word *modernity* appeared first: France. But postmodernity did not and does not refer only to a critical stance toward North Atlantic modernity. It asserts that all of us, "we," on the planet are also living *in postmodern times*, as typified by Jean-François Lyotard's concept of *postmodernity* and Fredric Jameson's theory of the logic of late capitalism. In other words, the West's particular ontology of history continues to assert its universality. One of the latest consequences is the universality of *posthuman*, which presupposes that all on the planet is posthuman when, in reality, modernity has reduced the majority of the population to quasi-human (see chapter 7).

## On Decoloniality after Decolonization

The argument reached the point of elucidating the meaning of decolonization and decoloniality. The conceptualization and analytic of coloniality—a
decolonial way of thinking and therefore of living, doing, sensing—came
into being as such at the same moment in which decolonization mutated into
decoloniality. Undoing is doing something; delinking presupposes relinking
to something else. Consequently, decoloniality is undoing and redoing; it is
praxis. After undoing comes redoing: re-existence, as Walsh argues in part I,
chapter 1. The goal of decoloniality in my conception is delinking, delinking what for? To engage in epistemic reconstitution (Quijano), in re-existing
(not only resisting, Adolfo Albán Achinte), engaging in forms of life that we
like to preserve rather than be hostage of the modernity's designs and desires,
and of nationalists' selection of the past of the nation; of resurgence in the
needs and conception of First Nations in Canada (Leanne Simpson); and last
but not least—and in a different sphere but similar political orientation of
delinking—cultural dewesternization and political re-emergence, as has been
articulated in Sharjah Biennial (Yuko Hasegawa). I explore this in more detail
in chapter 10.[20]

The goal was no longer to "take hold of the state" but to engage in epistemic and subjective reconstitution (see chapter 6). Although Quijano in his
foundational article still used the word *decolonization*, the argument changed
the meaning that the word had during the Cold War. The Online Etymological Dictionary locates the political meaning of the term in 1853 and explains
that it was previously a medical term. No more is said on the subject, but one
can imagine that it was related to the colon. When you Google "decolonization, definition," you find the following Wikipedia and Britannica.com first:
"Decolonization (US) or decolonisation (UK) is the undoing of colonialism,
where a nation establishes and maintains its domination over dependent territories" (Wikipedia). "Process by which colonies become independent of the
colonizing country. Decolonization was gradual and peaceful for some British
colonies largely settled by expatriates but violent for others, where native rebellions were energized by nationalism" (Britannica.com). In Quijano's argument,
*decolonization* takes a detour and means something related but different:

> The critique of the European paradigm of rationality/modernity is indispensable—
> even more, urgent. But it is doubtful if the criticism consists of a simple ne-
> gation of all its categories; of the dissolution of reality in discourse; of

the pure negation of the idea and the perspective of totality in cognition. It is necessary to *extricate* oneself from the linkages between rationality/ modernity and coloniality . . . epistemological decolonization, as decoloniality, is needed to clear the way for new intercultural communication, for an interchange of experiences and meanings, as the basis of another rationality that may legitimately pretend to some universality. Nothing is less rational, finally, than the pretension that a specific cosmic vision of a particular ethnicity should be taken as universal rationality, even if such an ethnicity is called Western Europe because this actually pretends to impose a provincialism as universalism.[21]

Ethnic groups who built their own imaginary on the idea of Europe, were also Indigenous. However, their own vocabulary tells us the indigenous are people originating in specific countries or regions outside of Europe. But the rhetoric of modernity made us believe that Indigenous were non-Europeans needing European universal religion and secular sciences and philosophy to become civilized and developed; that is, modern. The task of decoloniality after decolonization is redefined and focused on epistemology and knowledge rather than the state; or, in Western political theory that sustains the idea of the state. It still means to undo, but the undoing starts from "epistemological decolonization as decoloniality." And it means to build a praxis of living and communal organization delinking from the modern state and capitalist economy. The Zapatistas are a good example of what I have in mind, though it shall not be taken as a "model" to "apply" globally. The Zapatistas themselves will tell you so. What is to be followed is *what* they did and are doing, not *how* they did it, for the how is specific to local geopolitical and body-political histories.

Decolonization originally meant freeing a colony to allow it to become self-governing or independent; to build the former-colonized own nation-state. The latent question was: Who was/is the agent of decolonization? It was assumed that it was not the colonizers themselves—say, France decolonizing Algeria—that were ending colonialism but the Indigenous or Algerians themselves who were putting an end to French and British imperial/colonial domination. What happened after is the matter of a different argument.

In this sense, decolonization was widespread and connected with liberation struggles in Asia and Africa. *Decolonization and liberation* expressed an experience distinct from that expressed by *emancipation and freedom*, the preferred vocabulary of the eighteenth-century rhetoric of modernity. The former are the expressions for the emerging global political society, the latter the expression of the emerging European ethno-class, the bourgeoisie, in eighteenth-century Europe. The eighteenth century saw the secular emancipation of an emerging bourgeois ethno-class that, by the first half of the twentieth century, became the global/imperial bourgeoisie colonizing half of the planet, "human and natural resources."[22]

After Quijano it is possible to see that the cursory description of decolonization that I quoted above provides an understanding of decolonization as the undoing of colonialism and colonialism described as one nation-state establishing and maintaining its domination over dependent territories. There are many ambiguities in this description; it does not specify what kind of nations, which territories, when and where. However, since the concept of *decolonization* began to be commonly used after 1945, it seems the nations in question were not the Spanish or British monarchies but the secular nation-states that emerged after the Glorious and the French Revolutions. More recently, decolonization has been applied to earlier events called *revolutions* (e.g., the American and Haitian Revolutions) and *independence* struggles (e.g., South and Central American countries' Independence from Spain and Portugal in the nineteenth century)—showing, once more, the constant need for the conceptual elucidation of words, events, and phenomena. Thus conceived, decolonization is redefined from the perspective of decoloniality.

Which leads us to the word *revolution*. The word is used to refer to both the American and the Haitian Revolutions in the European colonies and to the Glorious and French Revolutions in Europe.[23] The revolutions in Europe and the colonies abroad do not have the same lineage. It makes more sense, consequently, to give the name *decolonization* (in the sense the word acquired during the Cold War) to the Haitian and U.S. uprisings and to view them in confrontation with the outcome of European colonialism. Instead, it would not make sense to describe the Glorious and French Revolutions as decolonization events. Thus, revolution is also redefined decolonially.

Homogenizing these first waves of revolution/decolonization and reordering the world order that emerged in 1500, show only half of the story that passes for the totality: the half of the story that self-builds the idea of modernity. By homogenizing them in this way, the differences and entanglements between imperial and colonial historical lineages are confused. Once a distinction is made, the separate lineages of imperialism and colonialism can come to light. And so thus coloniality, the hidden and darker side of modernity: revolutions and independence struggles in the colonies transformed outward coloniality (European direct control over the colonies) into internal colonialism (local elites managing the building of colonial nation-states according to the script of the European idea of modernity).

The word *decolonization* was established, if not necessarily invented, after World War II. Once the word was established it was retrospectively applied to similar phenomena in the past. Cases in point are that the revolutions and independence struggles in the Americas and the Caribbean (or the first wave of *decolonization*) have a different and inverse trajectory to *revolution*. Revolution, in modern vernacular languages, comes from the Latin *revolutio,* to turn around, like the planets orbiting the sun, which was then applied to social history to mean a fundamental change in political-economic organization and and cultural and subjectivity transformations. The first wave of decolonization (originally called revolutions and independences) happened in the Americas (North, South, Central, and Caribbean) and was led by Creole/Mestizo actors of European descent (Thomas Jefferson, Simón Bolívar, José de San Martín, Francisco de Miranda). The exception was the Haitian Revolution, whose actors were of African descent, and some African themselves (not born in Haiti). The uprisings of Túpac Amaru and Túpac Katari in the viccroyalty of Peru were suppressed, but they did not escape the attention of the Haitian revolutionaries. These revolts were no doubt struggles for decolonization in the sense in which the word acquires during the Cold War. However, contrary to the Haitian Revolution, they were stopped before control of the government could be ceased. Both struggles were connected, as evidenced by the fact that the island's name of Saint-Domingue was changed after the Haitian Revolution to the indigenous name of Ayiti. The common ground between the first and second wave of decolonization is the creation of nation-states after independence.[24]

The first wave of decolonization in the Americas responded to the same logic that motivated the second wave in Asia and in Africa: both series of decolonial struggles engendered at different historical moments and, consequently, different rhetoric of modernity and implementation of the logic of coloniality. The first wave corresponded with the imperial changes of hand in Europe: from Spain and Portugal, to Holland, France, England, and Germany. The rhetoric of modernity was based on progress and civilization. The second wave corresponded with the imperial change of hands from France and England to the U.S. The rhetoric of modernity was grounded on development and modernization. In between, the Russian Revolution was neither a revolution based on liberal ideas of the previous ones, nor corresponded with the ideals of decolonization after WWII, rejecting both liberalism and communism.[25] There were obvious differences, though, between the first and second waves of decolonization and the differences correspond with the specific transformations of the colonial matrix of power (CMP). The differences were not just local but global. The first wave responded to and reacted against the Spanish church and monarchy. And in this sense it was parallel to the Glorious Revolution in Britain and the French Revolution—against the church and the monarchy but also against the Spanish church and the monarchy. The first wave of decolonization ran parallel to the imperial ones. Parallel, but dependent! The second wave of decolonization, in Africa and Asia, was a response to the already-existing coloniality enacted by the modern bourgeois and European nation-states (mainly England, France, and Holland), but it was activated by the Indigenous population and not by Creoles and Mestizos of European descent as was the case in the Americas, with the exception of Haiti.

While the first wave was to some extent parallel to the European revolutions (Glorious and French) in their confrontations with the church and monarchy, the second wave was directed against the European imperial and bourgeois nation-states that emerged from the Glorious and French Revolutions. The Glorious and French Revolutions created the conditions for the emergence of European nation-states, at the same time that facilitated the historical foundations of the first modern-colonial nation-states in the Americas and in the long run motivated the second wave of colonization in Asia and Africa. Decolonization, both first wave in the Americas and second waves in Asia and Africa, has left the logic of coloniality intact. The changes were in the content not in the terms of the conversation. Decoloniality emerged from the shortcoming of decolonization.

The historical detour I've just taken was necessary for understanding the mutation from decolonization to decoloniality and the distinction between the de- and the post-. Coloniality of knowledge remained in place in all those cases, although transformed in their content and regulations, by means—in the Americas—of institutions like universities, museums, convents, and monasteries. The institutions that generated and transmitted the wisdom of ancient civilizations (Mayas, Incas, and Aztecs), were destroyed. What remains today is the survival mainly of oral conversations through generations and the recent emergence of Indigenous scholars, intellectuals and activist educated in Western institutions without knowing the knowledge and wisdom of their own languages and communities. In Africa and Asia was a different story. In China and India, in many regions where Islam was instituted, Western institutions had to coexist (then and now) with existing local instituted knowledge, local languages, belief systems and forms of life. Westernization was always half a way, then and now. Dewesternization and decoloniality emerged from the energies, knowledges and beliefs and praxis of living that were never destroyed. Delinking is possible, and border thinking necessary for both dewesternization and decoloniality, in spite of their differences already pointed out. Let me repeat: decoloniality aims are to delink from the colonial matrix of power (CMP, see chapter 6) in order to imagine and engage in becoming decolonial subjects. But delinking is only the first step. What follows is living decolonially: that is, assuming and engaging decolonial options. Dewesternization is an interstate-led project that disputes the control and management of the colonial matrix of power but doesn't question its very foundation.

The point is that decoloniality has changed the terrain from aiming at forming sovereign nation-states (decolonization) out of the ruins of the colonies to aiming at decolonial horizons of liberation (decoloniality) beyond state designs, and corporate and financial desires. The Zapatistas had through the years engaged praxis of living and knowing that did precisely what I am talking about.[26] There is no master plan and no privileged actors for decoloniality. There are, certainly, scales in the intensity of colonial wounds. Decoloniality is a multifaceted global enterprise in the hands of the people who act and organize themselves/ourselves as decolonial thinkers, actors, and doers. If coloniality is all over, decolonial praxis shall be over as well. Consequently, no experience of privilege could be claimed in the complexity of global decoloniality.

By conceiving of coloniality (CMP, see chapter 6) as a complex structure of management and control, one grasps that it is the "underlying structure" of Western civilization and of Eurocentrism and that fully understanding how it works is a necessary condition for delinking from coloniality. Eurocentrism is not a geographical issue, but an epistemic and aesthesic one (e.g., control of knowledge and subjectivities). In order to do so, it is necessary to think and act (doing, praxis) decolonially, both in the analysis of the colonial matrix of power—delinking subjectively and programmatically from it—and by engaging with projects and organizations that run parallel and in the same direction.

Decolonial delinking cannot be done all at once but shall focus on specific domains, levels and flows of the CMP and their relations with the rest. There is no master plan led by a privileged elite, avant-garde intellectuals or ego-identity politics that could do the job. Nor can it be done via state politics and regulation. Instead, it requires a political structure of governance (not the current nation-state) that rules and obeys at the same time (the Zapatistas have been doing it), that supports people's organizations and creativity, that could be thought of as part of a communal decolonial horizon. In the second decade of the twenty-first century, the number of organizations denying the authority of the colonial matrix of power and the empty promises of the rhetoric of modernity is growing around the planet. The horizon of doing needs horizons of thinking, which at the same time requires the actuality of doing.

Indeed, delinking today follows two routes: decoloniality and de-westernization. In both cases, although to different ends, epistemic and emotional (and aesthetic) delinking means conceiving of and creating institutional organizations that are at the service of life and do not—as in the current state of affairs—put people at the service of institutions. The recent conflict between Greece and the European Union is a clear example of what I mean. The officers of the European Union opted to defend and preserve the rules and institutions, and so to sacrifice the well-being of the Greek people. Putting life at the service of institutions is the basic principle of modernity/coloniality, of Eurocentrism, and of the colonial matrix of power. Decolonial being, thinking, and doing begin with such assumptions.

This book series is a publication of a university press written by two scholars, teachers and intellectuals who believe in the importance of praxical, conceptual, and analytic work. We assume the potential as well as the limit of a book series and do not pretend to make it be and do what it cannot.

We are aware that organizations are being reimagined and reinvented in many places and in different ways. Some of them have a decolonial import and dimension, though they might not define themselves as decolonial, and are remodeling knowledge, being, and communal relations in the following spheres of coloniality:

1   Racism and sexism, controlled by patriarchal/masculine (backed by Christian cosmology and white ethnicity) knowing, believing, and sensing;

2   Political and economic imperial designs, also controlled by a patriarchal/masculine conception of the world and society;

3 Knowledge and understanding, controlled by a local imaginary that poses as universal, and that includes sciences, philosophy, ethics, aesthetics, religion, and, of course, economics and politics (e.g., Eurocentrism);

4 Life in all its aspects, from human life to the life of the planet, controlled also by a patriarchal/masculine imaginary entrenched in politics and economy.

The decolonial option offers a particular frame and orientation for research, arguing, doing, and the praxis of living. A caveat is necessary: there is no safe place, even in decolonial praxis. Decoloniality could be invoked for personal gains in any domain of the CMP. Accusations could be used within the sphere of decolonial conversations, to disqualify a decolonial praxis that is not the one I think is the TRUE decolonial praxis because it is how a singular "I" understands it. Decolonial egos shall not yet be ruled out, and personal gains playing victim could be a temptation. This book series intends to contribute to enlarging the debate, learning and doing globally, including the important work carried on by racialized and sexualized "minorities" in the United States. Patriarchy, in the last analysis, is where racism and sexism originate and are maintained. There is a thin line connecting the civil society to the state, the corporations, and financial and religious institutions. Racism and sexism organize in the West in all spheres of life and have managed to impact non-Western societies. Racism as we understand it today is global because it is a fundamental component of the CMP and the CMP has been the tool of westernization since the sixteenth century.

For this reason, delinking today follows two major routes: decoloniality (delinking from state forms of governance) and dewesternization (delinking from westernization and confronting rewesternization by means of strong States). In both cases, although to different ends, epistemic and emotional (and aesthetic) delinking means conceiving of and creating institutional organizations that are at the service of life and do not—as in the current state of affairs—put people at the service of institutions. Putting life at the service of institutions is the basic principle of modernity/coloniality, of Eurocentrism, and of the colonial matrix of power. Decolonial being, thinking, and doing begin from disrupting these assumptions and the naturalization of death.

## On Dewesternization after the Cold War

To understand dewesternization, it is necessary to understand first westernization and its complicity with modernity. By westernization I mean the course of events and ideas that, around 1500, began to change the preceding global order and establish a new one whose cycle closed around 2000.[27] The first moment of westernization evolved around the invention of America; that is, a whole continent was invented symbolically, militarily, economically, politically, racially, sexually, aesthetically, and subjectively. It affected the subjectivity of both Europeans, and former civilizations of Aztecs, Mayas, Incas, Iroquois, Tainos, Arawaks, Mapuches, and so on. With time, its effects were extended to Asia and Africa.

Dewesternization is an outcome of the Bandung Conference of 1955. Although the Bandung Conference was the first international conference of "colored people" as President Sukarno specifies in its inaugural speech, it was a state-led conference. As explained before, decolonization during the Cold War was a state-led project as the newborn states were the outcome of the struggles for independence and liberation. The state politics of decolonization failed, and among the consequences are the failed modern/colonial nation-states created after independence, as seen today in several regions of Asia and Africa. On the other hand, Bandung Legacies succeeded when state formation, like that of Singapore and shortly after China, understood that political liberation depends paradoxically not on rejecting capitalism but on rejecting liberal and neoliberal principles and assumptions of Western capitalism. At that moment, the Bandung Legacies materialized in state politics of dewesternization. The state politics of dewesternization made possible the reorientation and recovery of the Russian Federation after the collapse of the Soviet Union. The formation of BRICS country was also possible because the politics and philosophy of dewesternization was already in place. Dewesternization also allowed Iran to find allies among non-Muslim states. Following this analysis, derived from the history of the CMP, we in the world and in the present are not in a new Cold War. The Cold War was a confrontation between two westernizing ideologies. Dewesternization on the contrary activates non-Western memories, languages, politics, religions, sensibilities and overall praxis of living that refuse to be submitted to neoliberal westernization.

The world became westernized not because people outside the spheres specified above became entirely converted to Christian, liberal, or Marxist values and visions all at once and totally, but because non-European regions, civilizations, and people were increasingly intervened in and interfered by Western civilization ideals, people, and institutions. The responses to westernization have varied throughout the history of the CMP and the narrative of modernity: they range from willing adaptation to silence to rejection to violence, and to a variety of epistemic, economic, political, religious, and aesthetic delinking projects. Those who endorsed and accepted westernization submitted to it and tried to assimilate. Those who did not like it rejected it and tried and are still trying to resist and delink. Although the attempts to protest and delink decolonial delinking can be traced back to the sixteenth century, it was only in the second half of the twentieth century that they became visible and irreversible. One of the venues for dissent and dispute of the control and management of the CMP is, as hinted at above, dewesternization. The other is decoloniality. Dewesternization is part of the analytic of decoloniality, and not decolonial allied. However, there are some issues common to both for, in the last analysis, decoloniality implies dewesternization by other means—not by state politics and capitalist economy.

The book series we are here initiating promotes decoloniality in two complementary venues. One is the *analytic of coloniality*—its history and the current dispute between rewesternization and dewesternization. This particular articulation comes out of the history of the CMP and decolonial analytics (see chapter 6). The dispute in question shall not be seen as an isolated binary opposition but as a particular unfolding of the CMP's complexity (political, economic, racial, epistemic, mediatic, and cultural at large). While westernization and rewesternization are ingrained in the same history and memories of Europe (Greece, Rome, Europe after the Renaissance) and the Anglo-Franco North Atlantic, dewesternization and decoloniality are grounded on *many local and diverse histories* being activated in response to the Western *local history*, in its diversity.[28] China, Russia, the other BRICS states, and Iran all ground their disputes and their refusal to be controlled in their own local histories. As for decoloniality, it presupposes the analytic of coloniality to understand its logic of management behind the rhetoric of modern salvation.

Dewesternization and decoloniality reached the points of no return over the ruins of the Cold War. Both Cold War contenders, liberal and socialists/communists, were caught up in the same Western history, only they bent it for different purposes, denying and erasing it where convenient. That is why the Soviets marginalized Orthodox Christianity and attempted to build a "modern" state, erasing the history of Russia before the revolution. That is also why Mao Zedong marginalized Confucius and all signs of religious revivals. By contrast, contemporary dewesternization is an intramural dispute for the control and management of the CMP—for the money and meaning that the CMP holds. The dispute is played out in the sphere of governance (interstate relations, economic and commercial agreements and organizations) and in the military confrontation that the dispute implies. On a less belligerent level, the dispute is at work in the cultural sphere (arts, museums, biennials).[29]

It is crucial to remember that, while dewesternization maneuvers in the sphere of state-regulated institutions and economic institutions (regulated or not), decoloniality works within the sphere of an *emerging global political society*. Distinct from the *civil society*, which is above all national, the *political society* today is driven by organizations independent of both nation-states and interstate relations.[30] But beyond all of that, decoloniality focuses on *changing the terms of the conversation*. Dewesternization, instead, *disputes the content of the conversation* and leaves the terms intact. That is, it leaves intact the structure of the CMP: for example, the modern state as the form of governance, and economic coloniality (capitalism) as the form of production, exchange, circulation, finances, and markets. Quijano has outlined the task of *epistemological decolonization*. That, precisely, is our starting point, and the irreversible call to *changing the terms of the conversation*.

The next chapter will be devoted to understanding how the CMP was built, transformed, and managed; hence how modernity/coloniality works. Understanding how modernity/coloniality works through the configuration of the CMP is always a decolonial undertaking and therefore of decolonial thinking and doing.

## Notes

Epigraph 1: Bob Marley, "Redemption Song," *Uprising*, Island/Tuff Gong, 1980.
Epigraph 2: Humberto R. Maturana, "Reality: The Search for Objectivity or the Quest for a Compelling Argument," *The Irish Journal of Psychology* 8, no. 1 (1988): 25–82.
1  *Undisciplinarity* was a trademark in the foundation of the project modernity/coloniality/decoloniality expressed in a collective volume coedited by Catherine Walsh,

Santiago Castro-Gómez, and Freya Schiwy, *Indisciplinar las ciencias sociales: Geopolíticas del conocimiento y colonialidad del poder* (Quito: Abya Yala, 2002). My own more recent article "Epistemic Disobedience, Independent Thought and Decolonial Freedom," *Theory, Culture and Society* 26, nos. 7/8 (2009): 1–23, http://waltermignolo.com/wp-content/uploads/2013/03/epistemicdisobedience-2.pdf, has its roots in the meeting that generated the book just quoted.

2    For an overview of this school of thought, see "Modernity and Decolonial-ity," *Oxford Bibliography Online*, 2011, accessed May 27, 2016, http://www.oxfordbibliographies.com/view/document/obo-9780199766581/obo-9780199766581-0017.xml.

3    Quijano's expression was introduced to account for the complexity of dependency during the debates of the 1970s in Latin America. He has recently revisited the concept. Milson Betancourt, "Anibal Quijano: Heterogeneidad histórico estructural. parte I," online video clip, YouTube, October 6, 2013, accessed May 23, 2016, https://www.youtube.com/watch?v=-okq89FNkTI. For more detail, see the collection of his works, Aníbal Quijano, *Antología esencial: De la dependencia histórico-estructural a la colonialidad/descolonialidad del poder*, selection and prologue by Alín Assis Clímaco (Buenos Aires: CLACSO, 2014), http://clepso.flacso.edu.mx/sites/default/files/clepso.2014_eje_8_pacheco.pdf.

4    Michel-Rolph Trouillot, "North Atlantic Universals: Analytical Fictions," *South Atlantic Quarterly* 101, no. 4 (2002): 839–58, accessed December 8, 2016, http://saq.dukejournals.org/content/101/4/839.

5    See Trouillot, "North Atlantic Universals."

6    Marc Fumaroli (preface and essay), *La querelle des anciens et des modernes* (Paris: Gallimard, 2001).

7    See Walter D. Mignolo, "The Enduring Enchantment (Or the Epistemic Privilege of Modernity and Where to Go From Here)," South Atlantic Quarterly 101, no. 4 (September 2002): 928–54.

8    For an overview see "Coloniality and Modernity/Rationality." In *Globalization and the Decolonial Option*, ed. Walter Mignolo and Arturo Escobar, 22–32 (London: Routledge, 2010). See also "Modernity and Decoloniality," *Oxford Bibliography Online*, 2011, accessed May 27, 2016, http://www.oxfordbibliographies.com/view/document/obo-9780199766581/obo-9780199766581-0017.xml.

9    For a critique of the ontology of the Global South unveiling the coloniality of geohistorical partitions, see Walter D. Mignolo, "The North of the South and the West of the East," *Ibraaz: Contemporary Visual Culture in North Africa and the Middle East*, November 2014, accessed May 30, 2016, http://www.ibraaz.org/essays/108.

10   Gloria Anzaldúa, *Borderlands/La Frontera: The New Mestiza* (San Francisco: Aunt Lute, 1987).

11   See Edgardo Lander, "Eurocentrism and Colonialism in Latin America Social Thoughts," *Nepantla: Views from South* 1, no. 3 (2000): 519–32; Aníbal Quijano,

"Coloniality of Power, Eurocentrism, and Latin America," *Nepantla: Views from South* 1, no. 3 (2000): 533–80. For an update of the question, see Walter D. Mignolo, "Spirit Out of Bound Return to the East: The Closing of the Social Sciences and the Opening of Independent Thoughts," *Current Sociology* 62 (July 2014): 584–602.

12  See, for example, "CNN Money," August 23, 2017, http://money.cnn.com/2017/08 /23/investing/the-impact-network-families/index.html.

13  See my *The Darker Side of the Renaissance: Literacy, Territoriality and Colonization* (Ann Arbor: The University of Michigan Press, 1995 [2nd ed. with new Afterword, 2003]).

14  Mignolo, Introduction to *The Darker Side of the Renaissance*.

15  "Colonialism," in *Online Etymology Dictionary*, 2001–2016, accessed May 23, 2016, http://www.etymonline.com/index.php?term=colonialism.

16  "Colonialism," in *Stanford Encyclopedia of Philosophy*, 2006, accessed May 23, 2016, http://plato.stanford.edu/entries/colonialism/.

17  Baudelaire, "The Painter of Modern Life" [1863], repr. in *The Painter of Modern Life and Other Essays* (London: Editorial Phaidon), accessed May 23, 2016, http://www.writing .upenn.edu/library/Baudelaire_Painter-of-Modern-Life_1863.pdf (emphasis mine).

18  Michelle K., "From Singapore, to Cambridge to Duke University," *Social Text Periscope*, 2013, accessed May 23, 2016, https://socialtextjournal.org/periscope _article/decolonial-aesthesis-from-singapore-to-cambridge-to-duke-university/.

19  "Progress," *Online Etymological Dictionary*, accessed July 20, 2017, http://www .etymonline.com/index.php?term=progress. Anthony Giddens provided a self-fashioning narrative (rhetoric) of modernity, hiding in a spectacular way the consequences of coloniality. See his *The Consequences of Modernity* (Stanford, CA: Stanford University Press, 1990).

20  Aníbal Quijano, "Colonialidad y modernidad/racionalidad," [1992] 2007; Adolfo Albán Achinte, "Pedagogías de la re-existencia: Artistas indígenas y afro-colombianos," in *La estética en la encrucijada decolonial*, ed. Zulma Palermo (Buenos Aires: Ediciones del Signo, 2009); Leanne Simpson, *Dancing on Our Turtle's Back: Stories of Nishnaabeg Re-Creation, Resurgence and Re-Emergence* (Winnipeg, Manitoba: Arbeiter Ring Publishing, 2012). On Yuko Hasegawa, see "Going Both Ways: Yuko Hasegawa in Conversation with Walter D. Mignolo and Stephanie Bailey," *Ibraaz: Contemporary Visual Culture in North Africa and the Middle East*, May 8, 2013, http://www.ibraaz.org/interviews/79; see also Walter D. Mignolo on Yuko Hasegawa curating Sharjah Biennial 11, "Re-Emerging, Decentering and Delinking: Shifting the Geographies of Knowing, Sensing and Believing," *Ibraaz*, May 8, 2013, http://www.ibraaz.org/essays/59/.

21  Aníbal Quijano, "Coloniality and Modernity/Rationality." *Cultural Studies* 21, nos. 2/3 (2007): 168–78.

22  The secular emancipation of this European ethno-class (the bourgeoisie) was not only political but also economic, subjective, artistic, religious. It birthed a new subjectivity, which Sylvia Wynter designates "Man2." See Wynter, *On Being Human as Praxis* (Durham, NC: Duke University Press, 2014).

23  See Jean Casimir, "Haïti et ses élites: L'interminable dialogue des sourds," *Worlds and Knowledges Otherwise*, 2008, https://globalstudies.trinity.duke.edu/wp-content/themes/cgsh/materials/WKO/v2d3_Casimir7.pdf.

24  This is not the place to engage with Benedict Anderson's argument in his classic book *Imagined Communities: Reflections on the Origins and Spread of Nationalism* (London: Verso, 1983). A revised edition was printed in 2016. The original argument was contested by a group of Latin American scholars, *Beyond Imagined Communities*, ed. John Chasteen and Sara Castro-Klarén (Baltimore: John Hopkins University Press, 2003).

25  "Neither Capitalism, nor Communism but Decolonization," *Critical Legal Thinking*, March 21, 2012, http://criticallegalthinking.com/2012/03/21/neither-capitalism-nor-communism-but-decolonization-an-interview-with-walter-mignolo/.

26  The Zapatistas have been from their very inception a strong point of reference to understand decoloniality. Whether the Zapatistas understand themselves as decolonial is another matter. See Mignolo, "The Zapatistas' Theoretical Revolution: Its Historical, Ethical and Political Consequences," *Review (Ferdinand Braudel Center)* 25, no. 3 (2002): 245–75. The consistent follow-up, 23 years later, is the Consejo Nacional Indígena and the participation of Luciano Concheiro. "Los pueblos Indígenas de México eligen a su vocera e irrumpen en el scenario politico nacional," *New York Times Es*, May 28, 2017, https://www.nytimes.com/es/2017/05/28/los-pueblos-indigenas-de-mexico-eligen-a-su-vocera-e-irrumpen-en-el-escenario-politico/?mcubz=3.

27  Serge Latouche, *L'Occidentalisation du monde* (Paris: La Découvert, 1989). In 1958 Edmundo O'Gorman, in Mexico, had already advanced what Latouche would argue thirty years later, not knowing O'Gorman's work. See his *La invención de América: El universalismo de la cultura de occidente* (Mexico City: Universidad Autónoma de México, 1958). The first offered a First World perspective, at the end of the Cold War, while the former offered a Third World perspective at the beginning of the Cold War.

28  See Walter D. Mignolo, *Local Histories/Global Designs: Coloniality, Subaltern Knowledges and Border Thinking*, 2nd ed. with a new preface (Princeton, NJ: Princeton University Press, 2012). See also the conversation with Catherine Walsh, "Las geopolíticas del conocimiento y la colonialidad del poder," in *Indisciplinar las ciencias sociales: Geopolíticas del conocimiemto y colonialidad del poder. Perspectivas desde lo andino*, ed. Catherine Walsh, Freya Schiwy, and Santiago Castro-Gómez (Quito: Abya Yala, 2002), http://www.oei.es/salactsi/walsh.htm.

29  See Walter D. Mignolo, "Enacting the Archive, Decentering the Muses," in *Ibraaz: Contemporary Visual Culture in North Africa and the Middle East*, November 2013, accessed May 24, 2016, http://www.ibraaz.org/essays/77, and "Re-Emerging, Decentering and Delinking."

30  On this issue, see part I of this volume, Walsh, "Decoloniality In/As Praxis." See also *Interculturalidad, estado, sociedad: Luchas (de)coloniales de nuestra*

*época* (Quito: Universidad Andina Simón Bolívar and Ediciones Abya-Yala, 2009), http://www.flacsoandes.edu.ec/interculturalidad/wp-content/uploads/2012/01 /Interculturalidad-estado-y-sociedad.pdf. See also Walsh and Mignolo, "Interculturality, State, Society: Catherine Walsh and Walter Mignolo in Conversation," *Reartikulacija,* 2010, accessed May 23, 2016, https://www.academia.edu/12871436 /Interculaturality_State_Society_Catherine_Walsh_and_Walter_Mignolo_in _conversation_Part_I.

# 6    The Conceptual Triad

*Modernity/Coloniality/Decoloniality*

## The Question of Knowledge and Its Institutions

What matters is not economics, or politics, or history, but knowledge. Better yet, what matters is history, politics, economics, race, gender, sexuality, but it is above all the knowledge that is intertwined in all these praxical spheres that entangles us to the point of making us believe that it is not knowledge that matters but really history, economy, politics, etc. Ontology is made of epistemology. That is, ontology is an epistemological concept; it is not inscribed in the entities the grammatical nouns name. If we could say today that beyond Western world-sense that privileges entities and beings (ontology; Martin Heidegger's Being), there are world-senses that privilege relations. A world-sense that privileges relations cannot be understood ontologically because relations are not entities (they are relations among entities). To name ontology a world-sense constituted by relations and not by entities (objects) is a Western misnomer equivalent to Hernán Cortés naming "Mosques" the buildings where the Aztec carry out their rituals.

Western civilization was built on *entities* and *de-notation,* not in *relations* and *fluidity.* The concept of *representation* is subservient to ontology. Decolonially speaking, ontologies are cosmologic/epistemic creations (storytelling about the creation of the world (cosmologies) and principles of knowing within a given cosmology (epistemology): it is through knowledge that entities and relations are conceived, perceived, sensed, and described. In this specific sense there are as many "ontologies" and "relationalogies" as there are cosmologies. Epistemologies are always derived from cosmologies. The Big Bang theory of the creation of the universe, for instance, is within Christian cosmology not within Islamic or Chinese cosmologies. *Epistemology*, the very word and concept, is a fragment of Western cosmology grounded on *objects* in the world and on *ideas* of their transcendence, like in Plato's philosophy or in one single *God*, which was the Christian translation of the idea of the *idea*. Thus, economy and politics are not transcendent entities but constituted through and by knowledge and human relations. It is knowledge weaved around concepts such as politics and economy that is crucial for decolonial thinking, and not politics and economy as transcendental entities.

It follows then that decolonizing knowledge and being (entity) to liberate knowing and becoming what coloniality of knowledge and being prevents to know and become, is at this point the fundamental task of *decoloniality*, while "taking hold" of the state was the fundamental task of *decolonization*. What has to be done is very clear, albeit the means of doing it and what to do after doing it are another matter. But now the questions are: If the fundamental task of decoloniality is to decolonize knowledge and being, how do you do it? You cannot "take" knowledge as the state was "taken" by armies of national liberation during the Cold War. You cannot decolonize knowledge if your do not question the very foundation of Western epistemology. And you cannot decolonize being if you do not question the very foundation of Western ontology. How do you decolonize Western political economy if you do not question and change the epistemic assumptions from which the edifice of political economy has been built since Adam Smith? Etc., etc.

I do not see another praxis than changing the terms (assumptions, regulations) of epistemic, ontological, and economic conversations. How do you decolonize the state and political theory if you do not open up your thinking to forms of governance beyond the nation-state? if you do not question the principles upon which Western political theory built its edifice and maintained it? In other words, the goal of decolonization of "taking hold" of the state did not prove to be sufficient, neither in the Soviet Union nor through decolonization in Asia and Africa during the Cold War. In all these cases decoloniality of knowledge, of knowing and understanding, was not yet seen and therefore decolonization failed.

Let's ask know, what is the *praxis* that leads to decolonizing knowledge and being? I do not see another way of responding to this question than by saying that the praxis has to be theoretical. Furthermore, in order to proceed in that direction, it is necessary to understand what coloniality of knowledge means, for you can hardly decolonize something about which you do not know how it works. The goal of this chapter is to lay down the bases for understanding *coloniality of knowledge and of being* (I return to this in chapter 7) and, therefore, for the doings (praxis) of knowing and understanding.

For what are economy, politics, and history if not the enactments of certain types and spheres of knowledge that frame the praxis of living in which economy is embedded and that is not limited by the technicalities of political economy? Economy, politics, and history (and we could add more to this list) become such only once a discourse that conceives of certain forms of doing and living (manufacturing, cultivating, producing, exchanging, organizing life among people, and telling stories about the creation of the world and the origination of the people, who in turn tell their own stories) gives meaning to a mix of interrelated activities within the praxis of living in conversation around taken-for-granted entities (economy, politics, art, religion, etc). Thus, it is through conversations (discourses and narratives, oral or written) that the amorphous activities of a people are distinguished, narrated, theorized, critiqued, and transformed into economics, politics, history, and so on.

All known organizations of people—civilizations, kingdoms, or cultures—create and transfer knowledge and understanding of their own praxis of living to the next generation. The more sophisticated the self-organization of a people is, the more institutions are needed to nurture and educate the younger generation in all the areas that an organization of the people (communal, societal) needs for its survival. In this process, institutions in one civilization could become the tool to manage and control knowing and understanding in other civilizations, which began to happened around 1500. The Aztecs, for example, had two central institutions: the Calmecac and the Telpochcalli. The first was for educating the children of the nobility (*pipiltzin*), while the second was for the education of people (*macehualtin*). In the Andes, the territory of the Incas, Yachaywasi (house [*wasi*] of wisdom [*yachay*]) was a center similar to the Calmecac. *Madrasa*, in the Islamic world, past and present, is a basic educational institution.[1] Not to mention education in the multimillennium histories of China and India. Western expansion was not only economic and political but fundamentally epistemic.

If we go to the kingdom of Aksum in Northern Ethiopia or the kingdom of Great Zimbabwe (two of the five or seven great kingdoms in Africa, beyond Egypt), we find that the achievement of these sophisticated organizations cannot be understood without an understanding of their own ways of knowing and education embedded in their praxis of living. Even ancient Greece had its own concept of education (*paideia*), and a specific institution where education took place (*gymnasium*). Medieval Christendom created its own institution, the *university*, which was transformed but maintained during the Renaissance. With the colonization of the New World, the *university* was transplanted (as today U.S. universities are transplanted) in what is today the Dominican Republic, the Viceroyalty of New Spain, the Viceroyalty of Peru, and the Viceroyalty of Río de la Plata (National University of Córdoba in Argentina). Harvard was the first such transplant in British America, in 1636.[2] Modernity/coloniaility means, in the sphere of knowledge, that Western institutions and philosophy encroached consistently over the wide and non-Western cultures and civilizations since 1500 whose praxis of living, knowing, and doing were mostly unrelated to Western civilization. And when they were—like Islam—Latin and Christian theology managed through time to impose their disavowal over Arab and Persian Islamic theology.

## The Conceptual Triad and the Darker Side of History

Violence is not a privilege of revolutions; it spreads all over to counterrevolutions. Violence is also enacted to prevent revolutions. When Marx chastised philosophers and told them that it is not enough to interpret the world, but it is necessary to transform it, it was a good advice. The problem was that subsequent generations reading Marx did not pay attention to the fact that this was precisely what Christianity and then secular liberalism were doing: they theorize the world in the process of changing it. Praxis is not a privilege of the Left. It is what the Right does too. Political and ideological positions identified since the French Revolution as Left and Right are second-order constructions based on experiences of people's self-organization and their preferences for transformation or preservation of their praxis of living.

Revolution needs vision. The implementation of vision when successful at some point would engender violence because it would introduce a disruption and a crack into the calm waters of "reality": that is, the commonsense created through coloniality of knowledge and of being (e.g., the world populated by object, laws, and living organisms). Nevertheless, before and after violence, there is much that can be accomplished if the vision is pursued with determination, open-mindedness, and resolution, as Frantz Fanon tells us in the conclusion of *The Wretched of the Earth* ([1961] 1968). *Vision* in this case is tantamount to theory, and theory is a fundamental component of revolutionary praxis. There cannot be revolutionary praxis without theory. Praxis without theory is blind; theory without praxis is sequestered. Both join forces in that long-lasting horizon we can call *vision* and, in this case, decolonial visions.

With this provisos in mind, what is the place of decoloniality in a world order at the limit of nuclear catastrophe? To oppose and confront the modern/colonial world order of today,, it is not necessary to be decolonial, Marxist, or an adherent to the theology of liberation. It requires an ethical commitment of the people who are not controlling and managing but are being managed and controlled. The rhetoric of modernity that aims to persuade you through promises of progress, growth, development, and newness of objects, composed of three interrelated domains: first, *a field of representation*, which grounds its power in the very idea that signs represent something existing, and, second, a *set of rhetorical discourses* aimed at persuading you that the world is as the field of representation tells you it is. The belief that signs represent something existing is based on the presupposition of universal naming. He who has the privilege of naming and implanting His naming is able to manage knowledge, understanding, and subjectivity. Accordingly, and in third place, the system of representation and the rhetoric conveying the promises of modernity support a *set of global designs* whose implementation would secure well-being and happiness for everyone on earth. If you were to translate these words into a diagram, the three domains would fall under the heading of Modernity. The three domains constitute what we might call, following Siba Grovogui, the *Instituted*.[3]

Let's approach the conceptual triad closely. Imagine yourself in front of a blackboard. You write the triad modernity/coloniality/decoloniality. The slash (/) between modernity and coloniality and between coloniality and decoloniality means that the three terms are simultaneously, since the sixteenth century, divided and united. They are indeed entangled: modernity/coloniality/decoloniality. The divisions and connections are constantly crossed by flows and energies that do not allow any one of these terms to be isolated and immutable (as the following section will explain in more detail). If there is no modernity without coloniality, if coloniality is constitutive of modernity, if the "/" at once divides and connects, then decoloniality proposes the undoing of modernity. That is, decoloniality implies demodernity.[4] At the same time, modernity/coloniality engender decoloniality. So there would be no decoloniality—and decoloniality would not be necessary—if modernity/coloniality had not created the need to delink from the rhetoric of modernity and the logic of coloniality.

Modernity names a set of diverse but coherent narratives, since they belong to the same cosmology. That cosmology is the Western Christian version of humanity, complemented by secular de-Goding narratives of science, economic progress, political democracy, and lately globalization: Reason displaced God.[5] That narrative originated during the European Renaissance, and manifested itself in two complementary trajectories. One trajectory narrated the re-naissance of Europe, the *colonization of time*, and the invention of Antiquity and the Middle Ages as the two previous periods upon which the rebirth was founded. This trajectory materialized the explicit celebration of the inward history of Europe.

The other trajectory was the invention of the New World and the *colonization of space*. In the first trajectory, the narratives of modernity are regenerated in a nonlinear appropriation of time that today is manifested by the prefix *post-*. Colonization of space and time were not military, financial, or state-politics activities: they were conceptual, that is, epistemic. Immanuel Kant couldn't have theorized space and time as he did without the colonization of time and space during the Renaissance.[6] In the second trajectory, the narratives of modernity are constantly regenerated through the celebrated idea of *newness* (and the keywords associated with it: *revolution, innovation*). *Newness* and *post-* are the two pillars with which the mythology of modernity captures the feelings and the imaginary of the population. I call this the *rhetoric of modernity*—rhetoric in the sense of discourse aimed at persuading an audience, as we all learned from Aristotle and Cicero. The rhetoric of modernity invented and regenerated the Instituted, the world as it presumably is.

Coloniality names the (un)intended consequences of the narratives of modernity—Anthony Giddens's missing chapters. It is the darker and hidden side of modernity. Coloniality names the *destitute* and the logic and processes of destitution. It is the task of decoloniality to unveil this logic and these processes. Coloniality is to decoloniality what the unconscious is to psychoanalysis, what surplus value is to Marxist political economy, and what biopolitics is to Foucauldian archaeology. The difference between coloniality and surplus value or biopolitics is that the latter concepts belong to the inward trajectory of European history and culture and originated in Europe. Coloniality, by contrast, originated in the Third World and belongs to the outward history of Europe. Coloniality is sensed in the trajectories of colonial histories, is inscribed in our bodies and sensibilities.

Coloniality is shorthand for *coloniality of power*. The expression suggests that what is imprinted in colonial cultures is the effect of the *imperiality of power*. And the imperiality of power in the modern/colonial world (i.e., not in the Roman Empire or in the Islamic Caliphate) is written not by guns and armies but by the words that justify the use of guns and armies, convincing you that it is for the good, the salvation, and the happiness of humanity. Such is the task of the rhetoric of modernity. What is at stake in the final analysis is the power of imperiality/coloniality—that is, the logic that underlines the differences, manifestations, and enactments of modern imperial/colonial formations (Spanish, Portuguese, Dutch, French, British, German, United States) and all its dimensions: knowledge (epistemic), economic, political (military), aesthetic, ethical, subjective (race, sex), spiritual (religious).

There is an implied complexity in the expression modernity/coloniality. On the one hand, this is because it could be written imperiality/coloniality, assuming that modernity is the discourse of Western imperialisms since the sixteenth century. On the other hand, if modernity is a narrative (or, better still, a set of narratives), coloniality is what the narratives hide or disguise, because it cannot be said explicitly. To say it explicitly would be to run against the very promises of modernity. It cannot be said explicitly that slavery is the exploitation of human beings for the benefit of other human beings. It cannot be said explicitly that the war in the Middle East or West Asia is for the control of territory and natural resources and not for the liberation or well-being of people. Slavery was justified via narratives that figured Africans as less than human so they could be treated like animals.

The invasion of Iraq could not have been explained as the need to depose the Iraqi leader, Saddam Hussein, for not following the dictates of the United States (coloniality); therefore it was explained instead as due to Hussain being an undemocratic leader "in possession" of weapons of mass destruction. Once weapons were fabricated to implement wars; the neoliberal inversion of the rhetoric of modernity consists in fabricating wars to implement and sell weapons. This inversion affects the entire sphere of life, from food to medicine (pharmacy and medical instruments). It was instigated by a minority at that time; now it is widespread. It was a global lie that shows the consequences of coloniality disguised by narratives of modernity. But it was done, and more of the same are in the horizon in May 2017 when I am finishing this manuscript. Coloniality names a complex structure of management and control that is explained in what follows.

## The Colonial Matrix of Power: Domains, Levels, and Flows

Quijano's groundbreaking concept of *coloniality* is shorthand for *coloniality of power*, and both are stand-ins for the *colonial matrix of power*, or the CMP. The use of one term or the other depends on how much detail we want to invoke with the expression.

The colonial matrix of power (the CMP) is a complex structure of management and control composed of domains, levels, and flows. Like *the unconscious* in Sigmund Freud or *surplus value* in Karl Marx, the CMP is a theoretical concept that helps to make visible what is invisible to the naked (or rather the nontheoretical) eye. Unlike Freud's unconscious or Marx's surplus value, though, the CMP is a concept created in the Third World—in the South American Andes, specifically.[7] It is not a concept created in Europe or in the U.S. academy. The concept was born out of theoretical-political struggles in South America, at the intersection between the academic and the public spheres. Driven by local criticism of development, the CMP bears the impulse of liberation theology and emerged out of the limits of dependency theory in the 1970s. These, of course, were also the years of the struggle for decolonization in Asia and Africa.

By highlighting *global coloniality*, I am underscoring that *global modernity* is only half of the story—the visible half of the whole. The other half (hidden) is global coloniality. Hence, again: modernity/coloniality. Surrounding the idea of modernity (in the period 1500 to 2000) is a discourse that promises happiness and salvation through conversion, progress, civilization, modernization, development, and market democracy. This discourse is tied up with the logic of coloniality, which circumscribes the progression of modernity within all the domains used to categorize and classify the modern world: political, economic, religious, epistemic, aesthetic, ethnic/racial, sexual/gender subjective.

Part of the significance of the CMP as a theoretical construct lies in its uncovering of the domains that the discourse of modernity produces in order to advance its overall project, hiding, destroying, demonizing, and disavowing whatever gets in its way. The advance of civilization is the justification of freedom and well-being for all the manifested goals. The rhetoric of modernity, for example, locates the historical foundation of political theory in ancient Greece, though this foundation was revamped from Machiavelli onward. On the other hand, there is no discourse on economy for the imaginary of modernity to find in Greece. Instead, this discourse emerged at the confluence of European local histories and its American colonies. This much is clear in the long section that Adam Smith devoted to colonialism in *The Wealth of Nations* (1776). Thus, decolonial tasks consist of undraping the positivity of political theory and political economy, and showing that the positivity of both is mounted on the negative consequences of their implementation.

But the question then becomes: What holds all the domains of the CMP together? To answer this question, we need to introduce the levels of the CMP. Within each domain are different levels of management and control. The rhetoric of modernity is heavily utilized within these levels, in order to convince the population that such-and-such a decision or public policy is for the betterment (i.e., the happiness and salvation) of everyone. While theological principles and philosophical-scientific truths have historically sustained the domains of the CMP, the mainstream media today plays an equally crucial role in disseminating the rhetoric of modernity and salvation in the face of ever-changing "enemies."

The actors and institutions that create, pronounce, and transform the designs that drive the idea of modernity are the same actors and institutions that (intentionally or not) keep all the domains interrelated and also keep these interrelations invisible. It is within this context that we must understand the creation of the figure of the "expert," who appears often in the mainstream media to explain this or that aspect of a news story and who knows a great deal about one domain but is ignorant of the others and of how all the domains are connected.

Outside the domains and their levels of management and control is a broader level where the domains themselves are defined, their interrelations legislated and authorized. We might call the domains themselves the *content* of the conversation, or that which is *enunciated*. Conversely, the broader level, where the domains are defined and interrelated, relates to the *terms* of the conversation, or "enunciation" proper. It is here that the patriarchy is located.

This broader level is also the level of *knowledge* in the deep sense of the word. It is composed of actors, languages, and institutions. The institutions involved are mainly colleges, universities, museums, research centers (think tanks), institutes, foundations, and religious organizations. At the same time, the enormous visibility of generous donors hides the detail that generosity is a fact of life for billions of people in the world, practiced on a much larger scale than elite/institutionalized philanthropy and its actors.

The actors involved in the CMP's domains are trained and experienced politicians, CEOS of banks and corporations, university presidents, museums directors, and so on. The actors that rule these institutions do not have a homogeneous view of the world and society, as we see today in the United States, in the positions of Democrats and Republics, or in Europe, where Poland

and Hungary are seeing Europe through their own right-wing eyes. What is common, across these differences, is the content of the conversation between the so-called Right (in different degrees) and the so-called Left (in different shades).

As for the languages in which the content of the conversation has been established and maintained, these have been and still are the six modern European imperial languages: Italian, Spanish, and Portuguese during the Renaissance; German, English, and French since the Enlightenment. For Russia and China to enter the conversation, the conversation has to be in English, French, or German. The reverse does not hold: leaders of the core European Union (of which Poland and Hungary are not part) can maintain their French, English, or German without needing to learn Russian or Chinese.

We might call the domains themselves the *content* of the conversation, or that which is *enunciated*. The domains are defined and interrelated with the *terms* of the conversation, or enunciation proper. It is at the level of the enunciation that the rhetoric of modernity is enunciated, transformed, legislated, and authorized. Consequently, decoloniality shall focus on changing the terms of the conversation that would change the content. The reverse does not obtain: changing the content of the conversations doesn't call the enunciation (the terms) into question.

For this reason, the essential feature to take notice of within the CMP's domains is the domain of knowledge. Knowledge has a privileged position: it occupies the level of the enunciated, where the content of the conversation is established, and it occupies the level of enunciation, which regulates the terms of the conversation. A pedagogical metaphor would help clarify the point I am making here. Think of a puppeteer: you do not see the puppeteer (the enunciator); you only see the puppets (the enunciated). You are drawn by the puppets, by their movements and dialogues. What you see and hear is the content of the conversation. In order to "see" the terms of the conversation, you would have to disengage from the illusion and focus on the puppeteer behind the scenes, who is regulating the terms of the conversation.

*Knowledge* in the CMP occupies two positions: knowledge is one of the puppets (one domain, and the domains are the content of the conversation, the enunciated), and knowledge also refers to the designs (the enunciation) that the puppeteer creates to enchant the audience. Coloniality of knowledge is enacted in that zone in which what you see and hear from the puppets that enchant you distracts you from the tricks and designs of the enunciator. Decoloniality of knowledge demands changing the *terms* of the conversations and making visible the tricks and the designs of the puppeteer: it aims at altering the principles and assumptions of knowledge creation, transformation, and dissemination. Dewesternization, by contrast, disputes the *content* of the conversation. It aims to change the puppets and the content of their conversation, not the terms. It disputes the place of the puppeteer not to replace it but to coexist next to the existing puppeteer.

The apparent paradox is that the domains of the CMP seem to be isolated and independent of one another, and knowledge seems to be separated from politics and economy, for example, while decolonially speaking there cannot be economy and politics without knowledge. The privileged position of knowledge being at the same time content and terms of the conversation explains the needs of *experts* within a given domain. These experts are unknowing not simply about other domains but about the logic (the terms of the conversation) that keeps all the domains interlinked. Experts in one domain are literally ignorant of other domains and, above all, about the interconnections between the domains and between domains and levels. The decolonial analytic of CMP aims precisely to reveal these interconnections that the rhetoric of modernity constantly hides.

Consequently, the CMP is held together by flows that emanate from the enunciation (from the terms of the conversation, the rhetoric of modernity). These flows interconnect all the domains and connect the domains with the actors and institutions, in the major languages of the European idea of modernity. Inevitably, the question of subjectivity and subject formation emerges: the CMP is involved in the creation of particular persons/subjects and institutions, but the CMP also takes on a life of its own, shaping and contorting the subjectivity (the reasoning and emotioning) of the person managing it. Because of coloniality, control of the terms of enunciation (i.e., control of knowledge) is necessary for controlling the domains, and controlling the domains means managing the people whose lives are shaped by the domains.


## Decoloniality, Delinking, and Border Thinking

There is no necessity for decoloniality without modernity/coloniality. Modernity/coloniality engendered decoloniality. As far as the promises of modernity legitimize coloniality, that is, oppression, exploitation, and dispossession, decoloniality is the response of and from people who do not want to be oppressed, exploited, and dispossessed. Decoloniality emerges out of the need to delink from the narratives and promises of modernity—not to resist, but to re-exist. In this sense, decoloniality is both an analytic of modernity/coloniality (its constitution, transformation) and a set of creative processes leading to decolonial narratives legitimizing decolonial ways of doing and living.

Seen as a complex structure of domains and levels, the CMP is spatial. However, Quijano has added the energies that keep the CMP in constant movement: domination/exploitation/conflict. And also temporality: formed in the sixteenth century the CMP is well and alive today. If the rhetoric of modernity (domination) legitimizes coloniality (exploitation), the latter engenders conflict and conflict generates responses. However, Quijano has added the energies that keep the CMP in constant movement: domination/exploitation/conflict. If the rhetoric of modernity (domination) legitimizes coloniality (exploitation), the latter engenders conflict and conflict generates responses. Dewesternization and decoloniality are two types of responses whose enactment and contours are shaped by local histories. The movements and mobility of the CMP through domination/exploitation/conflict put us in front of "history" being moved by the energy of this trialectic rather than by modern and postmodern dialectic. The movement of the conceptual triad is then trialectic rather than dialectic, and this conceptualization is always already decolonial, delinking from the good, the bad, and the ugly of modernity and postmodernity. Dewesternization like decoloniality, is one manifestation of the trialectic. However, as explained above, dewesternization disputes the control and magement of the CMP but doesn't question its very existence.

Decoloniality is first and foremost liberation of knowledge (for what I said above on the double location of knowledge, in the enunciation and the enunciated), of understanding and affirming subjectivities that have been devalued by narratives of modernity that are constitutive of the CMP. Its main goal is the transformation of colonial subjects and subjectivities into decolonial subjects and subjectivities. The expectation is not to convert the actors running the IMF, the World Bank, and the United Nations, nor expect them to run those institutions decolonially, which would in turn push every single state existing on the planet today to govern decolonially; nor is the expectation that the presidents and CEOs of all the global banks and corporations will run their finances and corporate designs decolonially.

The aim is to create rather than to be dependent on the creativity of the actors and institutions that produce and maintain the narratives of modernity. Re-existing means using the imaginary of modernity rather than being used by it. Being used by modernity means that coloniality operates upon you, controls you, forms your emotions, your subjectivity, your desires. Delinking entails a shift toward using instead of being used. It proposes to delink from the decolonial entanglement with modernity/coloniality.

The decolonial—in contradistinction to Christianity, liberalism, Marxism, and neoliberalism—is not another option for *global design* led by States, economic, financial, technological, and military institutions, but it is an option to delink from all global designs promoting local resurgences and re-emergences confronting and rejecting, unmasking their fundamentalism and pretense of "chosen" people to arrogate themselves the right to run the world. Decoloniality names the vision and energy of delinking (disconnect) to re-link (re-connect) with praxis of living, thinking, doing that we, decolonially speaking, want to preserve. Thus, re-existence, reemergence and reconstitution, resurgence are already populating the vocabulary of numerous and diverse decolonial projects. Decoloniality as conceived here therefore consists of two movements: one, its affirmation as an option among options (diverse and heterogeneous but grounded as any co-existing options, from Christianity, to neoliberalism to Marxism, Islamism); and two, the conception and enactment of the decolonial option, as an option among options in conflict or collabora-tion. The argument for decoloniality must at the same time work to wrestle decoloniality from the temptations of totalitarian totality. Decoloniality pro-motes pluriversality as a universal option—which means that what "should be" universal is in fact pluriversal, and not a single totality.

If we were to understand the configuration of the ancient Chinese or Aztec civilizations, as they mapped themselves and as they mapped the rest of the world in their own imaginary, we might not (or rather, we wouldn't) end up identifying the same domains specified here, or the same levels, or the same flows between domains and between levels. Today, however, we tend to look at ancient China and ancient Mesoamerica and ask questions about their knowledge, their being, their politics and their economy, their art and their re-ligion, and their perception of ethnic groups and sexual distinction based on our *own* categories of knowledge and being, because asking such questions and providing such answers is a consequence of being embedded and living in a Western imaginary enveloped in the process of becoming itself.

The narratives sustaining the imaginary of modernity make us believe that ontology is *represented* by epistemology:[8] we know what simply *is and exists*. Decolonially speaking, it is the other way around: it is epistemology that institutes ontology, that prescribes the ontology of the world. To say that non-Western civilizations have different ontologies means to project Western categories to non-Western thinking. Most of culture and civilizations on the planet *see relations while in the West we are taught to see entities, things. Relations* could not be called ontological. If the vocabulary wants to be preserved then one needs to talk about *relationalogy* (discourses on/about relationality of the living universe). What *there is* depends on how we have been programmed to name what we know. Hence, the coloniality of knowledge implies the coloniality of being; they move in two simultaneous directions. The coloniality of being is instituted by racism and sexism. However, if ontology is instituted by an epistemology that devalues certain human beings in terms of race and sexuality, there must be some force that sanctions the devaluation, since the devaluation is not itself ontological. The sanctioning comes from human beings who place themselves above those human beings who are devalued and dehumanized.

Coloniality of being therefore entangles both the enunciator and the enunciated.[9] Decoloniality of knowledge and of being, therefore, aims at the liberation of both, for if there is no enunciation instituting racial and sexual hierarchies (racism and sexism), then there is no racism and sexism. The battlefield for overcoming racism and sexism is, then, at the level of the enunciation, diverting the flows that hold together and sustain the four domains of the enunciated. Liberation is through thinking and being otherwise. Liberation is not something to be attained; it is a process of letting something go, namely, the flows of energy that keep you attached to the colonial matrix of power, whether you are in the camp of those who sanction or the camp of those sanctioned.

One outside evaluator of this manuscript wondered at this point, based on note 9, why María Lugones and Nelson Maldonado-Torres are mentioned, and not, for example, Enrique Dussel and Santiago Castro-Gómez. The reader thought it of interest to explain or account for different positionalities within the project. I have done this already in another publication.[10] The same reader also conjectured noting that Lugones, Maldonado-Torres, and Anzaldúa were rather Latinx than Latin American. This introduction is about concepts and arguments, not about people.

We could have added to the reader's list of Native American decolonial thinkers Canadian peoples and said more about Mayan, Aymaras, Quechuas, Quichuas, Mapuches, and so forth. We could have also extended our analysis to Australia and New Zealand, which I bring to the conversation in the conclusion. But, as we (Catherine and I) say in the introduction, we have not written an ethnography of who does decoloniality where and how, but a conceptual and political introduction derived from Quijano's concept of *coloniality*. Consequently it is not about "Latin American (de)coloniality" or "(decoloniality) in Latin America." It is just about—if aboutness is necessary to be explicit—modernity/coloniality/decoloniality in the praxis of living of the two of us who wrote the book: Catherine born and educated with English being her language of upbringing, Spanish a learned language; and Walter, who is the reverse, born and educated in Spanish, English being a learned language.

At this point I have arrived at a key juncture of the argument for understanding the relevance of the two levels (the level of the enunciated and the level of the enunciation) and the flows, on the one hand, between the domains and, on the other hand, between levels and domains: while the level of the instituted (the domains) consists of conceptual abstractions that posit an ontology in which there is no emotion, the level of the enunciation is where emotioning and reasoning take place and flow to the domains of the enunciated/instituted. The domains do not have their own emotions. Emotions lie within the actors of the enunciation who shape the enunciated: its domination, exploitation, conflicts. And it is the enunciation of these actors that makes the conflict appear. Conflict is not a given: for it to be visible, someone has to *speak* (with words or deeds) to mobilize the enunciation, be it by submitting, adapting, or confronting. Decoloniality is one type of confrontation, or *speaking to*, that delinks from the dictates of imperial enunciations.

Uncovering the level of the enunciation within the colonial matrix of power is always already a decolonial task and a contribution to the decoloniality of knowledge and of being. The analytic of the enunciation is not in itself a decolonial concept; it was first brought to light by French linguist Émile Benveniste.[11] But disclosing the level of the enunciation within the colonial matrix, hidden from the imaginary of modernity, is indeed a decolonial move.[12] The semiotic apparatus of enunciation (of any enunciation) has three components: actors, languages, and institutions. The question is, at what point has enunciation become the engine of modernity/coloniality? Or, better still, to what extent is modernity/coloniality the consequence of the formal apparatus of the enunciation becoming modern/colonial?[13]

It is not enough to change the content of the conversation (the domains, the enunciated); on the contrary, it is of the essence to change the *terms* (regulations, assumptions, principles managed at the level of the enunciation) of the conversation. Changing the terms of the conversation implies overcoming both disciplinary and interdisciplinary (which depends on maintaining the disciplines) regulations and conflicts of interpretations. It implies setting up regulations of and for decolonial knowledge that implies border thinking; not "between" disciplines but past the disciplines. As long as controversies and interpretations remain within the same rules of the game (the same terms of the conversation), the control of knowledge itself is never called into question. And in order to call the modern/colonial foundation of the control of knowledge into question, it is necessary to focus on the knower rather than on the known. This means going to the very assumptions that sustain our enunciations.

## Concluding Remarks

To sum up: the domains of the colonial matrix of power support one another. For instance, the flows that run from the domain of political authority (e.g., the state) to the economy (capitalism) enforce racial and sexual classifications and rankings. But those classifications and rankings are not inscribed in the domains ontologically. The domains do not exist independently, with tags saying "I am knowledge," "I am nature," "I am Black," "I am heterosexual," "I am gay," "I am politics," "I am finances," and so forth. All these domains have been invented by the rhetoric (the narratives) of modernity. They have come into existence through the various flows of the enunciation (scientific and media discourses, education and pedagogy from kindergarten to the university, etc.).

All domains are therefore interconnected by the logic of coloniality (the practical activations of state politics, economic organization, subjective social expectations, aesthetic regulated taste, and religious belief) while remaining hidden or disguised from and by the rhetoric of modernity (the imaginary discourse from institutions regulating social organization). You cannot grasp racial and sexual issues without grasping the underlying logic that activates the economy (e.g., slavery is a case in point yesterday and today) or the state politics, whose actors and managers institute economic values and orient behavior via particular racial and sexual classifications and hierarchies. And, in all such cases, everything goes back to knowledge, for it is through knowledge that the domains are instituted as *worlds* (ontologies) while the enunciation institutes itself as the *renderings* (description, explanation, representation, interpretation) of existing *worlds* and by so doing hides the fact that the worlds that the enunciation renders are not representations of existing worlds but instituted in and by the "doing" of the enunciation. The enunciation is a praxis that institutes the domains, without distinguishing the levels and hiding the flows. Modern/colonial apparatus of enunciation confound description and explanations of *worlds* with the worlds described and explained. For that reason, *representation* is a crucial concept of the rhetoric of modernity: makes us believe that there is a world out there that can be described independently of the enunciation that describes it. Removing the mask of the modern/colonial enunciation (the heart of the CMP) is a fundamental and basic task of delinking and decolonial thinking. That is, removing the mask can only be done by thinking, arguing, doing in communal *conversations* wherever and whenever we can engage and help to create what the rhetoric of modernity and the logic of coloniality prevent us from doing. Instituting management, which most of the time doesn't "feel" like we are managed, takes place at the very moment of enunciating the configuration of the domains—and of *deinstituting* whatever doesn't fit the model and the expectation of people's feeling, doing, and thinking. Dissenting within the CMP is one thing (e.g., Eurocentric critique of Eurocentrism) but what decoloniality means is to delink from both Eurocentric regulations and dissent within Eurocentrism. The rhetoric of modernity builds fields of representation to legitimize the instituted and justify the global designs that bulldoze (by diplomacy, debt, or war) whatever impedes their march, which is the march of coloniality. Domination presupposes exploitation, and both generate conflicts. The three spheres of influence operate in two dimensions: within European imperial states and in the European colonies. Therefore, the tasks of undoing and departing from Eurocentrism cannot be reduced to Eurocentric critic of Eurocentrism (e.g., demodernity), which is necessary but highly insufficient. What is essential at this point is the non-Eurocentric critic of Eurocentrism; which is decoloniality in its planetary diversity of local histories that have been disrupted by North Atlantic global expansions.

I will return to these issues in chapter 9. The next chapter is devoted to the Eurocentered image of the world resulting from the constitution, transformation, and management of the CMP.

## Notes

1  See the recent detailed Ebrahim Moosa study and autobiographical narrative, *What Is a Madrasa?* (Chapel Hill: University of North Carolina Press, 2015).
2  For a panoramic vista of this history, see my "Globalization and the Geopolitics of Knowledge: The Role of the Humanities in the Corporate University," in *The American Style University at Large*, 3–41 (Lanham, MD: Lexington Books, 2011).

Siba Grovogui, *Otherwise Human: The Institutes and Institutions of Rights*, accessed May 30, 2016, http://sibagrovogui.com/current-projects/otherwise-human-the-institutes-and-institutions-of-rights.

Aníbal Quijano, "Colonialidad del poder y subjetividad en América Latina," in *Decolonialidad y Psicoanálisis*, ed. María Amelia Castañola and Mauricio González, 11–34 (Mexico City: Ediciones Navarra and Colección Borde Sur, 2017).

Sylvia Wynter, "Unsettling the Coloniality of Being/Power/Truth/Freedom: Towards the Human, After Man—An Argument," *New Centennial Review* 3, no. 3 (2003): 257–337.

6   See "(De) Coloniality at Large: Time and the Colonial Difference," in Walter D. Mignolo, *The Darker Side of Western Modernity: Global Futures, Decolonial Options*, 118–48 (Durham, NC: Duke University Press, 2011); "The Moveable Center," in *The Darker Side of the Renaissance: Literacy, Territoriality and Colonization* (Ann Arbor: Michigan University Press, [1995], 2003), chap. 5; Daniel Astorga Poblete, "La colonización del Tlacauhtli y la invención del espacio en el México colonial," PhD dissertation, Duke University, 2015, http://dukespace.lib.duke.edu/dspace/handle/10161/10448; "Modernity and Decoloniality," *Oxford Bibliography Online,* 2011, accessed May 27, 2016, http://www.oxfordbibliographies.com/view/document/obo-9780199766581/obo-9780199766581-0017.xml.

7   For an update on the social struggles in the Andes that called for "coloniality," see Catherine Walsh's part I of this volume.

8   Postmodern critiques of *representation* have been eloquently advanced by Michel Foucault, *Les mots et les chose* (Paris. Gallimard, 1967) and by Richard Rorty, *Philosophy and the Mirror of Nature* (Princeton, NJ: Princeton University Press, 1982). For a decolonial critique of *representation*, see Rolando Vázquez, "Colonialidad y relacionalidad," in *Los desafíos decoloniales de nuestros días: Pensar colectivo*, ed. María Eugenia Borsani and Pablo Quintero, 173–97 (Neuquén, Argentina: Universidad del Comahue, 2014).

9   Research, analysis, and reflections on coloniality of being and of subjectivity (racism and sexism) are due to forward-thinking María Lugones and Nelson Maldonado-Torres. From Lugones, see "Heterosexualism and the Colonial/Modern Gender System," *Hypatia* 22, no. 1 (2007): 186–209, and "Toward a Decolonial Feminism," *Hypatia* 25 (2010): 742–59; from Maldonado-Torres, see "On the Coloniality of Being," *Cultural Studies* 21, no. 2 (2007): 240–70.

10   "Modernity and Decoloniality" *Oxford Bibliography Online,* 2011, accessed May 27, 2016, http://www.oxfordbibliographies.com/view/document/obo-9780199766581/obo-9780199766581-0017.xml.

11   For a detailed account of Émile Benveniste's displacement from the signified/signifier to the enunciation, see my "Epistemic Disobedience, Independent Thoughts and Decolonial Freedom," in *Theory, Culture and Society* 26, nos. 7/8 (2009): 1–23.

12   Mignolo, "Epistemic Disobedience."

13   Mignolo, "Epistemic Disobedience."

152 / WALTER D. MIGNOLO

The Invention of the *Human* and the
Three Pillars of the Colonial Matrix of Power

*Racism, Sexism, and Nature*

The previous section outlined the CMP—the apparatus that was built by a selected community of humans of a given religion (Christianity), in a continent
called Europe and around the fifteenth century, in the process of defining
themselves as humans. The question is not "what is human and humanity"
but rather who defined themselves as humans in their praxis of living
and applied their self-definition to distinguish and classify and rank lesser
humans. The self-definition became, subsequently, the self-identification of
living organisms that used their two upper extremities to build instruments
(that is, the extension of the hands) and cultivate their own food, build shelters
and have a global impact on Earth. The description and explanation of the
*human species* (a species of living organism) in recent history and specific
languages (Greek *anthropos*, Latin *humanus)* shall not be confused with the
point of origination (dates and places), which is the starting point in the
past invented in the present of the storytellers, whatever the present was
when the words *anthropos* and *humanus* were introduced. However, Greek
and Roman intelligentsia were not the only storytellers who created words
to describe themselves and their point of origination. The invention of the
model/human was fundamental in building, managing, and controlling
the CMP by silencing all other self-identification of the species.

This chapter explores the local and self-promoted emergence of *the
model/human* in the European Renaissance. The fictional conceptualization
was achieved through the (epistemic) invention of imperial and colonial differences. Western imperial subjects secured themselves and their descendant as
the superior subspecies. They invented also the idea of *nature* to separate their
bodies from all living (and the very life-energy of the biosphere) organisms

on the planet. Current conceptualization of posthuman and posthumanism carries the weight of its regional racial and sexual classifications and ranking. What follows is not an attempt to provide a true definition of human species, human, and humanity but to provide an answer to how it came to be the self-definition of certain praxis of living taken as model and horizon of all (e.g., universal) praxis of living. My argument is decolonial in the sense that it focuses on coloniality of knowledge (epistemology) constitutive of coloniality of being (ontology): the invention of the human.

### Before 1500 the World Order Was Polycentric and Non-Capitalist

What follows is not an ethnohistorical narrative, but a decolonial argument grounded on Aníbal Quijano's pioneering concept of *coloniality*. Coloniality redefined the concept of *modernity*, revealing its darker side, coloniality, as well as opening up the possibilities of reconceptualizing decolonialization into decoloniality, as argued in previous chapters. However, I bring into conversation strong conceptual formulations akin to the concept of *coloniality*: Frantz Fanon's *sociogenesis*, Sylvia Wynter's *Muni* and *Mana*, Gloria Anzaldúa's *border dwelling* and *la facultad,* the Andean concept of Sumak Kawsay, and Anishinaabe equivalent concept of *mino bimaadiziwin* (Leanne Simpson); the latter two underscore the resurgence of the communal, not individualistic, praxis living, sensing, thinking, doing, believing. I conceive them all as decolonial concepts with which my argument engages in respectful and, I hope, productive dialogue. By doing so I walk the roads, on the one hand, of decolonial analytics (the three pillars) and, on the other, of decolonial openings toward paths of delinking and relinking (re-existence).

Before 1500, most known cultures and civilizations on the planet (perhaps with the exception of Greece) were built on the assumption of the coexistence or complementarity of the opposite. It is known that, for example, Buddhist philosophy rejects the law of noncontradiction (which holds that "*A* is *B*" and "*A* is not *B*" are mutually exclusive and cannot coexist), and it is assumed that, in Greece, Heraclitus rejected it too. But Plato and Aristotle argued in favor of it.[1] On the contrary, all the inheritors today of the many cultures and civilizations in the territory named America, from the Mapuches in southern Chile to the Crees in Canada, conceived complementarity and not opposition. The law of contradiction or of noncontradiction (both terms are used to refer to it) seems to be the seed for the semantic construction of binary opposition in Western thoughts.

The story is well known, and this is not the place to repeat it.[2] What is necessary here is to understand how the narratives built around the idea of modernity, its rhetoric and goals, assumed the logic of noncontradiction and the semantic of binary opposition. It is this assumption that made and still makes it possible to tell stories and brand promises and build hopes of salvation, progress, development, democracy, growth, and so on; stories that hide and silences *coloniality*: the darker side of Western modernity. Decolonial thinking is akin to nonmodern ways of thinking grounded on cosmologies of *complementary dualities* (and/and) rather than on *dichotomies* or *contradictory dualities* (either/or). In Mesoamerican and Andean civilizations the consecration of the Sun and the Moon was a consecration of the necessary complementarity for the regeneration of life, of all life: the life of organisms that can tell stories and the life of organisms that are not telling stories but belong to the same world.

I argue that in the sixteenth century of the Christian era, many civilizations were organized and living within cosmologies that, in contradistinction with Greek cosmology reframed by Christian theology and the European Renaissance, did not operate in accordance with the logic of contradiction and even less with the logic of binary opposition. The idea of human and humanity was built upon this logic disguised as denotation of an existing entity. Human was a fictional noun pretending to be its ontological representation.

The system of oppositions and the logic of noncontradiction were set up, since the European Renaissance (antiquity, medieval) and since the Enlightenment (primitives, traditional) by chronology and by geography (Saracens, barbarians, uncivilized, underdeveloped, communists, terrorists). *Human* was the classifying entity in the process of defining itself as such. Since the Renaissance the *rhetoric of modernity was and continues to be built on the logic of coloniality: the denial and disavowal of non-European local times and spaces and non-European ways of life.* The rhetoric of modernity was built on the opposition between Christians and non-Christians, masculine and feminine, white and nonwhite, progress and stagnation, developed and underdeveloped, First and Second/Third World.

The chronology and geography of these denials are the constitutive act of coloniality, legitimized by the rhetoric (narratives) of modernity. In the next section, we will explore the constitutive acts of coloniality: the invention, transformation, and management of colonial and imperial epistemic and ontological differences.

### The Idea of the *Human* and *Humanity*: Exclusionary Logic and the Advent of a Monocentric World Order

Although Aristotle apparently thought that the law of contradiction was an ontological law and that binary oppositions were ontological oppositions, decolonially speaking oppositions are both imaginary entities created by the enunciator and the apparatus of enunciation (that is, actors, institutions, and languages) sustaining and building images of the world through storytelling, including logical and mathematical storytelling (e.g., Maya's mathematics continued to be ignored in the history of Western mathematics). The enunciation (actors, institutions, and languages) that created, transformed, and managed the colonial matrix of power (CMP) has hosted—since its foundation and through the centuries—many people. The mutual foundation of the enunciated (the domains) of the CMP and the enunciation that created the domains at the same time that it created itself as such, was founded on ceremonial acts and events. The CMP was put in place in the process of dealing with an unexpected situation (the invention of América) without the awareness that something different was being created. Singling out the level of the enunciated and its domains (governance, economy, knowledge, classification (racism and sexism, the invention of nature) and the level of the enunciation and its actors, languages, and institutions is a theoretical conceptualization that has emerged in recent years. It is a theoretical reconstruction of historical process. The "unconscious" in Sigmund Freud's work, to give a parallel example, was a reconstruction of what he thought operates in the human psyche. What one can say with confidence today is that the actors who created the CMP could not consciously know that they were creating what today we, in our analyticity, identify as such; but they certainly knew and believed that they were acting as *humans* in a world populated by lesser humans. Let's remember some etymologies from the *Online Etymology Dictionary*.

**human** (adj.)

mid-15c., humain, humaine, "human," from Old French humain, umain (adj.) "of or belonging to man" (12c.), from Latin humanus "of man, human," also "humane, philanthropic, kind, gentle, polite; learned, refined, civilized."

This is in part from PIE *(dh)ghomon-, literally "earthling, earthly being," as opposed to the gods (see homunculus). Compare Hebrew adam "man," from adamah "ground." Cognate with Old Lithuanian zmuo (accusative zmuni) "man, male person."

Human interest is from 1824. Human rights attested by 1680s; human being by 1690s. Human relations is from 1916; human resources attested by 1907, American English, apparently originally among social Christians and based on natural resources.

**human** (n.)

"a human being," 1530s, from human (adj.).

Latin *humanus* was the translation of Greek *anthropos*. But there is another noun in the languages of Western civilization (Greek, Latin, and modern vernacular and imperial European languages) that is relevant for the argument:

**man** (n.)

Old English man, *mann* "human being, person (male or female); brave man, hero; servant, vassal," from Proto-Germanic *manwaz (cognates: Old Saxon, Swedish, Dutch, Old High German man, German Mann, Old Norse maðr, Danish mand, Gothic manna "man"), from PIE root *man- (1) "man" (cognates: Sanskrit manuh, Avestan manu-, Old Church Slavonic mozi, Russian muzh "man, male").[3]

*Human* doesn't "represent" a given entity; it was an invention—who invented it? What was the purpose? Sylvia Wynter has argued, innovatively, that the constitution of Man1 (in the Renaissance imaginary) and Man2 (in the Enlightenment imaginary) stood for the humanity of the human.[4] The humanity of the human was universally postulated. What this meant was that those who conceptualized Man1 and Man2 as standing for the human were self-identified with the entity (Man1 and Man2 = Human) that they were describing. Wynter's argument carries the weight of African history and of the African diaspora in the Americas.[5]

In order for these actors to self-identify with the human, they needed to draw on differences with entities that were lesser than or nonhuman. Two spheres of meaning were available to this purpose in the early Renaissance: one was racial/religious, the other sexual. Racism and sexism emerged at that point—two constitutive pillars of the colonial matrix of power. In the sphere of religion, there were the Saracens, the Canaanites, and the Pagans; in the sexual sphere, a distinction was traced between necessary and dispensable women. Dispensable women invented by Human/Man were *witches*; necessary women were *wives* whose function was to secure the regeneration of the species.

When Christians encountered lands and people they did not know and baptized the people Indians and the land Indies, and when later on in the sixteenth century the trade of enslaved Africans began, it was necessary to situate the human and humanity in relation to people whom the Bible did not account for, and in relation to the massive contingents of enslaved Africans displaced to Indias Occidentales. If the inhabitants of Indias Occidentales became *Indians*, enslaved Africans became *Black* and, therefore, lesser beings in relation to the prototype of the (*White*) human. While in Europe racism manifested itself in the sphere of religion, in the New World (Indias Occidentales, and then America) racism was established in the secular realm, with people who, according to the Christians, had no religion.

Racism in the New World impinged upon sexism already established among Western Christians. Racism and sexism are inseparable and constitutive of the CMP. That is the beginning of *intersectionality* (a theoretical concept that identifies praxis of living enacting modernity/coloniality), and intersectionality is founded on the racial and sexual colonial differences (for the colonial difference, see the next chapter). If witches continued to be targeted in the New World, a significant difference in their categorization could not have gone unnoticed. *Witches* in Europe belonged to the same cosmology as *women*. The difference between the ideas of women and witches lay in the behavior Man attributed to them: the former complaisant, the latter disobedient. In the New World, however, neither Indian women nor African women belonged in the same cosmology as European women. Indian and African women were not properly considered women by Christian men, so that the women versus witches opposition that applied in Europe did not pertain in the New World: Indian and African females could be witches, but they could never be women. And that was the result of the ascendancy of racism over sexism, which has persisted to the present day and around the world. With Western expansion, colonial-racial differences encroached upon colonial-sexual differences.

But that was not all. There is one more facet in the procedural constitution of the human: the invention of *nature* and the degradation of life. *Nature* doesn't exist, or it exists as an ontological fiction—what there is is the relentless generation and the regeneration of life in the solar system from which processes emerged a species of living/languaging organisms. A limited sector of these creatures were able to define themselves as human and impose their self-referential description as standard for all living organisms of the same species. From life on Planet Earth to the other planets touring around the Sun, there is no single entity that could correspond to the noun *nature*. There is no such concept in other (non-Western) languages, from Aymara and Quechua to Tojolabal and Mandarin. If there is no such concept, it is because there was no conceptualization corresponding to what Europeans understood as nature. Indigenous peoples do not make this distinction,[6] and *Runa* in Kechua or *He* in Mandarin or *Bashar/Insan* in Persian means that living organisms who can describe themselves and the rest of the living system of the universe have a different way of conceptualizing than do the living organisms who dwelled in Greece and the outposts of the Roman Empire and spoke Greek and Latin.

Thus, as Wynter explains it, Man/Human, more than an existing entity, is an entity that "exists" (like Don Quixote or Madame Bovary) because those who named it defined themselves by looking at their image in the mirror. Decolonially, Man/Human must be located in the act of enunciation rather than in the entity that is enunciated. Focusing on the enunciation allows us to see who is behind the scene—who is manipulating the marionettes. Decolonially, we shall not be drawn by the mirage of the marionettes.

## The Fictional Ontology of *Nature*: Classifying and Shattering the Whole Diversity of the Living

Extractivism, possession, and dispossession have a long history in the formation and transformation of the CMP. From the sixteenth century through the nineteenth, extractivism targeted New World gold, exploiting and enslaving Indigenous and African peoples. After the Industrial Revolution, extractivism concentrated on those natural resources needed to feed the machines. And from the second half of the twentieth century to the present, extractivism has fueled the so-called Fourth Industrial (Technological) Revolution. What extractivism couldn't do was to "extract" the knowledge and the soul of the people. That is why, today, we are witnessing the powerful resurgence of Indigenous knowledges, philosophies of life, and ways of helping the world to realize how vicious and devilish the concept of nature and its proxy, *natural resources*, was and continue to be.

The point I want to make is that the CMP has been created by actors (languages and institutions) who saw and felt themselves as Man/Human and upon that belief built the *colonial differences*: racial, sexual, and the separation from *nature*.

Philippe Descola published an important book in 2013 titled *Beyond Nature and Culture*. He argues strongly that *nature* and *culture* are two concepts that make no sense beyond Western civilization and, I would add, beyond westernized anthropologists and educated persons outside of Europe and Anglo–United States tamed by Western education. Briefly, nature and culture are two Western fictions. Many of us in South and Central America and, of course, the Caribbean began to understand that in ancient civilizations in Mesoamerica and the Andes, the binary opposition *nature/culture* made no sense. There was no equivalent for such words. If there had been, it would mean something similar to "it is the nature of our human organism that generates culture." For ancient Mesoamerican and Andean people and for those who survived until today, nature and culture are two meaningless concepts.[7] How to get out of them is a decolonial question.

Proyecto Andino de Tecnologías Campesinas (PRATEC) began in Urubamba, Cuzco in November of 1986. It was led, and still is, by scholarly trained persons in collaboration with the knowhow of Indigenous and peasant communities. At that time, it was very common to see PRATEC as a romantic, new-age, irrelevant project to satisfy the non-Indigenous. One of the key points of PRATEC was to tell non-Indigenous readers that, among other things, nature and culture were irrelevant concepts in Indigenous philosophy (thinking). For PRATEC non-Indigenous leaders (Eduardo Grillo, Rengifo Vázquez, Valladolid Rivera), learning to think in and from—not about—indigenous concepts and engaging in their (indigenous) praxis of living means a radical shift in their thinking and subjectivities.[8] I am aware that counterfactuals are inconsequential for the trajectory that factually followed. Nevertheless, imagine that PRATEC would have had some strong support and funding institution using their financial privileges to appropriate their initiative. In that case, PRATEC would have ended enacting coloniality covered by the rhetoric of generosity of the founding institutions. However, since PRATEC did not enroll in modern global designs to enact coloniality, it remains less visible to the public eye, although decolonially effective in the sphere of its operation. Decoloniality to be defended cannot be funded.

What are we learning from PRATEC and what have its leaders learned from Indigenous philosophy and praxis of living?

> To nurture a *chakra* is not merely to domesticate plants and animals; it is to nurture lovingly and respectfully, in other words, to nurture ritually, together with the plants and animals, the soils, waters, microclimates and, in general, the whole land.[9]

These words were written by Julio Valladolid Rivera, co-founder of PRATEC. The claim is to revamp millenarian Andean ways of living together in the *chakra*. It is the whole where *Runas, sallqas, and huacas* interrelate in the process of *nurturing* (*nutrir*, "nutrients" in Spanish) and living—living requires nurturing, and nurturing regenerates living in all its dimensions. If you look up *nurture* in current dictionaries you would understand how coloniality of knowledge works: it is translated as and related to *development*, when indeed *chakra* is exactly the opposite. PRATEC was founded in 1987, during the years in which *development* was being radically critiqued. Its foundations offered a way of delinking from modernization and development.

*Chakra*, modern dictionaries will tell you, is a piece of land outside of the city where food is produced for city dwellers. Well, it is not what *chakra* means in ancient Andean cultures: *chakra* (also *chacra*) refers to *vincularidad* (interrelations) between *Runas, sallqas*, and *huacas*. *Runa* could not be translated as "human" because *human* in Western vocabulary was separated from *nature*, which is not the case in Indigenous philosophies. *Sallqas* are all living organisms, and *huacas* refers to the sacred, such as mountains or rivers that are also sallqas. Valladolid Rivera conceived *decolonization* in terms of delinking from Western cosmo-vision and relinking with Indigenous *cosmo-vivencia*. We need vocabulary that comes from many other experiences, not only from the Greek. There is no reason to continue privileging Greek and Latin sources. Epistemic disobedience means to recognize them and denaturalize them at the same time. Epistemic disobedience requires border thinking.[10] Yes indeed, nature and culture are two Western concepts only valid within Western cosmology. Indigenous scholars and intellectuals know it from their own memories and education. No need for them to read the discovery of an anthropologist from Le Collège de France.

Thus, for those of us who dwell in the Americas, who have been raised and educated in the Americas (regardless of our skin color, religious beliefs, migrant status, sexual preferences, etc.), and who have sensed through different aromas five hundred years of Western epistemic racism, it shall be evident that the classification and invention of "Indians"; the classification and invention of "Blacks" to homogenize the African population; the identification of the New World with "nature" and with the wealth of "natural resources" after the Industrial Revolution—all of these are epistemic invention of ontological natural and cultural entities. Ontology was created *by the diversity of a single Eurocentered story*: there were and are many stories but a single logic of coloniality hidden by the rhetoric of modernity.

Here is a tip to better understand what I am arguing:

**nature** (n.)

Late 13c., "restorative powers of the body, bodily processes; powers of growth;" from Old French nature "nature, being, principle of life; character, essence," from Latin natura "course of things; natural character, constitution, quality; the universe," literally "birth," from natus "born," past participle of nasci "to be born," from PIE *gene- "to give birth, beget" (see genus).

From late 14c as "creation, the universe"; also "heredity, birth, hereditary circumstance; essential qualities, innate disposition" (as in human nature); "nature personified, Mother Nature." Specifically as "material world beyond human civilization or society" from 1660s. Nature and nurture have been contrasted since 1874.[11]

"Restorative powers of the body." But not only Man/Human has a body: plants have bodies, fish have bodies, birds have bodies, vegetables have bodies, fruit have bodies. I will take body to be "living organisms." Living organisms deontologize the entity *body* (molecular self-regenerative system) and restore it to the irreducible processes in the praxis of living.[12] That is, every living organism and their regenerative processes have a *body* (that lives and dies). It is the materiality of the living that constitutes the body. The second definition of *nature* refers to "creation, the universe." Man/Human molecular organisms have been also created, along with the universe, but a great deal of the time "he" (Man/Human) acts as if "he" is only observing (with telescopes or experiments) the creation of the living.

For Acosta, as a good Jesuit, knowing and understanding *nature* had moral dimensions, and sacred dimensions as well. Knowing and understanding *nature* (energy of living and regeneration, not an object or entity) meant understanding and worshiping its Creator: the "Creator of the Universe," and of life, of course.[13] About twenty years later, Francis Bacon—an English philosopher, statesman, scientist, jurist, orator, and Viscount of St. Alban—was much less interested in understanding *nature* and in admiring and understanding its Creator like Acosta did. Bacon was the kiss of death for the living reduced to what became "natural resources" and more recently "human re-sources." He was riding a different wave: that of the secular humanists (Man2). Nature, for Francis Bacon, was out there, separated from him—something to be dominated and exploited.

Francis Bacon's injunction took hold in the secular scientific minds of the eighteenth century. This time, Georges-Louis Leclerc, Comte de Buf-fon, wrote the voluminous *Histoire naturelle, générale et particulière* (second half of the eighteenth century). Buffon assumed not only that nature was something separate from Man/Human, but also that she was subject to the chronological laws of human history, as narrated by Man/Human. He took literally the expression "New World" and argued that the New World was so young that not only its people but also *its nature* were behind the stages of history that Europe had already reached. Nature, for Buffon, and particularly the history of the New World, had the same status that the history of the state would have for G. W. F. Hegel, some fifty years later.

Responses from non-European Indigenous people (I am assuming here that European are Indigenous and are precisely the Indigenous Europeans who have problems with immigrants and refugees)[14] arose in different times, places, and vocabularies and political projects. In the South American Andes, *Pachamama* (Mother Earth) was always invoked by Indigenous people in spite and in front of the European idea of *nature*. Pachamama became in-creasingly meaningful to confronting the destruction of nature and its re-cent version, the *environment*, by transnational corporations exploiting and extracting *natural resources*. It acquired also a significant political meaning when it made its way into the Ecuadorian Constitution.

This Man/Human who created and managed the CMP, posited himself as master of the universe and succeeded in setting himself apart from other men/humans (racism), from women/humans (sexism), from nature (hu-manism), from non-Europe (Eurocentrism), and from "past" and "traditional" civilizations (modernity). Nature, in the domains of the colonial matrix of power, lies between the domains of economics and politics; it was invented by Man/Human in the process of him setting himself up in the locus of the enunciations (institutions, actors, and languages) that created, transformed, and managed the rhetoric (narratives) of modernity, and the necessary and concomitant logic of coloniality. He who governs does not obey, became the assumption in the growing affirmation of the secular *Ego* in Western civilization.

In Indigenous cosmologies, as I mentioned before, there is no such divide between *nature* and *culture*, a misleading formula, for nature is a cultural concept; and the *ego* is disseminated in the communal. That is, nature and culture are both cultural Western concepts that were established as ontologies. For that reason, current urgencies among Western scholars and intellectuals of moving "beyond nature and culture" is a regional and provincial Western urgency.[15] It is welcome of course, but it is not universal. Indigenous cosmologies do not present us with such urgency, for the simple reason that in this cosmology there are neither nature nor culture and even less a cultural structure of knowledge that needed to invent the concept of *nature* to highlight Man/Human as maker of culture.

## Stories of the Creation of the Cosmos and of the Living Species that Tell the Story of the Creation of the Ethnicity of the Storytellers

All known storytelling about the creation of the world (including scientific ones, like the Big Bang), and about the creation of the living species (including recent storytelling about the *anthropocene*) to which the narrators telling stories about the origin of the world belong, aim at and claim totality. It could not be otherwise. The narrators of the Popol Vuh, of the Legend of the Fifth Sun (as well as sacred books such as the Bible and the Qur'an) as well as of the many cosmological narratives of ancient China or ancient India, or of any other non-Western texts we might consider, would aim at the totality. Western Christian philosophers of the European Middle Ages formulated their own local totality in terms of *universals*. Universals, then, are a philosophical formulation within one specific cosmology (Christian) of the totality, for which this cosmology, as any other cosmology, aims.[16] The problem with universals is that, in aiming at the totality, they became totalitarian. What this means is that totalities are totalitarian if they succeed in overpowering or disavowing similar claims in other cosmologies. When that happened in the historical period we here describe as modern/colonial, a totalitarian totality provides a frame for coloniality of knowledge. *From being a local totality, Christian cosmology became a universal totality* (as redundant as this may sound). In eighteenth-century Europe it was translated into Western secular cosmology having science and philosophy as its two pillars. It is only for Christian believers that the world originated as the Bible story says.

And that is valid for any other cosmology, with the exception that Christianity became the leading story in the historical foundation of the CMP and its aftermath.

I would surmise that, for speakers of Aymaran, Anishinaabemowin, Osage, and Zapotec, as well as Chinese, Indonesian, Urdu, Bengali, Hindi, and so on, the above might sound a little strange—or at least as something that belongs to "those people, over there," to the west of Athens and to the west of Rome. To illustrate what I am arguing, I provide here one example from Persian and another from Kechua. Why do they have to surrender to the six modern European imperial languages and the knowledge built into them?

In Ali Shari'ati's discussions of the Holy Qur'an, he makes a distinction between *Bashar* and *Insan*: "By using *Bashar*, the Qur'an is talking about the two-footed creature that emerged at the end of the evolutionary chain. . . . *Bashar* is that particular being that contains physiological, biological and psychological characteristics which are shared by all *men* . . . . On the other hand *Insan* is that unique and enigmatic being that has a special definition that does not apply to any other phenomenon in nature. . . . *Bashar* is 'being' while *Insan* is becoming" (italics mine).[17]

I double-checked Shari'ati's definition of both terms (since I speak neither Arabic nor Persian), with Hamid Dabashi, Persian scholar and intellectual. Dabashi confirmed the definition through an email conversation:

> BASHAR and INSAN—both mean "human" in slightly different senses—they are both Arabic/Qur'anic that have entered Persian too; one might also add ADAM to it;
>> ADAM is the first *human being* God created—according to Qur'an;
>> BASHAR is the generic name for the corporeal body of the person;
>> INSAN is the generic name for the *humanistic* disposition of the person.
> (7/29/13) (italics mine)

Notice that the translation of Persian to Western languages requires the uses of *human* and *humanistic*, which doesn't mean that Western theology and epistemology got it right. It means that Western theology and epistemology became hegemonic, then dominant, and now are losing both, hegemony and domination. The decolonial option is contributing to such demise. In fact, it is a fundamental task of decolonial politics of scholarship. If we move from Persian to Kechua, we find that the noun *Runa* is often translated in modern European vernacular languages as "human" or "human being." But *Runa* is quite different from Man/Human. Man/Human, as we have seen, fashioned himself by cutting ties with "nature" and, by the eighteenth century, in an act of de-Goding (to use Sylvia Wynter's vocabulary), and also by setting up the rule of division between two things that are (or are represented as being) opposed or entirely different: Man and Woman, Human and Nature, Life and Death, Day and Night, Matter and Spirit, Mind and Body, and so on.

Runa cannot be flatly translated into Man/Human, and vice versa, for reasons that have to do more with power differential (and the entanglement the CMP generated) than with the problems of the incommensurability of translation. For people who conceived of themselves as Runa (parallel to other people who conceived of themselves as Man/Human, or as Bashar/Insan, or as Ren [人的]), this conceptualization implies a local universe of meaning.[18] Let's take Runa, to make a long story short, since we have already said something about the Persian Bashar/Insan.

Runa was and still is conceived in relation to and in *convivencia* (a literal translation would be "living-with-other-living-organisms," but the term is generally translated as "coexistence" or "conviviality")[19] with huacas (deities, entities of the sacred sphere), sallqa (all living organisms), and the Apu (the tutelary spirit that inhabits the snowed peaks of the mountains). These organisms are all weaved together, for the metaphor of *tejido* (weaving) is commonly invoked to express convivencia and vincularidad (translated as "relationality"). Convivencia, furthermore, is convivencia in the *ayllu* (equivalent to *oykos* in ancient Greek), a fluid structure of kinship—kinship not only among Runas, but also among huacas, sallqa, and Apu.

Consequently, in translating Runa into Man/Human you erase the convivencia of the living and the spiritual world and you "endow" Runa with the same violence that Man/Human has enacted in defining himself.[20] You then would continue the erasure that Man/Human started during the Renaissance in Europe and in the processes of epistemic conquest and the colonization of the world. Convivencia is not necessarily pacifistic, but it is a struggle in search of balance and harmony. Andean philosophy included the concepts of tinku and ayny. Tinku and ayni bring the opposite into the unity of complementary relations.[21]

It shall be pointed out here, that in introducing coloniality and distinguishing it from colonialism, Quijano reconceived decolonization as decoloniality: taking hold of the state apparatus is no longer the goal of decoloniality (see chapter 5). Decoloniality aims at epistemic reconstitution (see chapter 6). By doing so he meant that while colonialism referred to the military, political, and economic domination of other regions, coloniality illuminated

the cultural aspects and, of course, the epistemic and hermeneutical principles upon which Western religions, science, and philosophy were built. It was
through the control and management of knowledge that the colonial matrix
of power was created, managed, transformed, and controlled. There cannot
be military, political, and economic doing without an epistemic and hermeneutic framework—a framework of knowing and understanding upon which
Man/Human (as well as Runa, Anthropos, Ren, and Bashar/Insan) acts on
the world. Since the European Renaissance, it has been the self-definition of
Man/Human and the principles of knowledge and understanding that have
grounded both His affirmation in Western Christianity and in relation to
cultures and civilizations around the world.

Now, taking a cursory look at Daoism, one finds that the concept of *nature* in Western (west of Jerusalem) medieval Christianity, and in Western
civilization after it, hides more than it reveals. In this respect, it is similar to
the translation of *Runa* into Man/Human. *Qi* cannot be translated as "nature"; it must be translated as "energy": the energy of the living *in the* living
universe, named *Pacha* (cosmos) and Pachamama (Earth) in the Andean
civilizations and Gaia (the Earth) and Cosmos in ancient Greece—it is the
energy that enables living organisms that are able to define themselves in
relation to all other organisms in *convivencia*. In some cases, the relation is
convivial; in others, it is antagonistic.

*Qi* is the energy that must be governed by the complementarity and harmony of *yin-yang*: there is no yin without yang, there is no yang without yin
because movement is relentless; there is no masculine without feminine, there
is no day without night, there is no life without death, and so on. Like *tinku* in
Andean philosophy and other indigenous cosmologies in the great civilizations of the Americas shattered by European invasions, yin-yang involves the
constant search for harmony and equilibrium, and is the goal of living organisms endowed with the capacity to define themselves/ourselves as particular
entities in convivial or antagonistic relation to other living organisms.

In Taoist or Daoist philosophy, the diversity of living that Western epistemology reduced to *nature* does not exclude the spiritual and the social. In
this sense it is much like Andean philosophy: sallqa doesn't exclude Runa and
huacas, since Apu is at once sallqa and huaca. In more familiar terms, Apu is
both materially living entity and spiritual.

Convivial and/or antagonistic relations should not be understood *universally*, through Western notions of dichotomy and war. Struggle (e.g., the
struggle between yin and yang, between day and night) is not synonymous

with war. In Kechua language and Andean philosophy, *yanantin* and *masin-tin* are parallel to yin and yang.[22] What they have in common is the acknowledgment that there cannot be A without its opposite B. Once you acknowledge that these entities are inseparable (two moieties in movement), you have at least two options: either you can try to eliminate what you declare to be opposite; or you can recognize that you cannot forever eliminate or dominate your opposite—you can eliminate some of its manifestations but not its energy and living force. If you try to eliminate and control the opposite, you enter the realm of *war*; if you seek harmony and balance, you enter the realm of *struggle*, "weaving" relations (convivencia, vincularidad) with all that exists: rocks and mountains; spirits and plants; plants and mountains that are spirits; animals who do not speak Kechua, Hebrew, Latin, or any other of the known languages; and animals who do speak one or more languages.

## Changing the Terms (Principles, Assumptions, Regulations) by Changing the Questions Holding Up Western-Led Conversations

What does it mean to be human is no doubt a fundamental question for the twenty-first century. Why? For several reasons but mainly for the argument I am unfolding, because the very concept of *Human* is called into question by scholars and intellectuals who carry in their own bodies the traces of racialization and sexualization. I have identified myself with the *anthropos*, and have engaged in *barbarian theorizing* (this is what I do, this is my praxis of thinking in my praxis of living).[23] Both racialization and sexualization are systems of social classification that presuppose, on the one hand, a standard and superior idea of race and, on the other, a normal code of sexual relations between men and women. This normal code of sexual relations is established along the power differential between men and women. Crucially, both racial and sexual classifications presuppose a concept of the human that is both racially and sexually superior. Human and humanity are not only concepts; they are concepts created by agents who considered *themselves* humans and who were in a position to project their own image of themselves as humanity. Racial and sexual norms excluded from this territory all those "entities" that were less human or not quite human.

We can perhaps now begin to grasp what it means to be human and what it means to be Man as overrepresentation of Man/Human, in Wynter's powerful argument. *Human* is a noun we can pedagogically accept when referring to a living organism who can speak any of the thousands of spoken languages on the planet. This organism could equally be named *Runa* or *Ren* or *Bashar/ Insan*, or any of the other existing nouns that I haven't listed here; and also *human*. Regional humans have the right to exist next to the previous ones. But keep in mind that I am more interested in logic than in ethnography of naming. Naming in the CMP has been a parallel activity next to building statues, which are torn down for political inside fights (e.g., Stalin or Saddam Hussein) or for decolonial reclaiming (Rhodes in Cape Town, South Africa; Robert Edward Lee in Virginia, the U.S.). Accordingly, we can begin to grasp the role of the level of enunciation in building, transforming, and managing the CMP.

Let's recall from chapter 6, the *levels* of CMP: the level of the enunciation and the level of the enunciated. The enunciated is the level composed by the domains to be managed and controlled. The domains form the level ontologically constituted by the level of the enunciation. They do not exist by themselves, although we have the impression they do. That is, epistemology configures (and in that sense, creates) the domains' ontology. Racial and sexual ontologies, in Western civilization, emerge from classification and configuration (e.g., the features that identify ontological domains). Economy and politics, and of course nature, are constituted and configured by knowledge and the principles and assumptions upon which knowledge is a machine of world making. That is, epistemology creates ontological domains.

The enunciation is the level in which actors, languages, knowledge generation, and institutions enable the circumscription of the domains of the enunciated. Power of decision takes place in the enunciation, though there would never be consensual or homogeneous agreements between actors and institutions operating at the level of the enunciation. Democrats and Republicans control the enunciation, and though they do not agree on every policy and disagreements are common, the state enunciation is both Democratic and Republican. Nothing else. They share control of the enunciation since the state is a crucial institution controlling the political domain of the enunciated. Both levels (the enunciated and the enunciation) are *connected by flows of energy* in the spheres knowledge, subjectivities, and interests. The flows between the levels permeate the flows between the domains. Consequently, the separate domains—economics, politics, knowledge and subjectivity, racism and sexism, the domain of the living (or "nature")—cannot be grasped in isolation, for they are all interconnected.

The flows from the enunciation to the enunciated secure management, transformation, and control of the CMP—the flows from the enunciated to the enunciation, in turn, secure benefits and self-interest for all persons, institutions, and languages embedded in the enunciation. For instance, when in 2008 the media and other publications underscored the need to save capitalism, it meant saving institutions rather than saving the people who were thrown into the crisis. In terms of language use, if English is today the international language of communication, it is because the language of enunciation is always the language of the leading imperial state shaping the management and control of the CMP. At one point the leading language was Spanish, then French, then British English, and now U.S. English. Latin was never a global language: it was the language spoken in all the extensions of the Roman Empire but not in Asia. Sanskrit was the equivalent in Asia, but it was not known or spoken in Europe.

As already mentioned, problems arise when a concept belonging to *one* civilization is taken as a point of reference for similar concepts in *all* civilizations. That is truth without parentheses. Thus, once *human* and *humanity* were established as both the universality of the enunciated (the ontology of the human and of humanity) and the universality of the enunciation (the epistemology that invented the concepts of the human and humanity), all other equivalent concepts became subordinated to the human and humanity. Managing and controlling the idea of human and humanity allowed those who define and are allowed to identify as such, to establish a hierarchy among humans: racism and sexism served that purpose.

Human and humanity are today under attack from two perspectives. One is the postmodern conceptualization of the posthuman, and the endowment of a new history: the anthropocene, the era of the *anthropos*. The other arises from decolonial questioning. The aim of this chapter is precisely to show how Man/Human as a concept is embedded in the CMP and is the reference point in every domain: for example, *homo economicus*, *homo politicus* ("man is by nature a political animal," as Aristotle is often quoted as saying). Man/Human is the regulator of racial and sexual classification; the regulator of aesthetics and of spirituality through religious institutions; the regulator of knowledge and understanding through theology, science, and philosophy. Wynter's Man1 and Man2 as well as Fanon's sociogenesis are outstanding contributions toward changing the terms of the conversation, reducing the pretended ontology of Man/Human to size. This is one of the crucial tasks of decoloniality: to decolonize Man/Human, to liberate *pluriversal humanity*.

Exposing the analytic of the CMP is always already a decolonial task, aimed at the restitution (epistemic reconstitution, see chapter 10) of every aspect of life that Man/Human has displaced, negated, and destroyed through the manipulation of the CMP, and the covering up of this manipulation with the promises and the blinding lights of the narratives promoting modernity: conversion, progress, development. By asking what it means to be human, decolonial thinking rejects the ontology and the epistemology of the human and of humanity. As decolonial thinker, once I know what Human/Man means, I do not want to be human. But instead of simply rejecting its content and adding a prefix (posthuman), decolonial thinkers start by asking how these concepts came into being: when, why, who, and what for? And then moving toward molecular nervous system organisms who in their/our praxis of living liberated our hands and engaged in languaging and conversations to name and describe ourselves and, when possible, impose our descriptions on other organisms we want to control and dominate: the CMP emerged at a particular junction of the history of our ancestors (living biological-cultural organisms) that redirected praxis of living on the planet.

What, then, is the posthuman, once we have reduced Man/Human to size and stripped him of his universality by showing that it is merely the universalization of a regional vocabulary and a regional concept of unilinear time to name a certain species of organism for which every existing language and civilization has its own name, concept, and storytelling? Reading and reflecting on Wynter's argument on "towards the human, after Man" alongside (not in comparison to) Rosi Braidotti's argument on *the posthuman* might help in understanding the broad spectrum of two epistemic, intellectual, political, and ethical trajectories of our time.[24] Wynter's and Braidotti's concerns to a certain extent overlap: two women confronting Western hegemony (*overrepresentation* would be Wynter's term) of the idea of *human* and of its bodyguard, *humanism*. Posthuman is a Eurocentric critique of European humanism, while Wynter and Fanon open up for a decolonial critique of both the concepts of human and posthuman.

Humanism, as mentioned, is a set of discourses enunciated by agents who identify themselves as human and who project their self-fashioning ontology to a universal scale. Needless to say, the universal claim that universalized *human* in the European Renaissance had its genealogy in the European Middle Ages. The question that Sylvia Wynter posed when she dismantled the invention of Man1 in the Renaissance and its transformation into Man2 during the Enlightenment could be extended to Man3, the posthuman: what does the posthuman mean today, beyond the regional and limited concerns of Eurocentrism? If today it is meaningless to universalize the Man/Human, it is equally limiting to conceptualize posthuman beyond the regional scope of actors, institutions, and languages managing the CMP. Human, Man/Human, and Posthuman are three moments in the history of the CMP attempting to maintain control of epistemic meaning in the sphere of culture, parallel to the control of meaning and power in the sphere of economics and politics. The question of universality runs through the history of Man1, Man2, and Man3 (Posthuman).

The sources of the universality still paramount in Western cosmology (with consequences for other cosmologies) are located in ancient Greece.[25] There is no reason—as I mentioned above—why Greece (and the Western prefix *post-* on all things derived from Greece and Rome) shall be the universal origin of all storytelling of communities of living organisms engaged in conversations. One issue has been debated at length in Western philosophy. The question is—decolonially speaking—whether universals indeed exist or whether they are merely concepts taken as *representations* of what exists. Consequently, a second issue could be whether universals, in the event that they have substantial existence, are separated from sensible entities or are embedded in them; and the third issue to explore would be whether universals, if they exist separately from sensible entities, are corporal or incorporeal substances.[26] The medieval European problem of the universal is nothing more than a claim of totality for every cosmology. In order to establish one totality—a set of discourses that create an ontology—you have to debunk all other cosmologies that have a claim to totality. And in order to do this, you have to impose your own totality over all others. That is how truth without parentheses overrules the possibility of truth in parentheses, that is, living in a pluriversal rather than in a universal mode of existence. You have then not only to assert your own totality, but also to devaluate, demonize, and silence coexisting ones.

The course of action leading to the historical foundations of the CMP in the sixteenth century was not merely a question of physical actions (discovering, setting up institutions, managing indigenous civilizations, appropriating lands, exploiting labor, etc.). It was above all a massive conceptual (epistemic) machine: building and managing knowledge that the actors ruling institutions believed was superior or truer than others. Such beliefs authorized actors and institutions to promote their universality and to demonize and devalue praxis of living and knowledges, though they could not be destroyed. And they are re-emerging today. Decoloniality and dewesternization (see chapter 5) rely on knowledges that are embedded in praxis of living that generated such knowledges, before self-defined Westerners began to impose, since the sixteenth century, their narratives of their praxis of living (that they felt was the true one) around the planet. Praxis of living and knowledges that have been devalued and demonized are resurging today, even if the devaluation continues. A fundamental task of decoloniality enacting resurgences and re-existence of devalued and demonized praxis of living, whatever form they take in the myriad local histories that have been intervened by modernity/coloniality (e.g., CMP). There is no blueprint for it. This introduction is certainly not one. All we are saying is that resurgence and re-existence are taking place, on the planet. Ours, Catherine and Walter, is a singular trajectory of decolonial thinking and doing. It is neither a master plan nor a planetary ethnography.

One could say that modernity/coloniality is above all a question of knowing and knowledge and that coloniality is justified in and by the narratives of modernity (the enunciation: actors, institutions, languages that founded and maintained, though transformed, the rhetoric of modernity) that enact and transform existing knowledge systems and create a new one as the enterprise goes on. Indeed, one of the main assumptions guiding the actions of European Man/Human in the New World was the universality of his knowledge and his belief. If universal, then it was total: the knowledge and self-conception of Man/Human helped him in his advance toward the totality that Man/Human apprehended in the process of apprehending himself as such.

Quijano helps us in locating how the universal in medieval philosophy became crucial in building and justifying the narratives of modernity and enacting coloniality:

> In spite of its absence in the Cartesian paradigm, the intellectual necessity of the idea of totality, especially in relation to social reality was present in the European debate; early on in the Iberian countries (Victoria, Suárez) and in the preservation of power defended by the Church and the Crown, and in France somewhat later (eighteenth century), and then already as a key element of social criticism and of alternative social proposals.
>
> Above all, from Saint-Simon, the idea of social totality was spread together with proposals of revolutionary social change, in confrontation with the atomistic perspective of social existence then predominant among the empiricists and among the adherents of the existing social and political

order. In the twentieth century, totality became a perspective and a category generally admitted in scientific investigations especially those about society.[27]

*Human* and humanity (again), and all their derivations, were since the Renaissance the names by which those who identified themselves as human identified the rest of the inhabitants of the planet. The basic operation implemented to secure epistemic dominion was *social classification*. Social classification, rather than social class, is the foundational epistemic moment of the CMP. This is the theme of the next chapter.

## Notes

1   The *Stanford Encyclopedia of Philosophy* tell us that "according to Aristotle, first philosophy, or metaphysics, deals with ontology and first principles, of which the principle (or law) of non-contradiction is the firmest. Aristotle says that without the principle of non-contradiction we could not know anything that we do know." "Aristotle on Non-Contradiction," *Stanford Encyclopedia of Philosophy* (2007) 2–15, accessed July 21, 2017, http://plato.stanford.edu/entries/aristotle-noncontradiction/.

2   "Binary Opposition," accessed July 21, 2017, http://www.gutenberg.us/articles/binary_opposition.

3   "Human," *Online Etymology Dictionary*, accessed May 21, 2016, http://www.etymonline.com/index.php?term=human; "Man," *Online Etymology Dictionary*, accessed May 21, 2016, http://www.etymonline.com/index.php.

4   See Sylvia Wynter, "Unsettling the Coloniality of Being/Power/Truth/Freedom: Towards the Human, after Man, Its Overrepresentation. An Argument," *New Centennial Review* 3, no. 3 (2003): 257–337.

5   Memories and bibliographies are enormous on this topic. Since this is an argument doing theory, not an ethnographic report, I shall mention for interested readers Paget Henry's magnificent *Caliban's Reason: Introducing Afro-Caribbean Philosophy* (New York: Routledge, 2000).

6   Although *people* is plural, I pluralized anyway to underscore the diversity of human beings identified as *Indigenous*.

7   Philippe Descola, *Beyond Nature and Culture*, trans. Janet Lloyd (Chicago: University of Chicago Press, 2013).

8   See "On the History of PRATEC," accessed May 23, 2016, see http://www.globaltimes.cn/content/1021021.shtml.

9   "Andean Peasant Agriculture: Nurturing a Diversity of Life in the Chacra," in *The Spirit of Regeneration: Andean Culture Confronting Western Notions of Develop-*

*ment*, ed. Frédérique Apffel-Marglin with PRATEC (London: Zed Books, 1998), 57. The word *culture* is difficult to avoid in this context. However, if we start from *nurture and regeneration*, we would be able to avoid nature and culture.

10   *Cosmo-vivencia* could be translated as "cosmo-sense," which privileges all the senses, not only the eyes, like in cosmo-vision. See Simon Yampara, "Cosmovivencia Andina: Vivir y convivir en armonía integral," *Bolivian Studies Journal* 18 (2011), https://bsj.pitt.edu/ojs/index.php/bsj/article/view/42.

11   "Nature," *Online Etymology Dictionary*, www.etymonline.com.

12   Humberto Maturana and Ximena Dávila, "Cultural-Biology: Systemic Consequences of Our Evolutionary Natural Drift as Molecular Autopoietic Systems," 2016 (edited version of previous publication), http://www.univie.ac.at/constructivism/archive/fulltexts/3900.html.

13   José de Acosta took a hermeneutic detour in relation to Genesis, where it is said that "and the Lord said: Let us make Mankind in our image, after our likeness; and let them have dominion over the fish of the sea, and over the birds of the air, and over the cattle, and over all the earth, and over every creeping thing that creeps on the earth. So the Lord created Mankind in His own image, into the image of the Lord. He created Him, male and female" (Genesis 1:25–26). See *Natural and Moral History of the Indies*, trans. Frances López-Morillas (Durham, NC: Duke University Press, [1590] 2002).

14   For this argument see Walter D. Mignolo, "Coloniality Is Far from Over and, So Must Be Decoloniality," *Afterall* (spring/summer 2017), https://www.afterall.org/journal/issue.43/coloniality-is-far-from-over-and-so-must-be-decoloniality.

15   See Philippe Descola, *Beyond Nature and Culture*, trans. Janet Lloyd (Chicago: Chicago University Press, 2013).

16   For the continuity of the topic in contemporary philosophy, see Gabriele Galluzzo and Michael J. Loux, eds., *The Problem of Universals in Contemporary Philosophy* (Cambridge: Cambridge University Press, 2015), accessed May 25, 2016, http://assets.cambridge.org/97811071/00893/excerpt/9781107100893_excerpt.pdf.

17   Ali Shari'ati, *Man and Islam*, trans. Fatollah Marjari (North Haledon, NJ: Islamic Publications International, 2005).

18   Pluriversality promotes the coexistence, in cooperation among compatible universes based on truth in parentheses and in antagonism and conflict with universes of meaning based on truth without parentheses.

19   See note 10 above.

20   On "double translation" and the directionality that the CMP imposed and the erasure that coloniality enacts, see Walter Mignolo and Freya Schiwy, "Transculturation and the Colonial Difference: Double Translation," In *Translation and Ethnography: The Anthropological Challenge of Intercultural Understanding* (Phoenix: University of Arizona Press, 2003), 3–29.

21   A similar conceptualization was at work in Aztec philosophy. See James Maffie, " 'We Eat of the Earth Then the Earth Eats Us': The Concept of Nature in Pre-Hispanic Nahua Thought," *Ludis Vitalis* X (2002): 5–20. For more detail, see James Maffie,

*Aztec Philosophy: Understanding a World in Motion* (Denver: University Press of Colorado, 2014).

22 Tristan Platt, "Mirrors and Maize: The Concept of Yanantin among the Macha of Bolivia," in *Anthropological History of Andean Polities*, ed. J. V. Murra, N. Wachtel, and J. Revel, 228–59 (Cambridge: Cambridge University Press, 1986). See also Deisy Núñez del Prado Béjar, "Yanantin y masintin: La cosmovisión andina," in *Yachay: Revista Científica de la Universidad Andina del Cusco* 1 (2008): 130–36. Similarly in Aztec philosophy, the goal is the search for balance and harmony. The *Internet Encyclopedia of Philosophy* provides this helpful insight and bibliography information. "Because of this I suggest Nahua philosophy is better understood as a 'way-seeking' rather than as a 'truth-seeking' philosophy. 'Way-seeking' philosophies such as classical Taoism, classical Confucianism, and contemporary North American pragmatism adopt as their defining question, 'What is the way?' or 'What is the path?' In contrast, 'truth-seeking' philosophies such as most European philosophies adopt as their defining question, 'What is the truth?'" See James Maffie, "Aztec Philosophy," *Internet Encyclopedia of Philosophy*, accessed May 23, 2016, http://www.iep.utm.edu/aztec/. For a discussion, see David L. Hall and Roger T. Ames, *Thinking from the Han: Self, Truth and Transcendence in Chinese and Western Culture* (Albany: SUNY Press, 1998).

23 Santiago Slabodsky has pursued this line of reasoning as a "Jew of consciousness" in his book *Decolonial Judaism: Triumphal Failures of Barbaric Thinking* (New York: Palgrave Macmillan, 2014).

24 Rosi Braidotti, *The Posthuman* (Cambridge: Polity Press, 2013).

25 For an update on the problem of the universal, see Gyula Klima, "The Medieval Problem of Universals," *Stanford Encyclopedia of Philosophy*, fall 2013 ed., accessed May 25, 2016, http://plato.stanford.edu/entries/universals-medieval/#2.

26 Mauricio Beuchot, *El problema de los universales* (Mexico City: UNAM, 1981).

27 Aníbal Quijano, "Colonialidad del poder y classification social," 174.

# 8 Colonial/Imperial Differences

*Classifying and Inventing Global Orders*
*of Lands, Seas, and Living Organisms*

## Ontologies Are Epistemic Inventions

The issue at stake in this chapter is cultural classification, which includes social class. Cultural classifications are made, not ontologically inscribed in whatever is classified. Hence, classifications are cultural because they are inventions, not representations. Classifications are epistemic building of ontologies. Although classification is not privilege of any culture or civilization in particular, this chapter focuses on the type of classifications constitutive of modernity/coloniality. That is, classifications that built and activated by the CMP. For this reason, knowledge is the paramount domain of the CMP. Economy is knowledge organizing and legitimizing praxis. *Capitalism* names a type of knowledge that justified and justifies the subjugation of noncapitalist economies.

Hence, the basic, most fundamental, decolonial task is in the domain of knowledge, since it is knowledge that holds the CMP together and that con-form subjectivities whether of theological believers or of supposed free subjects of secular subjectivities, as I explained in chapter 6. Managing and controlling knowledge means managing and controlling subjects (subjecting them/us to the CMP) in all latitudes: the individuals who created, transformed, and managed the CMP and become subjected to their own pragmatic fantasies, as well as individuals subjected by the creators and managers of the CMP. Coloniality of knowledge is the invisible side of modernity, theological in the Renaissance; secular in the Enlightenment. Coloniality of knowledge here means schooling and training from elementary to higher education as well as the mainstream media that propagates and consolidates it, and, therefore, consolidates the working of the CMP in all the domains of the enunciated (from politics to economy, from racism to sexism, from aesthetics to the hard sciences, from the social sciences to the humanities, and then all the way down to the wide population consuming news and information) as well and mainly of the enunciation. Knowing and understanding how the CMP was built, managed, and controlled are paramount to the type of decolonial tasks we (Catherine and myself) are introducing in this volume.

It is generally taken for granted that the sixteenth century in Europe was a time of unprecedented changes. In relation to what, remains to be specified. But there is no reason to dispute that perception—except that it is only half of the story. Hence, the need to be specified. Indeed, only half of the unprecedented changes are located in the history of Europe itself. The other half, the missing chapter, is less visible when sixteenth-century Europe is celebrated. It involves the invention of America, the massive slave trade, the massive appropriation of land, the pulling to pieces of the great civilizations of Mesoamerica and the Andes, the two foundational genocides of Western civilization (of Indigenous people and enslaved Africans), and the historical foundation in the Atlantic (the Americas, South and North, the Caribbean, Africa, and Europe) of a new type of economy: economic coloniality, also known as capitalism. An enormous "change" in economic knowledge both in the regional history of Europe and in the changes that European expansion imposed in non-European economies.

Colonial and imperial differences were two major strategies that remain in place until today enacted by the United States, in a discourse that at once celebrated European achievements and hid and downplayed European crimes, justified because they were committed against lesser human beings. The turmoil of the EU and the decay of the European role in the world order shall not deviate our attention from the strength of its legacies, in Europe as well as around the world. Eurocentrism is not limited to the geography of former Western Europe. The point of origination and management is Europe. But Eurocentrism has infected subjectivities all over the planet. The problem of Eurocentrism is not its right to exist next to other geopolitical *centrisms* (Pan-Africanism, Pan-Asianism, [U.S.] Americanism); it is neither to deny its contribution to the histories of human species on the planet. The problem and the aberration were and are the arrogance and the self-legitimized right (passed into and appropriated by the Anglo-U.S.) to violate its own principles of sovereignty, its own declaration of human rights, its own defense of freedom, and its own promotion of democracy. To change the world, as Karl Marx stated, it is imperative to change the hegemonic knowledge that holds the interpretation of the world, in all dimensions of knowledge, from physics and biology to philosophy and theology, from political economy to political theory, from the hegemonic conception of the human (and its derivation, posthuman) to racism and sexism. The "world" cannot be changed if the "knowledge and the knower of the world" do not change. Let's walk into the hardwired model that makes us believe the world is like epistemic and hermeneutic hegemony said it is.[1]

As it is well known, since 1945 the United States took the baton from Western Europe to maintain and update the logic of cultural classifications. In the past, enslaved Africans were as "human" as the Europeans who invented the term, as were the inhabitants of the great civilizations of Mesoamerica and the Andes. But they became lesser humans (see chapter 7). Why? Because they were classified and ranked; they were not ontologically inferior. Who classified them? What made them inferior was knowledge. And who were in control of knowledge to place knowledge holders as the model and the rest as deficient to the model? Lesser humans did not classify as such themself, in the same way that Third World people did not decide that they were in third place. When Mao Zedong gave his own version of Three World distribution, he was already accepting the logic. He changed the content, not the terms of the classification. Cultural classifications and ranking is a strategy of the rhetoric of modernity enacting coloniality by disguising *colonial differences* (that we do not see) into cultural difference (that we are taught to see). Colonial differences established and still establish hierarchy and a power differential—from the Moors and the Jews in Europe to the Blacks and the Indians in the New World; from witches in medieval Europe to the invisibility of non-European women. But not only people were classified; regions were classified as well. From the medieval T-O map to the Three Worlds division that obtained from 1952 to the end of the Cold War, colonial and imperial differences have been the invisible mechanism of ontological configurations. Classification is knowledge (epistemology) not representation of existing ranked and organized partition (ontologies). Colonial and imperial differences are fundamental tools of Western global designs.

## Knowing Is Making Distinctions in Our Praxis of Living; Cultural Classifications Are Second-Order Distinctions

Classification is something that living organisms do in the very course of their/our living. I am not referring here to scientific classifications of whatever is classified. I am referring to the vital needs of any living organism (plants, mammals, vertebrates, reptiles), to classify and make distinctions. Otherwise no living organism could survive. Human beings (in the sense I outlined in the previous chapters), classify and make distinctions in languaging. These are first-order distinctions. Scientists who before becoming scientists are human beings making first-order distinction, classify following rules scientists have established to invent second-order classifications.

Through the act of classifying, each organism—the ant in the colony, the oak in the field, the fish in water, and the human on earth—creates its own niche.[2] To create our niche as a living organism means to classify what allows us to live and protect ourselves against what causes us harm. Humans are the only living organisms that not only classify (first order) but also reflect on and set rules for our own processes of classifying and living (second order). Colonial and imperial differences are classificatory devices shaped by the actors who put in place, transformed, and managed the CMP: both were built and operated as first- and second-order classification. Classifications are enacted mainly through and by conversations, oral and written, ascertained as empirical truth and legal regulations. But classifications are fictions, neither true nor legal beyond the belief of the community that accepts them as truth and legal.

The act of classifying, therefore, demands actors and means of classification. Without classifying and distinguishing what is biologically beneficial and detrimental for the organism, the organism will die. When it comes to cultural organization among humans, the most effective means of classification are discourses: oral conversations and visual discourses imprinted in some sign system (for example, ideograms), forms of alphabetic writings, discourses based on concepts and concepts based on assumptions, systems of beliefs (both religious and scientific), diagrams, visual narratives in moving or static images, and conceptual structures (religions) and theories (science, philosophy).

In a first foundational article, Aníbal Quijano brought to light the implications of race/racism in the formation (and transformation) of the CMP. For someone like Quijano, who came from Marxism, to introduce race/

racism over class/classism was a radical move. But, given the economic and cultural history of the South American Andes, it was not unexpected. Quijano drew on insights introduced by José Carlos Mariátegui in 1928. Mariátegui, a self-proclaimed Marxist despised by orthodox Marxists of his time, argued unequivocally that the problem of the Indian was economic and based on land, not industrial exploitation. He also argued that it presupposed racism:

> The assumption that the Indian problem is ethnic is sustained by the most outmoded repertory of imperialist ideas. The concept of inferior races was useful to the white man's West for purposes of expansion and conquest. To expect that the Indian will be emancipated through a steady crossing of the aboriginal race with white immigrants is an anti-sociological naiveté that could only occur to the primitive mentality of an importer of merino sheep. The people of Asia, who are in no way superior to the Indians, have not needed any transfusion of European blood in order to assimilate the most dynamic and creative aspects of Western culture. The degeneration of the Peruvian Indian is a cheap invention of sophists who serve feudal interests.[3]

Elaborating on Mariátegui's steps, Quijano stated that the "specific colonial structure of power" that emerged out of Europe with the invasion of America was justified by "specific social discriminations which later were codified as 'racial,' 'ethnic,' 'anthropological,' or 'national,' according to the times, agents, and populations involved."[4] The key term here is for Quijano *social classification*, distinguished from *social class*. Quijano was a trained sociologist so he sees *social* classifications. I was trained as a semiotician with an inclination of the biological foundation of language (culture). So my version is *cultural* classification.[5] Social classification, for Quijano, facilitates creating hierarchies and devaluing who/what doesn't fit (for whatever and multiple reasons) the scheme of who is classifying and ranking. In the sixteenth century, purity of blood and Christian religion were the two basic criteria for valuation: the first was clearly racial, the second, theological. Colonial and imperial differences unfolded, transformed, and grew out of these basic classifications.

In a second foundational article, "Coloniality of Power, Eurocentrism, and Social Classification," Quijano opens with the following statement: "What is termed globalization is the culmination of a process that began with the constitution of America[,][6] and colonial/modern Eurocentered capitalism as new global power."[7] One of the fundamental axes of the model of power outlined by Quijano is the social classification of the world's population around the idea of race, a mental construction that expresses the basic experience of colonial domination and pervades the more important dimension of global power, including its specific rationality: Eurocentrism.[8]

Quijano returns, in this passage, to the question of race, which he labels as "a mental category of modernity." If modernity is a set of fictional narratives that justified and legitimized the actions of those who told the story and built institutions that made the story credible, then *race* is one of its conceptual fictions, effective fictions nonetheless.[9] He underscored that "the idea of race in its modern meaning does not have a known history before the colonization of America."[10]

Indeed, *race* is a mental construct that in the Spanish Renaissance associated Moors and Jews with horses. *Pureza de sangre* (pure breed) mutated into *limpieza de sangre* (pure blood) when the Spanish Inquisition began to regulate mixing among Christians, Jews, and Moors, ensuring, above all, that those Jews and Moors who remained in Castile (after the expulsion of Moors and Jews in 1492) converted to Christianity. The term *converso* was used to refer to someone who was formerly Jewish and was now Catholic. Conversos converted for all kinds of reasons: some were forced; others went willingly toward Catholicism. Similarly, the term *morisco* was applied to Moors who remained in Castile and converted to Catholicism. The obsession Christians had with pureza or limpieza de sangre was nothing less than the historical foundation of modern racism. The Inquisition was one of the first modern institutions to regulate racial classification and hierarchy.

The first seed of modern racism was based on blood and religion. The second seed was planted in the Americas. Indians and Blacks (Africans) were the Spaniards' mental constructs for homogenizing the extreme diversity of the people inhabiting the New World (where the Mayas, Aztecs, and Incas all manifested a thousand years of heterogeneous history in their three areas). The first appellation, Indian, was a symptom of Christopher Columbus's confusion. The second, Black, was a novelty in the Americas, though it had a past in the memories of Western Christians.

Regulating racism was not only a question of institutions and rules. It also involved the formation of subjectivities that learned to hate and fear their territory (physical and cultural) being invaded, and, for the conversos and moriscos, the fear of being accused of not being true Catholics. Racism in this context was placed at the conjunction of blood and religion.

Quijano put into parallel and interlocking relation the configuration of labor, of knowledge, and of intersubjectivity. The configuration and control of labor were rooted in the racialization of the labor population: that is, in first establishing and then revamping the inferiority of Africans within Christian cosmology, in order to legitimize the slave trade. The vast genocide of Indians in the first decades of colonization was not caused principally by the violence of the conquest or by the plagues the conquistadores brought from Europe. It occurred because so many American Indians were used as disposable manual labor and forced to work until death. The elimination of this colonial practice did not end until the defeat of the *encomenderos* in the middle of the sixteenth century.[11]

Quijano sees in the New World the formation of a new pattern of labor management that involved the confluence of slavery, serfdom, petty commodity production, reciprocity, and wages—all labor centered and managed according to the interests of the holder of capital—and the opening of a global (a truly planetary commerce—unknown until then—began to be established connecting the Atlantic and the Pacific) marketplace for New World commodities. First to be commodified were the products of extractivism, gold, and silver; later came the products of the plantation economy in the Caribbean, both insular and continental (today, Brazil and Colombia). None of the existing forms of labor in Europe remained as they were, in their singularity. The vast opportunities for land appropriation/expropriation that the New World offered, combined with the new pattern of management of labor, created the conditions for a radical transformation in sixteenth-century Europe,[12] but also in China, with gold and silver from the colonies reaching China through Manila.[13]

For Quijano the fundamental link in the historical foundation of coloniality of power was established by the emergence of economic coloniality (capitalism in liberal and Marxist vocabulary) and the coloniality of knowledge. International law legitimized imperial appropriation and expropriation of land, and racism (epistemic social classification) legitimized imperial slave trade and exploitation of labor to produce commodities for the emerging global market. The radical shift introduced in the Atlantic commercial circuit through the massive appropriation of land and the massive exploitation of labor runs parallel to the radical epistemic shift introduced by Renaissance men in Europe. The epistemic revolution that was taking place in the European Renaissance was extended to the New World during colonization. Four universities following the European model were founded in the sixteenth century (in Santo Domingo, Mexico, Peru, and Córdoba), and one in the first half of the seventeenth century (Harvard). Colleges and convents abounded. The consequences were similar to that of the coloniality of economy: just as economic coloniality made destitute existing economic formations, so too did the coloniality of knowledge make destitute existing epistemic formations. Here, the narrative of modernity, of the renaissance era, established two of its pillars: the affirmation of a new type of economy, and the expansion of Renaissance knowledge into unknown territories until the end of the sixteenth century. As a matter of fact, America was an epistemic invention of the European Renaissance: no continent named America existed to be discovered. The name, invented after the name of Italian explorer Americo Vespucci, was an epistemic expropriation of the names the various civilizations of the continent had for their own territories. Like today's imperial monuments, "America" is a monument in litigation. Quijano summarizes these aspects of the colonial matrix of power as follows: "As the center of global capitalism, Europe not only had control of the world market, but was also able to impose its colonial dominance over all the regions of the populations of the planet, incorporating them into its world-system and its specific model of power."[14] The incorporation was above all epistemic, which justified the political and economic incorporation.

Colonial epistemic dominance over all regions of the planet was not achieved in the sixteenth and seventeenth centuries at once. From 1500 to 1650, approximately, there was certainly a global flow of commodities and of people, but the epistemically dominated regions were the regions of the Atlantic (the New World, Africa, and Europe). While the entire planet was mapped according to Western Christian perspectives and interests at the end of the fifteenth century and in the first half of the sixteenth,[15] it was only during the seventeenth century that the global economic flow increased, with the foundation of the British and Dutch East India Companies ("Indias Orientales" for the Spanish and Portuguese).

By the second half of the sixteenth century (and through all of the seventeenth), the world was totally mapped by European cartographers at their will. No one else on the planet participated. Their own territoriality was ignored and expropriated.[16] Cartography was one of the main weapons of epistemic control and racial classification. In many seventeenth-century maps, the classification and ranking of the planet's population appears on the cartouche in the four corners of the map.[17] In the upper-left corner appears Europe, well dressed and resting in a *locus amoenus*. In the upper-right corner, Asia is shown, sometimes seated on an elephant and sometimes on a camel. In a culture where writing goes from left to right, left is the marked end. In newspapers today, the relevant news appears in the upper-left corner. The two corners at the bottom of the map, America and Africa, exchange positions on different maps: sometimes Africa is on the bottom right; sometimes it is on the bottom left. In every case, Africa and America were personified by seminaked women seated on animals less noble than elephant or camels. In that overall epistemic-cartographic appropriation of the planet, political and economic expansions were routed from then to the twenty-first century. Dewesternization, however, is disturbing the fictional ontology of planetary Euro-centered partitions.

## Coloniality of Classifications: Colonial and Imperial Differences

We now have some of the elements necessary for understanding the makings, transformations, and consequences of colonial and imperial differences. Both were built upon racial classification, both of people and of planetary regions. Later in this book we will see how sexual classifications are results from enacting colonial and imperial differences as well.

All the narratives created by missionaries, men of letters, and soldiers (and, in the eighteenth century, travelers)[18] *about* the New World and, later on, *about* Africa and Asia and their inhabitants are framed by the assumed cultural differences between the European narrators and the regions and people being narrated. But these cultural differences, as discussed above, also became an indication of the lesser humanity of the narrated people and regions. In eighteenth-century Europe, it was assumed that the New World was indeed younger than the Old World, as revealed by the term *natural world* (see chapter 7 on the invention of *nature*).[19] This mode of ranking and classifying the planet and its people was translated into map-making practices. What was really being created here was the *colonial difference*—an epistemic mechanism with ontological consequences. Nature was severed from Man/Human and existing knowledge in the great civilizations that Europe reduced to "Indians" was ignored. Recently, biologists, anthropologists, and botanists are "discovering" that Gaia is a living system, but Pachamama was ignored; they are discovering now that "plants know," which Pueblos Originarios (First Nations) of the Americas knew forever, but it was ignored by missionaries, explorers, and eighteenth- and nineteenth-century European scientists.[20]

One such ontological consequence was embedded in the beliefs and assumptions of the languages and actors enacting the colonial difference. A particularly essential assumption in this regard is the mimetic or denotative philosophy of language that Christian theologians and, later on, secular philosophers inherited from Plato.[21] The "essence" of this philosophy of language presupposes that language represents something that is not language itself. Thus, the colonial difference makes us believe that the differences set up between the narrator, the narration, and the events and entities described and narrated exist *outside* the narrative that describes and tells the stories. Western philosophy of language is based on the belief and assumption of the mimetic or denotative function of language; decolonial thinking assumes that it is through language and sign systems that colonial differences are created and hidden at the same time. The rhetoric of modernity operates on denotation, and since there is no visible colonial difference to be denoted, then the colonial difference ontologically doesn't exist. Decolonial thinking looks for what denotation and re-presentations hide. Consequently, the concept of *the colonial difference* is a decolonial concept that brings to the surface what the rhetoric of modernity blurs.

The colonial differences I've been describing here are hidden strategies in the constitution of the CMP. They are located at the junction of knowledge, subjectivity, and racial classification. When racial classifications are not only descriptive but also hierarchical, racial classification turns into racism. It served European intellectuals, philosophers, and men of letters (and the integrated society at large) well to implement the colonial difference and racialize (i.e., to describe as inferior) both the Indigenous of the New World and Africans after doing the same with Moors and Jews; and later to encompass the Asian continent. Racialization of Moors and Jews served well to affirm Christian political, territorial-economic, and religious identity. In the New World it was necessary to legitimize land dispossession, slavery, and slave trade. And these, as Quijano argues, were necessary to organize the type of labor required by the conquest and colonization of the New World. Colonial differences that prop up racism were enunciated by actors in an institutional position for the purpose of asserting *their* enunciation over the enunciation of whoever is being classified. The European Renaissance was a time and a place where meaning making ran parallel to money making. The two reinforced each other, and continue to reinforce each other today, though some significant changes are taking place. I will return to these changes in chapter 9.

From the sixteenth century to the twenty-first, colonial differences did not stop being amplified, modified, and reproduced. The scenario of their persistence has been clearly described by Michel-Rolph Trouillot: "By North Atlantic universals, I mean words that project the North Atlantic experience on a universal scale that they themselves helped to create. North Atlantic universals are particulars that have gained a degree of universality, chunks of human history that have become historical standards. *They do not describe the world; they offer visions of the world.* They appear to refer to things as they exist, but because they are rooted in a particular history, they evoke multiple layers of sensibilities, persuasions, cultural assumptions, and ideological choices tied to that localized history."[22]

As Hegel anticipated in his narrative of universal history, the United States would be the future Europe of her time. Hence, the North Atlantic regional experience, as Trouillot observes, projected itself through its vocabulary onto a universal scale—a universal scale that did not exist prior to the words that created it and that was the creation of the words themselves. Thus, colonial differences do not describe the world but offer a *vision* of the world, falsely projected onto a universal scale. Like the world map, colonial narratives, descriptions, and arguments appropriated the world and condensed it into a house of *universal fictions*. We are still inside that house.

Universal fictions operate on our sensibilities; they have an *aesthesic* power, affecting our senses, driving our emotions and desires. For this reason, it is through knowledge that subjectivities (emotions, senses) were and still are managed, though contestations, dissenting, and delinking are increasing. It is this increase that opened up dewesternization and decolonization/decoloniality (see chapter 5, "Modernity and Globalism"). Trouillot continues:

> They come to us loaded with aesthetic and stylistic sensibilities; religious and philosophical persuasions; cultural assumptions ranging from what it means to be a human being to the proper relationship between humans and the natural world; ideological choices ranging from the nature of the political to its possibilities of transformation. There is no unanimity within the North Atlantic itself on any of these issues, but there is a shared history of how these issues have been and should be debated, and these words carry that history. And yet, since they are projected as universals, they deny their localization, the sensibilities and the history from which they spring.[23]

Epistemic colonial differences projected to a universal scale disguise the locality of their enunciation. For that reason, the geopolitics of knowing and understanding (and its corollary, the geopolitics of knowledge) is another helpful decolonial concept that serves to unveil the geohistorical location of abstract universals. But once universal fictions have been installed in the imagination of the people, in Europe and outside of Europe, they operate as *realities*—that is, as ontologies that are described and represented through and in language.

Colonial differences mutate in their content, all the while keeping their enunciation hidden. If, in the sixteenth century, purity of blood was one criterion for racialization, the bodies (actors) that enunciated this criterion were the bodies who wanted to keep their blood pure. However, the principles of limpieza de sangre to be defended had two different trajectories: one in the Iberian Peninsula and the other in the New World.

The first trajectory, already mentioned, is the origin of both colonial and imperial differences. If the Moors and the Jews were both communities expelled from the Iberian Peninsula (or forced to convert), they were not equal at the social level. The Moors were heirs of powerful Muslim caliphates, while the Jews were nomadic people without a central governing institution. In 711, Muslim forces invaded the Iberian Peninsula and in seven years had fully conquered it. The peninsula became one of the great Muslim civilizations, reaching its summit with the Umayyad Caliphate of Córdoba in the tenth century. Muslim rule gradually declined, however, and ended in 1492, when Granada was conquered. The Jews had a long history in the Iberian Peninsula but had no organization similar to the Umayyad Caliphate.

Purity of blood connected to religion, as seen above, was a fiction effective in tracing dividing lines between those who traced the lines and those who didn't (those who were "traced"). It was not only a question of the physical expulsion of the Moors and the Jews. It involved the kind of reasoning that *justified* the expulsion, a reasoning based on a hierarchical division: the colonial difference. The dismantling of the Umayyad Caliphate of Córdoba was similar to the dismantling of the Tlatoanate and the Incanate in the New World, except that the first occurred in the Iberian Peninsula, while the second occurred in the New World.

Colonial differences were established within Europe (against Muslims and Jews) and outside of Europe (Africa and the invented America). We might call them inward and outward colonial differences, respectively. The outward colonial difference projected on enslaved Africans had its own history, though, for enslaved Africans were not colonized. They were enslaved and brought into European imperial projects (by Portugal, Spain, Holland, France, and England). Africans were already cast out of Christian cosmology, for Africans were considered to be descendants of Ham, Noah's cursed son, while Shem was related to Asia, and Japheth to Europe. (Of course, this cosmology was *only* meaningful for Christians; it had no meaning or relevance for Africans, or anyone else who was not Christian.)

That Africa was the place that provided a massive enslavement market for European Christians in the sixteenth century was not only a result of its distance from the New World but also a result of the *aesthesis*, the sensibility of modern subjects and subjectivity. In other words, the making of colonial differences works in two directions: it makes the racialized person inferior to the person racializing, and it allows the racializing person to confirm him- or herself in his or her belief. Once enslaved and in the New World, the status of Africans changed dramatically. It was as if the Middle Passage had stripped them of Ham's stigma and converted them into ontological slaves—that is, "slaves by nature." Africans in the New World became "Black," and were marginalized alongside "Indians." The historical foundation of the outward colonial difference (epistemic and ontological) was projected onto Blacks and Indians in the New World.

The imperial difference (epistemic and ontological) was another creation of the Renaissance Man/Human. It was projected on the Ottoman Sultanate, the inheritor of the earlier Muslim caliphates. How does the imperial difference work? For one, it is projected onto people and civilizations that were not colonized. However, from the perspective of the emerging universal fictions, the Ottoman Sultanate was degraded in the narratives of the emerging Christian Empire of the Iberian Peninsula, centered mainly in Castile. The imperial difference meant that the Roman Empire's legacies and emperors (such as Charles V, Emperor of the Holy Roman Empire of the German Nations) were construed, by its own intellectual cast, as being above Suleiman the Magnificent, the Ottoman Sultan. Once the colonial and imperial differences were established, they would remain in place and become distinctive features of the history of the modern/colonial world order.

The eighteenth century witnessed interesting mutations of imperial and colonial differences. The mutations were part of the wave of decolonization (known as *revolution* in the United States and Haiti, and *independence* in the rest) in the New World and the waves of revolutions in Europe (the Great and French Revolutions). First of all, as Edward Said has shown, European philologists mainly, but also travelers and writers, engaged in the construction of the Orient.[24] The Orient was a mixture of colonial and imperial differences, for these differences are not ontologically fixed entities but rather changing contents of the rhetoric of modernity and the logic of coloniality. Colonial and imperial differences are strategies not ontologies.

Orientalism did well to rebuild the rhetoric of modernity around the civilizing mission that displaced, but did not replace, the Christian mission of conversion of the previous centuries. Orientalism ran parallel to the British and Dutch India Companies in South Asia and Southeast Asia, and prepared the way for many things to come: among them, British settlement in India by the mid-nineteenth century, and British (cum-French, and U.S.-supported) engagement in the Opium Wars of the 1840s and late 1850s. Orientalism, then, was a transformation of the colonial difference (now projected onto South Asia and Southeast Asia) and of the imperial difference (projected toward China). China, like the Ottoman Sultanate, was not colonized but was nonetheless disrupted by coloniality. Coloniality, in these two instances, was manifested in the creation and transformation of imperial differences.

The mutation of colonial and imperial differences also transformed the racial configuration upon which both were created and maintained. Once secularism displaced theology, racial configurations mutated from purity of blood and religious conflicts to skin color and "civilizing" ranking. Carolus Linnaeus's descriptive classification of skin colors by continents (Yellow in Asia, Black in Africa, Red in America, and White in Europe) was taken up by Immanuel Kant, who metamorphosed Linnaeus's descriptive classification into a racial ranking. Kant's ranking mirrors the ranking that we saw in the maps of the seventeenth century.[25] The reconfiguration of racism in turn served well to establish a racial world order based on colonial and imperial differences. Parallel to Orientalism was the making of the South of Europe. The South of Europe (the Spanish and Portuguese Empires, the Italian Renaissance, and Greece, the former cradle of Western civilization) was downgraded, losing its status as the Heart of Europe. What we have here is the creation, display, and enactment of the inward of the imperial difference.

Colonial and imperial differences were and still are powerful weapons of CMP. The making of the South of Europe was driven mainly by imperial differences. In the U.S. the colonial difference is manifested in the growing presence of white supremacy over the long-lasting Black/White divide and in the growing presence of Latinxs in the United States and of Trans/Queer/Two Spirits People in Europe, the U.S., and Canada.[26] While the imperial difference is manifested in the increasing conflicts on dewesternization and re-westernization: Ukraine, Syria, North Korea, Venezuela are the focus where the imperial differences are at work. In the twenty-first century, southern Europe was remapped by the colonial difference: Greece was colonized, not by settler colonialists but by EU's institutions. All the reports on the negotiations with the government of Alexis Tsipras are clear indication that Greeks are not seen and are not heard. That is basically how the colonial difference works—dehumanizing, disavowing, relegating equal human beings in front of you.

In the second half of the twentieth century and the first decades of the twenty-first, all of us on the planet have been witnessing not only a reconfiguration of colonial and imperial differences in an attempt to maintain control of the global order but also, and more significantly, a radical awakening and response to the wounds of imperial and colonial differences. Indeed, I have described rewesternization as the reconfiguration of colonial and imperial differences, and dewesternization and decoloniality as the awakening, resurgence, and reemergence of opposition, occurring at every level of the CMP. This resurgence and reemergence are driven by the wounds of racism and sexism—the two pillars of the hierarchical classification of people. The third pillar is the racialization and hierarchizing of regions (i.e., the invention of the Third World, developed and underdeveloped countries; emerging economies).

Colonial and imperial differences were and still are fundamental in securing the Eurocentered perceptions of the totality of knowledge, in driving westernizing designs for five centuries and in propelling rewesternization. Or, you can read it also in reverse: Eurocentrism and the North Atlantic were and are the consequences of the effective manufacturing of colonial and imperial differences. Rewesternization is still operating under the Western accumulation of meaning and money, during five centuries, that secures the accumulated meaning. Colonial and imperial difference were/are not *epistemicide* as the metaphor circulates today, for if they were, we would not have the potent and energetic resurgence of Indigenous thinking and doing through the Americas; and we would not have the legacies of Afro-Caribbean philosophy and politics that we have today. "You cannot kill ideas" is a dictum whose source is not well known. You can kill people—genocide—but you cannot kill ideas. The analogy is misleading for you could sideline and repress praxis of living, doing, and thinking but you cannot kill them. That is why resurgences and re-existences are flourishing today; there cannot be resurgence from death. The worldwide reemergence and revaluation of what modernity disavowed are the energy of re-existence that can no longer be suppressed, unless by nuclear annihilation. Ideas die by themselves when there are no longer actors that need them. But they cannot be killed while they are embodied by people living praxis who need them. Disbelief in the privilege of Eurocentrism (embedded in North Atlanticism) is mounting and with it grows also the embeddedness of decoloniality in our (those who identify with) praxis of living.

This is the theme of the next two chapters and of the conclusion to part II.

## Notes

1   *The Darker Side of the Renaissance: Literacy, Territoriality and Colonization* was my first effort to change the terms of hermeneutic conversations. I did not yet know of coloniality (CMP), but I was well aware of the first chapter of Western colonialism.

2   Eric H. Lenneberg, *Biological Foundations of Language* (New York: John Wiley, 1967).

3   Jóse Carlos Mariátegui, *Seven Interpretive Essays on Peruvian Reality,* Essay 2, 1928, accessed May 21, 2016, https://www.marxists.org/archive/mariateg/works/7 -interpretive-essays/essayo2.htm.

4   Aníbal Quijano, "Colonialidad y modernidad/racionalidad," *Perú Indígena* 13, no. 29 (1992): 11–20, accessed May 21, 2016, https://problematicasculturales.files .wordpress.com/2015/04/quijano-colonialidad y-modernidad-racionalidad.pdf.

5   Erick H. Lenneberg, *Biological Foundations of Language*, especially chap. 8 (New York: John Wiley, 1967); Humberto Maturana and Francisco Varela, *Autopiesis and Cognition* (Dordrecht: D. Reidel, 1972).

6   *Constitution* here means that America was not an entity discovered by Columbus, since America did not exist. It was invented about a decade after the confused Columbus landed on one of the Caribbean Islands. See Edmundo O'Gorman, *The Invention of America: An Inquiry into the Historical Nature of the New World and the Meaning of Its History* (Bloomington: Indiana University Press, [1958] 1961). See also Immanuel Wallerstein and Aníbal Quijano, "Americanity as a Concept or the Americas in the Modern-World System," *Institute for Scientific Information* 134 (1992).

7   Although Quijano maintains the term *capitalism*, I would say in this case *economic coloniality* for reasons that I will explain below in conjunction with *imperial difference.*

8   Aníbal Quijano, "Coloniality of Power, Eurocentrism, and Social Classification," [2000] in *Coloniality at Large: Latin America and the Postcolonial Debate*, ed. Mabel Moraña, Enrique Dussel, and Carlos A. Jáuregui, 186–24 (Durham, NC: Duke University Press, 2013).

9   Michel-Rolph Trouillot, "North Atlantic Universals: Analytic Fictions, 1492–1945," *South Atlantic Quarterly* 101, no. 4 (2002): 839–58, accessed December 8, 2016, http://saq.dukejournals.org/content/101/4/839.citation.

10  Aníbal Quijano, "Coloniality of Power, Eurocentrism, and Social Classification," 181.

11  *Encomendero* was a settler who received a grant of land and "Indians"—meaning, indigenous people to provide the labor; Aníbal Quijano, "Coloniality of Power, Eurocentrism, and Social Classification," 186.

12  Carlo Cipolla, *Money in Sixteenth-Century Florence* (Berkeley: University of California Press, 1989).

13  Dennis O. Flynn and Arturo Giraldez, *China and the Birth of Globalization in the 16th Century* (Farnham, UK: Ashgate, 2010).

14  Aníbal Quijano, "Coloniality of Power, Eurocentrism, and Social Classification," 188.

15  By the Treaty of Tordesillas (1494) Pope Alexander VI divided Indias Occidentales (the New World and related ocean's waters) and offered them to the monarch of Spain and Portugal. In 1529 the monarchs of Spain and Portugal divided among themselves Indias Orientales (East and Southeast Asia). Macao, Manila, and Formosa (today Taiwan) were the same Iberian post in the regions. The British East Indian Company and the Dutch East Indian Company were founded in 1601 and 1602 respectively.

16  See my *The Darker Side of the Renaissance*, chap. 5.

17  Accessed July 21, 2017, http://previews.123rf.com/images/megastocker /megastocker1111/megastocker111100150/11321440-High-quality-Antique-Map -Nicolas-Visscher-1652-Stock-Photo-map-world-old.jpg.

18  Mary Louise Pratt, *Imperial Eyes: Travel Writing and Transculturation* (London: Routledge, 1995).

19  Antonello Gerbi, *La Disputa del Nuovo Mondo. Storia di una polemica (1750–1900)* (Milan: Adelphi, 2000), accessed May 20, 2016, https://nuevomundo.revues.org/409.

20  See, for instance, the narratives of today in Nanuya-Colombian Abel Rodriguez, "El árbol de la abundancia," https://www.youtube.com/watch?v=DTXyXAqWEss. His knowledge is not university schooling and training but living with the plants, talking to the plants. In the scientific arena, see the interesting and well-written account by botanist Daniel Chamovitz, *What a Plant Knows: A Field Guide to the Senses* (New York: Farrar, Strauss and Giroux, 2013).

21  Raphael Demos, "Plato's Philosophy of Language," *Journal of Philosophy* 61, no. 20 (1964): 595–610, accessed July 27, 2017, http://www.jstor.org/stable/pdf/2023441 .pdf.

22  Michel-Rolph Trouillot, "North Atlantic Universals" (italics mine).

23  Trouillot, "North Atlantic Universals," 848.

24  Edward Said, *Orientalism* (New York: Pantheon House, 1978).

25  Emmanuel Chukwudi Eze, "The Color of Reason," in *African Postcolonial Philosophy* (Hoboken, NJ: Wiley-Blackwell, 1997).

26  See Sandeep Bakshi, Suhraiya Jivraj, and Silvia Posocco, eds., *Decolonizing Sexualities: Transnational Perspectives, Critical Interventions* (Oxford: Counterpress, 2016). Raúl Moarquech Ferrera-Balanquet, ed., *Erotic Sovereignty at the Decolonial Crossroads* (Durham, NC: Duke University Press, forthcoming).

# 9 Eurocentrism and Coloniality

*The Question of Totality of Knowledge*

## Imperial Eurocentrism

Eurocentrism is an epistemic phenomenon that received its name from the territorial location of actors, languages, and institutions that managed to project as universal their own world sense and worldview. The projection established the idea of modernity and its darker and hidden side: coloniality. Eurocentrism refers to the enunciation, the flows, and the domains constituting CMP (see chapter 6) *as if the* domains were mirrors of the world and the enunciations/enunciators the site where "true representation" of the world takes place.[1] It was not in itself misguided. All existing civilizations considered themselves the hub of the world. The problem was (and still is in its extension to Americanism and globalism) the pretense to be the planetary center and the desire and design to homogenize the world to its image and likelihood. Storytelling about the creation of the world and the ethnic group telling the story were centered on the ethnic group telling the story: Chinese-centric, Persian-centric, Islam-centric, Maya-centric, Inca-centric, Egyptian-centric, Mali-centric, Christian-centric, and so forth. What happened, for reasons explained in chapter 8, was Christian-centric knowledge that guided the invention of America toward the first image of the world composed of four continents.[2]

The enormous relevance of European cartography and its naming privileges must not, for all that, be underestimated. Tracing lines and naming were fundamental in anchoring an imaginary based on mapping masses of land and water, and complemented by the concurrent circumnavigation of the planet. No other civilization had done this before, or, if anyone had (as it has been argued that the Vikings, the Chinese, and the Africans had), those navigations and encounters with an unknown land had not generated, and apparently did not need, a cartographic record of the entire planet (*orbis ter-rarum*) and an alphabetic narrative in Latin and in Western European languages. It was knowledge that both prompted and guided European narratives promoting their own "discoveries." Neither Chinese nor Vikings and Africans (also invoked to have arrived to the continent before 1492), and even less Incas and Aztecs had the will, need, and knowledge to promote their own deeds to the most important event since the creation of the world, as told by Francisco López de Gómara, Adam Smith, and Karl Marx.[3] It was not the ontology of the event but the description, narratives and celebrations of the event, by Europeans, that confused what happened with the narration and explanation of what had happened.

Christian Europeans' conception and image of the world *were only their own conception and image of the world, and not the representation of a geohistorical ontology of the world.* This is what coloniality of knowledge means, and how coloniality of knowledge orients both geopolitical designs and body-political subjectivities (e.g., our senses, our emotions, our cosmo-vivencias). Obviously, Western Christian Europeans had the right to build their own image of the world, like anybody else who had done so before them. But it was an aberration to pretend and act accordingly as if *their specific image of the world and their own sense of totality was the same for any- and everybody else on the planet.* The strong belief that their knowledge covered the totality of the known brought about the need to devalue, diminish, and shut off any other totality that might endanger an epistemic totalitarianism in the making. Out of these needs emerged the colonial and imperial differences explored in the previous chapter (chapter 8).

It was from the Eurocentered epistemic assumptions that their New World or their America was the continent inhabited, according to their beliefs, by people without knowledge of God. Which was true, but it really did not matter at all, except for Europeans' coloniality of knowledge. In addition, the slave trade forcefully brought to the new continent the descendants of Ham, who was for Christians and for Christians only, Noah's willful son. Africa had already been devalued in the Christian imaginary; now it became entangled in the planetary imaginary slowly implanted by the colonial difference at work. The Christian continental imaginary was the necessary theological condition for the emergence of coloniality, and therefore of the colonial difference. The colonial difference tied up with the narrative of Renaissance *modernity*. This particular narrative of modernity presupposed a world that was new, or the New World—a name that introduced into the Christian trilogy (Asia, Africa, and Europe) the fourth continent created by God (but previously unknown to Christians).

The colonial difference—built upon the devaluation of enslaved Africans and ancient civilizations in Anahuac, Tawantinsuyu, Mayab, Turtle Island—was projected over Asia as soon as the Spanish, the Portuguese, and, at the beginning of the seventeenth century, the Dutch and the British began their incursions into South and Southeast Asia. Europe (Rome) became the center of the enunciation, and Eurocentrism was well on its way to existence. Euro-American-centrism and the North Atlantic (when London and the Greenwich Meridian replaced Rome as the center) are specifications that register superficial changes in the management and control of the enunciation and the enunciated, in the maneuvering of the flows of the CMP.

## Eurocentrism, the Colonial Matrix of Power, and Western Civilization

The geohistorical territory known as Europe was not an existing entity in which knowledge was produced, but one of the results of knowledge making itself: the enunciated is always invented by the enunciators (actors, institutions, languages), rather than the other way around. Humberto Maturana's dictum here acquires its full meaning: We do not see what there is; we see what we see.[4] For that reason, the materiality of the world (its ontology) is shaped by epistemology (world sense projected into storytelling and argument [logos]) coded, in every culture and/or civilization, as knowledge (epistemology). If I am not careful, I can break my nose running into a "standing piece of living wood" (ontology), but a *tree* is another story—it is a particular name given to the standing piece of living wood that occupies a particular place in human imagination who invented the concept of "nature." When it comes to *democracy*, *being*, *art*, and *religion*, the same principle applies, though the circumstances change: they depend on how universes of meaning are built. The CMP is one such powerful universe of meaning. It has "selected" from the vast invisible energy and visible materiality of the world what we should *see* (e.g., tree, America), from the imaginary of human beings what we should *believe* (e.g., democracy, religion), from all of human creation and effort what we should *enjoy* (e.g., art) and *accept* (e.g., capitalism or economic coloniality). The CMP created a powerful fiction, marked by a single totality.[5]

Quijano's reflections on the totality of knowledge focused on the eighteenth century; however, the eighteenth century is the logical consequence of European theological history of ideas and visions since the renaissance. The compound concept of *modernity/rationality* in his formulation was one of the foundational assumptions of the Western image of the totality of knowledge. Modernity/rationality is founded in both theological and secular assumptions. In that regard Quijano states that

> Western European modernity/rationality is constituted not only [by] disputatious dialogue with the church and with religion, but also in the very process of restructuration of power, on the one hand, in capitalist and urban social relations; and, on the other, in the colonization of the rest of the world.
>
> What does not cease to surprise, however, is that Europe succeeded in imposing that "mirage" upon the practical totality of the cultures that it colonized; and much more, that this chimera is still so attractive to so many.[6]

This, in a nutshell, is the question of the totality of knowledge. In 1500, theological Christianity was one among many cosmologies of the planet. The tendency to see their own epistemic totality as *the* epistemic totality established the foundations for the secular totality of knowledge in the eighteenth century at a moment when Europe was expanding all over the planet and secular science and philosophy were consolidating such beliefs. The question of the totality of knowledge therefore shows the double face of modernity/coloniality: (a) the consolidation of Eurocentrism as a system of interconnected knowledges (e.g., the epistemic domains of CMP: theology, philosophy, science, politics, economics, biology, culture; and (b) the dismissal and disavowal of principles of knowing and created knowledge in non-European languages and non-European systems of belief.

*Coloniality* is more than a word: it is shorthand for a complex configuration of building, managing, and controlling enacted by Western actors who, on the one hand, figure themselves as subjects guided by a totality of knowledge that they themselves have in fact generated and, on the other, their subjectivities (emotioning, sensing, reasoning) is shaped by what they themselves have created. Technology and Artificial Intelligence are today facets of the domain (coloniality of knowledge) that is taking over, including the actors and institutions generating them. Similar observations could be made on for instance global health or global ecology. This configuration underpins the CMP, with all its manifestations and mutations.[7]

Let's pause to understand the meaning *of matrix*. The definition provided by the Merriam-Webster dictionary is as follows:

**ma·trix**

*noun*\'mā-triks\

Something (such as a situation or a set of conditions), in which something else develops or forms.[8]

*Matrix* could then be visualized as a "structure" or a "flow of energies" that unfolds, grows, and transforms itself and all that falls into the structural management or force of the energies' flow. In more literal terms, Western Christianity mutated into Europe (the territory of Western Christians), and the European Atlantic monarchic state (from the sixteenth to the mid-eighteenth century) mutated into the builder and manager of coloniality (i.e., of the matrix of the flow of energies). This line of argumentation brought Quijano to see Eurocentrism as an epistemic rather than a geographic issue: "The Euro-centered capitalist (e.g., economic coloniality) was elaborated and formalized by the Europeans and established in the world as an exclusively European product and as *a universal paradigm of knowledge and of relations between humanity and the rest of the world*."[9]

To understand such tight formulation it suffices, for the time being, to speculate about two crucial institutions that secured the coloniality of knowledge and coloniality of being: the university and the museum. The institution called *university* is a Western medieval invention that runs parallel to the church. When I say *Western* all over my argument, I mean "west of Jerusalem," where Western Christians were dwelling and created the institution. The University of Bologna is considered one of the first universities of the Western world, founded around 1088.[10] The *Western world* (that is, Western Christendom) was not the only region that created institutions of learning, though. Every great civilizational complex of the time (China, India, Persia, the Aztecs, the Incas, the African Kingdom) had its own such institutions.

To take just a few examples: Nalanda, in India, was devoted to the study of Buddhism but also to other branches of learning, including health, astronomy, governance, and creative imagination (now called *art* in Western education, though in Bologna the term *artist* referred to scholars of medicine). In China, the Six Arts (in contemporary vocabulary: rites, music, archery, charioteering—today's "driving schools"—calligraphy, and mathematics) originated in Confucian philosophy. The ancient Aztec civilization had two schooling institutions, the Telpochalli and the Calmemac. The first was devoted mainly to military training for the *macehuales* (people not belonging to the ruling elite). The second was devoted to military training as well as to other aspects of Aztec life (writing, song and dance, astronomy, governance, manners). Islam, for its part, was experiencing its golden age at the time of the foundation of the University of Bologna.

Regarding Islam, the *Encyclopedia Britannica* reports that "the renaissance of Islamic culture and scholarship developed largely under the ʿAbbāsid administration in eastern Islam and later under the Umayyads in western Islam, mainly in Spain, between 800 and 1000. This latter period, the golden age of Islamic scholarship, was largely a period of translation and interpretation of Classical thoughts and their adaptation to Islamic theology and philosophy. The period also witnessed the introduction and assimilation of Hellenistic, Persian, and Hindu mathematics, astronomy, algebra, trigonometry, and medicine into Muslim culture."[11]

Museums are not as old as universities. But their role in consolidating the enunciation and, therefore, the coloniality of knowledge and being is enormous. At the same time, cracks exist where decoloniality can emerge, like the flowers in Middelburg, Netherlands, that shoot up from small cracks in the cement. Le Louvre was established in 1792, the British Museum in 1753. Essentially, museums are also a European invention—an invention of the second modernity, the Enlightenment—while universities were established in the Middle Ages and transformed during the Renaissance.

The Greek word *museion* means "place of study" or "library" and was translated into Latin as *museum*. The word comes from the Greek word *muse*, used to describe the seven daughters (the seven muses) of Mnemosyne, the goddess of memory. This kind of reverence toward the museum space as a place of learning was instrumental in building Western civilization's profile and identity, as we know it today. In this sense, the institution called *museum* could only collect artifacts representative of "other" memories; it could not collect the memories contained in those artifacts, removed and displaced from their cultural environment, their owners, and authors.[12]

Museums and universities are foundational institutions run by actors ingrained in and subjected to Western beliefs and effects of the totality of knowledge. But in the twenty-first century, both institutions can be appropriated to redirect the trend and decolonize and/or dewesternize the acceptance of the totalitarian totality of knowledge—that is, to rehabilitate the knowledge and ways of knowing that Western museums and universities displaced and transformed into objects that could be collected in museums or used to maintain colonial and imperial differences (e.g., Orientalism, area studies).

Quijano's critique of the modern concept of *totality* complements his critique of knowledge *located* in the individual, the "knowing subject" in front of a detached object (society, nature, the cosmos, other persons), isolated from the community of knowers. Although this critique could be found among Eurocentered critiques of modernity (psychoanalysis, early Frankfurt School), Quijano's open up the gates for decolonial critique of modernity and the consequent generation of decolonial knowledges.

## Eurocentrism: A Totalitarian Totality and the Reemergence of the Disavowed (Decoloniality)

*Totality* has two trajectories, and both have the same source: the epistemic distinction between knowing subject and known object. One trajectory runs through the inward history of Europe (for example, Max Horkheimer's notion of *traditional theory*); the object to be known is identified within a European sociohistorical context, and the knowing subject is assumed to be the European knower. The hall of fame that, together with universities and museums, consolidates and grounds the European knower is a hall of fame of thinkers (philosophers, theologians, writers, astronomers, mathematicians, legal theorists, "artists," etc.) from Greece and Rome all the way through to the European Middle Ages, the Renaissance, and the Enlightenment, the archive of Western knowledge and culture. But the encounter and invention of America, and the emergence of the Atlantic commercial circuits, brought a new dimension and the second trajectory into being. The assumption that knowledge is based on a subject/object relation suddenly made the rest of the world an extended object of European knowledge. Thus, European sense of the totality of knowledge and its totalitarian effect was devastating for the dignity and humanness of people in the rest of the planet. It was like everything that existed before Greece was stopped in their time and overcome by the new time, the time of the Renaissance and the Enlightenment. That was the meaning of the "New World." Once Western Christians arrived to the continent, the past stopped and became a New World in two senses: it was new in the sense that it was not known, and it was new because it was the new beginning of the continent: America was that new beginning.

Chronologically, the most critical moment in the process of fashioning the image of epistemic totality and ignoring or disguising its locality was the theological planetary extension through European history between the sixteenth and mid-eighteenth centuries. Within the reduced history of Europe itself, theology was the master epistemic code, governing the humanistic disciplines through the trivium and quadrivium system. It was theology and the trivium and quadrivium that together organized the structure of knowledge not only in Europe but also in the newly founded universities of the New World. Remember, for 250 years, since 1500, European planetary extension had unfolded mainly in the Americas; Dutch and British incursions into South and Southeast Asia had been mainly commercial. The starting point of British colonization in India is dated to 1858, in the midst of a second Opium War with China, when the Crown of England dissolved the East Indian Company and took over colonial management.

Theology, then, was the overarching cosmological frame for Western Christendom, which would become Europe. The trivium and quadrivium that framed humanistic high learning at its universities looked something like this:

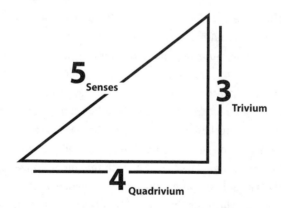

As this diagram shows, our body and mind interact with its niche through the five senses. The mind (reason) "applies" the *trivium* and *quadrivium* to organize the effects in our body of sensing the world daily in its cosmo-social dimensions. This process consists of several steps that enable us to a) understand how sensing relates to what we already know according to how we have been schooled and through our own praxis of living; b) explain our sensing to others in conversation (disciplinary or not); and c) explain how we preserve in our memory or store it in a material and methodical way.[13] The *trivium* consisted of General Grammar, General Logic and Rhetoric; the *quadrivium* of Arithmetic, Geometry, Music, and Astronomy. This structure of knowledge making was regional: it was a set of beliefs and principles shared by Western Christians and European Renaissance humanists, but not by Eastern Orthodox Christians. Nor was it shared by Buddhist believers or Confucian followers, or by followers of African ancient wisdom or that of the Incan, Mayan, Aztec, Iroquois, and First Nations that is today reemerging in the "New World."

Patrick Bowen tells a story that summarizes a global awareness of *local non-European histories and memories*, dated to when he was about nine or ten years old and living with his father in the Bushlands of Portuguese East Africa. His father wanted Patrick to join the missionary service in order to receive education and learn "white men's ways." At that time, Patrick had become friends with many children his age, principally Zulu, and through them had contact with wise elders. One of them was Mankanyezi. Patrick told Mankanyezi what his father wanted him to do, to which Mankanyezi responded as follows:

> Your teachers are doubtless learned men. But why do they strive to force their beliefs on us without first learning what our beliefs are? Not one of them, not even (Bishop) Sobantu, knows anything of our real belief. They think that we worship the spirits of our ancestors; that we believe our spirits, when we die, enter the bodies of animals. They, without proof or without enquiry, condemn us, the Isanusi, as deluders of our more ignorant brethren; or else they declare us to be wicked wizards having dealings with evil spirits. To show how ignorant they are, I shall tell you what we teach the Common Man (ordinary Native). We teach that he has a body; that within that body is a soul; and within the soul is a spark or portion of something we call Itongo, which the Common Man interprets as the Universal Spirit of the Tribe. We teach that after death the soul (*Idhlozi*) after hovering for a space near the body departs to a place called *Esilweni* (Place of Beasts). This is a very different thing, as you can see, from entering the body of a beast.
>
> In Esilweni, the soul assumes a shape, part beast and part human. This is its true shape, for man's nature is very like that of the beast, save for that

spark of something higher, of which Common Man knows but little. For a period that is long or short, according to the strength of the animal nature, the soul remains in Esilweni, but at last, it throws aside its beast-like shape and moves onward to a place of rest. There it sleeps till a time comes when it *dreams* that something to do or to learn awaits it on earth; then it awakes and returns, through the Place of Beasts, to earth and is born again as a child. Again, and again—does the soul travel through the body, through the Place of Beasts, to its rest, dreams its dream and returns to the body; till at last the Man becomes true Man, and his soul when he dies goes straight to its rest, and thence, after a space, having ceased to dream of earth, moves on and becomes one with that from which it came—the Itongo.

Then does the Man know that instead of being but himself, apart, he is truly all the tribe and the tribe, is he? This is what we teach, I say, for this is the utmost the Common Man is capable of comprehending; indeed, many have only a vague comprehension, even of this much. But the belief of us, Wiser Ones, is something far wider and greater, though similar. It is far too wide and great for Common Man's comprehension—or for yours, at present. But I may say this much, that we know that the Itongo is not the mere Spirit of the Tribe, but is the Spirit within and above all men—even all things; and that at the end, all men being one in Spirit, all are brothers in the flesh.[14]

This story was told to Bowen in the middle of the twentieth century. Within the context of my argument, it needs to be parsed.[15]

Western Christianity's *totality* had two outlets, so to speak. One was the *local hegemony* it attained. In the Middle Ages, no one in the Christian world believed in Christian cosmology in its double manifestation: the biblical narrative and the philosophical foundation that the Roman Algerian (in today's geography) Saint Augustine of Hippo (AD 354–430) had provided. Augustine mainly contributed to the assertion of Christian authority in the pagan Roman Empire. Later in the Middle Ages, though, the Italian Saint Thomas Aquinas (AD 1225–74) brought Christianity to its most systematic philosophical and theological expression. The separation from Eastern Orthodox Christianity here reached a point of no return. But—and this is the second outlet—the increasing assertion of the totality of knowledge reached its pinnacle at the crossroads of Greek philosophical legacies and medieval Western Christian concerns about universals.

The problem of universals is long and complex—it receives fuller treatment in an earlier section. Most crucial here is that it provided the foundations for what would become "the question of totality of knowledge" explored by Quijano. Let's take an example provided by the *Stanford Encyclopedia of Philosophy*:

> The universal features of singular things, inherent in these things them-selves, were referred to as *universalia in re* ("universals in the thing"), an-swering the universal exemplars in the divine mind, the *universalia ante rem* ("universals before the thing"). All these, universal concepts, universal features of singular things, and their exemplars, are expressed and signi-fied by means of some obviously universal signs, the universal (or com-mon) terms of human languages. For example, the term "man," in English is a universal term, because it is truly predicable of all men in one and the same sense, as opposed to the singular term "Socrates," which in the same sense, i.e., when not used equivocally, is only predicable of one man.[16]

Here is the crux of the matter: Western languages and thoughts con-ceived of *Man* as "truly predicable of all men in one and the same sense," without realizing that the name and idea they had for a given species of living organisms was only theirs; it was not global, and even less universal. What medieval Christian theological philosophers *locally* perceived and named as *Man* (in the sense of a human being, see chapter 7) gradually became hegemonic—standardly used to justify the conquering and imperial sub-jectivity of Western Man (Enrique Dussel's concept of the *ego conquiro*). In short, the local belief in universals was extended globally once Christianity encountered the unknown (the New World), providing the imperial founda-tion for the totality of knowledge.

The result is a double history of the belief in universals: one history is Euro-pean history itself, from medieval theology and philosophy to the eighteenth-century secularization of philosophy and marginalization of theology; the other is the Western Christian theological and Western secular philosophical foundation of knowledge in relation to non-Western systems of knowledge and belief—the foundation of the CMP in the sixteenth century and ever since. For although Asia and Africa were familiar places to Western Christians, the meaning the continents acquired for Christian theologians, philosophers, and men of letters in general changed drastically in the sixteenth century. Hence, the question of universals debated in the European Middle Ages provided the foundation for the question of the totality of knowledge.

Theologian philosophers in the New World, such as the Dominican Bar-tolomé de las Casas and the Jesuit José de Acosta, were founders of the encounter between medieval universals, the Renaissance geopolitics of knowledge, and the unknown "New World" of which they were making sense, to them, erasing the sense that the continent had for its inhabitants. The "detour" of the Atlantic, without which there would not have been the European Enlightenment, was ignored by enlightened philosophers themselves. They ignored (or repressed) what make them possible. Enlightened philosophers only saw the history line from Greece to Western Europe, through Rome. They were looking towards the East, while the West (New World, Indias Occidentales) was nourishing their bodies and mind. Indeed, the same limit exists in all histories and theories in Western Europe and the Anglo-disciplinary legacies of the United States that see *modernity* emerging in eighteenth-century Europe and hanging there like a floating garden without grounding. This detour was the veritable foundation of Eurocentrism. It was embedded in what Carl Schmitt has described as the emergence, in the sixteenth century and not the eighteenth, of the *second nomos of the earth*.[17]

The question of universals and their consequences, the totality of knowledge, then, is not only a metaphysical issue within the local history of European thought. It is also a problem of the *geopolitics of knowledge*: after European encounters with people of other continents, universals reinforced the sense of *epistemic totality* that was paired with *ontological racism*. For that reason, always approaching knowing and knowledge body- and geopolitically (who, where, why, when) is a decolonial necessity to relocate Western universals in their *local emergence* and restores them to their *local scope*. Now that the universal pretense has been reduced to size, let's consider David Hume and Immanuel Kant in their respective localities. In the eighteenth century, Hume wrote his infamous paragraph on "National Characters," which was later on taken up by Kant:

> I am apt to suspect the Negroes and in general all other species of men (for there are four or five different kinds) to be naturally inferior to the whites. There never was a civilized nation of any other complexion than white, nor even any individual eminent either in action or speculation. No ingenious manufactures amongst them, no arts, no sciences. On the other hand, the most rude and barbarous of the whites, such as the ancient Germans, the present Tartars, have still something eminent about them, in their valour, form of government, or some other particular.
>
> Such a uniform and constant difference could not happen, in so many countries and ages, if nature had not made an original distinction betwixt

these breeds of men. Not to mention our colonies, there are Negroe slaves dispersed all over Europe, of which none ever discovered any symptom of ingenuity; tho' low people, without education, will start up amongst us, and distinguish themselves in every profession. In Jamaica, indeed, they talk of one negroe as a man of parts and learning; but 'tis likely he is admired for very slender accomplishments like a parrot, who speaks a few words plainly.[18]

It has been noted that, in spite of statements such as the one above, Hume opposed the institution of slavery. What has been less explored is whether Hume's opposition was on moral or economic grounds. Hume's statement on "National Characters" was published in 1742.[19] By 1750 the campaign against slavery was reaching it highest point. "Humanitarians" had strong economic interests to defend, and slavery was working against them.[20]

## Border Thinking and Decoloniality

Let's now turn back to Mankanyezi. He had already absorbed Western concepts and images: Man and Spirit, for example. He had already had to confront "the question of the totality of knowledge." Conversely, actors believing in the totality of their own knowledge did not have to confront Mankanyezi and his African knowledge. Mankanyezi's knowing and knowledges were, in the eyes of totality of knowledge holders, superseded. As Mankanyezi says at the beginning, "they" do not know anything about it, and they do not care to know. Consequently, communication breaks down, because non-European rationalities and knowledges are disavowed and denied but not killed: their knowledge remains in the bodies, memories, and in the conversations of past, present, and future generations. The epistemic differential between regional knowledges taken for the totality and regional knowledges disavowed by stakeholders of the totality of knowledge, makes the question of epistemic totalitarianism visible and border (-dwelling and -thinking) epistemologies unavoidable and necessary: Mankanyezi knows and understands the genealogy of the thoughts he inhabits, and knows what the missionaries know, and knows the power differential between the two: that is, thinking is, of necessity, border thinking. Bishop Sobantu only knows the knowledge he inhabits; he doesn't recognize Mankanyezi's knowledge, because, for Sobantu, Mankanyezi is not a knowing subject. As Hume puts it, only the white man is a knowing subject (see quotations above).

The question of "the totality of knowledge" is not simply a question of what is known (for example, the encyclopedia). Mainly, it is a question of who is in a position to know, and to persuade the many that knowledge is universal, not local, and that the universality of knowledge is legitimized by actors and institutions that are in a position to assert it. The totality of knowledge is tantamount to universality, and both secure the Eurocentricity of the enunciation. The story of Mankanyezi and Sobantu is entangled with the totality of knowledge that is not theirs, that is imposed upon them, thus creating epistemic differentials that take the historical form of colonial or imperial differences: dwelling in/on the border and sensing the colonial epistemic and ontological difference bring about the necessary conditions of border dwelling, thinking, and doing. Border thinking and border epistemology emerge among *colonial subjects* (like Mankanyezi) who realize that their knowledge has been disavowed and denied.[21] That realization is the starting point of *becoming decolonial subjects*, or (as I will explain in chapter 10) of becoming dewestern subjects.

In Mankanyezi's words, Man and Spirit are Western concepts used to name certain types of experiences and sensibilities common to all human beings on the planet, but they do not capture the differential experiences and sensibilities of all human beings on the planet. As we have seen, it is the process of the Western totality of knowledge that created the idea and belief that Man and Spirit are universal, and that Western knowledge has the epistemic privilege to stand for the entire planetary humanity. Such is the main point that Mankanyezi is making, even though he has to use some Western vocabulary to do so. But the vocabulary does not fool him. He knows that even the reputed Bishop Sobantu doesn't understand, and doesn't even try to understand, the "totality" of African wisdom.

Knowledge and understanding cannot be killed. People, not knowledge, are killed, unless there is a total extermination of the people who carry ancestral knowledge in the present. Fortunately, non-Western knowledges and praxis of living-knowing were not killed, neither in the Americas and Africa, nor in China and India and in the vast territories of Islam. Because non-Western knowledge was not killed, today it is not only resurging and reemerging from the darker side of modernity, but if there is a hope to survive on the planet it would be due to memories and conceptions of life that westernization under the banner of modernity could never conquer and of course never kill. Mankanyezi is one example.

The distinction between knowledge and wisdom is a consequence of actors who believe in the totality of their own knowledge. *Knowledge*, since Western secularism, has become not only the totality of the known but also the only true way of knowing. Other knowledges, in the plural, were considered *wisdom*, or *witchcraft* (as in witch doctors, folklore, magic). Thus, "the question of the totality of knowledge" has two dimensions: the totality of the known (the enunciated) and the authority of the knower (the enunciation). It is this second aspect that legitimizes Hume's racist dictum.

Decoloniality (of knowing, sensing, believing in the praxis of living) takes its cues from the configuration of the CMP and the Eurocentric totality of knowledge. Its target is the level of the enunciation that maintains the configuration of the domains and the rhythm of the flows. Changing the terms of the conversation requires delinking from the enunciation and, therefore, from the fictional constituted domains, which are based on the belief that the world *is* what the domains makes us believe it is. Delinking from the enunciation and the enunciated and changing the terms of the conversation don't mean that states, the media, the banks, the IMF, the World Bank, and so on would all of a sudden also change the terms of the conversation.

For those of us in the world who engage decoloniality, in its different domains (the domains of the enunciated) and above all in delinking from the enunciation, the goal is not to convince the various egos manipulating the CMP to modify their control, or relinquish its control to those disputing it (like China and Russia, for example, and their followers). Rather, the goal is to engage in the domains ourselves and together can manage, in order to open up the gates to decolonial communal subjectivities.

This is the topic of the next and the final chapter.

### Notes

1   Michel Foucault, *Les mots et les choses* (Paris: Gallimard, 1966); Richard Rorty, *Philosophy and the Mirror of Nature* (Princeton, NJ: Princeton University Press, 1982).

2   For a cultural history account of the four continents focusing on the nineteenth century, see, Lisa Lowe, *The Intimacies of the Fourth Continents* (Durham, NC: Duke University Press, 2015).

3   For more details, see the afterword to the second edition of my *The Darker Side of the Renaissance: Literacy, Territoriality, and Colonization* (Ann Arbor: University of Michigan Press, [1995] 2003).

4   "The Meaning of the Earth Charter: Interview with Humberto Maturana and
    Ximena Dávila," Video, April 26, 2011, https://www.youtube.com/watch?v
    =GtEgtmo42Ls&list=PL6DoDC2BCE841549B.

5   "Looking at the theories of imperialism in Hobson and Lenin, you could understand
    the differences between the conceptualization of capitalism/imperialism on the
    one hand and coloniality of power (CMP) on the other." On Hobson and Lenin see
    Gallos 2007.

6   Aníbal Quijano, "Coloniality and Modernity/Rationality," *Globalization and the
    Decolonial Option*, ed. Walter Mignolo and Arturo Escobar (London: Routledge, 2010).

7   Quijano's expression in Spanish is "patrón colonial de poder." *Patrón* in Spanish
    means a person in a position of authority (e.g., a boss) or a pattern to model some-
    thing else:

        m. y f. 1. Protector, defensor. . . .
        Dueño de la casa o pensión donde uno se hospeda.
        Amo o señor de una finca o una heredad.
        Persona que emplea obreros, patrono.
        El que manda y dirige un pequeño buque mercante: *patrón de barco*.
        Modelo que sirve de muestra para sacar otra cosa igual: *hay que sacar el
            patrón del vestido para hacer otro.*
        (WordReference.com/*Online Language Dictionary*), accessed July 27, 2017.

8   "Matrix," *Merriam-Webster Dictionary*, www.merriam-webster.com/dictionary
    /matrix.

9   Aníbal Quijano, "Coloniality and Modernity/Rationality," (italics mine).

10  "The University from the 12th to the 20th century," Universita di Bologna, accessed
    July 21, 2017, http://www.unibo.it/en/university/who-we-are/our-history/university
    -from-12th-to-20th-century.

11  Hugh F. Graham, "Education," in *Encyclopaedia Britannica*, 11th ed., 2011, accessed
    May 23, 2016, http://www.britannica.com/EBchecked/topic/179408/education
    /47496/Major-periods-of-Muslim-education-and-learning. Keep in mind that the vo-
    cabulary is Western and that the equivalent terms in Arabic do not have the same
    meaning that, for example, algebra and trigonometry have in English. A very simple
    example of coloniality of knowledge: English (and the entire family of Western vo-
    cabulary based on Greek and Latin) hides the universes of meaning of non-Western
    languages translated into Western languages. There is always a "noisy silence,"
    and a different story, behind what appears as the totality that Western vocabulary
    names. See below the question of "totality" in Quijano.

12  While museums were crucial institutions during the westernization of the world,
    today museums are becoming one site where cultural dewesternization is taking
    place. See Walter Mignolo, "Enacting the Archive, Decentering the Muses," in
    *Ibraaz: Contemporary Visual Culture in North Africa and the Middle East*, Novem-
    ber 2013, accessed May 24, 2016, http://www.ibraaz.org/essays/77. On media,
    see Jim Curran and Myiun-Jin Park, eds., *De-Westernizing Media Studies* (London:
    Routledge, 2000).

13   From "The 7 Liberal Arts—Trivium, Quadrivium and Logical Fallacies," www
     .matrixwissen.de, accessed May 24, 2016, http://www.matrixwissen.de/index.php
     ?option=com_content&view=article&id=845:the-7-liberal-arts-trivium-quadrivium
     -and-logical-fallacies-en&catid=208&lang=en&Itemid=242.

14   Rene Guenon, "The Language of Birds," *Studies in Comparative Religion* 3,
     no. 2 (spring 1969) © World Wisdom, Inc., accessed May 27, 2016, http://www
     .studiesincomparativereligion.com/Public/articles/The_LanguageofBirds
     -byReneGuenon.aspx.

15   Catherine Walsh's argument in part I moves the argument in this direction,
     grounded in the local histories of the South American Andes.

16   Gyula Klima, "The Medieval Problem of Universals," in *Stanford Encyclopedia of
     Philosophy* (fall 2013), ed. Edward N. Zalta, accessed May 25, 2016, http://plato
     .stanford.edu/entries/universals-medieval/#2.

17   Carl Raschke, "What Is the 'New Nomos of the Earth'?: Reflections on the Later
     Schmitt," *Political Theology Today*, September 2016, http://www.politicaltheology
     .com/blog/what-is-the-new-nomos-of-the-earth-reflections-on-the-later-schmitt
     -carl-raschke/.

18   *Library of Economic Liberty*, search for word *negroes*, accessed May 23, 2016,
     http://www.econlib.org/cgi-bin/searchbooks.pl?searchtype=BookSearchPara&id
     =hmMPL&query=negroes.

19   Aaron Garrett, "Hume's Revised, Racism Revisited," *Hume Studies* 26, no. 1 (2000):
     171–78; Silvia Sebastiani, "Race and National Characters in Eighteenth Century
     Scotland: The Polygenetic Discourses of Kames and Pinkerton," *Cromhos: Cyber
     Review of Historiography* 8 (2003): 1–14 (see section 3 on Hume's national char-
     acters), http://weblaw.haifa.ac.il/en/Events/scottishenlightenment/Documents
     /Athanasia%20Glycofrydi%20-%20Hume%20on%20%E2%80%9CNational%20
     Characters%E2%80%9D.pdf.

20   This issue was clearly formulated by Eric Williams in his classic book *Capitalism and
     Slavery* (Chapel Hill: University of North Carolina Press, [1944] 1994), "The 'Saints'
     and Slavery," and "Slave and Slavery." For recent accounts see John Ashworth, "The
     Relationship between Capitalism and Humanitarians," *American Historical Review*
     92, no. 4 (1987): 813–28.

21   There are many other cases since the sixteenth century. Elsewhere are explored
     the thinking, doing, saying, and sensing of Guaman Poma de Ayala and Ottobah
     Cugoano.

## Colonality and the Anthropocene

The title of this section is a decolonial conceptualization of crossing narratives. One is the origination of humanness (the most recent is the origin and trajectory of the era of the anthropos, or the anthropocene). In any of these narratives, and the most recent of the anthropocene, it appears as if there is one and only one trajectory of orientation and "evolution" from our ancestors to us today. However and since looking at our present humans around the planet one suspect that there was not only one but many trajectories of in the era of the anthropos (anthropocene). The second narrative originates around 1500, a few decades earlier and a few decades later. It originated in the Atlantic, connecting the west coast of Western Europe, that of Africa, and the east coasts of a mass of land Europeans named Indias Occidentales, New World, America. This is the decolonial narrative of CMP. That is, of modernity/coloniality/decoloniality. As it was explained in chapter 5, coloniality is a decolonial concept as well as modernity/coloniality.

The fact that this narrative emerged in the Atlantic and around 1500 of the Christian era, means also was its absence: that did not appear in any other place of the planet and in any other time before. The sixteenth century in the Atlantic wrote a significant chapter in the history of humanness. For the first time in the history of the human species, the planet became known in its full extension. It was also the first time in the history of humanness that one ethnicity would be able to interfere and rule other ethnicities in the planet. As the invader and massive slave trader changed the praxis of living of many Africans and of the totality of the civilizations in the New World, the invading anthropos continued its task through the centuries, intruding in Africa and Asia as well. In the process they collected many collaborations from the places Western Europeans were intruding upon but they generated also many and strong oppositions, resentment, and anger. Neither collaborations nor oppositions placated; on the contrary, they increased. There are plenty of signs of both around the planet today. Dewesternization and decoloniality are two of the consequences of long and planetary trajectories of discontent.

The North Atlantic anthropos disrupted and projected on the rest of the planet increasing technologies that contributed to the separation between ourselves and the cosmos. The calendar became a counting of days and months mediating and obliterating the changing energies of the seasons, the circulation of the Sun and the Moon, and their impact in our daily living. The concept of "space" emerged in the rhetoric of modernity. Anthropos, in any place on the planet and in any moment of its trajectory on earth, had a sense of events that happened before the present in which the organism was living. Storytelling of a group of anthropos, for example, told stories about previous generations. Atlantic anthropos called that "time" and did not bother to learn that the invaded communities thought about themselves by means of narratives in which they told the stories of events that preceded the very present in which they were telling the story. "Time" is not universal but is the regional Western way of naming repetitions and transformations. The colonization of space and time were two fundamental pillars of the European praxis of living and, consequently, the changing direction of all non-Europeans invaded and confronted with praxis of living that were not theirs for centuries. Sun Yi, a student in one of my seminars on decoloniality, reminded me of Lu Xun's narrative of how much the Chinese conception of the body changed with the intrusion of Western biology and medicine. The ontology of the body was and continues to be similar (with superficial changes) from immemorial time to today. The neurons of the nervous systems and the cells of the organism did not change to the point in which bodies are no longer recognized as human bodies. What changed was the knowledge. This is why the target of decolonial thinking and doing is the hegemonic architecture of knowledge (content of the conversation) and the principles, assumptions, and rules of knowing (terms of the conversation). The option that decoloniality offers delinks, from the options articulated by modernity/coloniality and successfully established as the only option.

The biological praxis of living is common to all organisms on earth and earth as a living organism itself. Life in the planet could not have emerged from a dead planet!! Living organisms need water and food and oxygen, and sunlight and moonlight, and movement (rotations of earth around the sun and changing seasons above and below the equator, etc.). The biological praxis of living is common to plants, to grass, to insects, to lions, to our dog, and to ourselves. For billions of years the biological praxis of living has been recursive and expansive rather than evolutionary. The fact that in our present we have electrical stoves is not a sign of biological but cultural change. Whether we call that change "evolution of the species" or "extension of our praxis of living" is a matter of the assumptions in which we base our narratives. It is fair to surmise that our human species ancestors were doing the same thing we are doing now: eating, sleeping, nurturing and cooking, regenerating, loving and fighting. There was not evolution in this praxis of living; but there were extensions of our doing (cultural) in the way we do it now. If the size of our brains is larger than that of our ancestors because our cultural praxis of living expanded, there is not necessarily evolution but biological enlargement and strengthening of organs whose use has been preserved: "we" did not make our brain enlarge on purpose as "we" made our cooking more multifaceted or as pianists and guitarists strengthening the force and mobility of their fingers.

To understand the implications in and of the crossing of both narratives (the anthropocene and the CMP), some chronological references to our ancestors, to locate the moment in which the praxis of living guided by the rhetoric of modernity and the logic of coloniality emerged, would be here helpful and appropriate. In some accounts, our ancestors have been on Planet Earth for 6 million years. Other narratives place the living organisms of the anthropos species as we know them/us today about 200,000–250,000 years ago. Other narratives focus on the time in which many civilizations appeared on the planet about 6000 years ago. This chronology corresponds mutatis mutandis with the chronology of the Axial Age (see below on this concept). Last but not least, the historical formation of CMP, which became the overall pattern of management and control, emerged 500 years ago on the two sides of the Atlantic (the Americas, Europe and Africa) and expanded all over the planet since.

The closing of this introduction is the opening to wider roads for the series. In this last chapter of part II I am sketching the crossing paths between storytelling of the biological/cultural origin of humanness, of which the latest version is that of the era of the anthropos (the anthropocene, not known 30 years ago) and the historical foundation of modernity/coloniality, which here is rendered as the era of CMP. My own sketchy narrative of the origin of humanness is based on Alexander Marshack, *The Roots of Civilization*,[1] and the various works of Humberto Maturana, chiefly the summary of his view in *The Origins of Humanness and the Biology of Love*, cowritten with Gerda Verden-Zeller.[2]

These reflections are not new for me. Before my encounter with decolonial thinking in the mid-1990s, I was crossing my research on semiotics/semiology (since the early 1970s) and my research on the colonization of languages, space, and memories. I did not know about coloniality at the time, but I was well aware of colonization of signs and the consequences for the management of subjectivities, connected to political, economic, and military managements. At the end of the 1980s I was crossing, on the one hand, Maturana's languaging and Marshack's emergence of storytelling among our ancestors, with the emergence of the Greco-Latin alphabet, alphabetic writing, literacy, and literature on the other.[3] When I encountered coloniality and decolonial thinking (since coloniality is a decolonial concept), it took me to where I am now closing part II of this book and opening up future research and debates.

From where I am now, I can argue that the unilinear narratives of the origins of humanness or the era of the anthropos are narratives embedded in the regional epistemic frame of modernity; hence, they are inscribed in CMP. Consequently, they are not universal, as they pretend to be invoking the authority of "science" but are narratives based on epistemic assumptions in the frame of Western epistemology (what is known and principles of knowing), and therefore they reproduce epistemic coloniality. They hide, on the one hand, the plurality of trajectories in which our ancestors appeared on the planet and survived until today and, on the other hand, they ignore the radical transformation that a sector of the anthropos, at a given time and place (the Atlantic, 1500), fashioned a structure of management and a managerial style that formed the subjectivities of the actors involved and subjected to their own beliefs (the Papacy, European monarchies before the bourgeoisie) that took over toward the end of the eighteenth century, and expanded all over the planet. The anthropocene (the era of the anthropos) divided the waters at this point between a numerical minority located in Western Europe doing the managing and the immense majority increasingly being managed. In between the managers and the managed there are the stories of collaborators and self-convinced believers in the promises of CMP managerial structure.

Storytelling about tribal primitive hunters and about civilized European intellectuals are both secular storytelling. The first arose in the eighteenth century when Christian theological narratives of the origin of the universe made by God in seven days and the origin of humanness made also by God on the seventh day, were displaced by secular science and philosophy. Secular time displaced sacred/theological time narrative. *Primitives* were invented and located in time and displaced pagans and barbarians who were located in space. When primitives were invented (and hence the theory of evolution), the unilinear time narrative of humanness in a homogeneous abstract space unfolded in unison. The noun *primitive* was derived from Latin *primitivus*, which was an adjective. It became a noun to refer to aboriginal people in a land visited by Europeans. This meaning has been dated toward 1779 and interestingly enough it coincides with the advent of the word *civilization* to measure and determine uncivilized anthropos.[4] The second narrative (the anthropocene) appeared at the end of the twentieth century. It cannot be properly understood without the previous narrative that offers the frame from tribal primitives to urban civilized. The difference shows in the features that sustain each story. The first focuses on the evolution of the anthropos/ us and the second on the uses of the hands to transform the environment. This is not the place to put these narratives on trial, but it is the occasion to assume that the origination of humanness took place in different areas on the planet and in regional times. Instead, existing narratives are told as if it all happened homogeneously in one timeline and in an abstract and undif- ferentiated space. This frame, assumed in the nineteenth century, would have been unthinkable without the colonization of space and time during the Eu- ropean Renaissance.

Let us focus for a moment on the Axial Age (mentioned above) as a refer- ence point to substantiate decolonial reflections on, and delinking from, the frame of Western unilinear time narratives from primitives to civilized and of the era of the anthropos (anthropocene). German philosopher Karl Jasper has been credited for revamping an expression introduced in the nineteenth century.[5] By invoking this controversial thesis I intend neither to debate the issue nor to endorse the search for a common origin of all religions and, con- sequently, for a universal history (as the Axial Age intended to frame) that will legitimize the centrality of Europe (Eurocentrism). From the Axial Age hypothesis I accept the time frame in which many civilizations appeared on the planet. But I reject the hypothesis of one single origin, which is precisely an assumption that guarantees Eurocentric narratives of universal history.

Looking at the time frame in which Axial Age narratives have been lo- cated (8th- to 3rd-century BC) it becomes apparent that by that time frame the expanson of the brains, the extension in the uses of the hands (building fire, hunting, making instruments), and extension of languaging in storytelling have stretched out the overall praxis of living of our ancestors' appearance on earth, whether we count from 250,000 or 6,000 years ago. Now, limiting ourselves to the shorter time frame of the Axial Age, as we think about the narratives that the inhabitants of each of the many coexisting civilizations told about the origin of the earth and of themselves, the unilinearity of stories from primitives to civilized and of the anthropocene, collapses. Assuming, instead of a single and common origin someplace, sometime, that each local story about the origin of the universe and of their own ancestors, was told in China, India, Persia, in the later kingdoms of Africa, or among the Mayas, Incas, and Aztecs in the New World, the single origin and the single story of the origin of humanness cannot be sustained. It could be sustained as one among many narratives if it is specified that there are Western regional narratives that are valid for Westerners who believe in them and for non-Westerners who have been taught to despise their one and accept the "true" one, which is the Western local narrative. Introducing Asia, Africa, and the invented America into the picture (all locations that Hegel places at the margin or out of the unilinear unfolding of universal history) reduces to size the assumptions on a common origin of civilization flourishing during the Axial Age. Bringing space into the equation allows for underscoring the plurality of times and spaces (places) of origination of the species of living organisms engaging in languaging, building fires, cultivating, and cooking.

A cursory look at the knowledge we have of complex sociocultural organizations commonly referred to as "civilizations," between the Axial Age and 1500, confirms the intuition that the planet was populated by very sophisticated centers. In relation to their ancestors thousands of year ago, they have increased commerce, trades, and markets among their distinct civilizations. Let's take just one example of the trade routes that in the nineteenth century in Europe (controlling knowledge) was baptized the "Silk Road" (because of the obvious detail that silk was the major commerce of the road). The Silk Road was a quite impressive Eurasian network connecting the East and West and stretching from today's Korean peninsula and Japan to the Mediterranean Sea. There were both terrestrial and maritime routes connecting Asia and Europe. The time of its unfolding was during the Han dynasty, 207 BC–220 AD. In the New World, before it was "discovered," there was also active commerce and trade in the fifteenth century amid Andean and Mesoamerican civilizations as there was between the Iroquois in today's Northeast U.S. and the Osage Nations in the Great Plains, whose origins are dated to 700 BC. Briefly, the point I am making is that from the time of the Axial Age to 1500 the planet was inhabited by many civilizations, doing trade and commerce among them, making impressive buildings, telling stories, doing mathematics, regenerating the anthropos species, and engaging in many other endeavors, in their own local civilizations, but none of them was encroaching into any other civilizations. There were hierarchical domestic organizations in all of them, but no expansion to interfere with other civilizations. The planetary order was from the Axial Age up to 1500, a polycentric and noncapitalist world order. By 1500 one civilization emerged, Western civilization, that began to intrude, trespass, and violate other civilizations. It started with Spain and Portugal encroaching in a continent that was unknown to the intruders and that they named the New World and America. Shortly after, the benefit of the invention encouraged the participations of Holland, England, and France. The history of humanness or the anthropocene took a detour with the rise of CMP.

If we accept that that *Homo sapiens*, our closest ancestors unfolding from early hominids, appeared on earth around 200,000 to 250,000 years ago and we accept also that languaging biological capability triggered the cultural competence to coordinate behavior, then *Homo sapiens* became such when their organisms were able to engage in languaging and conversations to coordinate behavior. Whether the dates to locating the origination of languaging are accepted or disputed, the fact remains that at some point in time and in different regions of the planet, our ancestors engaged in languaging because their biological configuration allows them to do so. And we can surmise that if languaging arose with the communal life, coordination of behavior requires the extension of whatever means of interactions our ancestors had at that moment. But in any case, the origination of languaging is what counts here more than the decision of when it had originated, for if we humans are languaging organisms, at some point our languaging emerged among our ancestors. This imaginary moment of our ancestors' praxis of living coincides with current storytelling and invention of the anthropocene. The origination of CMP was not, however, a question of the origination of the anthropos but of Man/Human as I explain in chapter 7. This is precisely the point where the two narratives, that of the anthropocene and that of CMP crossed each other and the beliefs upon which they are built are exposed: decolonial analytics and narrative of CMP is an option that exposes its assumptions. The scientific narratives of the anthropocene are told under the presuppositions that it is not an option but that it is the true rendering (with diverse interpretations) of the appearance of the anthropos on earth and the cultural changes our ancestors, from immemorial time, infringed on the environment. Lions, for instance, have coexisted with anthropos for centuries if not millennia, but they did not engage in languaging and do not use their hands to extend their praxis of living. So they did not trespass on the harmony of their niches and, therefore, the aggregates of conditions in which living organisms are living ("environment" was Carlyle's translation of Goethe's *Umgebung*).[6]

The word *language* is derived from Latin *lingua*, which—any dictionary will tell you, and this is not trivial for my argument—is the organ with which we eat and talk. Eating and talking are verbs denoting praxis of living while food and language are nouns naming entities; the first is material and the second abstract or immaterial. We can eat raw food, but when we prepare food we use a verb to indicate that activity: the verb we use to name that activity is "cooking." Similarly, what we do with the abstract entity called language (in the restricted sense of activity done with the fleshy muscular organ we have in the mouth) is "languaging." Languaging is the praxis of living of organisms endowed with a nervous system using the tongue to generate chains of distinctive sounds coding meaning understood by other similar languaging living organisms in their relational living. When languaging arose among our ancestors, whether three million years ago or two hundred thousand year ago, there is preservation of the languaging as an activity but not evolution in the activity itself as performed by certain organisms (in spite of the millions of years lions are not yet languaging and anthropos continue to do so). Like our ancestors, we make modulated sounds communally coded. That is, the code was not created by one organism but in the coexistence and praxis of living of multiple organisms coordinating their mutual behavior.

Similar argument could be advanced regarding the uses of the hands to inscribe signs in flat surfaces like trees, tree bark, stones, paper, computers, and iPhone screens. Whether languaging capacity and engagement in storytelling and conversations was simultaneous, prior, or posterior to sign inscriptions on flat surfaces with the purpose of coordinating behavior, or as rudimentary storytelling, is beyond the scope of my argument here. What I am underscoring are two praxis of living of our ancestors that were preserved until today. Preservation takes us to different storytelling than those stories we can tell if we accept that there is evolution and that evolution is a universal account of human existence on earth from our ancestors to today and of all living systems: ants continue to build the same type of ant's nest they built millions of years ago and so do bees. Neither ants nor bees have architects yet.

Preservation puts emphasis on what remains within structural mutations in spite of surface changes. Enlargement of the brain size, what we can do with our hands, and the increasing complexity of storytelling (e.g., from oral storytelling to contemporary film, novel, and conceptualization of life and the universe), is what all existing human beings have been doing since their/our emergence on the planet. Take for instance the uses of the hands. To use an iPhone we use our hands and fingers in the same way that our ancestors years ago used their hands and fingers to inscribe signs on stone surfaces. Our (living organisms coexisting in languaging) structural biological composition has been modified but not changed to a degree in which our organisms are no longer recognized as one of the human species.

What has been changing is the *cultural making* of what we (human species) *make* with our *langue* (tongue) and our hands but not the biological capacity to use our hands and our tongue to engage in languaging. There has been extension and enlargements, but not evolution, of anthropos/us; *ability of doing with hands and tongue has been preserved.* What has changed is what we can do with our hands (from tools to plow to computers and iPods and tractors and the like) and what we can know through the extension and enlargement of our organs in the collective languaging capability, creating, preserving, and transforming what we know and do. Again, there is no *evolution* in the ability of our biological organisms to know, but there has been a remarkable *extension* of brain size and what we human species know. In parallel fashion, it has been a remarkable extension in the transmission of sounds from the copresence of interlocutors to the current possibility of speaking across countries with a simple iPhone. But there has not been *biological evolution* from the uses of the hands of our ancestors inscribing signs on the stone, and our current use of hands and fingers typing on computer or iPhone keyboards. It has been a remarkable *cultural extension* but not *biological evolution.* "Evolution" was an abstract fictional time-concept in the transformation of coloniality of knowledge in the late eighteenth and during the nineteenth century.

In the sphere of languaging, our ancestors engaged in two types of interrelated activities: conversations and storytelling. It would be fair to assume that our conversations and storytelling today are more complex not because of evolution but because of extension of vocabulary, knowledge, social organization, intrastate (domestic) or interstate (international relations). In any region of the United States, South Africa, China, or Bolivia (to name a few regions) our conversations and storytelling are more complex in everyday life in the countryside and in the city, at the university, and in the corporations, in the bank global network, and in governments. Since I am assuming that we human beings on the planet today are undertaking the same type of activities in languaging (conversation and storytelling), it's irrelevant to talk about evolution, but it is necessarily peremptory to recognize the remarkable extension in both activities. The CMP emerged at a particular time and place and under particular circumstances that made possible for a particular assembly of living organisms engaged in languaging to tell themselves and to others a story about their manifest destiny to rule, and destroy if necessary, cultures, and civilizations that they invented as dangerous for their own well-being. The late fifteenth and sixteenth centuries were the planetary chronology in which, from the many local histories in a polycentric world order, one location began to be erected as the privileged place in human history since God created the world.

Conversation and storytelling, in languaging, are two types of activities. Conversations in the sense I am using it here shall be distinguished from communication. Communication, entered the vocabulary of social sciences and the humanities after Norbert Wiener's groundbreaking books of cybernetics and control of communication in animals and machines.[7] Since then, language was conceived as a system to transmit information. Shortly after the impact of Wiener's book, Colin Cherry, a scholar of telecommunication and by then at University College London, published in 1957 a book on human communication,[8] and in 1963, the well-known Russian linguist Roman Jakobson, had several of his articles translated into French in a volume on general linguistics.[9] One chapter is devoted to linguistic theory of communication. His general linguistic theory was then extrapolated to the understanding of linguistics and poetics: aesthetics was transferred to communication and furthering the separation between aesthetics (a philosophical theory of taste and genius in Western and non-Western praxis called art in Western narratives) and *aesthesis* (a Greek word referring to the senses).

### Cultural Praxis of Living

The CMP emerged from and slowly implanted cultural praxis of living in one region of the planet (the Atlantic, connecting the west coasts of Europe and Africa with the "discovered" continent). It emerged from new cultural-historical conditions in the praxis of living of Christian Western Europeans actors. The drivers of these historical and regional chapters in the era of the anthropos (theologians, missionaries, merchants, continental monarchies, scholars, and mapmakers) propagated their own regional praxis of living all over the population of the continent they named New World, Indias Occidentales, and America. The model was extended in the subsequent centuries to Asia and Africa, while Holland, France, and England were displacing Spain and Portugal in the endeavor of projecting their global designs. As we know, settlements and global designs did not transform local populations into Western persons. Local praxis of living, in their splendid diversity, were disrupted ever since, but never cloned. Local non-Western histories, in their diversity, had to accommodate their own praxis of living to the ones implanted by the settlers, actors, and institutions.

However, the implantation of CMP doesn't mean that everyone on the planet became European or (U.S.) American once they were interfered with by North Atlantic universal fictions and invited or forced to obey.[10] It means that local praxis of living has been forever disturbed all over the planet, with all the consequences it entails. Look at today's Afghanistan and Iraq, for example, to have an idea of what has happened in five hundred years of Western Europeans settled in the Americas, and then in South and Southeast Asia, and disrupted forever China's history without settling in China. Now mechanical weapons and soldiers are the settlers managed from distant shores by computers and drones. Colonialism is one thing, coloniality another (see next chapter, "Closing Remarks"). China was not colonized but did not escape coloniality. Carl Schmitt's apt metaphor of "global linear thinking" provides the formula for 500 years of Western history since the renaissance impinging all over the planet.[11]

At this point I can affirm with confidence that the anthropocene (the time period of the anthropos on earth) is not a single line of "evolution" of one tribe of anthropos, but a multiplicity of time lines of anthropos inhabiting what are today Asia, Africa, Europe, the Americas, Australasia. Geopolitics of the anthropocene's narrative consists in silencing geopolitics. The narratives are embedded in the rhetoric of modernity and the logic of coloniality that frame them. If we assume that the era of the anthropos is a history that leads to the North Atlantic, its presence in time and location in space, we are just updating Hegel.

The embedding of CMP praxis of living on the planet beyond the North Atlantic, has to be lived in the awareness that someone or something is telling them/us how to live or how to do what is right and what is wrong, what is it that the transcendental unfolding of universal history requires. That analytic awareness in the praxis of living, which doesn't need investigations supported by grants, is the moment in which decolonial thinking germinates. Once the words and concepts (decolonization and decoloniality) emerged in the second half of the twentieth century, it was possible to understand that the sensing, thinking, and praxis of living in the borders that the words describe, arose at the very moment in which Europeans invaded local histories for the first time.[12] The starting point is the confrontation with and delinking from the fiction of the totality of knowledge, which is tantamount to Eurocentrism. Thus, decolonial praxis of living in the border means decolonial praxis of knowing, sensing, and believing. It means also the surge of the will to liberate oneself from the subjectivities and from the CMP self-entitled to subject other people to their regional praxis of living. That is what Bob Marley, rephrasing Marcus Garvey, tells us in his famous "Redemption Song": "Emancipate yourself from mental slavery/None but ourselves can free our minds."

If you expect decoloniality today to be a remake of decolonization during the Cold War, you would be deceived by my argument. We are no longer in the Cold War. The Cold War was driven by the confrontation of liberal capitalism with state communism. No longer. The world order isn't anymore divided into First, Second, and Third Worlds; the First being liberal and capitalist, the Second being communist and statist, and the Third underdeveloped and either or both desiring development and fighting for decolonization and liberation from both, capitalism and communism. Today capitalism is global, but escaped the control of liberal or neoliberal Western political management. If this were not the case, then there would be no problem between the North Atlantic on the one hand and China and Russia and Iran on the other. Decolonization, as argued in chapter 5, was successful in sending the colonizer home but it was a failure, for it ended up creating nation-states that remained within the management of CMP even if imperial settlers were no longer in the terrain. Knowledge was not called into question, but it was accepted as if decolonization could be achieved without delinking from the knowledge of political theory and political economy, and the corresponding subject-formation that these knowledges entail. The defeat of capitalism was intended several times in the name of Marxism. And several times it failed because Marxism remained within the frame of CMP: it opposed the content but did not question the terms (assumptions, principles, regulations) of the type of knowledge within which capitalism would not exist. For the time being and for a foreseeable future, capitalism endures; it will for a time that cannot be anticipated. However, capitalist economy has made possible political dewesternization.

The interstate confrontation between rewesternizing global designs and dewesternizing resolve to delink from rewesternization is very visible in 2017, in Ukraine, Syria, and North Korea. Because of the mutation of the world order, decoloniality today had to reformulate the goals of decolonization during the Cold War: the goals are not, as they were, liberation to form nation-states ruled by Indigenous (or Native) populations. *The goals of decoloniality are delinking from* CMP *to engage in epistemic reconstitution* in search of patterns of re-existence not subjected to what rewesternization and dewesternization designs wants and expect. The option that decoloniality offers is not to overturn rewesternization and dewesternization and the overwhelming force of the mass media still dominated by rewesternization to (dis)orient the population and engage in media war with dewesternizing media. Decolonial thinking and doing has a hard task to germinate coexisting with overpowering forces. However, the growing need and desire to delink in order to to re-exist is a driving force from the Zapatistas and Peasant Way to intellectuals, artists, and people in general reinventing organization.[13]

I argue here that the option that decoloniality offers shall be understood and activated in three different and interrelated spheres of our biological and cultural praxis of living. Decoloniality is an option called to intervene in (a) the system of disciplinary management of knowledge (all the disciplines in the social sciences, humanities, and natural sciences, as well as professional schools); (b) the system of beliefs (religions); and (c) the systems of ideas (liberalism, conservatism, and socialism). One of the major tasks, if not the major, is to change the terms (assumptions, regulations, principles) of the conversations implanted by CMP that brings about our knowing, sensing, believing, and competing: the task is to delink from modern/colonial praxis of living and knowing, and to walk toward re-existing in the borderland and the borderlines in decolonial praxis of living, knowing, sensing, and of loving.[14] Decolonial love implies it is enacted with dignified anger confronting the dismantling of the social fabric of civilizational tendencies that promote competition and war. Decolonial love moves in two simultaneous directions: one confronting and delinking from the meanings that the word *love* has in liberal and Christian discourses, both of them embedded in CMP, and the other, accepting that re-existence and building communalities of all kinds demands respects, listening, cooperation, and care. This is the direction that decolonial love is taking in rebuilding what the principles and goals in the name of modernity destroyed and continue to destroy.

## Options and Imperatives

It has been suggested that decoloniality should be understood as an imperative rather than an option, for option may imply voluntarism. My argument is that in CMP there is nothing but options, options within the imaginary of modernity and options within decolonial imaginaries. Accordingly you choose an option in full awareness of the chart or you are chosen by one of the existing options that you take, willingly or not, as the truth, the correct or right one. Decoloniality is an option articulated in decolonial analytics of modernity/coloniality. Its aim is decolonial liberation from CMP. There are many other projects of liberation that are not and do not have to be decolonial. Decolonial liberation is a particular conception of the praxis of living in its biological and cultural interrelated spheres.

You may be enacting some options without knowing you are, because you think, or have been educated to believe, that there is only one option (cf., totality of knowledge) that corresponds to reality, and what is left is to engage in the conflict of interpretations within the logic of what seems to be the only option. However, from the moment you realize that what seems to be reality, objectivity, and truth is nothing but a dominant or hegemonic option, you are already stepping out and inhabiting the decolonial or other liberating options. Each option has its imperative. Kant's imperatives are categories in its universal conceptions of (liberal) morality. "Immanuel Kant (1724–1804) argued that the supreme principle of morality is a standard of rationality that he dubbed the 'Categorical Imperative' (CI). Kant characterized the CI as an objective, rationally necessary and unconditional principle that we *must always follow* despite any natural desires or inclinations we may have to the contrary" (emphasis added).[15] Decoloniality is not a mission, an option that cannot be dominating and imperative, but I have to be confident, convincing, and empowering. Kantian imperatives justified what modernity/coloniality achieved: management, control, and unidirectional cosmopolitanism.

Furthermore, it cannot be imperatives in abstract unless you assume the universality of your own imperatives. If decolonial imperatives are thinkable they cannot be detached from decoloniality as an option among coexisting modern/colonial options (with their own imperatives), some antagonistic and some compatible in their claim for liberation rather than progress, development, and subjection. Once it is understood that modernity is a set of fictional narratives that hide and enact coloniality, once it is understood that CMP operates by ejecting all that is perceived (or said to be perceived) as attempting against civilization, paths of liberation, reconstitution, and re-existence could be devised and activated. But to move in that direction, to delink from the praxis of living that CMP embedded, to engage in decolonial praxis of living, it is necessary to build decolonial paths of knowing, disobeying the epistemic regulations and subjectivities managed by the CMP level of enunciation. If coloniality is a frame of subjection, decoloniality shall be the opening path of liberation. But this cannot be achieved without epistemic disobedience and the creative joy of knowing beyond the disciplines, the modern/colonial system of ideas and institutionalization of belief that colonized (manage) spirituality. If, however, decoloniality is the option to be enacted to delink from the CMP in all its domains, but above all from the level of the enunciation that controls and manages knowledge and knowing, sensing and believing, then decoloniality is an imperative for whoever engages with the decolonial option, but cannot be a missionary imperative to control and dominate. And above all, it is neither a claim that decoloniality is the option where the final truth without parentheses is housed.

## Notes

1   Alexander Marshack, *The Roots of Civilization* (New York: Moyer Bell Limited, 1991).

2   Gerda Verden-Zöller and Humberto Maturana, *The Origin of Humanness and the Biology of Love* (Tulsa, OK: Imprint Academy, 2008).

3   Walter D. Mignolo, "(Re)modeling the Letter: Literacy and Literature at the Intersections of Semiotics and Literary Studies," in *On Semiotic Modeling*, ed. Myrdene Anderson and Floyd Merrell, 357–95 (Berlin: Mouton de Gruyter, 1991).

4   Mignolo, "Coloniality at Large: Time and the Colonial Difference," in *Time in the Making and Possible Futures*, ed. Enrique Larreta, 237–72 (Rio de Janeiro: UNESCO, 2000). A revised version was printed in chapter 4 of *The Darker Side of Western Modernity: Global Futures, Decolonial Options* (Durham, NC: Duke University Press, 2011). A summary of the chapter could be found here, http://ucritical.org/time-and-the-colonial-difference/.

5   Andrew Smith, "Between Facts and Myths: Karl Jasper and the Actuality of the Axial Age." *International Journal of Philosophy* 76, no. 4 (2015): 315–34.

6    R. Jessop, "Coinage of the term *environment*, a word without authority and Carlyle's displacement of the mechanical metaphor," *Enlighten Publications* (Glasgow: University of Glasgow, 2012), http://eprints.gla.ac.uk/69879/.

7    Norbert Wiener, *Cybernetics: Or Control and Communication in the Animal and the Machine*, 2nd ed (Cambridge, MA: MIT Press, 2017).

8    Colin Cherry, *On Human Communication: A Review, a Survey, and a Criticism* (Cambridge, MA: MIT Press, 1957).

9    Roman Jakobson, *Essais de linguistique generale:* Tome 1. *Les fondations du langage* (Paris: Edition de Minuit, 1963).

10   Michel-Rolph Trouillot, "North Atlantic Universals: Analytical Fictions, 1492–1945," *South Atlantic Quarterly* 101, no. 4 (2002): 839–58, accessed December 8, 2016, http://saq.dukejournals.org/content/101/4/839.citation.

11   Carl Schmit, *The Nomos of the Earth in the International Law of Jus Publicum Europaeum* (New York: Telos Press, 1993).

12   Walter Mignolo, "Epistemic Disobedience and the Decolonial Option: A Manifesto," *Transmodernity* 1, no. 2 (2011): 44–66.

13   Frederic Laloux, *Reinventing Organization: A Guide to Creating Organizations Inspired by the Next Stage of Human Consciousness* (Oxford: Nelson Parker Publishing, 2014). The book is interesting for both the ethnographic documentation and the vision and ambition of foreseeing the next stage of human consciousness. The vision is a call mainly for the middle class, which is losing its privileges. No State, Bank, or Corporation would listen to the call at this point.

14   I elaborate on this issue in my *Decolonial Politics: Border Dwelling, Re-Existence, Epistemic Disobedience* (Durham, NC: Duke University Press, forthcoming). See also one of my sources, Gerda Verden-Zöller and Humberto Maturana, *The Origin of Humanness and the Biology of Love* (Tulsa: Imprint Academy, 2008).

15   "Kant's Moral Philosophy," *Stanford Encyclopedia of Philosophy*, July 7, 2016, accessed July 21, 2017, https://plato.stanford.edu/entries/kant-moral/.

# Closing Remarks

The preceding argument introduces and updates key concepts derived from Aníbal Quijano's groundbreaking proposal. *Coloniality* is, in the first place, a concept that came into being from the former colonies of the South American Andes, at the closing of the Cold War (geopolitics of knowing). It brought to light the global consequences of the invention of the Americas for the planetary world order since then. Modernity, Quijano taught us, is half of the story. The other half is coloniality. Both together engender decolonial responses: epistemic reconstitutions, the legacies that Guaman Poma de Ayala left to us and to the world. Coloniality (shorthand for the CMP) is a concept that uncovers the underlying logic of Western civilization, its formation and planetary expansion since the sixteenth century. In second place, Quijano introduced a radical distinction between *coloniality* and *colonization*. Consequently, and this is crucial for the argument of this book and for the goals of the book series, the distinction between *decoloniality* and *decolonization*.

If by coloniality we mean the underlying logic common to all Western colonialisms and therefore the darker side of modernity, decoloniality means both the analytic of such underlying logic rather than the historic-socio-economic analysis of colonization. Decolonial analytics is at the same time the history of formation, transformation, management, control, and current dispute of the CMP. But the analytic is one aspect of decoloniality. The other is the prospective, the praxis of knowing and living oriented by the decolonial analysis. The analytic is necessary to orient our delinking and relinking to re-exist. For that, epistemic reconstitution is the first step, Quijano taught us to think. Reducing to size Western disciplinary apparatus and the institutions (university, museums, theological institutions) that created and maintain North Atlantic universal fictions, is unavoidable and necessary to open up the coexistence of epistemic and ontological pluriversality. Multiple ontologies are only possible if multiple epistemologies are possible. There cannot be multiple ontologies "recognized" by the benevolence of one universal epistemology. In the politico-economic level of interstate relations, the world order can no longer be monopolar with one State being the commander in chief regulating monopolarity. We are already at the inception of a multipolar world order and witnessing the pressing mutation of the United Nations to become a real United States of the Planet instead of United States of America ruling the United Nations and the planet.

Parallel to the tsunami reordering interstate relations, is the epistemic planetary tsunami reordering the ways of worlds making, mutating the imaginary that the propagation of modern imaginary invited us to see ourselves, our nationals, the others, the non-national, the living organisms with whom we coexist and the life-energies not produced by industry that made possible living (so far) in the planet. The entities that political theory and political economy theorize are not "things" but conceptual structures guiding the conversations, the emotioning and reasoning of politicians, economists, bankers, corporations' CEOs and, at its turn, guiding the behavior of the vast majority of voters and consumers. The alienation that Western knowledge created by conceptualizing and celebrating competition and individualism (which destroys the social fabric), has to be overcome by visions and conceptions of communal praxis of living that puts love and care as the final destiny of the human species and our relations with the living universe (including planet earth). It has become too evident that the turmoil at the global scale (including unnatural disasters), are all signs of the collapse of a system of knowing and being in the world (CMP) and at the same time signs of war are emerging, which are irreversible. In my analysis, those two global heterogeneous orientations are dewesternization and decoloniality. Similarities and differences, analyzed in chapter 5, are the roads toward a multipolar world order (dewesternization) and epistemic and ontological pluriversality (decoloniality).

While the goal of decolonization was marked by the struggle of the native or indigenous population to expel the settler from their colonies and to form their own sovereign nation-states on the ruins of the former colonies, decoloniality's aims are no longer those of decolonization. Decoloniality's goal and orientation, in the shift introduced by Quijano, are *epistemic reconstitution*. Epistemic reconstitution cannot be achieved by setting up a "new" school of thought within Western cosmology. It requires two simultaneous tasks: to open up to the richness of knowledges and praxis of living that the rhetoric of modernity demonized and reduced to tradition, barbarism, folklore, underdevelopment, denied spirituality in the name of reason, and built knowledges to control sexuality and all kind of barbarians. Second, and necessarily, epistemic reconstitution requires delinking from the bubbles of modern thoughts from the left and from the right. Decoloniality then is the constant double movement of the analytics of the CMP, of reducing North Atlantic universals to size and building reemergences and resurgences of the disavowed. Epistemic reconstitution means to delink from the CMP in order to relink and to re-exist. There is no decolonial master plan for that. Each trajectory will be molded and modeled in the praxis of living of those who engage in doing it.

These are the tasks that Quijano's invited us, all of us who would like to join, to pursue. This book, parts I and II, and the book series are reinstating that invitation.


## Modernity's Splendors and Miseries

It is common to hear defenses of modernity invoking its contributions rather than its nefarious consequences. It is also common of people who did not read our work (and many of the scholars and intellectuals who engage coloniality/ decoloniality) to imagine that we are preaching not to read any European authors. Personally, to write *The Darker Side of the Renaissance: Literacy, Territoriality and Colonization* (1995), I needed to read many European authors, some of them critical of their own civilization. But my endeavor and critique was not theirs. There may be someone someplace who recommends not to read European authors. Catherine and I are not responsible for that. Whoever that person is or may be, we do not recognize them in our conversation with our project. The choice is not whether to read works by authors who are European, Eurocentric, or critical of Eurocentrism, but how to read them.[1] The question is from where you start. When I read works by European authors of all kind, I do not start from them. I arrive to them. I start from thinkers and events that were disturbed by European invasions. Even if European thinkers are aware of that and critique colonialism, well, that is half of the story. The other is the critique of modernity from its receiving end, the darker side of modernity, the decolonial praxis of living. Decolonially we draw on the experiences and narratives of events and thinkers in the former colonies in Asia (East, South, Southeast, West, and Central), Africa (Maghreb and sub-Saharan) and from there go to the encounter of events in Europe and European thinkers, from the left and from the right, reading them from the backstage rather than admiring them (even if they are admirable) from the audience.

Without reading the European canon, Enrique Dussel could not have been making the arguments he has been making all along in his career. The contributions that Europe made to the world under the name of modernity have not been called into question. What we call into question is the aberration: the aberration of pretending to submit the planet to the wonderful achievements and visions of the Eurocentered idea of modernity and the torch passed on to the United States, increasingly belligerent. The aberration has been clearly articulated by Dussel a few years after Quijano's foundational article. In his Frankfurt lectures, Dussel stated without equivocation the following:

> Modernity is, for many (for Jürgen Habermas or Charles Taylor, for example) an essentially or exclusively European phenomenon. In these lectures, I will argue that modernity is, in fact, a European phenomenon but one constituted in a dialectical relation with a non-European alterity that is its ultimate content. Modernity appears when Europe affirms itself as the "center" of a *World* History that it inaugurates; the "periphery" that surrounds this center is consequently part of its self-definition.
>
> . . .
>
> It is a question of uncovering the origin of what I call "the myth of modernity" itself. Modernity includes a rational "concept" of emancipation that we affirm and subsume. But, at the same time, it develops an irrational myth, a justification of genocidal violence. The postmodern criticize modern reason as a reason of terror; we criticize modern reason because of the irrational myth it conceals.[2]

It was the air of the time, we could say. In fact, what Dussel was showing was the visible and invisible (colonial) faces of modernity: the emancipating will and the genocidal violence. The first is a sign of the rhetoric of modernity; the second of the necessary and hidden logic of coloniality. Thus, after distinguishing colonialism from coloniality, the second assumption of decolonial thinking is that there is no modernity without coloniality. We write modernity/coloniality. Consequently, affirming and subsuming emancipation doesn't mean to wait for Europeans to liberate non-Europeans first from the Devil (theology), second from barbarism (civilizing mission), third from underdevelopment (the drive to modernization, accepting the universality of modernity), and last from terrorism (globalism and U.S. neo-nationalism). These four projects mentioned are the basic global designs of Western imperial/modernity from 1500 to 2017. Decolonial epistemic praxis

targets the conceptual narratives that sustain and legitimize the implementation of Western global designs. But targeting only the content (the domains
of the CMP), without questioning the terms (the enunciation of the CMP)
that "naturalizes" the content, will not do. If socialism in the Soviet Union
and decolonization during the Cold War failed, one of the reasons is that
both projects confronted the content, not the terms of the conversation. Dewesternization, instead, maintains the domains (the contents) but disputes
the unilateral management of the CMP, not by *opposing* liberal capitalism,
but by *appropriating* capitalism and rejecting liberalism and neoliberalism.[3]

In the Americas and the Caribbean, which are the colonial histories and
legacies that propelled the concept of coloniality; and which are also Catherine's and my histories—see the "After-Word(s)", nation-states were formed
during the nineteenth century mainly.[4] Furthermore, one crucial difference
between decolonization in the second half of the twentieth century and the
same phenomenon in the Americas, but called instead "revolutions" and "independences," is that in Asia and Africa the natives or indigenous were the
ones who fought and managed to build their own nation-states. In the Americas, instead and with the exception of Haiti, all the revolutions and independences were in the hands of people of European descent (Creoles rather than
Natives or Indigenous).

These are the demographic genealogies to which Catherine and I fit in.
Quijano was well aware of it, particularly in the Andes, where First Nations
people are the majority of the population. He was also well aware of the simultaneous confrontation of the West and the Soviet Union, on the one hand,
and the decolonization in Africa and Asia on the other. Decoloniality (epistemic reconstitution) in his formulation emerged from dissention within the
demographic composition Creoles and Mestizo/as of European descent and
with the awareness that brings forward our responsibility in redressing the
wrongdoings of our European colonial or late immigrant ancestors, be they
from the Iberian peninsula, France, England, Italy, or the Netherlands.

Decolonial epistemic reconstitution(s) (re-existence, reemergence) in
whatever form it takes and whomever are the actors in their respective
local histories to engage in it/them cannot be thought out as a global universal but as global pluriversal. No universal decoloniality can be mapped
by one single local history and one single project. This was precisely the
aberration of modern global designs. And this is precisely the aberration of Western modernity, of westernization, and rewesternization (see
chapter 5).

## The Case for Colonialism and the Unawareness of Coloniality

The arguments advanced in this book, and in the series, will have also an important role to play in confronting emerging tendencies underscoring positive sides of colonialism claiming the benefit of its return. From here to right wing's (Alt-Right and other versions) arguments there is only one step. In the years preceding the invasion of Iraq, Canadian author, academic, and former politician Michael Grant Ignatieff published several articles and a book arguing for the need for "soft imperialism."[5] Not surprisingly, Ignatieff's call was not forgotten. Recently Bruce Gilley, a political science professor, argued for the return of colonialism.[6] In both cases, it is evidently the continuation of a seed that was planted several decades ago by Rudyard Kipling's "The White Man's Burden: The United States and the Philippine Islands," a poem published in 1899 exhorting the United States to follow the path of England and European nations to take on the "burden" of empire.

Before I go on, a clarification is necessary: the article by Gilley I am commenting on here was taken off circulation shortly after it was published. I have written what follows before it was taken down. Fortunately, I downloaded and saved a copy. What it is available to the general public today are the reasons why it was taken off circulation, the reasons for the resignation of a significant number of board members of *Third World Quarterly*. My comment bellows are neither concerned with the reasons it was published nor for the reasons taken off circulations (which is an internal issue of *Third World Quarterly*). I am concerned with the argument that would still stand if the scholarship were not questioned. Or, putting it differently: the claim for the benefit of colonialism shall be uncoupled from the valuation of scholarship, for the claim would still stand if scholarship were accepted, by the board members, as sound scholarship. The reason I focus on the claim of the benefits of colonialism today is because I has been around for a while. I thank Gilley for making public and explicit what is in the mind of many people: the benefit that colonialism and modernity brought to uncivilized barbarians and lesser human beings. These claims, not made public, are only looking at one side of the story: colonialism brought modernity to the world without looking at how modernity also brought coloniality to the world. There is no modernity without coloniality, and there is no colonialism without all kinds of violence (physical, psychological, racist, sexist) and without the arrogance of the colonizer. All of this is overlooked in Gilley's argument.[7]

Both Ignatieff and Gilley address different circumstantial scenarios to make the same type of argument. Ignatieff wrote several articles and a book before and after 2003 justifying the (unjustifiable) invasion of Iraq. The United States invaded Iraq on March 20, 2003. On January 5, 2003, the *New York Times* published an op-ed by Ignatieff significantly titled "The American Empire; The Burden."[8] The argument, 104 years after Kipling, is the same: only the years have changed, the circumstances, and a few proper names. More striking though is that Kipling was making his request at the time in which the United States was asserting (one hundred and twenty years after its constitution as nation-state) its right to become a global power. The Sino-Japanese War (July 1894–April 1895) and the Spanish-American War, April–August 1998) are signposts of the transformation of the global order, and the restructuration of CMP, in which the United States and Japan became uninvited global players. Recently, however, Condoleezza Rice stated in an interview that democracy was not the reason why the United States invaded Iraq. The "white man burden" mutated into the "white man mission."

After World War II and the defeat of Japan, the United States became the hope for the recovering of Europe (Marshall Plan), the champion of modernization and development in Latin America (the Alliance for Progress), and the supporter of freedom in the fight for decolonization in Africa and Asia. The invasion of Iraq led many to rethink the role of the United States as a global leader—and Ignatieff argued the need for "soft imperialism" in the name of freedom. WMD were one of the excuses (what has to be destroyed); the other was to remove Saddam Hussein, a tyrant, to spread democracy. On November 3, 2003 (about six months after the invasion), George W. Bush "laid out a broad vision of an American mission to spread democracy throughout the Middle East and the rest of the world, saying, 'Freedom can be the future of every nation.'"[9]

Gilley's argument brings up many issues Catherine and I have addressed in this book, but of course from a different perspective. I will retain only two: one is to show the different narratives that can be construed if your assumptions lead you to reasoning from the regulations of disciplinary formations (in Gilley's case political sciences) or if your assumptions lead you to reasoning from the principles of decolonial thinking. The following comments on Gilley's argument intend to clarify and strengthen the points made in previous chapters. The second is to show the argumentative strength of decoloniality when it delinks from disciplinary strictures and becomes an undisciplinary and liberating path of thinking guiding our doing and becoming on the planet.

What I have in mind with my observations on becoming is Argentinian philosopher Rodolfo Kusch who, learning from Aymara's thinking, expressed it in an Argentine Castilian formula that has no translation into English, French, or German: *estar siendo*. Estar siendo is Kusch's understanding of Aymara's thought in confrontation with the modern/colonial state of mind of the Latin American middle class whose horizon was *querer ser* (wanting to be what they are not). Estar siendo is at once resistance and re-existance: to be being in their own praxis of living. "Estar siendo" is akin to decoloniality today, for the project of decolonization during the Cold War was driven by an "ought to be free" through the creation of a nation-state, which was falling into the trap of coloniality without colonialism. I am not saying that leaders of decolonization should have adopted the estar siendo position. I am just describing Aymara's responses of resistance in re-existence as understood by Kusch, which I think is the planetary scenario today. It is in this sphere of praxis of living that decoloniality could make a contribution that is not trapped in the spider web of the nation-state, capitalism, rewesternizing neoliberalism and dewestern affirmation by appropriating the economy of accumulation. Dewesternization is an unavoidable outcome of five hundred years of westernization. Decoloniality acts as the cracks of the interstate conflict between re- and dewesternization. In this scenario, there is no way to revamp colonialism even soft imperialism as Ignatieff dreamed. Ukraine and Syria as well as the Belt and Road changed the CMP's scenario forever.

Gilley's point is to show the benefits of returning to colonialism. Beyond his analysis of the failures of decolonization during the Cold War he has also, as a political scientist, recommendations to make for recolonization work to the benefit of both former Western settlers and for the local population. It is not clear in his argument, but given the experiences of decolonization and its aftermath, that the local elites in complicity with sectors of the former colonizer would end up being reproduced if Gilley's proposal materializes. Local elites will, as they did, take advantage of their privileges and disregard the "nations" of their "state." Imperial elites will benefit from the colonial collaborators and perhaps promote their own ethics contributing to the development of the underdeveloped. Or perhaps Gilley is just making an argument for debate among disciplinary political scientists, argument that will not have any bearing in imperial public policies. Perhaps the argument could make the elites of some former colonized country happy and reassured to be protected and nourished by former imperial countries. But let's suppose, for the sake of argument, that Gilley's proposal could materialize.

Gilley's argument focuses on colonialism in Africa mainly with some examples from Asia, before the United States took over world leadership. His scenario is basically the scenario that decolonization struggle during the Cold War dismantled—this was the victory of decolonization although building nation-states was a failure. Gilley invites us to imagine what a benevolent neocolonialism would be for former imperial countries and local colonial elites.

> Gilley invites us to image that the government of Guinea-Bissau were to lease back to Portugal the small and uninhabited island of Galinhas that lies ten miles off the mainland and where the former colonial governor's mansion lies in ruins. The annual lease should be US$1 so that the Portuguese spend their money on the island and the Guinea-Bissau government is not dependent on a lease fee. Suppose, then, that the US$10 million to US$20 million in foreign aid wasted annually on the country were redirected to this new offshore colony to create basic infrastructure. As part of the deal, the Portuguese would allow a certain number of Guinea-Bissau residents to resettle on the island each year. Portuguese institutions and sovereignty would be absolute for the term of the lease—say 99 years as was the case with the mainland parts of Hong Kong. A small European state would grow up on the African coast.
>
> At 60 square miles, Galinhas could, over time, wisely accommodate the entire population of Guinea-Bissau. If successful, it would attract talent, trade and capital. *The mainland parts of Guinea-Bissau would benefit from living next to an economic dynamo and learning to emulate its success, while symbolically escaping from the half-century anticolonial nightmare of Amilcar Cabral. The same idea could be tried over the coastlines of Africa and the Middle East if successful. Colonialism could be resurrected without the usual cries of oppression, occupation, and exploitation.*[9] (emphasis mine)

I do not want to mislead the reader with a quotation out of context. In the paragraph after the quotation the author wonders whether his example could be considered preposterous. He underscores, in full awareness of the controversial aspects of his argument, that it may not be so much preposterous if one thinks about anticolonial ideology that in the past 100 years (which would be since 1920, or the end of World War I fought among European states for their own Scramble for Africa), "has been hurting the lives of hundreds of millions of people in the Third World. A hundred years of disasters"—he concludes—"is enough. It is time to make the case for colonialism again."[10] Gilley has a point that I have also addressed in chapter 5 and at the beginning of these "Closing Remarks": the failure of decolonization in building sovereign modern/colonial nation-states after independence, in spite of the victory of sending the settlers home. So, the ideal lab experiment of Galinhas should be taken as an invitation to imagine forms of governance that would end the 100 years of the decolonizing ideology hurting the lives of millions of people in the Third World, in the quoted sentences in this paragraph. These are for Gilley the consequences of recolonization.

Before moving forward, I need to underline a few missing pieces of the puzzle that Gilley tries to put together, when you go at them from decolonial assumptions and that in consequence are crucial for decolonial arguments. The first missing piece shows up in Gilley's historical reference to past colonialisms.

> The case for the past record of Western colonialism—usually referring to British, French, German, Belgian, Dutch, and Portuguese colonies from the early nineteenth to mid-twentieth centuries—rests on overturning two distinct lines of criticism: that it was objectively harmful (rather than beneficial); and that it was subjectively illegitimate (rather than legitimate). There is in addition, a third line of criticism that merits revision: that it offends the sensibilities of contemporary society.[11]

Albeit the dates noted by Gilley are the early nineteenth to mid-twentieth centuries, it is surprising that he names Portuguese but not Spanish colonialism. One of the reasons may be that his entire argument is framed from the eighteenth century on and, the other, already mentioned, *is that Gilley only sees colonialism but not coloniality*. In this regard, Spanish colonialism from Indias Orientales to Indias Occidentales (from 1500 to 1898 when Spaniards lost their last colonies in the Caribbean and the Philippines) established—in conjunction with the Pope and the Portuguese monarchy—the historical foundations of both the salvation rhetoric of modernity and the hidden logic of control and domination (politically, economically, epistemically, esthetically, ethnically, sexually). Coloniality is more, much more, than political-economic "good" administration bringing material benefits for some at the expense of misery and humiliation for others. Dutch, British, and French colonialism in the nineteenth and twentieth centuries were just a continuation of this earlier historical foundation. The changes are substantial if you focus on colonialism. If instead you look for coloniality and you are aware of the history of the CMP they are circumstantial.

In her celebrated TED Talk, ("The Danger of a Single Story"), Chimamanda Ngozi Adichie has a couple of powerful recommendations on this topic:[12] Storytelling could be used—Adichie observes—to denigrate and mislead but it can also be put to work to empower and demystify. But when there is a single story that people believe, the question is not whether to empower or denigrate but from where to start the story. If you start from—say—the failure of Africans to build successful nation-states, you will arrive at certain conclusions, akin to Gilley's argument. If you instead start from the fact that nation-states, the very idea of uniform nationality, was a European imperial imposition, you will arrive at a different conclusion, akin to the one we are making in this book. Gilley started from the Africans' failure to build nation-states; we start from the second, the problems that the creation of nation-states meant for Europe (think about Nazism) as well as for the former colonies that fell into the trap of wanting their own nation-states.

Gilley takes a quotation from the memoirs of Chinua Achebe (who is Nigerian as well as Adichie) to support his argument, and Adichie's underscoring of the danger of a single story is helpful. Achebe's quotation follows:

> Here is a piece of heresy: The British governed their colony of Nigeria with considerable care. There was a very highly competent cadre of government officials imbued with a high level of knowledge of how to run a country. This was not something that the British achieved only in Nigeria; they were able to manage this on a bigger scale in India and Australia. The British had the experience of governing and doing its competently. I am not justifying colonialism. But it is important to face the fact that British colonies, more or less, were expertly run.[13]

Indeed, Achebe recognizes, explicitly, that the British were careful administrators (we could say the same for their administration of *their* plantations in the Caribbean). It means, tacitly, that nation-states after decolonization were not as well run as the British ran the colonies. Which brings us back to Adichie's point: it all depends from where you start. If you start from the British good administration running their own business, you conclude that

Africans are incompetent to run the model administration that the British left behind when running their own business. But if instead you start from the fact that Africans received (without asking for it) and were left with an administrative structure totally alien to their millenarian praxis of living, you have to conclude that the British good administration disrupted the praxis of living Africans had (in the territory British mapped and named Nigeria) before they had imposed upon them the expertise and administrative experience in Britain. Africans did not invite the British to transform their territory into well-run British colonies.

Perhaps the most pernicious colonial legacy since and after the eighteenth century was the idea that to one state corresponds only one nation. It worked in Europe because the population was relatively homogeneous. But the Holocaust showed to the world the problem of the idea that one state corresponds to one nation (or vice versa). Immigrants and refugees in Europe and the United States are showing again that the formula is not working. The opening up in Bolivia and Ecuador toward plurinational states, although it doesn't question the state-form of governance, shows that in the former colonies one-nation–one-state formula was a formula for trouble.[14] One-nation–one-state formula could not have worked out when the British invented the territory of Nigeria. The majority of British people were white and Christians under one kingdom, although some were Catholic and others Protestant. However, the nation grouped people of the same ethnicity, language, and Western memory. In Nigeria, beyond the high number of ethnic groups, it proved to be more than difficult bringing together Hausa-Fulani, Yoruba, and Igbo under the idea of *one nation*. The British model of governance based on British historical trajectory did not work in Nigeria nor in many other regions where the idea of "plurinational" offers the possibilities (to those interested in it) of saving the state form of governance

Nonetheless it is unavoidable to recognize that decolonization during the Cold War failed, and it failed for many reasons: one of the reasons is that local elites wanted something (the nation-state) that was alien to them but that was desirable because of the persuasive rhetoric enticing people to become modern and jump on the bandwagon of universal history. The second reason is that the elites founding, and controlling the newly formed nation-state took also the opportunity of the personal advantage that decolonization offered to them. All the dreams of Amilcar Cabral and Patrice Lumumba were taken away from them and distorted by the elites trapped in the interstate system web regulated by the CMP. Recognizing that decolonization failed leaves us today with two options: to return to the colonial administration as Gilley argues or to move away from *decolonization* toward *decoloniality*. The second path is what this book and the book series intends.

## Decoloniality meets Biology of Cognition and Cultural Biology

Catherine and I started the introduction addressing relationality/vincularidad as the horizon of knowledge and understanding that will take us, on the planet (if there is time left), away from Western ontological totalitarianism. And I argued through part II that coloniality of knowledge and of being is the target of decolonial work: decolonial knowledge shall restore many issues that coloniality of knowledge and the narratives of modernity disavowed and relegated to the past and to tradition and it shall also open up the imagination without restriction to avoid and undermine the latest technological advance of coloniality in the name of modernity (progress, salvation, freedom, and the like). Retrieving the nonmodern in its planetary diversity doesn't mean that all the nonmodern shall be retrieved. Like with the tradition of modernity, there are many issues and experiences that we do not want to preserve: we do not want to preserve racism, sexism, genocide, arrogance, inequalities that goes with the territory of modernity.

Entities and objects populate Western epistemologies and, consequently, "representation" became a key word of the rhetoric of modernity to free the known from the knower, attributing to the ontic an existence independent from the knower that "represents" ontologically. This is the issue I underscored with Maturana's epigraph in chapter 5. Theology populated the world with abstract entities and secular empirical sciences and the corresponding philosophy populated the world and the universe with objects and matter. It was precisely at that junction that Immanuel Kant and then Martin Heidegger came up with the concept of ontotheology. Epistemology and ontology are two Western concepts that you do not find in any non-Western ways of thinking . . . until Western theology, science, and philosophy invaded those systems. The conjunction of Christian theology and Western secularism shattered experiences of seeing and sensing relations/vincularidad in the living energy of the universe. Today non-Indigenous people around the world begin to realize the trap of Western modern epistemology and the consequences of coloniality of knowledge and of being: that means coloniality of ontology or ontological coloniality (see chapters 7 and 8).

At this point of the closing remarks, decoloniality meets biology of cognition in the sphere of humanness (see chapter 7). Biology of cognition moves us away from the basic assumptions of secular hard sciences, parallel to the way in which decolonial thinking moves us away from the social sciences and the humanities. Decoloniality joins biology of cognition also in the similarity of goals: to delink from the traps of Western epistemic ontology and to open up to epistemic pluriversality and therefore to ontological coexistence leading to epistemic pluriversality. Maturana's foundational article changing the logic of the questions that all Western disciplines ask was published in 1970. I quote from a 1980 reprint. Here is the entry arguing for the biological foundation of cognition:

> Man knows and his capacity to know depends on his biological integrity; furthermore, he knows that he knows. As a basic psychological and, hence, biological function *cognition* guides his handling of the universe and *knowledge* gives certainty to his acts; *objective knowledge* seems possible and through *objective knowledge* the universe appears systematic and predictable. Yet *knowledge* as an experience is something personal and private that cannot be transferred, and that which one believes to be transferable, objective knowledge, must always be created by the listener: the listener understands, and *objective knowledge* appears transferred, only if he is prepared to understand. Thus, *cognition* as a biological function is such that the answer to the question, *'What is cognition?'* must arise from understanding knowledge and the knower through the latter's capacity to know.[15]

To make a long story short, decoloniality meets biology of cognition at the point where the biological constitution of a species of living organisms endowed with nervous systems can engage in praxis that non-other living organisms can: (a) to use the hands to cultivate and cook their own food as well as to make instruments that extend the uses of the hands (e.g., the hammer and the computer keyboard where I am typing now); and (b) to engage in languaging in order to coordinate behavior with other members of the same species. Languaging made possible storytelling to imagine the creation of the universe as well as the origination of the ethnic groups telling the story of the universe and of themselves, from the earlier records to the contemporary narratives of the Big Bang. There is no *evolution* in the uses of the hand and engaging languaging but *expansion* of the activities that can be performed by the combined praxis of both. In Western vocabulary the word *human* names the class of living organisms I am referring to. But "human" is a regional concept that was extended to other languages and civilization, ignoring that each language and civilization has their distinctive ways of conceiving and naming the species of living organisms standing erect on two extremities, using their hands and engaging in languaging.

Once it is understood that cognition is biologically embedded in all living organisms[16] and that there is a class of living organisms able to use their/our upper extremities to build shelters, cultivate our own food and cook it, to make instruments enlarging the capacity of our hands, it is no longer necessary to engage in debates about mind/body, masculine/feminine, and above all nature/culture dichotomies. The so-called human body (see chapter 6) is a moving and living relational organism that can only exist for a period of time (from birth to death) in relation to planetary energies of life (sun, moon, rain, water, oxygen, plants, animals) and the niche (the particular configuration of a given organism with its needs outside of itself) without which the organism will not survive. Cognition is presupposed in the basic and elemental praxis of living. Therefore, concepts such as "culture," "mind," "soul," "women," "men," "god" are all conceptual consequences of our human capacity for languaging. "Culture" could only have been conceived because of "nature": that is, the biological constitution of certain living organisms (nature) made possible the invention of both the concept of culture and its opposite, the concept of nature (see chapter 7). Conversely, the biological constitution of the organisms becomes embedded in the "culture" that languaging organisms create in (second-order, disciplinary) conversations.

Biology of cognition comes to assist decolonial thinking in its endeavor of reducing Western knowledge (scientific, philosophical, theological) to size and opening it up to pluriversal epistemic ontologies (multiversal in Maturana's vocabulary). Biology of cognition is achieving in the sphere of Western sciences and education (see chapter 10) what decoloniality aims to achieve in the social sciences and humanities, including the artistic spheres (curatorial, art history, and criticism)[17] and the sphere of education.

It is not by chance that Maturana's scientific investigation has led him to work in education and with psychologists and social workers once he began to further explore the biological dimension of biology and the cultural aspects of culture. "Cultural biology" is the formula that he and Ximena Dávila created to describe the collaboration between a scientist and a psychologist and social worker.[18] Education is a battleground between, on the one hand, modern/colonial *schooling* to maintain the CMP and, on the other, decolonial education/pedagogy delinking from the CMP schooling practices. When land becomes the basis and guidance for First Nations pedagogy[19] it will not be accepted by the secretary of education of any known mononational state, university presidents, museum directors, on the leaders of other institutions of public or private education.[20] Biology of cognition/education and decolonial pedagogies cannot be expected to be endorsed and promoted by the state, the university, the museum, or the church. These institutional spaces can be taken and used in the seminars we teach, workshops we can organize, and conversations we can maintain and initiate, when necessary. However, initiatives mapping the horizons of cultural biology and decolonial thinking have to come and are coming from the emerging global political society of which this book and the series aimes to belong.

## Notes

1    I ally myself here with the clear statement by Syed Farid Alatas on reading Europeans authors; without reading them one could not point out their limitations. However, the genealogies of thought in former colonies are not the same as the genealogy of European thoughts even when they critique their own Eurocentrism. See Syed Farid Alatas and Vineeta Sinha, *Sociological Theory Beyond the Canon* (London: Palgrave MacMillan, 2017); Wang Hui, *China from Empire to Nation-State* (Cambridge, MA: Harvard University Press, 2014).

2    Enrique Dussel, "Eurocentrism and Modernity (Introduction to the Frankfurt Lectures)." *Boundary 2* 20, no. 3 (1993): 65–76.

3    "Western Liberal Democracy Will Be Wrong for China." *Intelligence2: The World of Debate.* YouTube, 2012, https://www.youtube.com/watch?v=EwM9CuGcBgl.

4    Benedict Anderson, *Imagined Communities: Reflections on the Origin and Spread of Nationalism* (London: Verso, 1983). See also from the other side of the line, Sara Castro-Klarén and John Chastin, eds., *Beyond Imagined Communities: Reading and Writing the Nation in Nineteenth Century Latin America* (Washington, DC: Woodrow Wilson Center Press, 2003).

5    Michael Ignatieff, "The American Empire: The Burden," *New York Times*, January 5, 2003, http://www.nytimes.com/2003/01/05/magazine/the-american-empire-the-burden.html. See also by Ignatieff *The Lesser Evil: Political Ethics in the Age of Terror* (Princeton, NJ: Princeton University Press, 2005).

6    Bruce Gilley, "The Case for Colonialism," *Third World Quarterly*, September 8, 2017, http://www.tandfonline.com/doi/full/10.1080/01436597.2017.1369037.

7    I am thankful to Lisa Ann Richey, editorial board resigning member, for a long personal conversation in Chapel Hill, NC, in which she explained the avatars that

led to the publication of the article and the resignation of several of the editorial board members and provided me with several links on the follow up. Here is a chronology of the event: https://storify.com/ComDev/third-world-quarterly -the-colonialismdebate; http://blogs.lse.ac.uk/impactofsocialsciences/2017/09 /19/clickbait-andimpact-how-academia-has-been-hacked/. Lisa also generously provided me with letters of resignations and provided me with the link for another article by Gilley on Chinua Achebe and the positive legacies of colonialism, which is part of the argument the author made in "The case for colonialism": https:// academic.oup.com/afraf/articleabstract/115/461/646/2236096?redirectedFrom =fulltext.

8   Ignatieff, "The American Empire," http://www.nytimes.com/2003/01/05/magazine /the-american-empire-the-burden.html.

9   Maura Reynolds, "Bush Said America Must Spread Democracy," *Baltimore Sun*, November 7, 2003, http://www.baltimoresun.com/news/bal-te.busho7novo7-story .html; see also Condoleezza Rice, "US Wars in the Middle East Were Not Supposed to Bring Democracy," *Newsweek*, May 12, 2017, http://www.newsweek.com/us-war -middle-east-bring-democracy-rice-608640.

10  Gilley, "The Case for Colonialism."

11  Gilley, "The Case for Colonialism."

12  Gilley, "The Case for Colonialism."

13  Chimamanda Ngozi Adichie, "The Danger of a Single Story." TED Talk, October 7, 2009, https://www.youtube.com/watch?v=D9Ihs241zeg.

14  Chinua Achebe, *There Was a Country* (London: Penguin Books, 2012), 43.

15  Sofía Cordero Ponce, "Estados plurinacionales en Bolivia y Ecuador: Nuevas ciudadanías, más democracia." *Nueva Sociedad*, 2012, 134–48, http://nuso.org /articulo/estados-plurinacionales-en-bolivia-y-ecuador-nuevas-ciudadanias-mas -democracia/.

16  Humberto Maturana, *Biology of Cognition: Biological Computer Laboratory Research Report BCL 9.0* (Urbana: University of Illinois, 1970); reprinted in *Autopoiesis and Cognition: The Realization of the Living*; Dordrecht: D. Reidel, 1980, 5–58. At that time Maturana, as many others, wrote "Man" for "Human." That has been changed in his latest work, at least since the late nineties.

17  Abel Rodriguez, *El árbol de la abundancia*. YouTube, April 4, 2014 (a living perspective). https://www.youtube.com/watch?v=DTXyXAqWEss; see also Daniel Chamotivtz, *What a Plant Knows: A Field Guide to the Senses (a scientific perspective)* (New York: Farrar, Straus and Giroux, 2013).

18  Walter D. Mignolo and Rolando Vázquez, "Decolonial AestheSis: Colonial Wounds/ Decolonial Healings." *Social Text Online*, July 2013, https://socialtextjournal.org /periscope_article/decolonial-aesthesis-colonial-woundsdecolonial-healings/.

19  Humberto Maturana and Ximena Dávila, "Cultural-Biology: Systemic Consequences of Our Evolutionary Cultural Drift as Molecular Autopoietic Systems." CEPA e-print 3900, 2016, http://www.univie.ac.at/constructivism/archive/fulltexts/3900.html.

20  Leanne Simpson, "Land as Pedagogy: Nishnaabeg Intelligence and Rebellious Transformations." *Decolonization: Indigeneity, Education and Society*. 3, no. 3 (2014): 1–25, http://decolonization.org/index.php/des/article/view/22170/17985.

21  See "Learning from the Land: Indigenous Land-based Pedagogy and Decolonization," *Decolonization: Indigeneity, Education and Society* 3, no. 3 (2014).

# After-Word(s)

At the beginning was the word. Catherine and Walter drew a map of our vision of the series, the volumes, and the two parts and the chapters of this book that each one of us would write. Then each of us proceeded to write our respective parts. When we were done we cowrote the introduction. Then came the period of responding to outside evaluators and editing according to comments and suggestions we both considered relevant. We exchanged again our respective parts to cowrite an afterword or *after-words*, literally the "words after."

As we explained in the introduction, this book opens the series "On Decoloniality" in two voices, each with their own accent, perspective, and positionality, but in conversation and relation. In fact, our intention is just this. It is to make evident a methodology of cothought and corelation, a methodology-in-as-pedagogy that does not just describe decoloniality but more crucially enacts decoloniality in the very process of analysis, concept making, concept revising, and praxis-based thinking. Our intention is to evince decolonial thinking/doing as neither individual nor finished processes; they are always conversational, relational, and becoming. The intention is also to place in tension our own authority and places of enunciation. As we said in the introduction, this book in no way assumes that our perspectives are the only valid ones for understanding decoloniality. We are not "experts." Rather, we are engaged intellectuals still learning to unlearn in order to relearn; to challenge our own histories, herstories, privileges, and limitations. For us, decoloniality means thinking, doing, sharing, and collaborating with people in different parts of the globe engaged in similar paths, people striving—as both of us are—in their own local histories confronting global designs. Thus while the book takes as its ground Quijano's idea/concept of *the coloniality of power*, the project and proposition are broader: in essence, they point to the ways that coloniality and decoloniality are options, perspectives, and practices for an otherwise of being, thinking, sensing, doing, and living in the world.

In consonance with this project, proposition, and intention, we choose to close the book together, in two voices, with the following after-words that further weave our ongoing conversation.

**CATHERINE:** It is interesting, Walter, how each of us, in somewhat similar ways, think from and with the ideas (and-as-analytics, and-as-postures, and-as-practices) of resurgence and re-existence. I open the book in chapter 1 with reflections on the significance of re-existence and resurgence for understanding decoloniality in/as praxis, particularly in Abya Yala or the Americas, and you close the book in chapter 10 with reflections that also give centrality to both with regard to decoloniality's analytic and praxis. The fact that we did not plan this connection is in and of itself interesting. However, what I find important to once again emphasize and highlight for our readers here is how these postulates-practices make especially evident the lived meaning and ongoing nature of decoloniality. Resurgence and re-existence signify the praxical and the actional (in the Fanonian sense). Moreover, they make present and bring to the fore the relational lifeblood of decoloniality as prospect and project.

**WALTER:** It is interesting indeed. In my case, I always read Quijano's call to "desprenderse del patrón colonial de poder" (delinking from the colonial matrix of power) together with his statement after the call for delinking: it is urgent and necessary, Quijano said in the first foundational articles of what became a project, to engage in *epistemic reconstitution*. As we know Quijano was trained in sociology, and he taught in several academic institutions. However, I never saw Quijano's work as academic work. He always was—and still is—a scholar/activist. So *epistemic reconstitution* did not mean a reconstitution to "save" sociology, but to save ourselves from the modern/colonial academic epistemology that permeates our lives beyond the university. Then came Adolfo Albán Achinte, who offered to the collective the crucial concept of *re-existence*. So for me, epistemic reconstitution now has a nephew or a niece: re-existence introduced a new dimension, and we had two powerful concepts to overcome the limits (although also the necessity) of resistance. Then came Leanne Simpson, from whom I learned the meaning of resurgence in the epistemic, political, and ethical struggles of First Nations in Canada rejecting the colonial settler state project of recognition. Then, in another sphere, the sphere of cultural dewesternization that I mentioned in chapter 5 (although we do not address the question of art, museums, and biennials here), the need of reemergence proved to be necessary. Briefly what I see is that, on the one hand, there is the need and urgency of delinking and, on the other, the need and urgency of relinking. Otherwise, delinking leaves you in front of a precipice. Now the question is what to relink with; well, that would depend on people organizing themselves/ourselves in different regions and locales of the world, people who feel the need to delink from the colonial matrix of power in order to relink to their own praxis of living. I think you theorize in part I, relinking from different geopolitical and body-political venues. My understanding here is that together our two parts enact decoloniality in its two complementary faces: the analytic to know how, when, from what aspect of CMP to delink and consequently how and what to relink.

**CATHERINE:** Exactly. I agree that re-existence and resurgence (along with what I describe in chapter 2 as insurgence) take resistance to another level. In essence, they point to, reveal, and construct struggles not just against the CMP but for the possibilities of an otherwise. Here delinking and relinking as you describe them, and seen as both individual and collective processes, are interwoven in the political, epistemic, ethical, and existence-based work of affirmation, affirmation as opposed to negation. Affirmation of life against the project of death which increasingly defines global coloniality today. I recall a conversation we had after the election of Trump in the United States and with respect to the rise of the extreme Right in South America and elsewhere, a conversation about the need to more deeply analyze and consider the constitution and operation of the global CMP today. Certainly such analysis is part of the work to be done. It is also part of the work occurring in collectives, organizations, and communities in many regions of the world; the recent seed-bed seminar of the Zapatistas that I mention in chapter 2 is only one such example. Still, and returning to the context of our book and these after-words of conversation, I want to say two things. The first has to do with what I consider as the openness and ongoing usefulness of Quijano's thought. I recall Maria Lugones's argument in her now classic text on the colonial/modern gender system. For Lugones, Quijano's historical theory and framework of social classification and coloniality's model of power are not closed; rather, they invite additions and contributions that build upon his original conceptualizations. This understanding is fundamental. Not only does it underscore the collective nature of the project of modernity/coloniality/decoloniality in its various situated and incarnated perspectives, manifestations, and groupings, but it also incites and encourages theoretical, conceptual, and praxistical work that can help to elucidate and extend comprehensions of the complex and reconstitutive matrix of colonial/modern power. Such understanding disputes the all-authoritative, definitive, and individualized property-related tenets of Western academic knowledge. It unravels arguments—including among some who associate themselves with decolonial thought—about the limitations of Quijano's thought. And it furthers the recognition, present throughout this book, of the ways that Quijano's conceptualization of the coloniality of power continues to promote and provoke decolonial thinking and doing.

The second and related point that I wanted to bring into these afterwords, is about the relation of epistemic reconstitution (as conceptualized by Quijano) and re-existence. Here I am thinking with Albán's postulate, with the existence-based thought of Caribbean intellectuals such as Frantz Fanon, Sylvia Wynter, Lewis Gordon, Paget Henry, Nelson Maldonado-Torres, and Jacqui Alexander, with the propositions of decolonial feminists, particularly those of color, and with the many struggles *from below* in the Souths of the world (including the Souths in the North) that, as the Pakistani feminist Corinne Kumar reminds us (see chapter 1), break the mind constructs and walk new political imaginaries, new meanings, new moorings. I think you would agree, Walter, that this is part of our project in this book and the series that will soon follow.

**WALTER:** I do in fact agree. In the second part I tried to walk the years since Aníbal Quijano published his foundational article for the project (the project, of course, not being his intention), and reflect on where we are now on the planet. Since you mentioned in the previous paragraph several thinkers who are in and related to our project (like "shifting the geography of reason," the logo of the Caribbean Philosophical Association), I would like to continue that line of reflection at a global scale. Always keeping with Quijano's initial intention and formulation: what happened in the Atlantic in the sixteenth century and the invention of America extended all over the planet, into Asia and Africa in the subsequent centuries. Global coloniality is not only political, economic, and military but epistemic and cultural in all its domains as well. I am interested in understanding decolonial responses to coloniality in local histories where the West (Western Europe and later on the Anglo–U.S.), intervened, interfered and disrupted.

Take, for example, the collapse of the Soviet Union and with it the transformation of Eastern Europe. We will have contributions in this series by Madina Tlostanova (Cherkessian) and Ovidiu Tichindeleanu, both working on several dimensions of postsocialism and decoloniality, in politics, arts, genders, and sexuality. Both are connected to Maria Lugones; Ovidiu was her student. Madina is connected as well with Sylvia Marcos, and follows the work of Gloria Anzaldúa in dialogue with feminism in Central Asia. At this very moment I am writing these lines in Ho Chi Minh City, where there is a group of artists, curators, and philosophers interested in our conception of coloniality/decoloniality in conversation with local theorists like Kwan-sing Chen in Taipei and Wang Hui in Beijing. I was just in Taipei a few weeks ago with Joyce C. H. Liu at the Center for Inter-Asia Cultural Studies, to which Kwan-sing belongs. In South Africa, Sabelo J. Ndlovu-Gatsheni is doing interesting work starting from the local histories of Africa in dialogue with coloniality/decoloniality. Each of them have, of course, their own versions of what we call coloniality grounded their own local histories intervened in by global designs.

There is another aspect that has been unfolding among those who embrace modernity/coloniality/decoloniality: decolonial aesthetics/aesthesis. There is a considerable work done in this aspect. As a matter of fact, Adolfo (Albán Achinte) raised the aesthetic issue in the colonial matrix of power many years ago in the PhD program that you created at the Universidad Andina Simón Bolívar in Quito. Many people have been exploring expanding this venue both as artists, curators, art critics and historians, and activists. I hope also to have a volume on the topic in the series. I have been working with Pedro Pablo Gómez (Colombia), Alanna Lockward (Berlin–Dominican Republic), Rolando Vázquez (Mexico–the Netherlands), and several artist and curators in Europe gathered around the Middelburg Decolonial Summer School and Be.Bop 2012–18 (Black Europe Body Politics). In Argentina there is also an interesting unfolding of decolonial aesthesis led by Zulma Palermo (in Salta), María Eugenia Borsani (in Neuquén) and Pablo Quintero

(Venezuela-Argentina-Brazil). Briefly, I hope that the series will continue the ramification of dialogues and doing in our daily decolonial praxis of living.

**CATHERINE:** The presence of decolonial pluriversals and interversals is growing in the world as people struggle to find ways of being, thinking, sensing, feeling, knowing, creating, and existing—of living—in the borders and cracks of the CMP, and what the Zapatistas refer to as the capitalist hydra, the Storm or catastrophe brewing, and the war against life. As I describe in chapter 4, the decolonial cracks have become, for me, the place and space of my thinking-doing. Opening, making, and widening the cracks, along with sowing seeds within the cracks, are, without a doubt, part of the work to be done.

Most recently, and after reading your part II, Walter, I have thinking about the relation between the borders and the cracks, between border thinking and the thinking-doing from, with, and towards the decolonial cracks, including the actions of decolonial crack making. Such relation has prompted me to read and reread Gloria Anzaldúa, particularly her text *Light in the Dark/Luz en lo oscuro*, written in the last decade of her life and edited in 2015 by Analouise Keating. In this text, Anzaldúa relates the borders with the cracks. She speaks of the "cracks between the worlds" and of "dwelling in liminalities" as part of negotiating borders and becoming *nepantleras*. "We must *choose* to occupy intermediary spaces between worlds," Anzaldúa says, "*choose* to move between the worlds like the ancient chamanas who *choose* to build bridges between worlds, *choose* to speak from the cracks between the worlds, from las rendijas [the crevices]." Moreover, and as she goes on to argue, "We must *choose* to see through the holes in reality, *choose* to perceive something from multiple angles."[1] The cracks, in this sense, are spaces of creativity, consciousness, and choice, spaces that contest boundaries and binaries, spaces that for Anzaldúa also contest "simplistic colonialist notions of racial difference."[2] They are spaces of knowing and being.

As Keating points out in her introduction to the text, Anzaldúa expands here her idea of the border and of border thought, complicating it with the in-between place of *nepantla* and with the perspective(s) from the cracks. For Keating, Anzaldúa uses the perspectives from the cracks "to question 'consensual reality' (our status quo stories) and develop alternative perspectives—ideas, theories, actions, and beliefs[—]that partially reflect but partially exceed worldviews. They invent relational theories and tactics with which they can reconceive and in other ways transform the various worlds in which we exist."[3] As I read these words after finishing my part I, I cannot help but think how Anzaldúa gives further sense and meaning to the cracks, but also how she synthesizes, in a sense, our shared intention in this book.

**WALTER:** It is very interesting what you said here, Catherine, for it brings to light connections that do not surface until they surface. This was the case with words like reconstitution, re-existence, resurgence, and reemergence: the *re*-words highlight the necessary complement of the *de*-words. Your narrative in the previous paragraph highlights connections that now are surfacing.

I read Anzaldúa, *Borderlands/La Frontera: The New Mestiza* shortly after it was published in 1987. At that point I did not know about Quijano, and Quijano's concept of *coloniality* was not yet born. It was a shock for many reasons, but the most important is that it brought me from the semiotic abstraction I was doing, down to earth: I realized that I was made "Hispanic" (the word still used at the time from the discourse that classifies you), and I realized that in Argentina I was Italo/Argentinian. I understood, with the corresponding scale differences, what Fanon meant by *sociogenesis*. When you feel that you have been classified, that you are not what you think you are, you become part of the gaze of the classifier. The awareness of dwelling in the border brought immigrant consciousness and that affected my body, I "felt" like an immigrant in Argentina, in France I was classified as Sudaka, and then in the U.S. I became Hispanic and Latino, an ambiguous Latino for the classifier since I have white skin and blue eyes. Borderland and border-lines brought the concept of *pluritopic hermeneutic* in *The Darker Side of the Renaissance*, which I finished writing in 1993. Anzaldúa is in the introduction next to Raimon Panikkar. The second shock was Anzaldúa's revamping the concept of Nepantla (which at the time I had encountered in my research in colonial México). So in *The Darker Side* I traced the line between *feeling nepantla* as a Nahuatl speaker was reported to say around 1550 and *nepantilism* in the twentieth-century borderland.

It was a third shock how she brings the bleeding of the Third World grating with the First World, the bleeding of borderlands. But borderlands are not geopolitical; they are much more than that: they are racial and sexual, they are in Ciudad Juárez and El Paso but also in Chicago and Durham, North Carolina. All that is what I took from Anzaldúa and carry with me, in my senses, since then. So next to my immigrant consciousness was also my

Third World consciousness, educated in the trying years of the sixties in Argentina and then going to France to become a Sudaka when Parisians were enjoying "le dernier gadget d'outremer," the new Latin American novel, the exoticism of South America.

By 1995 we started, at Duke University Press, the book series *Latin America Otherwise*. The intention was to break up the closed circle of *Latin America* (that I addressed in *The Idea of Latin America*). We invited as two of the three editors, Sonia Saldívar Hull, and Irene Silverblatt. Sonia wrote an introduction to the 1999 edition of Anzaldúa's book. The book by Keating that you mentioned was published in *Latin America Otherwise*. It was Sonia's work to get Keating's book into our series.

Thus, a few years later, I could articulate (with the help of Franz Hinkelammert) the concept of *pluriversity*, a natural consequence of *pluritopic hermeneutic*.[4] By the early nineties I "discovered" Rodolfo Kusch, an immigrant like myself but of German descent. However, his immigrant consciousness threw him into the depth of Aymara thinking and, without talking about borders, all his work came to emanate from dwelling in the border lines between modernity and coloniality, modernity/coloniality. The "/" is for me the borderland, the borderland where I dwell. In that sense *The Darker Side of the Renaissance* is an autobiographical book trying to understand myself in order to find and work kindred Spirits: border dwellers.

When I encountered Quijano and the concept of *coloniality*, it was another shock; it gave what I did not have: a way to understand what I was doing (investigating colonialism in the sphere of language, memories, and space) in the larger scheme, the colonial matrix of power. Thus, I could connect my praxis of living with linear border thinking, Carl Schmitt's concept on which I elaborate in chapter 10, and explored in more details in chapters 3 and 4 of *The Darker Side of Western Modernity*. Global linear thinking makes the borders in international law; it is the foundation of colonial and imperial differences, the foundation of racism and sexism. I began to understand that there is no outside of CMP and that the first decolonial step is to understand where we have been classified, how we have been identified. Since then, all my work focuses on CMP. Like the unconscious for Sigmund Freud and Jacques Lacan, or surplus value for Karl Marx, CMP became the overall horizon of my praxis of living, my teaching, writing, lecturing. So part II shall be read as an update and a summary of a long process that I just described. When you become aware that you dwell in the border, your praxis of living changes because it becomes difficult to return to dwell in the territory where you dwelled but sensed that it was not your place.

But there is one more crucial aspect: Humberto Maturana, not his concept of *autopoiesis* that has been unduly transplanted to the social sciences and the humanities, but his removal of objectivity, reality, and truth and his dictum "everything said is said by an observer," which connects with my interest (obsession) with the enunciation and the elimination from my vocabulary of *representation*, for representation belongs to the family of truth, objectivity, and reality that are somehow *represented* in the conflict of interpretation. Maturana is also embedded in *The Darker Side of the Renaissance* from the very title of the introduction: "Describing ourselves describing ourselves." The book has several reviews, but none of the reviewers picked up on the "call" I made in the title of the introduction. Maturana and Anzaldúa were walking side by side in the introduction. They both again were in company in one of the key chapters of *Local Histories/Global Designs* titled "Bilanguaging Love." Languaging comes from Maturana, but the *bilanguaging* highlights the borderland and borderline between Spanish and English, thus coloniality of language/knowledge between imperial languages (cfr. imperial linguistic difference mutated into colonial linguistic difference). *Love* in the title crossed by bilanguaging refers to the borderland/borderline disrupting the homogeneity of monolanguaging love: love for the nation, love for the territory, love for homogeneity enclosed within the frontier.[5]

Thus, Maturana's distinction between truth without parentheses and truth in parentheses (which I elaborate on in *The Darker Side of Western Modernity*, chapter 1), brings us back to *pluriversality*, which in Maturana's words is the *multiverse*. Obviously, decolonially speaking the question is not which one is the true one, or the one that represents reality or is objective. None of this is relevant decolonially. Decolonially speaking what is relevant to me is how a scientist (biologist) could be meaningful for decolonial thinking. Well, it is for parallel reasons to why Western canonical sciences and particularly physics are relevant to *New Materialism*. At this point we continue . . . [the] parallel routes of postmodern thinking (*New Materialism*),[6] and decolonial thinking (what you and myself have done and what we are doing here, in this book and in the series).

To summarize: if I have to identify a few pillars of thinking in my praxis of living these would be, in chronological order: borderland/borderline/*la frontera*, modernity/coloniality and delinking as epistemic reconstitution, decolonial truth in parentheses, pluriversality (or multiverse in Maturana's vocabulary), which shall be distinguished from *multipolarity*. Multipolarity is a concept in political theory and interstate relations, a crucial concept among social scientists and journalists promoting dewesternization and a multipolar world order. I explain in several chapters, that decoloniality is not, and cannot be at this moment, a state-led project. Decoloniality is a project of the emerging global political society of which this book *enacts* . . . in the very process of writing it. The book series, in my view, shall be a contribution to global decoloniality.

**CATHERINE:** Thanks, Walter, for these reflections. Certainly they help bring home how and why this book is not just a description of decoloniality but, more crucially, an enacting of decoloniality in which our own processes of becoming are necessarily part. I think this is crucial for the reader to understand, most especially because it reveals once again that decoloniality is not a new abstract universal, but a way of being, thinking, sensing, and doing, a conscious way of existence—of re-existing—that is ongoing; to use the Zapatistas' phrase, it is a way that walks asking.

In part I, I allude to some of my own routes, most especially with regard to praxis. I will briefly expand on them here so that readers can more clearly see our differences of coming to coloniality/decoloniality, our crossing of paths, and some of our walking together.

As I have described elsewhere, I first began to think about what we now term *coloniality* in the late 1970s and the decade of the 1980s, with relation to the still colonial relationship of the U.S. and Puerto Rico, and most specifically the struggles of Boricuas in the continental U.S. This thinking began in the context of western Massachusetts, where I lived, studied, and worked at the time, a region, community, and graduate studies program with a strong Puerto Rican presence. This lived reality became central to my intellectual-activist work. I collaborated with community-based popular education programs, with parent and teacher collectives in the schools, with intellectual-activists at the Center for Puerto Rican Studies at Hunter College in New York, and worked with legal advocacy groups, including the Puerto Rican Legal Defense and Education Fund, the Lawyers' Committee for Civil rights, and the Multicultural Education Training and Advocacy project in the areas of linguistic, cultural, and educational rights and against the ongoing weight of structural racism, colonialism, and difference. These three interrelated spheres (which we now understand within the frame of CMP) became the focus of my doctoral dissertation and later my first book: *Pedagogy and the Struggle for Voice: Issues of Language, Power and Schooling for Puerto Ricans* (1991). Pedagogy here, and in my subsequent work, was never limited to the system of education or the transmission of knowledge; rather, it was understood as part of the practices, processes, and struggles of social and political transformation. The years spent in dialogue with Paulo Freire and with colleagues in efforts toward what we then termed *critical pedagogy*, helped me understand the pedagogical significance of struggle against colonial structures and conditions, and for an otherwise. Work with African American, Latino and Latina, Haitian, Cape Verdean, Chinese, and Southeast Asian communities and collectives in these years pushed further these understandings.

In the early 1990s, the National Confederation of Indigenous Nationalities of Ecuador asked me to *think with* them in the creation of an Indigenous University. My relationship with Ecuador had begun long before, but this process began another phase in my coming to think from and with coloniality/decoloniality. How to think an Indigenous University in ways that delink from the dominant Western frames of higher education and of knowledge, in ways that think *with and from* Indigenous cosmologies, and construct interepistemic relation? Such experience urged my own learning how to unlearn, a beginning to relearn in radically distinct ways. My permanent move to Ecuador in the mid-1990s impelled further shifts, shifts not only in and of geopolitical and body-political locations, but also in in the praxistical processes of thinking, being, sensing, knowing, and living, in existence itself.

It was in 1998, I believe, that our paths crossed in Cochabamba, Bolivia, in a seminar where we were both invited to speak. I recall our amazement at the relatedness of the titles and contents of our talks. Months later you invited me to a meeting at Duke with Quijano and others, and from there we began to give form to what became known as the collective project of modernity/coloniality (with decoloniality introduced some years later). In all of this I want to emphasize your protagonism, Walter, in bringing similarly minded folks together, then and now, and in encouraging, nurturing, and pushing the concept, analytic, and praxis of global decoloniality, a praxis that has never been individual but always thought with others, in dialogue and conversation.

Certainly there is much more that could be said in these after-words. I could speak about our shared practices, spaces, and places of intellectual work, of shared seminars and workshops, shared teaching, and of course the never-ending shared conversations. However, I think, and particularly for the readers' sake, that we should probably find a way to conclude. I'll leave that to you.

**WALTER:** Yes, indeed, it was in Cochabamba that our paths first crossed and if not 1998, around that time. It was serendipity because we got to that meeting from different routes. I learned several months after the meeting that Luis Macas was there with other indigenous leaders. I remember in general your path from pedagogy of liberation to decoloniality, but I am grateful that your narrative refreshed my memory. From then to now has been a continuous conversation, both in person, and from the distance. But my visiting Quito to teach at the PhD on Latin American Cultural Studies that you created and spirited, and your several visiting positions at Duke, allowed for more sustained conversations. Without these sustained conversations and collaborating with graduate students' dissertations, this book and the book series would not have been possible. And we have to thank Gisela Fosado for suggesting the idea of having a book series on decoloniality. The topic she suggested became the title of the series. So, I think this is the proper way to conclude the "words after," bringing Gisela, the silent voice here, into the project.

**CATHERINE:** Yes!

## Notes

1   Gloria Anzaldúa, *Light in the Dark, Luz en lo oscuro: Rewriting Identity, Spirituality, Reality*, ed. Analouise Keating (Durham, NC: Duke University Press, 2015), 93.
2   Anzaldúa, *Light in the Dark*, 73.
3   Keating in Anzaldúa, *Light in the Dark*, xxxvi.
4   Walter D. Mignolo, "The Zapatistas' Theoretical Revolution: Its Historical, Ethical, and Political Consequences," *Review (Fernand Braudel Center)* 25, no. 3 (2002): 245–75. A translation into Spanish was published by Raymundo Barraza at CIECI, San Cristobal de Las Casas, and a revised version is reprinted in *The Darker Side of Western Modernity: Global Futures, Decolonial Options*, Durham, NC: Duke University Press, 2011. The Zapatistas' dictum "A world in which many would coexist," reduces Western universality to size: it becomes one of many.

5   See Chela Sandoval's *Methodology of the Oppressed: Theory Out of Bounds* (Minneapolis: University of Minnesota Press, 2000). This concept is addressed in Part 4, "Love in the Postmodern World: Differential Consciousness III." It was published the same year as *Local Histories/Global Designs*, thus I could not take it into account. However, the fact that *love* was surfacing as a concern is interesting to note.

6   *New Materialism: Interviews and Cartographies* (Ann Arbor, MI: Open Humanities Press, 2012).

# Bibliography

Achebe, Chinua. *There Was a Country*. London: Penguin Books, 2012.

Acuerdo del Consejo de Desarrollo de Nacionalidades y Pueblos del Ecuador (CODENPE), No. 2884. Quito: CODENPE, December 4, 2013.

Adichie, Chimamanda Ngozi. "The Danger of a Single Story." *TED Talk*, October 7, 2009. Accessed May 28, 2016. https://www.youtube.com/watch?v=D9Ihs241zeg.

Alatas, Syed Farid, and Vineeta Sinha. *Sociological Theory beyond the Canon*. London: Palgrave Macmillan, 2017.

Albán Achinte, Adolfo. "Epistemes 'otras': ¿Epistemes disruptivas?" *Revista Kula* 6 (2012): 22–34.

———. "¿Interculturalidad sin decolonialidad? Colonialidades circulantes y prácticas de re-existencia." In *Diversidad, interculturalidad y construcción de ciudad*, ed. Wilmer Villa and Arturo Grueso, 64–96. Bogotá: Universidad Pedagógica Nacional/ Alcaldía Mayor, 2008.

———. *Más allá de la razón hay un mundo de colores: Modernidades, colonialidades y reexistencia*. Santiago de Cuba: Casa del Caribe y Editorial Oriente, 2013.

———. "Pedagogías de la re-existencia: Artistas indígenas y afrocolombianos." In *Pedagogías decoloniales: Prácticas insurgentes de resistir, (re)existir y (re)vivir*, vol. 1, ed. Catherine Walsh, 443–68. Quito: Ediciones Abya-Yala, 2013.

Alexander, M. Jacqui. *Pedagogies of Crossing: Meditations on Feminism, Sexual Politics, Memory, and the Sacred*. Durham, NC: Duke University Press, 2005.

Alfred, Taiaiake. *Peace, Power, Righteousness*. Oxford: Oxford University Press, 2008.

Almendra, Vilma. "PalabrAndando: Entre el despojo y la dignidad." In *Pedagogías decoloniales: Prácticas insurgentes de resistir, (re)existir y (re)vivir*, vol. 2, ed. Catherine Walsh, 209–44. Quito: Ediciones Abya-Yala, 2017.

Alvira Briñez, Yamile. "El lugar del canto y la oralidad como prácticas estético-pedagógicas para la reafirmación de la vida y su existencia en los Andes-Cajamarquinos." In *Pedagogías decoloniales: Prácticas insurgentes de resistir, (re)existir y (re)vivir*, vol. 2, ed. Catherine Walsh, 245–72. Quito: Ediciones Abya-Yala, 2017.

Anderson, Benedict. *Imagined Communities: Reflections on the Origins and Spread of Nationalism*. London: Verso, 1983.

Anderson, Myrdene, and Floyd Merrell, eds. "(Re) modeling the Letter: Literacy and Literature at the Intersections of Semiotics and Literary Studies." *On Semiotic Modeling*. Berlin: Mouton de Gruyter, 1991, 357–95.

Anzaldúa, Gloria. *Borderlands/La Frontera: The New Mestiza*. San Francisco: Aunt Lute, 1987.

———. *Light in the Dark, Luz en lo Oscuro: Rewriting Identity, Spirituality, Reality*. Edited by Analouise Keating. Durham, NC: Duke University Press, 2015.

Archibal, Linda. *Decolonization and Healing: Indigenous Experiences in the United States, New Zealand, Australia and Greenland*. Ottawa: Aboriginal Healing Foundation, 2006.

Arias, Arturo, Luis Cárcamo-Huechante, and Emilio Del Valle Escalante. "Literaturas de Abya Yala." *Lasa Forum* 43, no. 1 (winter 2012): 7–10.

"Aristotle on Non-Contradiction." *Stanford Encyclopedia of Philosophy* (2007): 2–15. Accessed July 21, 2017. http://plato.stanford.edu/entries/aritotle-noncontradition/.

Ashworth, John. "The Relationship between Capitalism and Humanitarians." *American Historical Review* 92, no. 4 (1987): 813–28.

Astorga Poblete, Daniel. "La colonización del Tlacauhtli y la invención del espacio en el México colonial," PhD. Dissertation, Duke University, 2015. Accessed May 21, 2016. http://www.worldcat.org/title/la-colonizacion-del-tlacauhtli-y-la-invencion-del-espacio-en-el-mexico-colonial/oclc/923881277&referer=brief_results.

Bakshi, Sandeep, Suhraiya Jivraj, and Silvia Posocco, eds. *Decolonizing Sexualities: Transnational Perspectives, Critical Interventions*. London: Counterpress Publishing House, 2016.

Basheer, Varsha. "Decolonial Feminisms: Exploring Religion as Methodology." Accessed September 10, 2017. https://www.youtube.com/watch?v=3Jq8JVRcal4.

Baudelaire, Charles. "The Painter of Modern Life" [1863]. Reprint in *The Painter of Modern Life and Other Essays*. London: Editorial Phaidon. Accessed May 23, 2016. http://www.writing.upenn.edu/library/Baudelaire_Painter-of-Modern-Life_1863.pdf.

Bautista, Rafael. "Bolivia: Del estado colonial al estado plurinacional." January 21, 2009. Accessed September 13, 2017. https://www.servindi.org/actualidad/opinion/6774.

Becker, Marc. "The Children of 1990." *Alternatives* 35 (2010): 291–316.

Betancourt, Milson. "Aníbal Quijano: Heterogeneidad histórico estructural. Parte I." Online video clip. *Youtube*, October 6, 2013. Accessed May 23, 2016. https://www.youtube.com/watch?v=-okq89FNkTI.

Beuchot, Mauricio. *El problema de los universales*. Mexico City: UNAM, 1981.

"Binary Opposition." Accessed July 21, 2017. http://www.gutenberg.us/articles/binary+opposition.

Borsani, María Eugenia. "Introducción." In *Ejercicios decolonizantes en este sur*, ed. María Eugenia Borsani. Buenos Aires: Ediciones del signo, 2015.

Borsani, Maria Eugenia, and Pablo Quintero, eds. *Los desafíos decoloniales de nuestros días: Pensar colectivo*, 173–97. Neuquén, Argentina: Universidad del Comahue, 2014.

Braidotti, Rossi. *The Posthuman*. Cambridge: Polity Press, 2013.

Branche, Jerome. "Malungaje: Hacia una poética de la diáspora africana." In *Pedagogías decoloniales: Prácticas insurgentes de resistir, (re)existir y (re)vivir*, vol. I, ed. Catherine Walsh, 165–87. Quito: Ediciones Abya-Yala, 2013.

———. *The Poetics and Politics of Diaspora: Transatlantic Musings*. New York: Routledge, 2015.

Cabnal, Lorena. "Acercamiento a la construcción de la propuesta de pensamiento epistémico de las mujeres indígenas feministas comunitarias de Abya Yala." *Feminismos diversos: El feminismo comunitario*. Madrid: Acsur–Las Segovias, 2010, 11–25.

Cariño, Carmen, Aura Cumes, Ochy Curiel, María Teresa Garzón, Bienvenida Mendoza, Karina Ochoa, and Alejandra Londoño. "Pensar, sentir, y hacer pedagogías descoloniales: Diálogos y puntadas." In *Pedagogías decoloniales: Prácticas insurgentes de resistir, (re)existir y (re)vivir*, vol. 2, ed. Catherine Walsh, 509–636. Quito: Ediciones Abya-Yala, 2017.

Casimir, Jean. "Haïti et ses élites: L'interminable dialogue des sourds." In *Worlds and Knowledges Otherwise*, 2008. Accessed May 24, 2016. https://globalstudies .trinity.duke.edu/wp-content/themes/cgsh/materials/WKO/v2d3_Casimir7.pdf.

Césaire, Aimé. *Discourse on Colonialism*. Translated by Joan Pinkham. New York: Monthly Review Press, [1955] 2000.

Chamovitz, Daniel. *What a Plant Knows: A Field Guide to the Senses*. New York: Farrar, Straus and Giroux, 2013.

Chasteen, John, and Sara Castro-Klarén, eds. *Beyond Imagined Communities*. Baltimore: John Hopkins University Press, 2003.

Chen, Kwan-sing. *Asia as Method: Toward Deimperialization*. Durham, NC: Duke University Press, 2010.

Cherry, Colin. *On Human Communication: A Review, a Survey, and a Criticism*. Cambridge, MA: MIT Press, 1966.

Cipolla, Carlo. *Money in Sixteenth-Century Florence*. Berkeley: University of California Press, 1989.

"CNN Money." Accessed August 23, 2017. http://money.cnn.com/2017/08/23/investing /the-impact-network-families/index.html.

Colby, Gerard, and Charlotte Dennet. *Thy Will Be Done: The Conquest of the Amazon: Nelson Rockefeller and Evangelism in the Age of Oil*. New York: HarperCollins, 1995.

"Colonialism." In *Online Etymology Dictionary*, 2001–16. Accessed May 23, 2016. http://www.etymonline.com/index.php?term=colonialism.

"Colonialism." In *Stanford Encyclopedia of Philosophy*, 2006. Accessed May 23, 2016. http://plato.stanford.edu/entries/colonialism/.

Comisión de la Sexta del EZLN. *Pensamiento crítico frente a la hidra capitalista 1*. Chiapas, Mexico: EZLN, 2015.

CONAIE—Confederación de Nacionalidades Indígenas del Ecuador. "Políticas para el Plan de Gobierno Nacional: El mandato de la CONAIE." Manuscript. Quito: CONAIE, 2003.

———. "Propuesta de la CONAIE frente a la Asamblea Constituyente: Principios y lineamientos para la nueva Constitución del Ecuador." Manuscript. Quito: CONAIE, 2007.

———. *Proyecto político*. Quito: CONAIE, 1997.

CONAIE-ICCI. *Amawtay Wasi: Casa de la sabiduría. Universidad Intercultural de las Nacionalidades y Pueblos del Ecuador. Propuesta de camino en camino*. Quito: CONAIE-ICCI, 2003.

CONAIE, ONIC, and SAIIC. "A Call to Indigenous People: 500 Years of Resistance." *Native Web*, South and Meso American Indigenous Information Center, April 1989. http://www.nativeweb.org/papers/statements/quincentennial/quincentennial .php.

Concheiro, Luciano. "Los pueblos Indígenas de México eligen a su vocera e irrumpen en el scenario politico nacional," *New York Time en Español*, May 28, 2017. Accessed May 28, 2017. https://www.nytimes.com/es/2017/05/28/los-pueblos-indigenas -de-mexico-eligen-a-su-vocera-e-irrumpen-en-el-escenario-politico/?mcubz=3.

Constitución de la República del Ecuador, 2008. Accessed July 19, 2019. http://pdba .georgetown.edu/Constitutions/Ecuador/english08.html.

Coronil, Fernando. "¿Globalización liberal o imperialismo global? Cinco piezas para armar el rompecabezas del presente." *Comentario Internacional, Revista del Centro Andino de Estudios Internacionales*, no. 5 (2004): 103–32.

Coulthard, Glen. *Red Skin, White Masks: Rejecting the Colonial Politics of Recognition*. Minneapolis: University of Minnesota Press, 2014.

CRIC-Consejo Regional Indígena de Cauca. *¿Qué pasaría si la escuela . . . ? 30 años de construcción de una educación propia*. Popayán, Colombia: CRIC, 2004.

CSUTCB. "Tesis política 1983." In *Oprimidos pero no vencidos: Luchas del campesinado aymara y qhechwa 1900–1980*, ed. Silvia Rivera Cusicanqui, 184–201. La Paz: Hisbol, 1986.

Curiel, Ochy. *La Nación Heterosexual*. Bogotá: Brecha Lésbica and *en la frontera*, 2013.

Curran, Jim, and Myiun-Jin Park, eds. *De-Westernizing Media Studies*. London: Routledge, 2000.

de Acosta, José. The *Natural and Moral History of the Indies*. Translated by Frances Lopez-Morillas. Durham, NC: Duke University Press, [1590] 2002.

del Prado, Béjar Deisy Núñez. "Yanantin y masintin: La cosmovisión andina." *Yachay: Revista Científica de la Universidad Andina del Cusco* 1(2008): 130–36.

Doxtater, Michael G. "Indigenous Knowledge in the Decolonial Era." *American Indian Quarterly*. Special Issue on *The Recovery of Indigenous Knowledge* (summer 2004): 618–33.

Dunbar-Ortiz, Roxanne. *An Indigenous Peoples' History of the United States*. Boston: Beacon Press, 2014.

Dussel, Enrique. "Eurocentrism and Modernity." *boundary 2* 20, no. 3 (1993): 65–76.

——. *16 Tesis de Economía Política: Interpretación filosófica*. Mexico City: Siglo XXI, 2014.

Escobar, Arturo. "Beyond the Third World: Imperial Globality, Global Coloniality and Anti-globalization Social Movements." *Third World Quarterly* 25, no.1 (2004): 207–30.

——. "Worlds and Knowledge Otherwise." *Cultural Studies* 21, nos. 2/3 (2007): 179–210. Special issue, *Globalization and the Decolonial Option*, ed. Walter D. Mignolo.

——. "Worlds and Knowledges Otherwise: The Latin American Modernity/Coloniality Research Program." In *Globalization and the Decolonial Option*, ed. Walter Mignolo and Arturo Escobar, 33–64. New York: Routledge, 2010.

Espinosa Miñoso, Yuderkys, Diana Gómez Correal, and Karina Ochoa Muñoz. "Introducción." In *Tejiendo de "otro modo": Feminismo, epistemología y apuestas decoloniales en Abya Yala*, ed. Yuderkys Espinosa Miñoso, Diana Gómez Correal, and Karina Ochoa Muñoz, 13–40. Popayán, Colombia: Universidad de Cauca, 2014.

Esteva, Gustavo. "Reclaiming our Freedom to Learn." *Yes Magazine*, November 7, 2007. Accessed October 23, 2015. http://www.yesmagazine.org/issues/liberate-your-space/reclaiming-our-freedom-to-learn.

Eze, Emmanuel Chukwudi. "The Color of Reason." In *African Postcolonial Philosophy*. Hoboken, NJ: Wiley-Blackwell, 1997.

Fanon, Frantz. *Black Skin, White Masks*. New York: Grove Press, 1967.

——. *The Wretched of the Earth*. New York: Grove Press, 1968.

Federici, Silvia. *Caliban and the Witch: Women, the Body and Primitive Accumulation*. New York: Automedia, 2004.

Ferrera-Balanquet, Raúl Moarquech, ed. *Andar erótico decolonial*. Buenos Aires: Ediciones del Signo, 2015.

——. *Erotic Sovereignty at the Decolonial Crossroads*. Durham, NC: Duke University, forthcoming.

Flynn, Dennis O., and Arturo Giraldez. *China and the Birth of Globalization in the 16th Century*. Farnham, UK: Ashgate, 2010.

Fonseca, Vanessa. "América es nombre de mujer." *Reflexiones* 58, no. 1 (1997): 1–19.

Foucault, Michel. *Les mots et les choses*. Paris: Gallimard, 1966.

Freire, Paulo. *Pedagogy of the Oppressed*. New York: Continuum, 1974.

——. *The Politics of Education: Culture, Power, and Liberation*. Translated by Donaldo Macedo. South Hadley, MA: Bergin and Garvey, 1985.

Fumaroli, Marc. *La querelle des anciens et des modernes*. Paris: Gallimard, 2001.

Galindo, María. *Feminismo urgente: ¡A despatriarcar! Mujeres creando*. La Paz: Lavaca, 2014.

Gallos, Dimitri. "Comparison of Lenin's and Hobson's Theory on Imperialism." *Centre for Media Alternatives-Quebec*, October 22, 2007. Accessed February 22, 2018. http://archives-2001-2012.cmaq.net/en/node/28392.

Galluzzo, Gabriel, and Loux, Michael J., eds. *The Problem of Universals in Contemporary Philosophy*. Cambridge: Cambridge University Press, 2015. Accessed May 25, 2016. http://assets.cambridge.org/97811071/00893/excerpt/9781107100893_excerpt.pdf.

García Salazar, Juan, and Catherine Walsh. *Pensar sembrando/Sembrar pensando con el Abuelo Zenón*. Quito: Cátedra de Estudios Afro-Andinos, Universidad Andina Simón Bolívar y Ediciones Abya-Yala, 2017.

Garrett, Aaron. "Hume's Revised Racism Revisited." *Hume Studies* 26, no. 1 (2000).

Gerbi, Antonello. *La Disputa del Nuovo Mondo. Storia di una polemica (1750–1900)*. Milan: Adelphi, 2000. Accessed May 20, 2016. https://nuevomundo.revues.org /409.

Giddens, Anthony. *The Consequences of Modernity*. Stanford, CA: Stanford University Press, 1990.

Gilley, Bruce. "The Case for Colonialism." *Third World Quarterly*, September 8, 2017. Accessed May 20, 2016. http://www.tandfonline.com/doi/full/10.1080/01436597 .2017.1369037.

Glissant, Édouard. *Poetics of Relation*. Ann Arbor: University of Michigan Press, 1997.

Gordon, Lewis. *Existentia Africana: Understanding Africana Existential Thought*. New York: Routledge, 2000.

——. *Fanon and the Crisis of the European Man*. New York: Routledge, 1995.

——. "A Pedagogical Imperative of Pedagogical Imperatives." *Thresholds* (2010): 27–35.

Gordon, Lewis, and Jane Anna Gordon. "Introduction: Not Only the Master's Tools." In *Not Only the Master's Tools: African-American Studies in Theory and Practice*, ed. Lewis Gordon and Jane Anna Gordon, ix–xi. Boulder, CO: Paradigm, 2006.

Graham, Hugh F. "Education." In *Encyclopaedia Britannica*, 11th ed., 2011. Accessed May 23, 2016. http://www.britannica.com/EBchecked/topic/179408/education /47496/Major-periods-of-Muslim-education-and-learning.

Grande, Sandy. "Red Pedagogy: The Un-Methodology." In *Handbook of Critical and Indigenous Methodologies*, ed. N. Denzin, Y. Lincoln, and L. T. Smith, 233–54. London: SAGE, 2008.

Greer, Margaret, Walter D. Mignolo, and Maureen Quilligan, eds. *Rereading the Black Legend: The Discourses of Racial and Religious Differences in the Renaissance Empires*. Chicago: University of Chicago Press, 2008.

Grovogui, Siba. *Otherwise Human: The Institutes and Institutions of Rights*. Accessed May 30, 2016. http://sibagrovogui.com/current-projects/otherwise-human-the -institutes-and-institutions-of-rights/.

Grueso, Libia. "Escenarios de colonialismo y (de)colonialidad en la construcción del Ser Negro: Apuntes sobre las relaciones de género en comunidades negras del Pacífico colombiano." *Comentario Internacional: Revista del Centro Andino de Estudios Internacionales* 7 (2006–7): 145–56.

Guenon, Rene. "The Language of Birds." *Studies in Comparative Religion* 3, no. 2. (spring 1969) © World Wisdom, Inc. Accessed May 27, 2016. www.studiesincomparative religion.com. http://www.studiesincomparativereligion.com/Public/articles/The _Language_of_Birds-by_Rene_Guenon.aspx.

"Gunnar Myrdal." *The Concise Encyclopedia of Economics*. 2008. http://www.econlib .org/library/Enc/bios/Myrdal.html.

Hall, David L., and Roger T. Ames. *Thinking from the Han: Self, Truth and Transcendence in Chinese and Western Culture*. Albany: SUNY Press, 1998.

Hasegawa, Yuko. "Going Both Ways: Yuko Hasegawa in Conversation with Walter D. Mignolo and Stephanie Bailey." *Ibraaaz: Contemporary Visual Culture in North Africa and the Middle East,* May 8, 2013. Accessed May 23, 2016. http://www .ibraaz.org/interviews/79.

"Hay que sacar el patron del vestido para hacer otro." WordReference/com/Online Language Dictionary. Accessed July 27, 2017.

Haymes, Stephen Nathan. "Pedagogy and the Philosophical Anthropology of African-American Slave Culture." In *Not Only the Master's Tools: African-American Studies in Theory and Practice*, ed. Lewis Gordon and Jane Anna Gordon, 173–204. Boulder, CO: Paradigm Publishers, 2006.

Henry, Paget. *Caliban's Reason: Introducing Afro-Caribbean Philosophy*. New York: Routledge, 2000.

Hobsbawm, Eric. "Barbarism: A User's Guide." *New Left Review* I, no. 206 (July–August 1994): 44–54.

Hobson, John A. *Imperialism: A Study*. New York: James Pott, 1902.

hooks, bell. *Teaching to Transgress: Education as the Practice of Freedom*. New York: Routledge, 1994.

Huanacuni Mamani, Fernando. *Vivir Bien/Buen Vivir: Filosofía, políticas, estrategias y experiencias regionales*. 6th ed. La Paz: Instituto Internacional de Integración (III-CAB), [2010] 2015.

Hui, Wang. *China from Empire to Nation-State*. Cambridge, MA: Harvard University Press, 2014.

"Human." *Online Etymology Dictionary*. Accessed May 21, 2016. http://www.etymonline .com/index.php?term=human.

Hunt, Sarah. *An Introduction to the Health of Two Spirit People: Historical Contemporary and Emergent Issues*. Prince George, BC: National Collaborating Center of Aboriginal Health, 2016.

Husserl, Edmund. *The Crisis of European Sciences and Transcendental Phenomenology*, 1–20, 103–86. Translated by David Carr. Evanston, IL: Northwestern University Press, 1970.

Igelmo Zaldivar, Jon. "La Universidad de la Tierra en México: Una propuesta de aprendizaje convivencial." In *Temas y perspectivas sobre educación: La infancia ayer y hoy*, ed. José Luis Hernández Huerta, Laura Sánchez Blanco, and Iván Pérez Miranda, 285–98. Salamanca, Spain: Globalia, Ediciones Anthema, 2009.

Ignatieff, Michael. *The Lesser Evil: Political Ethics in the Age of Terror*. Princeton, NJ: Princeton University Press, 2005.

Jakobson, Roman. *Essais de linguistique generale: Tome 1 les fondations du langage*. Paris: Edition de Minuit, 1963.

Jessop, Ralph. "Coinage of the term *environment,* a word without authority and Carlyle's displacement of the mechanical metaphor." *Enlighten Publications*. Glasgow: University of Glasgow, 2012. http://eprints.gla.ac.uk/69879/.

K., Michelle. "From Singapore, to Cambridge to Duke University." *Social Text Periscope*, 2013. Accessed May 23, 2016. https://socialtextjournal.org/periscopearticle /decolonial-aesthesis-from-singapore-to-cambridge-to-duke-university/.

"Kant's Moral Philosophy." *Stanford Encyclopedia of Philosophy*. July 7, 2016. Accessed July 21, 2017. https://plato.stanford.edu/entries/kant-moral.

Klima, Gyula. "The Medieval Problem of Universals," "2. The Emergence of the Problem." *The Stanford Encyclopedia of Philosophy*, ed. Edward N. Zalta (fall 2013). Accessed May 25, 2016. http://plato.stanford.edu/entries/universals-medieval/#2.

Kumar, Corinne. Introduction to *Asking We Walk: The South as New Political Imaginary. Book One, In the Time of the Earth*, ed. Corinne Kumar, xiii–xxii. 2nd ed. Bangalore: Streelekha, 2010.

Kusch, Rodolfo. *Indigenous and Popular Thinking in América*. Translated by Maria Lugones and Joshua Price. Durham, NC: Duke University Press, 2010.

Laloux, Frederic. *Reinventing Organization: A Guide to Creating Organizations Inspired by the Next Stage of Human Consciousness*. Oxford: Nelson Parker Publishing, 2014.

Lander, Edgardo. "Eurocentrism and Colonialism in Latin American Social Thought." *Nepantla: Views from South* 1, no. 3 (2000): 519–32.

Larreta, Enrique, ed. "Coloniality at Large: Time and the Colonial Difference." In *Time in the Making and Possible Futures*, 237–72. Rio de Janeiro: UNESCO, 2000.

Latouche, Serge. *L'Occidentalisation du monde*. Paris: La Découvert, 1989.

Lenin, Vladimir. *Imperialism: The Highest Stage of Capitalism*, written January– June 1916. Accessed May 25, 2016. https://www.marxists.org/archive/lenin /works/1916/imp-hsc/.

Lenneberg, Erick H. *Biological Foundations of Language*. New York: John Wiley, 1967.

León, Edizon. "Acercamiento crítico al cimarronaje a partir de la teoría política, los estudios culturales y la filosofía de existencia." PhD diss., Universidad Andina Simón Bolívar, Quito, Ecuador, 2015. http://repositorio.uasb.edu.ec/ handle/10644/4679.

Lorde, Audre. *Sister Outsider*. Berkeley: Crossing Press, [1984] 2007.

Lowe, Lisa. *The Intimacies of the Four Continents*. Durham, NC: Duke University Press, 2015.

Lozano Lerma, Betty Ruth. "El feminismo no puede ser uno porque las mujeres somos diversas: Aportes a un feminismo negro decolonial desde la experiencia de las mujeres negras del Pacífico colombiano." *La manzana de la discordia* 5, no. 2 (2010): 7–24.

——. "Neo conquista y neo colonización de territorios y cuerpos en la región del Pacífico colombiano." Talk given at Universidad Andina Simón Bolívar, November 2014.

——. "Pedagogías para la vida, la alegría y la re-existencia: Pedagogías de mujeres negras que curan y vinculan." In *Pedagogías decoloniales: Prácticas insurgentes de resistir, (re)existir y (re)vivir*, vol. 2, ed. Catherine Walsh, 273–90. Quito: Ediciones Abya-Yala, 2017.

———. "Tejiendo con retazos de memorias insurgencias epistémicas de mujeres ne-gras/afrocolombianas: Aportes a un feminismo negro decolonial." PhD diss., Universidad Andina Simón Bolívar, Quito, 2016. http://repositorio.uasb.edu.ec/handle/10644/4895.

Lugones, María. "The Coloniality of Gender." *Worlds and Knowledges Otherwise* 2 (2008): 1–17.

———. "Heterosexualism and the Colonial/Modern Gender System." *Hypatia* 22, no. 1 (2007): 186–209.

———. "Toward a Decolonial Feminism." *Hypatia* 25, no. 4 (2010): 742–59.

Macas, Luis. "Diversidad y plurinacionalidad." *Boletín ICCI-ARY Rimay* 6, no. 64 (2004). Accessed December 6, 2016. http://icci.nativeweb.org/boletin/64/macas.html.

———. "Presentación." In *Interculturalidad crítica y (de)colonialidad: Ensayos desde Abya Yala*, by Catherine Walsh, 5–6. Quito: Ediciones Abya-Yala, 2012.

Maffie, James. "Aztec Philosophy." *Internet Encyclopedia of Philosophy*. Accessed May 23, 2016. http://www.iep.utm.edu/aztec/.

———. *Aztec Philosophy: Understanding a World in Motion*. Denver: University of Colorado, 2014.

———. "'We Eat of the Earth Then the Earth Eats Us': The Concept of Nature in Pre-Hispanic Nahua Thought." *Ludis Vitalis* 10 (2002): 5–20.

Maldonado-Torres, Nelson. *Against War: Views from the Underside of Modernity*. Durham, NC: Duke University Press, 2008.

———. "On the Coloniality of Being." *Cultural Studies* 21, no. 2 (2007): 240–70.

———. "Frantz Fanon and CLR James on Intellectualism and Enlightened Rationality." *Caribbean Studies* 33, no. 2 (July–December 2005): 149–94.

———. "On the Coloniality of Being: Contributions to the Development of a Concept." In *Globalization and the Decolonial Option*, ed. Walter Mignolo and Arturo Escobar, 94–124. London: Routledge, 2010.

———. "Thinking through the Decolonial Turn: Post-Continental Interventions in Theory, Philosophy, and Critique—An Introduction." In *Transmodernity: Journal of Peripheral Cultural Production of the Luso-Hispanic World*. Accessed May 24, 2016. http://escholarship.org/uc/item/59w8jo2x#page-2.

"Man." *Online Etymology Dictionary*. Accessed May 21, 2016. http://www.etymonline.com/index.php?term=man&allowed_in_frame=0.

Marañón Pimentel, Boris, and Dania López Córdoba. "Solidaridad económica, buen vivir y (des) colonialidad del poder." *Sociedad y Discurso* (2014): 153–78. Accessed May 27, 2016. www.discurso.aau.dk.

Marcos, Sylvia. "La realidad no cabe en la teoría." In *El pensamiento crítico frente a la hidra capitalista III*, ed. EZLN, 15–29. Mexico City: EZLN, 2016.

Mariátegui, Carlos. *Seven Interpretive Essays on Peruvian Reality*. Essay 2, 1928. Accessed May 21, 2016. https://www.marxists.org/archive/mariateg/works/7-interpretive-essays/essay02.htm.

Marley, Bob. "Redemption Song." In *Uprising*. Island/Tuff Gong, 1980.

Marshack, Alexander. *The Roots of Civilization*. New York: Moyer Bell Limited, 1991.

Martínez Andrade, Luis. "Entrevista a Ramón Grosfoguel." *Analéctica*, December 2013. Accessed July 24 2017. http://www.analectica.org/articulos/mtzandrade -grosfoguel/.

"Matrix." *Online Etymology Dictionary*. Accessed May 20, 2016. http://www.etymonline .com/index.php?term=matrix.

"Matrixwissen." Accessed May 25, 2016. www.matrixwissen.de.

Maturana, Humberto. *Biology of Cognition: Biological Computer Laboratory Research Report BCL 9.0*. Urbana: University of Illinois, 1970.

——. "Reality: The Search for Objectivity or the Quest for a Compelling Argument." *Irish Journal of Psychology* 8, no. 1 (1988): 25–82.

Maturana, Humberto, and Ximena Dávila. "Cultural-Biology: Systemic Consequences of Our Evolutionary Natural Drift as Molecular Autopoietic Systems." CEPA e-print 3900, 2016. Accessed May 23, 2016. http://www.univie.ac.at/constructivism /archive/fulltexts/3900.html.

Maturana, Humberto, and Ximena Dávila. "The Meaning of the Earth Charter." Interview with Humberto Maturana and Ximena Dávila. Video. April 26, 2011. https://www .youtube.com/watch?v=GtEgtmo42Ls.

Maturana, Humberto, and Francisco Varela. *Autopiesis and Cognition*. Dordrecht: D. Reidel, 1972.

"The Meaning of the Earth Charter: Interview with Humberto Maturana and Ximena Dávila." Video, April 26, 2011. Accessed May 23, 2016. https://www.youtube.com /watch?v=GtEgtmo421Ls&list=PL6DoDC2BCE841549B.

Melito, Leandro. "Doutrinação: Página de Paulo Freire na Wiki é alterada em rede do governo." *UOL educação*, June 29, 2016. Accessed July 19, 2017. http://educacao .uol.com.br/noticias/2016/06/29/doutrinacao-paulo-freire-na-wikipedia-e -alterado-por-usuario-do-governo.htm.

Mendez, Xhercix. "Notes toward a Decolonial Feminist Epistemology: Revisiting the Race/Gender Matrix." *Trans-Scripts* 5 (2015): 41–59.

Mignolo, Walter D. "Coloniality at Large: Time and the Colonial Difference." In *Time in the Making and Possible Futures*, ed. Enrique Larreta, 237–72. Rio de Janeiro: UNESCO, 2000.

——. "Coloniality Is Far from Over, and So Must Be Decoloniality." *Afterall* (spring/summer 2017). https://www.afterall.org/journal/issue.43/coloniality-is-far-from-over -and-so-must-be-decoloniality.

——. "The Communal and the Decolonial." *Turbulence: Ideas in Movement*. 2010. Accessed May 26, 2016. http://turbulence.org.uk/turbulence-5/decolonial/.

——. *The Darker Side of the Renaissance: Literacy, Territoriality and Colonization*. Ann Arbor: University of Michigan Press, [1995] 2003.

——. *The Darker Side of Western Modernity: Global Futures, Decolonial Options*. Durham, NC: Duke University Press, 2011.

——. *Decolonial Politics: Border Dwelling, Re-Existence, Epistemic Disobedience*. Durham, NC: Duke University Press, forthcoming.

———. "Decolonial Thinking and Doing in the Andes: An interview with Catherine Walsh, a propos of *Interculturalidad, Estado, Sociedad: Luchas (de)colonials de nuestra época*." *Reartikulacija*, Slovenia, January 2011.

———. "Enacting the Archive, Decentering the Muses." In *Ibraaz: Contemporary Visual Culture in North Africa and the Middle East*, November 2013. Accessed May 24, 2016. http://www.ibraaz.org/essays/77.

———. "The Enduring Enchantment (Or the Epistemic Privilege of Modernity and Where to Go From Here)." *South Atlantic Quarterly* 101, no. 4 (September 2002): 928–54.

———. "Epistemic Disobedience, Independent Thoughts and Decolonial Freedom." *Theory, Culture and Society* 26, nos. 7/8 (2009): 1–23. http://waltermignolo.com/wp-content/uploads/2013/03/epistemicdisobedience-2.pdf.

———. "Foreword: Anomie, Resurgences, and De-Noming." In *The Anomie of the Earth: Philosophy, Politics, and Autonomy in Europe and the Americas*, ed. F. Luisetti, J. Pickles, and W. Kaiser, vii–xvi. Durham, NC: Duke University Press, 2015.

———. "Globalization and the Geopolitics of Knowledge: The Role of the Humanities in the Corporate University." In *The American Style University at Large*, 3–41. Lanham, MD: Lexington Books, 2011.

———. *The Idea of Latin America*. Malden, MA: Blackwell, 2005.

———. "Islamophobia/Hispanophobia: The (Re) Configuration of the Racial Imperial/Colonial Matrix." *Human Architecture: Journal of the Sociology of Self-Knowledge*. 5, no. 1 (2006).

———. *Local Histories/Global Designs: Coloniality, Subaltern Knowledges and Border Thinking*. 2nd ed. with new preface. Princeton, NJ: Princeton University Press, 2012.

———. "The North of the South and the West of the East." *IBRAAZ: Contemporary Visual Culture in North Africa and the Middle East*, November 2014. Accessed May 30, 2016. http://www.ibraaz.org/essays/108.

———. "Re-Emerging, Decentering and Delinking: Shifting the Geographies of Knowing, Sensing and Believing." *IBRAAZ: Contemporary Visual Culture in North Africa and the Middle East*, May 2013. Accessed May 27, 2016. http://www.ibraaz.org/essays/59.

———. "(Re)modeling the Letter: Literacy and Literature at the Intersections of Semiotics and Literary Studies." In *On Semiotic Modeling*, ed. Myrdene Anderson and Floyd Merrell, 357–95. Berlin: Mouton de Gruyter, 1991.

———. "Spirit Out of Bound Return to the East: The Closing of the Social Sciences and the Opening of Independent Thoughts." *Current Sociology* 62 (July 2014): 584–602.

———. "The Zapatistas' Theoretical Revolution: Its Historical, Ethical, and Political Consequences." In *The Darker Side of Western Modernity: Global Futures, Decolonial Options*, 213–51. Durham, NC: Duke University Press, 2011.

———. "The Zapatistas Theoretical Revolution: Its Historical, Ethical, and Political Consequences." *Review (Fernand Braudel Center)* 25, no. 3 (2002): 245–75. *JSTOR*. Accessed May 20, 2016. www.jstor.org/stable/40241550.

Mignolo, Walter, and Arturo Escobar, eds. *Globalization and the Decolonial Option*. London: Routledge, 2010.

Mignolo, Walter, and Freya Schiwy. "Transculturation and the Colonial Difference: Double Translation." *Translation and Ethnography: The Anthropological Challenge of Intercultural Understanding*, 3–29. Phoenix: University of Arizona Press, 2003.

Mignolo, Walter D., and Rolando Vázquez. "Mexico Indigenous Congress: Decolonising Politics." *Al-Jazeera*, September 27, 2017. Accessed September 27, 2017. http://www.aljazeera.com/indepth/opinion/mexico-indigenous-congress -decolonising-politics-170926093051780.html.

"Modernity and Decoloniality." *Oxford Bibliography Online*, 2011. Accessed May 27, 2016. http://www.oxford. bibliographies.com/view/document/obo -9780199766581/obo-9780199766581-0017.xml.

Moosa, Ebrahim. *What Is a Madrasa?* Chapel Hill: University of North Carolina Press, 2015.

Morales Ayma, Evo. *Discurso inaugural del Presidente Evo Morales Ayma (22 de enero de 2006)*. La Paz: Publicaciones de Cancillería, January 10, 2006. Accessed September 12, 2017. http://saludpublica.bvsp.org.bo/textocompleto/bvsp /boxp68/discurso-jefes-estado.pdf.

Moraña, Mabel, et al. *Coloniality at Large: The Postcolonial Debate in Latin America*. Durham, NC: Duke University Press, 2013.

Muyolema, Armando. "De la 'cuestión indígena' a lo 'indígena' como cuestionamiento: Hacia una crítica del latinoamericanismo, el indigenismo y el mestiz(o)aje." In *Convergencia de tiempo: Estudios subalternos/contextos latinoamericanos, estado, cultura subalternidad*, ed. Ileana Rodríguez, 327–63. Amsterdam: Rodopi, 2001.

Nandy, Ashis. *The Intimate Enemy: Lost and Recovery of the Self under Colonialism*. Delhi: Oxford University Press, 1983.

Ndlovu-Gatsheni, Sabelo J. *Coloniality of Power in Postcolonial Africa: Myths of Decolonization*. Dakar: CODESRIA, 2013.

———. "Why Decoloniality in the 21st Century?" *The Thinker for Thought Leaders* 48 (2013): 10–15.

"Neither Capitalism, nor Communism but Decolonization." *Critical Legal Thinking*, March 21, 2012. Accessed May 24, 2016. http://criticallegalthinking .com/2012/03/21/neither-capitalism-nor-communism-but-decoloniztion-an -interview-with-walter-mignolo.

Noboa, Patricio. "La matriz colonial de poder, los movimientos sociales y los silencios de la modernidad." In *Pensamiento crítico y matriz (de) colonial de poder: Reflexiones latinoamericanas*, ed. Catherine Walsh, 71–109. Quito: Universidad Andina Simón Bolívar and Ediciones Abya-Yala, 2005.

O'Gorman, Edmundo. *La invención de América: El universalismo de la cultura de occidente*. Mexico City: Universidad Autónoma de México, 1958.

———. *The Invention of America: An Inquiry into the Historical Nature of the New World and the Meaning of Its History*. Bloomington: Indiana University Press, [1958] 1961.

Olvera, René. "Pedagogías de la resistencia: De los *cómo* sembrar vida donde está la muerte." In *Pedagogías decoloniales: Prácticas insurgentes de resistir, (re)existir y (re)vivir)*, vol. 2, ed. Catherine Walsh, 195–208. Quito: Ediciones Abya-Yala, 2017.

"On the History of PRATEC." Accessed May 23, 2016. http://www.globaltimes.cn/content /1021021.shrml.

Oviedo Freire, Atawallpa. "El neocolonialismo de fe." *Plan V. Ideas*, May 27, 2015. http://www.planv.com.ec/ideas/ideas/el-neocolonialism-fe.

Pacari, Nina. "La incidencia de la participación política de los pueblos indígenas: Un camino irreversible." In *Las vertientes americanas del pensamiento y el proyecto des-colonial*, ed. Heriberto Cairo and Walter Mignolo, 45–58. Madrid: Tramas editorial, 2008.

———. Talk given in the Forum on the "World Crisis and the Exhaustion of Progressive Models," Universidad Andina Simón Bolívar, Quito, October 12, 2015.

Panikkar, Raimon. "Religion, Philosophy, and Culture," *Polylog*, 2000. Accessed April 15, 2016. https://them.polylog.org/1/fpr-en.htm.

Paredes, Julieta. "Hilando fino desde el feminismo comunitario." La Paz: Comunidad de Mujeres Creando Comunidad and CEDEC, 2008.

———. *Hilando fino: Desde el feminismo comunitario*. Querétaro: Colectivo Grietas, 2012.

Patzi Gonzáles, Felix. "Los ayllus siguen vivos en el norte de Potosí." http://www.katari .org/pdf/potosi.pdf.

Patzi Paco, Félix. "Sistema comunal: Una propuesta alternativa al sistema liberal." In *Las vertientes americanas: Sistema comunal: Una propuesta alternativa al sistema liberal*, ed. Heriberto Cairo-Carau and Walter Mignolo, 61–84. Madrid: Trama Editorial, 2008.

Pérez, Emma. *The Decolonial Imaginary: Writing Chicanas into History*. Bloomington: Indiana University Press, 1999.

Planetary Decolonial Feminisms (Dossier).*Qui Parle: Critical Humanities and Social Sciences* 18, no.2 (spring/summer 2010).

Platt, T. "Mirrors and Maize: The Concept of Yanantin among the Macha of Bolivia." In *Anthropological History of Andean Polities*, ed. J. V. Murra, N. Wachtel, and J. Revel, 228–59. Cambridge: Cambridge University Press, 1986.

Pluriversidad Amawtay Wasi. "Quienes somos." Accessed September 7, 2015. http:// www.amawtaywasi.org.

Ponce, Sofía Cordero. "Estados plurinacionales en Bolivia y Ecuador: Nuevas ciudada-nías, más democracia." *Nueva Sociedad* (2012): 134–48. Accessed May 21, 2016. http://nuso.org/articulo/estados-plurinacionales-en-bolivia-y-ecuador-nuevas -ciudadanias-mas-democracia/.

Pratt, Mary Louise. *Imperial Eyes: Travel Writing and Transculturation*. London: Routledge, 1995.

"Progress." *Online Etymological Dictionary*, ed. Douglas Harper. Accessed July 20, 2017. http://www.etymonline.com/index.php?term=progress.

Quijano, Aníbal. *Antología esencial: De la dependencia histórico-estructural a la colonialidad/descolonialidad del poder*. Selection and Prologue by Alín Assis Clímaco. Buenos Aires: CLACSO, 2014. http://clepso.flacso.edu.mx/sites/default /files/clepso.2014_eje_8_pacheco.pdf.

——. "Colonialidad del poder y subjetividad en América Latina." *Decolonialidad y Psicoanálisis*, ed. María Amelia Castañola y Mauricio González, 11–34. Mexico City: Ediciones Navarra and Colección Borde Sur, 2017.

——. "Colonialidad y modernidad/racionalidad." *Perú Indígena* 13, no. 29 (1992): 11–20. https://problematicasculturales.files.wordpress.com/2015/04/quijano -colonialidad-y-modernidad-racionalidad.pdf.

——. "Coloniality and Modernity/Rationality." In *Globalization and the Decolonial Option*, ed. Walter Mignolo and Arturo Escobar, 22–32. London: Routledge, 2010.

——. "Coloniality of Power, Eurocentrism, and Latin America." *Nepantla: Views from South* 1, no. 3 (2000): 533–80.

——. "Coloniality of Power, Eurocentrism, and Social Classification." In *Coloniality at Large: Latin America and the Postcolonial Debate*, ed. Mabel Moraña, Enrique Dussel, and Carlos A. Jáuregui, 181–224. Durham, NC: Duke University Press, 2008.

Quijano, Aníbal, and Immanuel Wallerstein. "Americanity as a Concept or the Americas in the Modern-World System." *Institute for Scientific Information* 134 (1992).

Quintero, Pablo, ed. *Alternativas decoloniales al capitalismo colonial/moderno*. Buenos Aires: Ediciones del Signo, 2015.

——. "Refractando la modernidad desde la colonialidad: Sobre la configuración de un locus epistémico desde la geopolítica del conocimiento y la diferencia colonial." *Gazeta de Antropología* 25, no. 2 (2009), article 52. Accessed July 27, 2016. http://www.ugr.es/~pwlac/G25_52Pablo_Quintero-Ivanna_Petz.html.

Raschke, Carl. "What Is the 'New Nomos of the Earth': Reflections on the Later Schmitt." *Political Theology Today*. September 2016. Accessed May 20, 2016. https://www .politicaltheology.com/blog/what-is-the-new-nomos-of-the-earth-reflections-on -the-later-schmitt-carl-raschke/.

Reynolds, Maura. "Bush Said America Must Spread Democracy," *Baltimore Sun*, November 7, 2003. Accessed May 25, 2016. http://www.baltimoresun.com/news/bal-te .busho7novo7-story.html.

Rice, Condoleezza. "US Wars in the Middle East Were Not Supposed to Bring Democracy," *Newsweek*, May 12, 2017. Accessed May 12, 2017. http://www.newsweek .com/us-war-middle-east-bring-democracy-rice-608640.

Rise Stronger. "It Takes Roots Red Lines Action," April 2017. Accessed July 17, 2017, https://www.risestronger.org/events/it-takes-roots-red-lines-action.

Rivera Cusicanqui, Silvia. *Ch'ixinakax utxiwa: Una reflexión sobre prácticas y discursos descolonizadores*. Buenos Aires: Tinta limón, 2010.

——. "La raíz: Colonizadores y colonizados." In *Violencias encubiertas en Bolivia: Cultura y política*, ed. Xavier Albó and Raúl Barrios, 27–139. La Paz: CIPCA-ARUWIYIRI, 1993.

———. *Oprimidos pero no vencidos: Luchas del campesinado aymara y qhechwa 1900–1980*. La Paz: Hisbol, 1986.

———. "Violencia e interculturalidad: Paradojas de la etnicidad en la Bolivia de hoy." *Revista Telar* 15 (July 2016): 49–70. http://revistatelar.ct.unt.edu.ar/index.php /revistatelar/article/view/18.

Roberts, Neil. *Freedom as Marronage*. Chicago: University of Chicago Press, 2015.

Rodriguez, Abel. "El Arbol de la Abundancia." Accessed May 26, 2016. https://www .youtube.com/watch?v=DTXyXAqWEss.

Rorty, Richard. *Philosophy and the Mirror of Nature*. Princeton, NJ: Princeton University Press, 1982.

Said, Edward. *Orientalism*. New York: Pantheon House, 1978.

Sandoval, Chela. *Methodology of the Oppressed: Theory Out of Bounds*. Minneapolis: University of Minnesota Press, 2000.

Sandoval, Rafael. "La epistemología zapatista y el método del Caminar Preguntando." In *La escuelita Zapatista*, 7–16. Guadalajara: Grietas Editores, 2014.

Sanjinés, Javier. *Mestizaje Upside Down*. Pittsburgh: University of Pittsburgh Press, 2004.

Santos, Boaventura de Sousa. "Para leer en 2050: Una reflexión sobre la utopía." Document circulated on the Internet, September 2015.

Sayyid, S. *Recalling the Caliphate: Decolonization and World Order*. London: Hurst, 2014.

Schiwy, Freya, and Michael Ennis, eds. "Dossier: Knowledges and the Known: Andean Perspectives on Capitalism and Epistemology." *Nepantla: Views from South* 3, no.1, 2002.

Sebastiani, Silvia. "Race and National Characters in Eighteenth Century Scotland: The Polygenetic Discourses of Kames and Pinkerton." *Cromhos: Cyber Review of Historiography* 8 (2003): 1–14. Accessed May 20, 2016. http://weblaw.haifa.ac.il/en /Events/scottishenlightenment/Documents/Athanasia%20Glycofrydi%20-%20 Hume%20on%20%E2%80%9CNational%20Characters%E2%80%9D.pdf.

Segato, Rita Laura. "La perspectiva de la colonialidad del poder." In *Aníbal Quijano: Textos de fundación*, ed. Zulma Palermo y Pablo Quintero, 10–42. Buenos Aires: Ediciones del Signo, 2014.

———. "Patriarchy from Margin to Center: Discipline, Territoriality, and Cruelty in the Apocalyptic Phase of Capital." *South Atlantic Quarterly* 115, no. 3 (2016): 615–24.

"The 7 Liberal Arts—Trivium, Quadrivium and Logical Fallacies." Accessed May 24, 2016. http://www.matrixwissen.de/index.php?option=com_content&view=article&id =845:the-7-liberal-arts-trivium-quadrivium-and-logical-fallacies-en&catid =208&lang=en&Itemid=242.

Shari'ati, Ali. *Man and Islam*. Translated by Fatollah Marjari. North Haledon, NJ: Islamic Publications International, 2005.

Silverblatt, Irene. *Moon, Sun, and Witches: Gender Ideologies and Class in Inca and Colonial Peru*. Princeton, NJ: Princeton University Press, 1987.

Simpson, Leanne. *Dancing on Our Turtle's Back: Stories of Nishnaabeg Re-Creation, Resurgence and New Emergence*. Winnipeg, Manitoba: Arbeiter Ring, 2012.

———. "Land as Pedagogy: Nishnaabeg Intelligence and Rebellious Transformation." *Decolonization: Indigeneity, Education and Society* 3, no. 3 (2014): 1–25.

———. "Queering Resurgence: Taking on Heteropatriarchy in Indigenous Nation-Building." *Mamawipawin: Indigenous Governance and Community Based Research Space*, June 2012. Accessed September 1, 2017. https://www.leannesimpson.ca/writings/queering-resurgence-taking-on-heteropatriarchy-in-indigenous-nation-building.

Slabodsky, Santiago. *Decolonial Judaism: Triumphal Failures of Barbaric Thinking*. New York: Palgrave Macmillan, 2014.

Slater, David. "Spatial Politics/Social Movements: Questions of (B)orders and Resistance in Global Times." In *Geographies of Resistance*, ed. Steve Pile and Michael Keith, 258–76. London: Routledge, 1997.

Smith, Adam. *The Wealth of Nations*. London: Wordsworth Editions, [1776]. 2013.

Smith, Andrew. "Between Facts and Myths: Karl Jasper and the Actuality of the Axial Age." *International Journal of Philosophy* 76, no. 4 (2015): 315–34.

Smith, Linda Tuhiwai. *Decolonizing Methodologies: Research and Indigenous Peoples*. London: Zed, 1999.

Subcomandante Insurgente Marcos. "Comunicado del CCRI-CG del EZLN: Comisión sexta-comisión intergalática del EZLN." September 2008. http://www.ezln.org.

———. "Comunicado del Comité Clandestino Revolucionario Indígena-Comandancia General del Ejército Zapatista De Liberación Nacional del 21 de diciembre del 2012." Accessed July 22, 2017. http://enlacezapatista.ezln.org.mx/2012/12/21/comunicado-del-comite-clandestino-revolucionario-indigena-comandancia-general-del-ejercito-zapatista-de-liberacion-nacional-del-21-de-diciembre-del-2012/.

———. "Entre la luz y la sombra." Chiapas, Mexico: EZLN, May 25, 2014. http://enlacezapatista.ezln.org.mx/2014/05/25/entre-la-luz-y-la-sombra/.

Taiaiake, Alfred. *Peace, Power, Righteousness*. Oxford: Oxford University Press, 2008.

———. *Waspase: Indigenous Pathways of Action and Freedom*. Toronto, Ontario: University of Toronto Press, 2005.

Tlostanova, Madina, Suruchi Thapar-Björkert, and Redi Koobak. "Border Thinking and Disidentification: Postcolonial and Postsocialist Feminist Dialogues." *Feminist Theory* 17, no.2 (2016): 211–28.

Torres, Rosa María. "Adiós a la educación comunitaria y alternativa." *Línea de fuego* (November 2013). Accessed September 6, 2017. https://lalineadefuego.info/2013/11/14/adios-a-la-educacion-comunitaria-y-alternativa-por-rosa-maria-torres/.

Trouillot, Michel-Rolph. "North Atlantic Universals: Analytical Fictions, 1492–1945." *South Atlantic Quarterly* 101, no. 4 (2002): 839–58. Accessed December 8, 2016. http://saq.dukejournals.org/content/101/4/839.citation.

Universidad Intercultural Amawtay Wasi. *Aprender en la sabiduría y el buen vivir/Learning Wisdom and the Good Way to Live*. Quito: UNESCO/Universidad Intercultural Amawtay Wasi, 2004.

"The University from the 12th to the 20th century." Università di Bologna. Accessed July 21, 2017. http://www.unibo.it/en/university/who-we-are/our-history /university-from-12th-to-20th-century.

Valladolid, Julio. "Andean Peasant Agriculture: Nurturing a Diversity of Life in the Chacra." In *The Spirit of Regeneration: Andean Culture Confronting Western Notions of Development*, ed. Frédérique Apffel-Marglin with PRATEC. London: Zed Books, 1998.

Vázquez, Rolando. "Colonialidad y relacionalidad." In *Los desafíos decoloniales de nuestros días: Pensar colectivo*, ed. María Eugenia Borsani and Pablo Quintero, 173–19. Neuquén, Argentina: Universidad del Comahue, 2014.

———. "Towards a Decolonial Critique of Modernity: *Buen Vivir*, Relationality and the Task of Listening." In *Capital, Poverty, Development: Denktraditionen im Dialog: Studien zur Befreiung und Interkultalitat* 33, ed. Raúl Fornet-Betancourt, 33:241–52. Wissenschaftsverlag Mainz, Germany: Achen, 2012.

Vázquez, Rolando, and Walter D. Mignolo. "Decolonial AestheSis: Colonial Wounds, Decolonial Healings." *Social Text Periscope Online*, July 15, 2013. Accessed May 28, 2016. http://socialtextjournal.org/periscope_article/decolonial -aesthesis-colonial-woundsdecolonial-healings/.

Verden-Zöller, Gerda, and Humberto Maturana. *The Origin of Humanness and the Biology of Love*. Tulsa, OK: Imprint Academy, 2008.

Villa, Wilmer, and Ernell Villa. "Donde llega uno, llegan dos, llegan tres y llegan todos: El sentido de la pedagogización de la escucha en las comunidades negras del Caribe Seco colombiano." In *Pedagogías decoloniales: Prácticas insurgentes de resistir, (re)existir y (re)vivir*, vol. 1, ed. Catherine Walsh, 357–99. Quito: Ediciones Abya-Yala, 2013.

Walsh, Catherine. "Afro In/Exclusion, Resistance, and the 'Progressive' State: (De)Colonial, Struggles, Questions, and Reflections." In *Black Social Movements in Latin America: From Monocultural Mestizaje to Multiculturalism*, ed. Jean Muteba Rahier, 15–34. New York: Palgrave Macmillan, 2012.

———. "The (De)Coloniality of Knowledge, Life, and Nature: The North American-Andean Free Trade Agreement, Indigenous Movements, and Regional Alternatives." In *Globalization and Beyond: New Examinations of Global Power and Its Alternatives*, ed. Jon Shefner and Patricia Fernández-Kelly, 228–48. University Park: Pennsylvania State University Press, 2011.

———. "Decolonial Pedagogies Walking and Asking: Notes to Paulo Freire from AbyaYala." *International Journal of Lifelong Education* 34, no. 1 (2015): 9–21.

———. "(De)Construir la interculturalidad: Consideraciones críticas desde la política, la colonialidad y los movimientos indígenas y negros en el Ecuador." In *Interculturalidad y Política*, ed. Norma Fuller, 115–42. Lima: Red de Apoyo de las Ciencias Sociales, 2002.

———. *Existence Otherwise: Decolonial Movement in Abya Yala*. Durham, NC: Duke University Press, forthcoming.

——. *Interculturalidad, Estado, Sociedad: Luchas (de)coloniales de nuestra época.* Quito: Universidad Andina Simón Bolívar/Ediciones Abya-Yala, 2009.

——. "¿Interculturalidad? Fantasmas, fantasias y funcionalismos." In *Ecuador: Desafíos para el presente y futuro*, ed. César Montúfar and Fernando Balseca, 269–82. Quito: Universidad Andina Simón Bolívar and Ediciones de la Tierra, 2015.

——. "Introducción: Lo pedagógico y lo decolonial: Entretejiendo caminos." In *Pedagogías decoloniales: Prácticas de resistir, (re)existir y (re)vivir*, vol. 1, ed. Catherine Walsh, 23–68. Quito: Ediciones Abya-Yala, 2013.

——. "Las geopolíticas de conocimiento y la colonialidad del poder: Entrevista con Walter Mignolo." In *Indisciplinar las ciencias sociales: Geopolíticas del conocimiento y colonialidad del poder: Perspectivas desde lo andino*, ed. Catherine Walsh, Freya Schiwy, and Santiago Castro-Gómez. Quito: UASB/Abya Yala, 2002. Accessed May 26, 2016. http://www.oei.es/salactsi/walsh.htm.

——. "Life, Nature, and Gender Otherwise: Feminist Reflections and Provocations from the Andes." In *Practising Feminist Political Ecologies: Moving beyond the "Green Economy*,*"* ed. Wendy Harcourt and Ingrid L. Nelson, 101–28. London: Zed, 2015.

——. "Life and Nature 'Otherwise': Challenges from the Abya-Yalean Andes." In *The Anomie of the Earth: Philosophy, Politics, and Autonomy in Europe and the Americas*, ed. F. Luisetti, J. Pickles, and W. Kaiser, 93–118. Durham, NC: Duke University Press, 2015.

——. *Lo pedagógico y lo decolonial: Entretejiendo caminos.* Querétaro, Mexico: En cortito que's pa' largo, 2014.

——. "On Gender and Its 'Otherwise.'" In *The Palgrave Handbook on Gender and Development Handbook: Critical Engagements in Feminist Theory and Practice*, ed. Wendy Harcourt. London: Palgrave, 2016.

——. "Pedagogical Notes from the Decolonial Cracks." *e-misférica* 11, no. 1 (2014). Accessed May 24, 2016. http://hemisphericinstitute.org/hemi/en/emisferica-111-decolonial-gesture/walsh.

——. "Political-Epistemic Insurgency, Social Movements and the Refounding of the State." In *Rethinking Intellectuals in Latin America*, ed. Mabel Moraña, 199–211. St. Louis: Washington State University, 2010.

——. "The Politics of Naming: (Inter)cultural Studies in De-Colonial Code." *Cultural Studies* 25, nos. 4–5 (2011): 108–25.

——. "The (Re)Articulation of Political Subjectivities and Colonial Difference in Ecuador: Reflections on Capitalism and the Geopolitics of Knowledge." *Nepantla: Views from South* 3, no. 1 (2002): 61–97.

Walsh, Catherine, and Juan García Salazar. "(W)riting Collective Memory (De)spite State: Decolonial Practices of Existence in Ecuador." In *Black Writing and the State in Latin America*, ed. Jerome Branche, 253–66. Nashville: Vanderbilt University Press, 2015.

Walsh, Catherine, and Edizon León. "Afro-Andean Thought and Diasporic Ancestrality." In *Shifting the Geography of Reason: Gender, Science and Religion*, ed. Marina

Paola Banchetti-Robino and Clevis Ronald Healey, 211–24. Newcastle, UK: Cambridge Scholars Press, 2006.

Walsh, Catherine, Freya Schiwy, and Santiago Castro-Gómez. *Indisciplinar las ciencias sociales: Geopolíticas del conociemiento y colonialidad del poder.* Quito: Abya Yala, 2002. Accessed May 26, 2016. http://www.oei.es/salactsi/walsh.htm.

Walsh, Catherine, and Walter Mignolo. "Interculturality, State, Society: Catherine Walsh and Walter Mignolo in Conversation." *Reartikulacija*, 2010. Accessed May 23, 2016. https://www.academia.edu/12871436/Interculaturality_State_Society _Catherine_Walsh_and_Walter_Mignolo_in_conversation_Part_I.

"Western Liberal Democracy Will Be Wrong for China." *Intelligence2: The World of Debate. YouTube*, 2012. https://www.youtube.com/watch?v=EwM9CuGcBgl.

Williams, Eric. *Capitalism and Slavery.* Chapel Hill: University of North Carolina Press, [1944] 1994.

Wynter, Sylvia. "No Humans Involved: A Letter to My Colleagues." *Forum NHI: Knowledge for the 21st Century* 1, no. 1 (1994): 42–71.

———. *On Being Human as Praxis.* Durham, NC: Duke University Press, 2014.

———. "Towards the Sociogenic Principle: Fanon, The Puzzle of Conscious Experience, of 'Identity' and What It's Like to Be 'Black.'" In *National Identities and Sociopolitical Changes in Latin America*, ed. Mercedes Durán-Cogan and Antonio Gómez-Moriano, 30–66. New York: Routledge, 2001.

———. "Unsettling the Coloniality of Being/Power/Truth/Freedom: Towards the Human, After Man, Its Overrepresentation: An Argument." *New Centennial Review* 3, no. 3 (2003): 257–337.

Yampara, Simón. "Cosmovivencia Andian: Vivir y convivir en armonía integral." *Bolivian Studies Journal* 18 (2011). Accessed May 24, 2016. http://bsj.pitt.edu/ojs/index .php/bsi/article/view/42.

———. *El Ayllu y la territorialidad en los Andes: Una aproximación a Chamba Grande.* La Paz: Inti Andino, 2001.

Zapata Olivella, Manuel. *Las claves mágicas de América.* Bogotá: Plaza and Janes, 1989.

———. *Rebelión de los genes: El mestizaje americano en la sociedad futura.* Bogotá: Altamira Ediciones, 1997.

# Index

Lee, Robert E., 169
Legend of the Fifth Sun, 164
León, Edizon, 43
Leyenda de los Soles, 107
Leyva, Xochitl, 52n19
LGBT, 11, 40, 47, 190. *See also* gender
Liberal Institute (Brazil), 89–90
liberation theology, 139, 142
Linnaeus, Carolus, 190
Liu, C. H., 249
Lockward, Alanna, 249
logocentrism, 27–28, 62–64
Londoño, Alejandra, 95
López de Gómara, Francisco, 195
Lorde, Audre, 7, 8, 17
Lozano Lerma, Betty Ruth, 35–36, 39, 40;
    on "blackwomen," 36, 41–42, 95; on
    *cimarronaje*, 42; on pedagogies, 95
Lu Xun, 212
Lugones, María, 8, 39, 100, 148, 247–49
Lumumba, Patrice, 238
Lyotard, Jean-François, 119

Macas, Luis, 59, 61, 76, 256; on colonial
    yoke, 18, 69, 99
Machiavelli, Niccolò, 142
Macron, Emmanuel, 5
Madre Montaña, 65
Mahan, Alfred Thayer, 11
Maldonado-Torres, Nelson, 8, 15, 148,
    248; on coloniality, 23; on decolonial
    attitude, 17; on Fanon, 92
Man/Human, 65, 159–73, 185–86, 189,
    204, 217
Mankanyezi (Zulu elder), 202–3, 206–7
Mao Zedong, 130
Mapuche, 38, 128, 154
March of Indigenous Peoples (Bolivia), 25
Marcos, Sylvia, 19, 52n19, 249
Mariátegui, José Carlos, 181
Marley, Bob, 105, 222
marronage. See *cimarronaje*
Marshack, Alexander, 213, 214

Marshall Plan, 233
Marx, Karl, 3, 89, 138, 195; on hegemonic
    knowledge, 178–79; on surplus value,
    10, 142, 252
*masintin*, 168
mathematics, 156, 199
*Matrix, The* (film), 114–15
Maturana, Humberto, 196, 213–14,
    239–41, 253
Mayas, 124, 128, 160, 182, 202; cosmol-
    ogy of, 155, 194, 216; language of, 38;
    mathematics of, 156
McLaren, Peter, 89
Melucci, Alberto, 34
Mendez, Xhercis, 53n19
Mendoza, Bienvenida, 95
Mendoza, Breny, 53n19
*mestizaje*, 39, 62, 123, 124, 231. *See also*
    race
Mexico, 38, 138, 160; universities of, 72–74,
    80n43. *See also* Aztecs; Zapatistas
*mino bimaadiziwin*, 154
Miranda, Francisco de, 123
modernity, 117–19, 154, 229–39; Baude-
    laire on, 118; darker side of, 106–12,
    122–23, 140, 154, 229–31; Dussel on,
    230; economic development as, 67;
    Giddens on, 132n19, 140; "myth" of,
    230; options of, 224; promises of, 4,
    139, 141, 145–46; Quijano on, 182, 197;
    Renaissance and, 118–19, 139–40,
    183–84, 195–96; tradition and, 118;
    violence of, 1. *See also* rhetoric of
    modernity
modernity/coloniality, 3–5, 76, 107, 230,
    255; education and, 74; Quijano on,
    112, 114–16, 120–21, 227; research on,
    8, 25–29; Third World and, 111–12.
    *See also* coloniality
modernity/coloniality/decoloniality triad,
    8, 107–9, 116, 138–41, 149, 211, 255
monotheism, 136
monotopism, 77n8

Moors, 182, 186, 188
Morales, Evo, 33, 51n3, 78n16
Mother Earth, 6, 163, 167; "Red Line
    Action" for, 35. See also *Pachamama*
Mouffe, Chantal, 34
Mujeres Creando (collective), 99–100
Multicultural Education Training and
    Advocacy project, 254
multiculturalism, 44; decoloniality and,
    99; interculturality versus, 57–58;
    neoliberalism and, 57–58; politics of
    recognition and, 57–58, 61
multipolarity, 6, 228, 254
"Muntu," 92, 97n25
museums, 199–200, 209n12, 241
Muyolema, Armando, 22

Nahuatl, 38, 176n22, 251. See also Aztecs
naming practices, 22, 26, 139, 169;
    cartography and, 194–95; Greek/Latin
    vocabulary and, 113–14
National Confederation of Indigenous
    Nationalities of Ecuador, 255
National Council of Evaluation, Accredita-
    tion, and Insurance of Quality in Higher
    Education (CEAACES), 71–72
National Indigenous Organization of
    Colombia (ONIC), 21–22
nationalism, 68, 230–31; African, 237–38;
    decolonization and, 235, 237–38;
    democracy and, 25; logocentrism of,
    62–64; pluriversal/intercultural views
    of, 75–76. See also plurinational states
National Liberation Army (ELN), 51n4
naturalization of life, 10
natural resources, 157, 159, 162, 163
nature, 25, 65, 185; Bacon on, 162–63;
    commodification of, 38; concept of,
    153, 158–64; culture versus, 65, 155,
    160–64, 175n9, 187, 241; etymologies
    of, 159, 161, 162; naturalization of life
    and, 10; race/gender and, 157–60;
    rights of, 65

Ndlovu-Gatsheni, Sabelo J., 249
neocolonialism: intellectual, 69–70
neoliberal globalism, 5, 6, 222
neoliberalism, 38, 106, 111, 231; geopoli-
    tics and, 5–6; Indigenous movements
    and, 58–59, 63–64; interculturality
    and, 57–59, 63–64; rewesternizing
    of, 234; as rhetoric of modernity, 141;
    Trump on, 5. See also capitalism
*nepantla* (in-between places), 82–83,
    250–51
New Zealand, 26, 61, 148, 221
Nicaragua, 80n43
Nigeria, 237–38
9/11 attacks, 106. See also terrorism
noncontradiction, law of, 154–56, 174n1
nurture, 161, 175n9

Ochoa, Karina, 39, 52n19, 95
Olvera Salinas, René, 48–49
ontotheology, 239
Opium Wars, 190, 201
Orientalism, 190
Osage people, 165, 216–17
Ottoman Empire, 189, 190
Oviedo Freire, Atawallpa, 72

Pacari, Nina, 1, 12n1, 26–27, 33–34, 60
*Pachamama*, 90, 163, 167, 185; Ecuador's
    Constitution and, 63, 65. See also
    Mother Earth
*palabrandar* (walking words), 37, 101
Palermo, Zulma, 62, 249
Panama, 21–22
Panikkar, Raimon, 58, 251
Paredes, Julieta, 40–41, 81–82, 100
patriarchy, 38–41, 126–27; *cimarronaje*
    and, 42; colonialism and, 99–100; In-
    digenous women and, 81; Lugones on,
    100; violence of, 47. See also gender
*patrón*, 209n7, 246
Patzi Paco, Félix, 1, 12n1
"pedagogization," 88, 91–96

pedagogy, 21, 245; of activism, 83; Alexander on, 90–91; *cimarronaje* as, 93; collective memory and, 93–94; critical, 89, 255; decolonial, 88–96, 241–42, 256; of Freire, 88–90; land as, 94; slave, 42

Pérez, Emma, 34–35

Persia, 138; cosmology of, 159, 165–66, 194; science of, 113, 199, 216

Peru, 38, 40, 123, 138. *See also* Incas

Plato, 136, 154, 186, 204

plurinational states, 63–64, 238; CONAIE on, 61–63; Zapatistas on, 68. *See also* nationalism

pluritopic hermeneutic, 251, 252

pluriversality, 147, 170, 172, 175n18, 240–41, 254

pluriversals/interversals, 2, 3, 69, 74–76, 250

pluriversity, 70, 72, 251

Poland, 143–44

Popol Vuh, 107, 164

Portugal, 235, 236

posthuman, 119, 154, 171–72

postmodernity, 112, 119, 253

pragmatism, 50, 176n22, 177

primitivism, 155, 215

Procesos de Comunidades Negras (collective), 86

progress, 123, 139–40, 239; as economic development, 10, 142, 155; etymology of, 119

Proyecto Andino de Tecnologías Campesinas (PRATEC), 160–61

Pueblos en Camino (collective), 37, 48, 223

Puerto Rico, 83, 254–55

*qi* (energy), 167

quadrivium/trivium, 113–14, 201–2

Quijano, Aníbal, 4, 228–29; on capitalism, 183, 184, 198; on codification of difference, 23; on coloniality/decoloniality, 6, 23, 66, 99, 106–7; on colonial matrix of power, 146, 184; on decolonization, 120–21, 130; on dependency theory, 112, 131n3; on Enlightenment, 173–74; on epistemic reconstitution, 246; on globalization, 181–82; on "heterogeneous historical-structural node," 109; on modernity/coloniality, 112–16, 120–21, 182, 197, 227; on outside/inside, 74; on racism, 23, 180–81; on Renaissance, 173, 186–87; on totality of knowledge, 197, 204

Quintero, Pablo, 249

Qur'an, 164, 165

race, 25, 181; "blackwomen" and, 36, 41–42, 95; classifications of, 185, 186, 190, 250; ethnicity and, 81–82, 121, 164, 181; gender and, 94, 157–60; mixed, 39, 62, 123, 124, 231; privileges of, 21, 81; violence and, 93–94. *See also mestizaje*

racism, 75, 188; Bautista on, 79n33; Hume on, 205–6, 208; Mariátegui on, 181; ontological, 205; Quijano on, 23, 180–81; religion and, 182, 186–89; sexism and, 10, 15, 82, 126–27, 148, 157–60, 168; Spanish Inquisition and, 182; Zapata Olivella on, 92

recognition politics, 26, 31n35, 57–58, 61

Red Mariposas de Alas Nuevas Construyendo Futuro, 36

reemergence of disavowed, 200–206, 229

re-existence, 95–96, 99, 246–47, 254; Albán Achinte on, 3, 7, 18, 35–39, 94, 120, 246; definitions of, 18, 106; epistemic reconstitution as, 231; *estar siendo* as, 234; in relation, 35–39

relationality, 11n1; feminist views of, 17; re-existence and, 35–39; *vincularidad* and, 1–2, 239

*Ren* (human), 166, 167, 169

Wiener, Norbert, 220

wisdom, 22, 76, 92; African, 202, 207–8; Aztec, 176n22; house of, 69–74, 137; knowledge versus, 124–25, 202, 208; Macas on, 56; Zulu, 202–3

witches, 158, 179, 208

Workers' Party (Brazil), 90

World Bank, 58, 146

World Conference against Racism (2001), 51n7

world order, 222, 228; monocentric, 156–59; polycentric, 154–56

Wynter, Sylvia, 8, 17, 34, 50, 132n22, 248; on "de-Goding," 139–40, 166; on Man1/Man2, 154, 157, 159, 170–72

Yachay University, 72

Yachaywasi (house of wisdom), 137

yanantin, 168

yin-yang, 167, 168

Zapata Olivella, Manuel, 24, 92

Zapateándole el Mal Govierno (collective), 86

Zapatistas, 15, 25–26, 33, 254; on "capitalist hydra," 29, 46–47, 100, 250; decoloniality and, 49, 133n26, 223; on plurinational nation-state, 68; praxis of, 46–50, 121, 125; schools of, 73, 86–88; seed-bed seminars of, 100–101, 247; on thinking-doing, 20

Zapotecan, 38, 165

Zavalla, Iris, 22

Zenón. *See* "Abuelo Zenón"

Zimbabwe, 137

Zulus, 202–3